Clinical Behavior Therapy and Behavior Modification
Volume Two

Clinical Behavior Therapy and Behavior Modification

Editor-in-Chief

Reid J. Daitzman, Independent Practice, Stamford, CT; and Connecticut Center for Behavioral and Psychosomatic Medicine, New Haven, CT

Editorial Consultants

Clinical Behavior Therapy and Behavior Modification

Volume Two

Reid J. Daitzman, Ph.D.

Editor-in-Chief

Garland STPM Press

New York and London

Library of Congress Cataloging in Publication Data
  Main entry under title:
  Clinical behavior therapy and behavior modification, ed. by Reid
    Bibliography: p.   J. Daitzman.
    Includes index.
    1. Behavior therapy. 2. Behavior modification.
  I. Daitzman, Reid J. [DNLM: 1. Behavior therapy—
  Periodicals. W1 CL 668LM]
  RC489.B4C58   616.8'914   79-14455
  ISBN 0-8240-7217-0 (v. 2)

Published by Garland STPM Press
136 Madison Avenue, New York, New York 10016

Printed in the United States of America

To Eleanor, Norman, and Donna

Contents, Volume One

Contents, Volume Two

Contributors

Andrew Christensen
University of California at Los Angeles
Los Angeles, California

Daniel J. Cox
University of Virginia
School of Medicine
Charlottesville, Virginia

Harry Lando
Iowa State University
Ames, Iowa

Paul J. Margolies
Harlem Valley Psychiatric Center
White Plains, New York

Gayla Margolin
University of Southern California
Los Angeles, California

Barry S. Reynolds
University of California at Los Angeles
Los Angeles, California

R. Taylor Segraves
The University of Chicago Hospitals and Clinics
Chicago, Illinois

Douglas W. Thomas
University of Virginia
School of Medicine
Charlottesville, Virginia

Acknowledgments

This series has depended upon the support and encouragement of many individuals and organizations. I want to thank George Narita, Editor-in-Chief of Garland STPM Press, for his continued support, advice, gentle prodding, and enthusiasm for this series. His confidence in my ability to put the series together has continued to motivate me in its preparation. I also want to thank all my teachers (you know who you are) and clients for giving me the opportunity to listen, share, and learn. I especially want to thank Arnold H. Buss, presently at the University of Texas at Austin, William Groman of Virginia Commonwealth University, and Marvin Zuckerman at the University of Delaware for serving as mentors during the formative stages of my academic and professional development.

Introduction

Purpose of the Series

Reid J. Daitzman

This present volume, part of an ongoing series, is written for students and clinicians in all areas of mental health who have a serious interest in the efficient therapeutic application of behavior therapy and behavior modification. *Clinical Behavior Therapy and Behavior Modification* is for the psychiatrist, clinical psychologist, counselor, psychiatric social worker, occupational therapist, physical therapist, psychiatric nurse, and paraprofessional in these professions.

Empirically based assessment methods and standardized clinical prescriptions (*see* Goldstein and Stein, 1976) are a relatively recent development. *Clinical Behavior Therapy and Behavior Modification* assumes that interpersonal skills, empathy, rapport, placebo, timing, and transference are part of all therapies *in addition to empirically based prescriptive behavioral interventions based upon adequate diagnosis.* Regardless of therapeutic orientation, diagnosis is a prerequisite to effective and ethical intervention. The series uses the American Psychiatric Association Diagnostic and Statistical Manual of Mental Disorders DSM–II (1968) as a convenient and standardized conceptualization of mental disorders.

With these facts and background in mind, the purpose of the series is twofold:

1. If you are a clinician with limited experience in the chapter topic area, a study of the chapter will allow you to proceed with an empirically based strategy(ies) for intervention.
2. If you are a student or researcher reviewing crucial published (and unpublished) works in the chapter topic area, referencing the chapter will allow you to proceed with a well-designed project that is timely, relevant, and practical.

Outstanding researchers and clinicians were contacted and requested to submit chapters cross-referenced with the DSM–II. Each chapter has a common outline. In turn, an international editorial board reviewed each contribution for completeness, clarity, and quality.

Each chapter of the series is divided, more or less, into ten sections:

1. Introduction and scope of diagnostic category
2. Theoretical analysis, both behavioral and nonbehavioral
3. Assessment—projective, objective, behavioral
4. Proven treatment procedures based upon literature search
5. Prototype clinical prescription
6. Sample case report illustrating clinical prescription
7. Ethical and legal issues and need for special equipment instrumentation
8. Suggestions for future clinical and experimental investigation(s)
9. One-thousand word summary
10. References and (optional) bibliography.

These ten sections outline the following six questions that the reader of a chapter should be able to answer:

1. What specific intervention(s) and strategies are the treatment(s) of choice for the specific disorder?
2. What is the empirical basis of these intervention strategies and *how well designed was the research?*
3. How are the intervention strategies best applied and what further education, supervision, and equipment is needed for best results?
4. How strong is the relationship between assessment(s) and treatment(s)? Is there discriminant and convergent validity of the various dependent assessment/intervention measures?
5. How can the optimal treatment methods be better standardized and what types of research can be designed in the near future to further refine the necessary and sufficient assessment/intervention variables?
6. What are the legal and ethical considerations and constraints to be considered before, during, and after implementation of the optimal treatment strategies?

There were some diagnostic categories that did not lend themselves to a precise 10-section outline. However, in every case the six questions could be answered after reading the chapter.

THE ROLE OF DIAGNOSIS AND THE
NEED FOR A STANDARDIZED TEXT

The *Clinical Behavior Therapy and Behavior Modification* series will include all of the current DSM-II diagnostic categories under the following major topic areas:

1. Mental Retardation (310-315)
2. Psychoses Associated with Organic Brain Syndromes (290-294)
3. Nonpsychotic Organic Brain Syndromes (309)
4. Neuroses (300)
5. Personality Disorders and Certain Other Nonpsychotic Mental Disorders (301-304)
6. Psychophysiological Disorders (305)
7. Special Symptoms (306)
8. Transient Situational Disturbances (307)
9. Behavior Disorders of Childhood and Adolescence (308)
10. Conditions Without Manifest Psychiatric Disorder and Nonspecific Conditions (316-318).

The decision to cross-reference *Clinical Behavior Therapy and Behavior Modification* with the 1968 DSM-II was based upon a number of practical considerations. Although the rationale and importance of diagnosis has been criticized (e.g., McLemore and Benjamin, 1979; Ward, Beck, Mendelson et al., 1962; Zigler and Phillips, 1961a, b), at the grass-roots level a primary and secondary diagnosis is required for record keeping, research, insurance carriers, workmen's compensation, legal consent and competency, and in private and university hospitals for budgeting and grant requests. Labeling and pigeonholing a client's covert and overt behaviors into confusing and unreliable diagnostic categories may be a necessary evil of the 1970s, especially with the formulation of a comprehensive National Health Insurance Plan now pending. In addition, many medical schools obviously continue to emphasize the medical model to their third-year clerkship psychiatric students and psychiatric residents.

Finally, and perhaps most important, the divergent professional disciplines of mental health care delivery suffer from an unavailability of an organized and unified standard text. Most professional textbooks advance a theoretical position and treatment is dependent upon the personality theories, developmental theories, psychopathology, and treatment parameters that are consistent with that model. Although the orientation of the present series is behavioral, other positions are represented to the extent that their literature and methods contribute to the prescriptive eclecticism advanced in this series. What is hoped for is the eventual development of a mental health reference similar to such medical volumes as the *Physician Desk Reference* (PDR) or *Merck Manual.* Since most physicians refer to the annual PDR when seeking information on a particular drug, it is hoped that mental health practitioners, when seeking information on the assessment, diagnosis, and treatment of mental disorders will consult this series.

An obvious criticism of cross-referencing this series with the DSM-II is that by the time the series appears it may be outdated by DSM-III. However, the DSM-III is not without its own problems and critics (*see* Schacht and Nathan, 1977).

> No longer will a clinician simply select the one or two categories into which the patient or client seems to fit best. Instead, it will be necessary to relate explicitly the primary diagnostic *axis,* based on presenting dysfunction, to other features also termed axes.
>
> The five axes that will be referenced in diagnosing an individual are (1) clinical psychiatric syndromes and other conditions, (2) personality disorders (adult) and specific developmental disorders (children and adolescents), (3) nonmental medical disorders, (4) severity of psychosocial stresses, and (5) highest level of adaptive functioning in the past year. (McLemore and Benjamin, 1979, p. 17)

The following includes an example of each axis as it might appear for a single patient (from Schacht and Nathan, 1977, p. 1019).

Axis I: 296.80 Atypical Depressive Disorder
Axis II: 301.81 Narcissistic Personality Disorder
Axis III: Diabetes, Hypertension
Axis IV: *Psychosocial stressors:*5, severe (business failure)
Axis V: *Highest Adaptive Behavior past year:*3, good.

From a practical standpoint, many of the primary and sub-axes are easily cross-referenced with the DSM-II, with treatment following accordingly. However, a major improvement in the DSM-III over the DSM-II is in the operational criteria for diagnosis. For example, compare the two criteria for "Phobia":

> *300.2 phobic neurosis (DSM-II)*
> This condition is characterized by intense fear of an object or situation which the patient consciously recognizes as no real danger to him. His apprehension may be experienced as faintness, fatigue, palpitations, perspiration, nausea, tremor, and even panic. Phobias are generally

attributed to fears displaced to the phobic object or situation from some other object of which the patient is unaware. A wide range of phobias has been described. (DSM–II, p. 40)

300.24 simple phobia—all should be present (DSM–III)

A. Avoidance of the irrationally feared object or situation. If there is any element of danger in these objects or situations, it is reacted to in a fashion out of proportion to reality.

B. The avoidance has a significant effect on the patient's life adjustment.

C. The patient has complete insight into the irrational nature of his fear.

D. The phobic symptoms do not coincide with an episode of Depressive Disorder, Obsessive Compulsive Disorder, or Schizophrenia, nor are they limited to a period of two months prior to, or two months after such an episode. (DSM–III Draft Version, 1968)

DSM–III operational criteria for phobia is clearer and less dependent on a theoretical orientation to mental health (e.g., psychodynamic). *I suggest that the readership of this series consult and cross-reference the appropriate DSM-III operational criteria for the chapter topics included in this series.*

The DSM–III also includes additional diagnostic categories not clearly covered in DSM-II. For example, in the area of the sexual dysfunctions, male secondary impotence/erectile dysfunction is not included in DSM-II (although there will certainly be a chapter in this area in the series). If, as a clinician, your own bias is that erectile dysfunction is a vascular disorder of deficits in myotonic vasocongestion, then in DSM-II you would diagnose it as a psychophysiological genito-urinary disorder (305.6). However, if you feel that erectile dysfunction is primarily dependent upon anxiety, then you may diagnose it as anxiety neurosis (300.0). Or you may wish to bypass the problem and classify it as a "Special Symptom Not Elsewhere Classified" (306.9).

The DSM–III contains a catchall diagnostic category that probably includes primary and secondary erectile dysfunction, premature ejaculation, retarded ejaculation, primary and secondary orgasmic dysfunction, dyspareunia, and vaginismus. These disorders are classified as "Psychosexual Disorders, Psychological Dysfunction." However, as any sex therapist soon realizes, this category does not take into account the problem of low sex drive or ejaculatory incompetence.

Sharpe, Kuriansky, and O'Connor (1976) propose a classification of functional human sexual disorders. Their system is based upon objective behavior and reports of distress. Five categories of disorders are proposed:

1. Disturbances of the physiological sexual response cycle
2. Disturbances of perceptual component of the sexual response cycle
3. Disturbances of subjective satisfaction in the sexual response cycle
4. Distress concerning sexual functioning associated with false beliefs or lack of sexual knowledge
5. Socio-sexual distress.

Within this nomenclature, the label of "low sex drive" would fall under category 2. Likewise, ejaculatory incompetence would also be classified under category 2. This category includes three components: (1) hypersexual feelings (e.g., "nymphomania"); (2) hyposexual feelings (e.g., low sex drive), and (3) anesthesia (e.g., ejaculatory incompetence). Only within such an original diagnostic system would these diagnoses be easily classifiable.

The basic point to be emphasized here is that the jury is still out concerning the classification of mental health problems, and that all diagnostic manuals will have critics and problems. In the meantime, this series will continue to cross-reference with the DSM-II and, where appropriate, with DSM-III. Perhaps future editions of clinicians and books will be reorganized under the DSM-IV that will be introduced in 20 years.

THE DESIGN QUALITY RATING (DQR)

Once a diagnosis is established, the resulting treatment(s) should be empirically based upon well-designed clinical and experimental research. Until the publication of this series, no one publication has systematically measured the design quality of the literature upon which the treatment was based. The contributors were asked to assign a design quality rating (Gurman and Kriskern, 1978) to each investigation in the chapter. Sometimes this proved to be extremely difficult. Not only were individual papers difficult to score, but entire diagnostic areas were hazy as to experimental design. Where the assignment of the DQR scores proved to be virtually impossible, it is assumed that the probable total score would be in the 0–10 range (poor).

The DQR involves the summation of 13 separate scores. In turn, those scores which have a value of "5," "3," "1," or "½" are totaled for the DQR. A 0–0 is poor; 10½–15 is fair; 15½–20 is good; and 20½–32 is very good. The 13 criteria and their individual scores follow.

1. *Controlled assignment to treatment conditions:* random assignment, matching of total groups or matching in pairs (5)
2. *Pre-post measurement of change* (5)

3. *No contamination of major independent variables,* e.g., therapists' experience levels, number of therapists per treatment condition, and relevant therapeutic competence, e.g., a psychoanalyst using behavior therapy for the first time offers a poor test of the power of a behavioral method (5)
4. *Appropriate statistical analysis* (5)
5. *Follow-up:* none (0), 1–3 months (½), 3–12 months (1), 13–18 months (3), more than 18 months (5)
6. *Treatments equally valued:* i.e., tremendous biases are often engendered for both therapist and patient when this criterion is not met (1)
7. *Treatment carried out as described or expected:* clear evidence (1), presumptive evidence (½)
8. *Multiple change indices* used (1)
9. *Multiple vantage points* used in assessing outcome (1)
10. *Data on other concurrent treatment:* evidence of no treatment; or of such treatment without documentation of amount or equivalence (½)
11. *Equal treatment length* in comparative studies (1)
12. *Outcome assessment allowing for both positive and negative change* (1)
13. *Therapist-investigator nonequivalence* (1).

Most behavior therapists would think that the DQR of our research would be higher than the DQR of their (nonbehavioral) research. In general, however, quality of experimental design had little to do with the theoretical orientation of the investigator or the fact that it was published in "better" journals.

PRESCRIPTIVE BEHAVIORAL ECLECTICISM

All therapies must be taken in the context of culture, subject and organismic variables, moderator variables, setting, and relationship variables. Modern behavior therapy has evolved a package of techniques that, when systematically applied by trained personnel, tend at least to produce equal results with other nonbehavioral interventions (*see* Dimond, Havens, and Jones, 1978; Sloane, Staples, Cristol, et al., 1975). The ultimate criteria for the choice of one method over another, one school over another, or one therapy over another often is based upon nonrational information (most recent book or workshop attended, favorite professor, orientation of supervisor, or personal philosophy (*see* Daitzman, Chapter 1, Volume 1). Whether there is an ultimate therapy based upon Truth is not as important as trying our best as individual therapists in applying what we know (as derived from the Truth of the Scientific Method) to the real problems of real people seeking our help.

To this extent, the readership of this series is assumed to be familiar with the *techniques* of implementation given the proper input (from this series and others) as to how best to apply behavioral prescriptive eclecticism (*see* Goldstein and Foa, 1980). The social and natural sciences, desensitization, assertive training, psychopharmocology, biofeedback, thought stopping, sensate focus, family therapy, token economy, personality theory, psychopathology, psychophysiology, history and methodological design, developmental biopsychology, endocrinology, physical rehabilitation, and psychoanalysis are areas that every reader, independent of degree or orientation, should have a general knowledge of, both theoretically and clinically.

Volume 2 of *Clinical Behavior Therapy and Behavior Modification* has 6 chapters, selected for their quality, comprehensiveness, and timeliness. Subsequent volumes will include six to eight chapters of other diagnostic categories from DSM-II or DSM-III published every 10–12 months.

REFERENCES

Committee on Nomenclature and Statistics of the American Psychiatric Association. *DSM-II diagnostic and statistical manual of mental disorders.* Washington, D.C.; American Psychiatric Association, 1968.

Dimond, R. E., Havens, R. A., and Jones, A. C. A conceptual framework for the practice of prescriptive eclecticism in psychotherapy. *American Psychologist,* 1978, *33,* 239–248.

Garfield, S. and Bergin, A. (eds.), *Handbook of psychotherapy and behavior change,* 2nd ed. New York: John Wiley, 1978.

Goldstein, A. and Foa, E. B. *Handbook of behavioral interventions.* New York: Academic Press, 1980.

Goldstein, A. and Stein, N. S. *Prescriptive psychotherapies.* New York: Pergamon Press, 1976.

Gurman, A. S. and Kriskern, D. P. Research on marital and family therapy: Progress, perspective and prospect. In S. Garfield and A. Bergin (eds), *Handbook of psychotherapy and behavior change,* 2nd ed. New York: John Wiley, 1978.

Kazdin, A. E. *History of behavior modification: Experimental foundations of contemporary research.* Baltimore: University Park Press, 1978.

McLemore, C. W. and Benjamin, L. S. Whatever happened to interpersonal diagnosis? A Psychosocial Alternative to DSM-III. *American Psychologist,* 1979, *34,* 17–34.

Schacht, T. and Nathan, P. E. But is it good for psychologists? Appraisal and status of DSM-III. *American Psychologist,* 1977, *32,* 1017–1024.

Sharpe, L., Kuriansky, J. B., and O'Connor, J. F. A preliminary classification of human functional sexual disorders. *Journal of Sex and Marital Therapy,* 1976, *2,* 106–114.

Sloane, R. B., Staples, F. R., Cristol, A. H., et al. *Psychotherapy versus behavior therapy.* Cambridge, MA: Harvard University Press, 1975.

Task Force on Nomenclature and Statistics, American Psychiatric Association. *Diagnostic and statistical manual of mental disorders* (3rd ed.; draft version of January 15, 1978). Available from Task Force on Nomenclature and Statistics, American Psychiatric Association, 722 W. 168 Street, New York, New York 10032.

Ward, C. H., Beck, A. T., Mendelson, M., et al. The psychiatric nomenclature: Reasons for diagnostic disagreement. *Archives of General Psychiatry,* 1962, *7,* 198–205.

Zigler, E. and Phillips, L. Psychiatric diagnosis and symptomology. *Journal of Abnormal and Social Psychology,* 1961a, *63,* 69–75.

Zigler, E. and Phillips, L. Psychiatric diagnosis: A critique. *Journal of Abnormal and Social Psychology,* 1961b, *63,* 607–618.

1
Early Infantile Autism

Paul J. Margolies

"One of the biggest problems in writing about autistic children is that doctors and other professional people tend to differ in the words they use to describe and name the condition" (Wing, 1972, p. 3). To date, there is no definition or description of early infantile autism that receives universal recognition by researchers, clinicians, and scholars. Since 1943, when Kanner initially delineated a dozen clinical features of the syndrome, numerous systems of diagnostic criteria have been introduced.

Rutter's (1978) definition of early infantile autism has been one of the most recent to appear in the literature. He points to four essential criteria in relation to the child's behavior before the age of five. These are: (a) onset before the age of 30 months; (b) impaired social development that has a number of special characteristics, including a lack of attachment behavior and a lack of or unusual use of eye-to-eye gaze, and is out of keeping with the child's intellectual level; (c) delayed and deviant language development that has certain defined features, including little social imitation and echolalia with associated I–you pronoun reversal, and is out of keeping with the child's intellectual level; and (d) insistence on sameness which includes stereotyped play patterns, abnormal preoccupations, and resistance to change.

Major systems of criteria have also been developed by Kanner (1943), Eisenberg and Kanner (1956), Ward (1970), DeMyer, Churchill, Pontius, and Gilkey (1971), and Ornitz and Ritvo (1976), and they will be reviewed later in this chapter. The point is that agreement in diagnosis, even among experts, cannot be expected when different individuals are using different sets of criteria. The implication is that there is no guarantee that the characteristics of the children studied in the numerous reports cited in this chapter are identical.

The age of onset of the disorder is between birth and 2½ years of age (Wing, 1972). Ornitz and Ritvo (1976) note that subtle signs are frequently apparent during the child's first year. Autism is diagnosed in 4 children per 10,000 (Hermelin & O'Connor, 1970) with a male : female ratio of approximately 2.5 : 1 reported by Hermelin and O'Connor and 4 or 5 : 1 reported by the National Society for Autistic Children (1978).

Prior to the introduction of behavioral interventions, the prognosis for the disorder was generally quite poor. For example, DeMyer, Barton, DeMyer, Norton, Allen, and Steele (1973) followed 120 autistic children for 12 years and found that most remained educationally retarded. Of those 120 children, 1 to 2 percent recovered normal functioning; 5 to 15 percent were found to function at a borderline level, 16 to 25 percent at a fair level, and 60 to 75 percent at a poor level; and 42 percent remained institutionalized. In addition, upon examining long-term follow-up data concerning children studied by Kanner, Creak, and Maudsley Hospital, Rutter (1974) concluded that two-thirds of the children remained severely handicapped while one-sixth obtained regular paid employment and another one-sixth made a fair social adjustment. About half of these children remained without speech and even those who gained speech continued to evidence language disabilities.

It appears that the best prognostic indicator has been the ability to communicate verbally (i.e., speech and language skills) (Stark, 1972; Lotter, 1974; Rutter, 1974).

THEORETICAL ANALYSIS
Psychodynamic/Psychogenic

Thirty years ago Kanner (1949) remarked that, in his experience, the parents of autistics were almost always very successful in their careers. They were generally highly intelligent, not comfortable in the company of people, and demonstrated little affection. Such observations led to speculation that autism develops in response to these qualities.

For example, Fraknoi and Ruttenberg (1971) theorized that inadequate mothering is central to the etiology of the syndrome. They characterize this inadequate mothering as aloof, insensitive, and ambivalent, and hypothesize that it is due to unresolved conflicts from the mother's own early history. Such mothering leaves the infant unrelieved of tension, insecure, and overwhelmed by stimuli. The infant attempts to relieve this discomfort through repetitive movements and self-stimulation. The authors note that such infants may evidence congenital weaknesses; however, these weaknesses are etiologically related to the disorder only in that they set the stage for the inadequate mothering to occur. "Autism is, therefore, understood as a defensive position which the congenitally vulnerable child works out for himself in order to cope with undue stress and frustration—a function which under normal circumstances the mother would be assuming" (p. 736).

Ward (1970), in his review of the autistic syndrome, suggests that early infantile autism develops due to a lack of varying, novel, patterned stimulation in the child's early developmental history. This lack of stimulation results in a "behavioral ego," a deviant ego which consists of repetitive, stereotyped activities. L'Abate (1972) questions Ward's conclusions, observing that Ward cites no direct evidence to support his theory and asserting that Ward's coverage of the literature is selective and incomplete.

Two studies have recently appeared which question the notion that parents of autistics differ from parents of nonautistics. Cox, Rutter, Newman, and Bartak (1975) found no differences between parents of autistic boys and parents of dysphasic boys with respect to parental warmth, emotional responsiveness, sociability, and psychiatric condition. Cantwell, Baker, and Rutter (1977) found no differences between mothers of autistic boys and mothers of dysphasic boys with respect to patterns of communication with their sons. The mothers did not differ regarding level of language usage, pattern of functional interaction, or overall clarity of communication. These two studies suggest that parents of autistics cannot be distinguished from parents of dysphasics on variables hypothesized to be relevant to the etiology of autism.

Kanner's (1949) observations are open to question today. Indeed, the Cox et al. (1975) and Cantwell et al. (1977) studies seem to imply that even if Kanner's observations were accurate, such qualities may not be limited to parents of autistics. Furthermore, no data has been found to suggest that early infantile autism develops as a result of either parental behavior or characteristics; it is as likely that these alleged qualities arise as a result of the experience of raising such a child.

Rutter (1974) concludes, "there is so much evidence against the view that autism is a primarily psychogenic disorder, that it would not seem worthwhile to investigate it further" (p. 152).

Genetic/Biochemical/Neurological

The role of genetics is unclear. Whereas Hanson and Gottesman (1976) reviewed relevant literature and concluded that no strong evidence exists for genetic transmission of the disorder, Folstein and Rutter (1977) studied 11 monozygotic and 10 dizygotic twin pairs and concluded that there are important hereditary influences concerning a cognitive deficit (i.e., probably involving language) associated with autism. Both of these articles suggest, in addition, that biological hazards and congenital anomalies (e.g., viral infection during prenatal life, neonatal convulsions, delay in breathing of at least 5 minutes after birth) are sufficient to cause autism.

Moore and Shiek (1971) view autism as due to faulty imprinting. They theorize that certain fetuses with an inherited high potential for intellectual superiority actually become imprinted within the uterine environment rather than postnatally. Once born, these infants exhibit autistic symptomatology. No data are presented, however, and Webb (1972) seriously questions whether imprinting is possible under such circumstances and whether intellectual potential is indicative of precocious development.

There has been much speculation concerning biochemical and hematologic influences upon autism, especially the role of a disturbance in serotonin metabolism (Boullin, Coleman, & O'Brien, 1970; Rimland, 1972). Ritvo, Rabin, Yuwiler, Freeman, and Geller (1978) reviewed the growing literature and found it difficult to make general conclusions. They comment, "even a cursory analysis of the studies we have reviewed reveals difficulties caused by lack of diagnostic specificity and objective clinical ratings" (p. 179).

Several theorists have hypothesized pathology of the central nervous system to account for the development of the syndrome. Gold and Gold (1975) present data to support the notion that autism is due to a malfunction in basic alerting and attentional mechanisms of the central nervous system. The child inappropriately analyzes incoming stimuli as non-novel and insignificant, often resulting in the absence of an appropriate orienting response. Ornitz (1978) suggests, after presenting relevant supportive data, that a disturbance of the child's vestibular system is responsible for difficulties in sensorimotor integration that result in the autistic repertoire. Rutter and Bartak (1971) suggest that a cognitive defect involving an impairment in language comprehension, in control functions associated with language, and with processing of symbolic or sequenced information is a primary characteristic of autism. Social and behavioral abnormalities are viewed as secondary consequences. Although the central nervous system appears to be implicated in such a defect, Rutter (1974) is careful to point out that the biological basis of the cognitive defect remains unknown.

Behavioral

Ferster (1961) speculated that the behavioral repertoire of the autistic child is learned in the same way that other behavior is learned. That is, the child is born with the capabilities to develop normally but, due to his specific learning experiences, develops the autistic repertoire. Prolonged extinction and intermittent reinforcement act to prevent the permanent acquisition of speech and social behavior. The parents, being the predominant sources of reinforcement for the child, are the agents of this extinction and intermittent reinforcement. As a consequence of this learning history, secondary reinforcers such as praise and attention exert little or no control over the child.

Previously Phillips (1957) used Miller's (1944) approach–avoidance conflict theory to account for the development of the syndrome. The approach gradient was equated with assertiveness and the avoidance gradient with denial of experience. Conflict creates tension, which results in the autistic symptomatology.

Comment

Psychodynamic, physiological, and behavioral theories of autism have been developed over the years to account for this puzzling phenomenon. The accumulation of data to date leaves the puzzle far from being understood. As Rutter (1978) concludes in his recent review, "lastly, of course, the cause or causes of autism and the psychological mechanisms that underlie its development have still to be established" (p. 156).

ASSESSMENT

> Confusion and disagreement in the diagnosis of autism is widely recognized in the field. It can be found in the literature and at professional meetings when the research findings for autistic children from one study do not coincide with those reported in another because criteria for diagnosis are different. It can also be seen at the clinical level, when discord is reflected in the treatment decisions for a child. (Schopler, 1978, p. 137)

This chapter began by stating that universal agreement as to the diagnostic criteria for early infantile autism has yet to be found. Then

Rutter's (1978) four essential criteria were presented. It is useful at this point to examine several other major systems of classification.

The earliest attempt at diagnostic criteria is Kanner (1943), who proposed 12 features of autism. These were:

1. The autistic child is always aloof.
2. The child looks normal, alert, and expressive.
3. Motor coordination seems normal.
4. The child avoids eye contact and lacks visual or auditory responses to others.
5. There is no physical reaching out in infancy.
6. The child does not initiate sounds or gestures.
7. Speech is not used for communication.
8. The child has a marked facility with objects, in contrast to his response to people and to language.
9. Psychometric performance indicates that cognitive potentialities are masked by the basic disorder.
10. There is an obsessive desire to maintain sameness.
11. Bedwetting, thumbsucking, nailbiting, and masturbation are rarely associated with autism.
12. The rate of occurrence is less than 1 percent in the general population.

Continued research led Eisenberg and Kanner (1956) to conclude that all of the original diagnostic criteria except two also were found in other childhood disorders. These two major features of autism were the lack of object relations and the maintenance of sameness via stereotyped behaviors.

Ward's (1970) diagnostic standards are: (a) lack of object relations from birth, (b) lack of use of speech for communication, (c) maintenance of sameness via stereotyped behavior, and (d) lack of neurological dysfunction. DeMyer, Churchill, Pontius, and Gilkey (1971) present the following criteria: (a) emotional withdrawal from people before the age of three, (b) lack of speech for communication, (c) nonfunctional, repetitive use of objects, and (d) failure to engage in role playing alone or with other children. Finally, Ornitz and Ritvo (1976) conceptualize autism as consisting of disturbances of perception, developmental rate, relating (e.g., poor eye contact, delayed or absent social smile), speech and language (e.g., muteness, echolalia), and at times motility (e.g., swaying, headbanging, moving of hands within the visual field).

The differential diagnosis of autism from childhood schizophrenia has received some attention in the literature. Most authors agree that behaviorally it is difficult to distinguish the two. It has been suggested that the critical variable is the level of functioning before the onset of the disorder (Eisenberg & Kanner, 1956; Ward, 1970). Childhood schizophrenia is generally seen as a withdrawal from a previously adequate level of functioning, whereas autism represents inadequate functioning from the start. However, even here there is less than perfect agreement.

It follows that the assessment of autism would be dependent upon the system of criteria that the assessor utilizes. Regardless of the specific system utilized, however, assessment would generally incorporate behavioral observation and history taking. In order to facilitate this process, a number of scales have been devised to aid the clinician. It is noteworthy that when four popular scales (Creak, 1964; Lotter, 1966; Polan & Spencer, 1959; and Rimland, 1964) were used to diagnose the same group of 44 children referred consecutively to a clinical center, DeMyer et al. (1971) found only a 35 percent degree of correspondence among them.

For the behavioral clinician, assessment consists of more than merely establishing a working diagnosis. It is the assessment that identifies the targets for treatment. The child's behavioral repertoire is examined to identify undesirable or maladaptive behaviors which are to be reduced or eliminated, and behavioral deficits indicative of adaptive responses which are to be established or increased. Potential primary and conditioned reinforcers are also identified for use in the program to be developed.

BEHAVIORAL TREATMENT PROCEDURES
Evaluating Treatment Reports

Therapeutic interventions are presented in the literature in many ways, from the uncontrolled case study to methodologically sophisticated group designs. The degree of confidence that one places in the findings of a report is directly related to the methodological rigor of the experimental design.

Each of the reports which follows in this section has been evaluated for its experimental rigor through the use of the Design Quality Rating scale (DQR). Table 1 presents the DQRs of treatment reports grouped by intervention target in this section.

Eliminating Maladaptive Behaviors

The autistic repertoire often contains responses that are maladaptive or undesirable in some way. Some responses can have dangerous consequences for the child and for those around him; others may

Table 1. Design quality ratings of treatment reports, grouped by target.

Target	Author(s)	Date	No. of Ss	DQR[a]
Self-destructive	Wolf, Risley, & Mees	1964	1	9
behavior	Wolf et al.	1967	1	7
	Yeakel et al.	1970	1	1
Tantrums	Davison	1965	1	7
	Wetzel et al.	1966	1	8
	Jensen & Womack	1967	1	8
	Schell & Adams	1968	1	8
	Martin et al.	1968	4	8
Aggressive and	Wolf et al.	1964	1	9
disruptive behavior	Wolf et al.	1967	1	7
	Jensen & Womack	1967	1	8
	Brown, Pace, & Becker	1969	1	10
	Tramontana & Stimbert	1970	1	1
	Husted, Hall, & Agin	1971	4	12
Self-stimulation	Lovaas et al.	1965	2	9
	Koegel & Covert	1972	3	20
	Foxx & Azrin	1973	4	21
	Koegel et al.	1974	2	20
	Wells et al.	1977	2	20
Toilet training	Marshall	1966	1	8.5
	Wolf et al.	1967	1	7
	Ando	1977	5	9
	Matson	1977	1	7
Eye contact	McConnell	1967	1	13
	Brooks et al.	1968	1	12
Imitation	Metz	1965	2	10
	Hewett	1965	1	2
	Hingtgen et al.	1967	2	11
	Stark et al.	1968	1	8
	Marshall & Hegrenes	1970	1	9
	Craighead et al.	1973	1	14

[a]Note that a single report may earn different DQR scores for different treatment targets and thus may be listed more than once.

preclude more adaptive functioning until they are significantly reduced or eliminated. Self-destructive behavior, tantrums, aggressive and disruptive behavior, and self-stimulation have all been targets of behavioral interventions. As Lovaas, Koegel, Simmons, and Long (1973) have pointed out, such interventions have involved one or more of the following: (a) contingent reinforcement withdrawal (e.g., time-out rooms, looking away from the child), (b) contingent aversive stimulation, and (c) reinforcement of incompatible behavior.

Table 1. *(Continued)*

Target	Author(s)	Date	No. of Ss	DQR[a]
Verbal imitation and functional speech	Wolf et al.	1964	1	9
	Hewett	1965	1	5
	Wetzel et al.	1966	1	9
	Jensen & Womack	1967	1	8
	Schell et al.	1967	1	9
	Fineman	1968a	1	7
	Fineman	1968b	1	7
	Martin et al.	1968	4	8
	Stark et al.	1968	1	9
	Halpern	1970	15	15
	Marshall & Hegrenes	1970	4	10
	Tramontana & Stimbert	1970	1	3
	Jellis & Grainger	1972	1	7
	Sailor & Taman	1972	3	21
	Stevens-Long & Rasmussen	1974	1	19
	Coleman & Stedman	1974	1	8
Communication with sign language	Fulwiler & Fouts	1976	1	9
	Bonvillian & Nelson	1976	1	9
	Salvin et al.	1977	1	15
	Casel	1978	4	15.5
	Brady & Smouse	1978	1	18
Peer interaction and prosocial behavior	Lovaas et al.	1965	2	16
	Wetzel et al.	1966	1	8
	Schell & Adams	1968	1	8
	Means & Merrens	1969	1	8.5
Classroom behavior	Rabb & Hewett	1967	2	9
	Martin et al.	1968	4	9
	Koegel & Rincover	1974	8	20
	Russo & Koegel	1977	1	14

Self-destructive Behavior. Headbanging, face scratching, and self-slapping are often associated with the autistic condition. The child's physical survival often rests upon the clinician's ability to eliminate such behavior. The learning of adaptive behavior is often difficult, if not impossible, while the child engages in this activity.

Wolf, Risley, and Mees (1964) used a time-out room to eliminate headbanging and face scratching in a 3½-year-old autistic boy. The child was placed in the room contingent upon the onset of such behavior, and he remained there until the behavior had ceased. This proved effective in eliminating the problem, as a 6-month follow-up demonstrated. The same procedure later proved equally effective in eliminating selfslapping in the child, as reported by Wolf, Risley, Johnston, Harris, and Allen (1967).

Contingent aversive stimulation was utilized in the treatment of constant head banging in a 14-year-old autistic girl by Yeakel, Salisbury, Greer, and Marcus (1970). A helmetlike device was developed which absorbed the impact of the blows without harming the girl's wrists and delivered a shock to her arm whenever she hit her head. The authors observed that the headbanging was rapidly eliminated by the helmet when it was worn, only to return to full strength when the device was removed. No data were presented, however.

Lovaas (1970) commented upon his approach to the problem, which generally involved the use of contingent shock;

> To summarize the result of our treatment projects, I would say that we are probably best, most efficient and most reliable, at removing behavior. This is particularly true in the case of self-destructive behavior where, seemingly independently of how badly the child is mutilating himself or how long he has been doing so, we can essentially remove the self-destructive behavior within the first minute. (p. 38)

The studies and comments reviewed seem to indicate that behavioral techniques, including time-out rooms and contingent aversive stimulation, are effective in the treatment of the autistic child's self-destructive behavior. However, the relatively low DQRs presented in Table 1 indicate that these reports fall somewhat short of being methodologically sound. Studies falling within the realm of experimental or quasi-experimental design (Campbell & Stanley, 1963) are needed to support undeniably the effectiveness of these procedures.

Tantrums.   Tantrum behavior is maintained by its consequences (Bandura, 1969). Williams (1959) showed that the removal of attention contingent upon such behavior resulted in the extinction of the response in a nonautistic infant.

Wetzel, Baker, Roney, and Martin (1966) attempted to deal with the tantrums of a 6-year-old autistic boy by using isolation as a time-out procedure. The child was given an initial warning and then kept in a room until the tantrum had ceased for 3 minutes. Within one month, the tantrums almost completely disappeared. Jensen and Womack (1967) effectively used a time-out room to eliminate the tantrums of a 6-year-old autistic boy within a 10-week period. Schell and Adams (1968) taught parents to extinguish tantrums in their 3-year-old child by ignoring him and using a time-out room. Martin, England, Kaprowy, Kilgour, and Pilek (1968) ignored tantrum behavior and then reinforced quietness in a classroom setting. This program proved effective by the end of the 12-week training period. Davison (1965) emphasized the use of explanations as well as extinction in reducing the tantrums of a 9-year-old verbal autistic boy.

The literature tends to support the notion that tantrum behavior can readily be eliminated through the effects of time-out and related techniques. Caution should be taken, however, since the proper experimental controls are all but absent in this body of work.

Aggressive and Disruptive Behavior. As aggressive and disruptive behavior is reduced, the child becomes viewed in a more positive manner. The elimination of such behavior increases the likelihood of the child finding a responsive environment.

The use of time-out procedures has been well documented in this area. Wolf et al. (1964) significantly reduced the throwing of eyeglasses by a 3½-year-old and later reported (1967) eliminating the same child's tendency to pinch other children and teachers. Tramontana and Stimbert (1970) controlled disruptive behavior in a 7-year-old autistic boy, and Husted, Hall and Agin (1971) eliminated physical aggression and running from the living unit in four children, three of whom were autistic, during a 14-month program. Husted et al. reported that comparisons with baseline measures showed time-out to be highly effective. The target responses resumed, however, when contingencies were dropped.

Jensen and Womack (1967) successfully used immediate contingent punishment on a 6-year-old child over a period of 10 weeks to eliminate such aggressive behaviors as spitting, stepping on others, and hitting. Punishment consisted of an immediate slap, brief restraint, or verbal disapproval. Verbal negativism was the target of a program devised by Brown, Pace, and Becker (1969). After baseline recordings were made, the child was forced to comply with simple instructions. The same responses were then contingently reinforced with tokens, and later with tokens and praise. Data taken at each of these phases indicated that the verbal negativism was greatly reduced by the end of treatment.

Although this group of studies is suggestive of therapeutic effectiveness, once again, the lack of experimental rigor precludes definitive conclusions.

Self-stimulation. Stereotyped self-stimulatory activity is a frequent characteristic of autism. Hand flapping, rhythmic rocking, and the twirling of objects in front of the eyes are rather typical components of the repertoire. It has been suggested that the child's ability to learn is diminished during periods of self-stimulation (Koegel & Covert, 1972; Koegel, Firestone, Kramme, & Dunlap, 1974). "Autistic children appear to be most unresponsive to their environment when engaged in ritualistic stereotyped behaviors" (Koegel & Covert, 1972, p. 381). These authors conclude that "functionally, the data suggest that if one attempts to teach a new behavior to an autistic child, it is important to ensure that the child does not engage in self-stimulatory behavior" (p. 387).

Attempts to eliminate self-stimulation have varied. Suppression during experimental sessions has been achieved through verbal reprimand, slapping, briefly immobilizing the part of the body involved in the response (Koegel & Covert, 1972; Koegel et al., 1974), and contingent electric shock (Lovaas, Schaeffer, & Simmons, 1965). Lovaas (1970) has acknowledged, however, that suppression generalized with great difficulty, although such attempts were successful during experimental manipulations, and he has hypothesized that internal reinforcement is responsible for maintaining the behavior. Foxx and Azrin (1973) developed the *overcorrection procedure,* which requires the child to practice more adaptive forms of behavior that use the body part in question contingent upon the onset of self-stimulation. Comparisons made between overcorrection and alternatives such as physical punishment and reinforcement for nonself-stimulatory behavior found overcorrection to be most effective, rapid, and enduring. Finally, Wells, Forehand, Hickey, and Green (1977) successfully used overcorrection to reduce stereotyped behaviors displayed by two autistic children: one of the children even displayed a marked increase in the adaptive behavior practiced during overcorrection, compared to baseline activity.

It can be concluded that overcorrection and other behavioral means have been found to be effective in reducing autistic self-stimulation. The literature has been of a generally high quality, as reflected in Table 1.

Expanding the Behavioral Repertoire

In addition to maladaptive and undesirable responses, the autistic child demonstrates a gross deficit in adaptive behavior. Absent from the child's repertoire may be such skills as proper toilet training, eye contact, imitation, verbal behavior and language, peer interaction, and classroom behavior. Such a limited repertoire may result in difficulty for the child in dealing effectively with his environment and significant others.

The behavior modification literature offers a number of strategies that have been found to be effective in expanding the repertoires of a wide range of populations. These have included reinforcement of successive approximations (i.e., shaping) with primary or conditioned reinforcers, the use of instructions, modeling, guided participation, behavior rehearsal, and negative reinforcement (Bandura, 1969; Rimm & Masters, 1974).

Toilet Training. Shaping and contingent reinforcement were major components of a program developed by Marshall (1966) to treat a nonverbal autistic boy who defecated in his pants approximately 95 percent of the time. The criterion response was reduced to a set of components (e.g., approach to the toilet, removal of clothing, proper body posture, straining), each of which was reinforced in turn. In addition, punishment in the form of a slap on the buttocks was employed, contingent upon soiled pants. By the end of therapy, the rate of soiling was reduced to 30 percent of the time. The child's mother was trained to continue treatment after termination and was successful in completely toilet training her son. Shaping and contingent reinforcement also were utilized by Wolf et al. (1967), along with guided instruction, to toilet train their subject successfully.

Ando (1977) utilized operant procedures, contingent reinforcement, and punishment to attempt to teach five severely autistic boys aged 6 through 9 to urinate in the toilet. Some success was achieved for four of the children, although none completely eliminated inappropriate urination. The author concluded that "the results of the study show that operant conditioning techniques can be used to change the urination behavior of profoundly retarded autistic children even where other methods have failed" (p. 151).

Finally, Matson (1977) reported on the successful application of the *simple correction* procedure for eliminating encopresis and establishing appropriate toilet use in a 16-year-old autistic boy. This procedure required the child to clean up after himself upon soiling, and it made verbal praise contingent upon appropriate toilet use. At baseline, the child averaged 3.6 soils per day. Treatment lasted for 2 weeks and at a 3-month follow-up there had been no accidents since the end of treatment.

As Table 1 indicates, these reports offer no true experimental evidence as to the efficacy of the techniques employed. They do, however, suggest positive consequences for the interventions. Needless to say, more rigorous experimental data would be of great value.

Eye Contact. Autistic children show little eye contact in response to other human beings. If allowed to continue, this behavior can decrease the probability of effective social interaction and minimize treatment opportunities. Brooks, Morrow, and Gray (1968) commented, "As long as gaze aversion is typical in a subject, normal social interaction is not possible. Once visual attention responses are established, the work of training other social skills can begin" (p. 309). McConnell (1967) demonstrated, through the use of an equivalent time-samples design, the effectiveness of praise and smiling contingent upon eye contact in a 5½-year-old autistic boy. Primary reinforcement in the form of candy was used by Brooks et al. (1968) to establish visual attention in a 19-year-old deaf autistic girl. Measures taken during baseline, continuous reinforcement, variable ratio reinforcement, extinction, and variable ratio conditions once again demonstrated the power of the contingencies. Hartung (1970) suggested beginning the shaping process by holding the primary reinforcer directly in front of the therapist's face: the child would tend to look at the reinforcer and thereby attend to the therapist's face as well.

Thus it has been demonstrated that contingent reinforcement can establish and maintain eye contact in the autistic child. From this point other social skills become a potential reality.

Imitation. Autistic children are less likely than other children to imitate the actions of those around them. As Hingtgen, Coulter, and Churchill (1967) have suggested, this absence of imitation may contribute to the child's limited behavioral repertoire. Since imitation facilitates the learning process, learning to imitate can play an important role in further expanding the child's repertoire.

Metz (1965) used passive demonstration (i.e., physically guiding the child through the act), shaping, and fading to teach two autistic children to imitate specific behaviors. It was found that autistics are capable of learning imitation, such learning can generalize to similar but new situations, and the generalized response persists over time. Shaping was also used in studies by Hewett (1965), Stark, Giddan, and Meisel (1968), Marshall and Hegrenes (1970), and Hingtgen et al. (1967). As the DQRs presented in Table 1 indicate, however, these studies are not without methodological difficulties. In an experimental study, Craighead, O'Leary, and Allen (1973) used food and praise to teach a 4-year-old boy diagnosed as autistic to follow verbal instructions. The child learned to follow the instructions presented, and the response generalized to new people and instructions and continued when the original intervention was withdrawn.

Verbal Imitation and Functional Speech. Autistic children are generally mute or echolalic; rarely are they found to employ adaptive, functional speech. Consequently, there has been a growing literature that attempts to demonstrate that these children can be taught to communicate verbally.

Verbal learning is not possible without the ability to communicate. Once generalized imitation skills have been established, nonvocal imitation has been extended to include use of the mouth, tongue, jaws, and lips (Marshall & Hegrenes, 1970; Stark et al., 1968). Lovaas et al. (1973) explained the process of establishing verbal imitation in the following way:

> Briefly, verbal imitation was established in five steps: (1) The child received reinforcement for vocalizing in order to increase the frequency of speech sounds. (2) We then established a temporal discrimination. The child received reinforcement only for those vocalizations that were emitted within a five-second period after the therapist made a vocalization. (3) The therapist now began to demand similarity for vocalizations between himself and the child. For example, the therapist gave reinforcement for a sound only after the therapist had just emitted that sound himself. (4) After the child reliably emitted one sound, the therapist introduced a second sound and reinforced reproductions of that sound. These first two sounds were then presented in a random order so that the child was required to discriminate between the two vocalizations. (5) A third sound was presented, requiring increasingly fine discriminations. (p. 135)

Labels for objects are established through the use of shaping, prompting, and fading. The shaping process begins with sounds already in the child's repertoire and is extended until the proper labels are verbalized. Echolalic children are prompted through the use of questions, and gradually the prompts are faded until the child is properly labeling objects. Generalization is maximized by having the child use speech in settings other than the one in which it was learned. Closer and closer approximations to functional speech are shaped as pronoun use and other aspects of language are programmed in (Lovaas et al., 1973; Risley & Wolf, 1967).

A large number of studies have appeared in the last 15 years supporting the notion that verbal imitation and functional speech are legitimate targets for these behavioral techniques. For example, Fineman (1968a, 1968b) and Jellis and Grainger (1972) were able to increase the frequency of vocalizations in mute autistics through the use of contingent changes in the visual display of a color organ and a projected kaleidoscope pattern.

Hewett (1965) reported on a program to teach verbal skills to a 4½-year-old mute autistic boy: Imitation skills were developed, verbal imitation was shaped, object labels were learned, appropriate answers to questions were taught, and generalization was maximized. The child's vocabulary grew to 150 words. Schell, Stark, and Giddan (1967) prompted and shaped the verbal behavior of a 4-year-old nonverbal autistic boy and taught him to follow verbal instructions in a 15-week program. Stark, Giddan, and Meisel (1968) utilized imitation training and fading to establish verbal labeling. In this manner, the child learned to use such words as knee, eye, and pie properly. The authors remarked that by the end of 8 months, considerable progress was evident and the use of language had acquired secondary reinforcing properties. Other studies which have reported on the acquisition of functional speech by previously nonverbal autistics include Marshall and Hegrenes (1970) and Halpern (1970).

Still other studies have attempted to shape functional speech in autistics who were somewhat verbal or echolalic before the intervention began. Wolf et al. (1964) shaped verbal responses in a child who could mimic. Food was used as a reinforcer to establish object names. Wetzel et al. (1966) taught command following and object naming to a 6-year-old echolalic boy through prompting and fading. By the end of treatment, the child was capable of naming nearly 100 objects and of following 70 to 80 commands. Similarly, Jensen and Womack (1967), as part of their 10-week treatment program for a 6-year-old autistic, taught the child proper object names and complete sentence usage. Martin et al. (1968) employed prompting and fading to teach seven autistics who were able to mimic to answer properly questions asked of them over a 12-week period. Tramontana and Stimbert (1970) did the same with a 7-year-old autistic boy. In a multiple baseline design, Stevens-Long and Rasmussen (1974) demonstrated the use of contingent reinforcement and imitative prompts to establish simple and compound sentence usage. Coleman and Stedman (1974) used shaping and modeling by a peer (i.e., another child) to train a 10-year-old echolalic girl to speak at a normal voice volume, acquire a labeling vocabulary of 100 words, learn the alphabet, and respond to specific questions with complete sentence answers.

Finally, Sailor and Taman (1972) illustrated the training of prepositional usage in three autistic children under "ambiguous" and "nonambiguous" stimulus conditions. Ambiguous conditions employed the same stimulus objects to train use of both *in* and *on*; nonambiguous conditions employed different stimulus objects for each preposition. The results for two of the children indicated the superiority of the nonambiguous condition. Results for the third child suggested that initial training with nonambiguous stimuli might contribute to accurate responding under ambiguous conditions later.

This large body of work certainly supports the contention that verbal imitation and functional speech can be established in mute and echolalic autistics. However, an examination of Table 1 leads to the conclusion that evidence of a methodologically sound nature is scarce; indeed, most of the studies cited fall short of true experimental control. In addition, it is important to realize that although some verbal skills appear to have been learned, the degree to which meaningful language has been taught is questionable. Lovaas (1970) comments:

> With respect to building behavior, it is certainly true that with the older and mute autistic children, our progress has been quite limited. As an example, the program we have for building speech in these children has been fairly well limited to establishing elementary vocabularies for requesting wants. In the case of echolalic children, we have been more successful. (p. 39)

Communication with Sign Language. An alternative to the development of vocal speech has been the recent emphasis upon the acquisition of manual sign language (e.g., American Sign Language), especially for mute autistics. As the following studies suggest, signing may very well be an adaptive means of communication for some autistics.

Fulwiler and Fouts (1976) spent 20 hours teaching American Sign Language to a 5-year-old nonverbal autistic boy. The therapist spoke each word while demonstrating, molding, or prompting the sign. It was found that the child did acquire use of the signs and such usage spontaneously generalized to new situations. In addition, increased signing led to increased vocal speech and resulted in increased social interaction. Bonvillian and Nelson (1976) taught a 9-year-old mute autistic boy to communicate through American Sign Language over a 6-month period through the use of molding (i.e., the teacher shaped the child's hands and guided them through the proper motion) and imitation (i.e., modeling and behavior rehearsal). The authors concluded that "Ted's success in both producing and comprehending sign language suggests that his cognitive and linguistic abilities had been relatively untapped by previous speech-oriented family and therapeutic settings" (p. 345).

In a more rigorously controlled study, Salvin, Routh, Foster, and Lovejoy (1977) attempted to teach a modified form of American Sign Language to a mute 5-year-old autistic boy who had previously failed in attempts to learn spoken language. At the end of 20 sessions of prompting, manual guidance, and reinforcement, the child had mastered 12 signs. At a 6-month follow-up, he demonstrated a receptive vocabulary of approximately 30 signed words and an expressive vocabulary of approximately 10 words, and was capable of responding to approximately 20 spoken words. In another well-controlled study, Casel (1978) taught mothers of autistic children to use manual signs with verbalizations to foster appropriate communicative behavior and to reduce maladaptive behavior in their children. A multiple baseline design indicated that as a result of the intervention, communicative behaviors increased and inappropriate behaviors decreased as compared to baseline for each child.

Brady and Smouse (1978), after having found that an approach that utilized both manual signing and vocal speech training was more effective than either of those procedures alone, cautiously concluded that "the recent enthusiasm for signing as a treatment with autistic children should be tempered with recognition that there may be significant variation among autistic children which would dictate the preferred mode of language training for a given child" (p. 279).

Peer Interaction and Prosocial Behavior. Social withdrawal seems to characterize the autistic child. The absence of peer interaction is typical. Wetzel et al. (1966) increased approach behavior with a 6-year-old in a 3-month program. Adult attention was used to shape the desired response, and success was indicated by a sign'ficant increase over baseline measurements. Means and Merrens (1969) in working with a 3½-year-old boy shaped approach and parallel play. Lovaas et al. (1965) presented data to support the use of electric shock to build social behavior. Using the shock as a negative reinforcer, approach responses to adults brought about a reduction in the aversive stimulus. As a result of the treatment, the authors noted increases in affectionate and other social behaviors toward adults. Schell and Adams (1968) reported teaching play behavior to a 3-year-old autistic boy through the use of modeling, behavior rehearsal, and imitation of successively closer approximations to the desired goal.

These four studies suggest that prosocial behavior can be established through behavioral means. Table 1 reflects, however, that only the Lovaas et al. (1965) study offers firm empirical support. In addition, the establishment of prosocial responses becomes inconsequential unless generalization to the daily life of the child is accomplished. Breger (1965), commenting upon the work of Lovaas et al. (1965), concluded that little lasting generalization actually did occur. It seems necessary to bring prosocial responses under the control of social reinforcement in order to maintain gains made in the laboratory.

Classroom Behavior. Rabb and Hewett (1967) in a preliminary report found that tokens made contingent upon appropriate attention and classroom activity performance were effective in maintaining these target behaviors. Martin et al. (1968) shaped classroom behavior by beginning with a 1:1 student:teacher ratio in a small room, and gradually moving to a more typical classroom setting and increasing the ratio to 7:1. Tokens were used to teach appropriate behaviors, including sitting quietly at a desk, tracing, and copying. The procedure was successful in varying degrees for 7 of the 10 children involved. Koegel and Rincover (1974) taught basic classroom tasks to eight autistics in a 1:1 student:teacher ratio; fading procedures successfully maintained these behaviors for larger student:teacher ratios. Finally, Russo and Koegel (1977) utilized a multiple baseline design to demonstrate that contingency management procedures could allow a 5-year-old autistic girl to attend a normal public school classroom successfully. Training her teachers in behavioral techniques was sufficient to maintain appropriate behavior throughout kindergarten and the first grade.

Generalization and Maintenance of Change

Successful intervention will not simply establish the desired target responses; these responses should occur in settings other than the learning environment and should be durable over time. *Generalization* refers to appropriate responding in extra-therapy settings and *maintenance* to the subsequent continuation of such responding (Koegel & Rincover, 1977). Nordquist and Wahler (1973) noted that successful treatment in the laboratory is no guarantee that the response will transfer to the child's natural environment. Breger (1965) argued that generalization of behavior learned by autistics should not be expected. He stated, "In a sense, the autistic child seems to be that rare organism that behaves according to strict S–R principles. He cannot make use of past experience in any integrative fashion" (p. 112).

Rincover and Koegel (1975) found generalization to be a problem of antecedent stimulus control; generalization was likely to occur when the antecedent stimulus that was functional during the learning experience was introduced into the extra-therapy environment. Koegel and Rincover (1977) found maintenance to be more likely when partial reinforcement schedules were used in the treatment environment and noncontingent reinforcers were present in the extra-therapy setting.

Without an appropriate post-treatment environment, treatment effects may easily extinguish. Lovaas (1970), for example, found that those children discharged from his program to institutions where they received little treatment regressed to pretreatment levels of functioning within months.

As Rincover and Koegel (1975) and Koegel and Rincover (1977) have noted, generalization and maintenance are possible if programmed into treatment. This programming may involve teaching the new response under a number of stimulus situations and altering the child's everyday environment to offer the appropriate contingencies (Risley & Wolf, 1967; Schell & Adams, 1968; Tramontana & Stimbert, 1970). Indeed, Lovaas et al. (1970) found such efforts to meet with success.

An Evaluation

Much of the work presented in this section lacks the methodological controls of experimental or quasi-experimental designs (Campbell & Stanley, 1963). Indeed, 70 percent of the entries in Table 1 earned DQR scores within the "poor" range. What can be concluded? Margolies (1977), in his review of the treatment literature, suggests:

> This is not to say, however, that behavioral interventions were found ineffective. Rather, true experimental conclusions were precluded by the frequent lack of experimental rigor. However, the large volume of preexperimental data supporting the effectiveness of behavior modification cannot be taken lightly. Although one case study suggests little, a large volume of preexperimental reports confirming the utilization of behavioral intervention does suggest that something positive may be occurring. It will take better controlled experimental work to confirm this assertion. (p. 261)

CLINICAL PRESCRIPTION

The assessment serves two basic functions: to establish the diagnosis and to identify targets for behavioral intervention. History taking, behavioral observation, and the use of an empirically validated diagnostic scale (e.g., Rimland, 1964) all contribute data for the clinician to consider in choosing the appropriate diagnosis.

The identification of targets for treatment rests largely upon an examination of the child's behavioral repertoire. Undesirable or maladaptive behaviors in need of reduction or elimination may include self-destructive behavior, tantrums, aggressive and disruptive behavior, and stereotyped self-stimulation. Behavioral deficits, which suggest adaptive responses needing to be established or increased, may include improper toilet training, the absence of appropriate eye contact, poor imitation skills, muteness or echolalia, and social isolation.

At this point in the assessment, potential primary and conditioned reinforcers are identified for use in the programs to be developed.

Maladaptive behaviors are generally reduced or eliminated through contingent reinforcement withdrawal (e.g., time-out rooms), contingent aversive stimulation, and reinforcement of incompatible behavior. Self-destructive behavior, including headbanging and self-slapping, has been treated with contingent shock and time-out procedures. Time-out and reinforcement of alternative behaviors are recommended for tantrums and aggressive behavior. Overcorrection procedures appear to offer promise in the suppression of self-stimulation.

The behavioral repertoire is capable of being expanded through the use of several behavioral procedures: shaping with primary or conditioned reinforcers, instructions, modeling, guided participation, behavior rehearsal, and negative reinforcement. Appropriate toilet behavior often can be established through the use of guided participation, shaping, and contingent aversive consequences for inappropriate responding (e.g., simple correction procedures). Eye contact has been established with shaping and contingent reinforcement. Imitation and the use of functional speech have been established through the use of guided participation, prompting, shaping, and fading, as has the use of sign language communication. Shaping and negative reinforcement have been shown to establish prosocial behavior, and shaping and fading procedures have placed autistics in classroom settings.

The clinician should take steps to insure that therapeutic gains generalize to post-treatment settings and then are maintained over time. Such steps may include teaching the new response under a number of stimulus conditions and altering the child's post-treatment environment to offer contingencies that will maintain the newly learned behavior. Teaching parents and other caretakers behavioral principles should be helpful in this respect.

How much change can the clinician expect? Margolies (1977) notes, "Clearly, these children are not made normal. Speech and classroom behavior, for example, only grossly approximate that of the normal child. However, considering the state of the child's repertoire before intervention, it has been suggested that behavior modification has indeed produced real change" (p. 261).

CASE REPORT

The literature offers many case studies that illustrate the use of behavioral procedures with autistic children. The following case, presented by Jensen and Womack (1967), was chosen because of the diversity of target behaviors and the fact that therapeutic gain was made after other treatment approaches had been exhausted.

Jerry was a 7-year-old autistic boy whose prenatal history and birth were apparently without incident. At 2 months, his mother noticed that he did not respond to cradling as his siblings had. He began to walk and hum tunes at 16 months and was toilet trained at 2 years. Temper tantrums began roughly at age 2; he became easily upset with changes in his environment or patterns of handling. He generally avoided human contact, showed no preference for family members over strangers, and spent much time engaged in stereotyped behaviors. He was somewhat verbal, having learned the one-word names of some foods.

He had spent the previous 12 months participating in a psychodynamic treatment program which consisted of milieu therapy on a treatment ward five days a week, play therapy two or three times a week, and psychotherapy for his mother. By the end of the 12 months some gains were evident, including the development of some relationships with significant others, response to some instructions, and an increased attention span. However, therapists and ward staff were of the belief that he had reached a plateau, with little actual change during the past several months. For this reason, behavioral procedures were viewed as a logical next step in the treatment plan.

The behavior therapy program lasted for 10 weeks. It began with the assessment of potential reinforcers (e.g., ice cream, attention from nurse), behaviors to be increased in frequency (e.g., peer interaction, verbal behavior), and behaviors to be minimized or extinguished (e.g., temper tantrums, stereotyped behaviors, aggressive behavior).

Prior to the 10-week program, Jerry was generally oblivious to the activities of his peers, and prosocial activity was absent. Peer interaction was shaped in the program through brief positive statements such as "good" or "fine" and a touch with the hand or a brief embrace. "Within several weeks Jerry was making several daily contacts with peers involving sustained interaction sequences" (pp. 31–32).

Verbal behavior was trained in daily 20-minute sessions. Since Jerry already had a vocabulary of one-word object labels, training consisted of shaping the use of phrases and sentences. "In the ensuing weeks he began using words and word combinations spontaneously. . . . His increased language generalized to use at home as well" (p. 32).

Temper tantrums occurred as often as 10 times a day during baseline. The use of a time-out room with the door opened contingent upon his quieting resulted in tantrums becoming a rarity after several weeks. Stereotyped behaviors, including handwaving and staring at toys or objects, were successfully reduced by contingent withdrawal of the therapist's attention. Aggressive behavior was reduced by contingent aversive consequences consisting of a verbal "no" and/or a brief restraint or immediate mild slap.

In order to facilitate generalization and maintenance, the child's mother was instructed in operant reinforcement principles and techniques. The authors concluded that, "on the basis of this clinical assessment, it appeared that we had succeeded with this child in modifying specific behavior patterns to a considerable degree" (p. 34).

ETHICAL CONSIDERATIONS

Two major objections have appeared in the literature concerning the ethics of behavior modification with autistic children. The use of aversive stimulation, especially electric shock, has been challenged and the seemingly mechanistic nature of the approach has been criticized.

Rimland (1978) notes five common objections to the use of aversive stimulation with autistics: ideological opposition, fear of overuse or abuse, belief that its use is not helpful, confusion with punishment, and dread of electric shock. He suggests that abuse of aversives should be handled by establishing safeguards defining appropriate use and prohibiting misuse. In addition, he notes the growing literature supporting the utility of aversives with certain selected targets (i.e., they are helpful) and points out that electric shock poses no danger to the child, unlike alternatives such as medication and permitting self-destructive behavior to continue. Punishment of autistic children is not the aim of using aversives; the aim is to build a more rewarding repertoire. Finally, he concludes that ideological opposition is simply not rational.

Lichstein and Schreibman (1976) reviewed 12 relevant articles and concluded that the majority of reported side effects of electric shock are actually of a positive nature. These side effects include response generalization, increases in social behavior, and positive emotional behavior. The National Society for Autistic Children (1975), after considering the available evidence, made the following recommendation:

> Clearly, electric shock should not be used when less aversive reinforcers can be used effectively. Moreover, safeguards should be used, including both parental and professional supervision for planned, carefully monitored, and time-limited periods. . . . When alternatives have been exhausted, safeguards against abuse have been employed, and the aversive techniques found helpful in a particular case, it can be the

treatment of choice. To deprive an autistic child of this opportunity for improved survival for any reason not limited to his own welfare is not in his best interest. (pp. 2–3)

Murray (1974) notes that humanistic psychologists have often criticized the mechanistic, "artificially motivated" results of behavior modification. Schreibman and Lovaas (1974), in a rejoinder to Murray, express their belief that such criticism is due simply to a limited understanding of the nature of behavior modification. The National Society for Autistic Children (1975) addresses this issue as well.

We should also remember that it is difficult for autistic children to be spontaneous, and that behavioral techniques do not completely transform the symptoms of their disability. Those who have complained that autistic children have been turned into robots may have overlooked the fact that stereotyped behavior patterns are a basic part of the autistic syndrome (p. 2).

SUGGESTIONS FOR FUTURE RESEARCH

By now it has become apparent that we are only beginning to understand this phenomenon of early infantile autism. It has been little more than 35 years since the problem was first delineated by Kanner; yet today, a technology has developed which has apparently resulted in concrete therapeutic gain in numerous target areas. Nevertheless, this gain is merely a beginning.

The diagnostic criteria used to identify the disorder have yet to be agreed upon universally; an operational definition of early infantile autism needs to be developed. Indeed, it is unclear whether we are dealing with one clearly recognized syndrome or rather a collection of somewhat related phenomena.

Although there is some data supporting various physiological explanations of autism, the etiology of the disorder remains far from clear. Continued research in this area will no doubt contribute to our understanding of the development and maintenance of the disorder.

Considerable research remains to be done in evaluating treatment procedures. Our Design Quality Rating system found that 70 percent of the studies presented were methodologically poor, 13 percent were fair, another 13 percent were found good, and only 3 percent were judged very good. The most recent reports are somewhat superior: of those published since 1975, 44 percent are judged to be poor, 22 percent are fair, and 33 percent receive a good rating. Although a large bulk of preexperimental literature does offer some support for the treatment procedures reviewed, firm conclusions must await data resulting from improved, methodologically superior studies.

SUMMARY

At the present time there is no universal agreement on an operational definition of early infantile autism. Numerous sets of diagnostic criteria have been developed since 1943, when Kanner first delineated the syndrome. Rutter's recent definition is illustrative. He points to four essential criteria in relation to the child's behavior before the age of 5. These are: (a) onset before the age of 30 months; (b) impaired social development, including a lack of attachment behavior and a lack or unusual use of eye-to-eye gaze, which is out of keeping with the child's intellectual level; (c) delayed and deviant language development, including little social imitation and echolalia, which is out of keeping with the child's intellectual level; and (d) insistence on sameness which includes stereotyped play patterns, abnormal preoccupations, and resistance to change.

The age of onset is between birth and 2½ years of age. Autism is diagnosed in 4 children per 10,000 and is seen more frequently in males than females. Prior to the introduction of behavioral interventions, the prognosis was generally quite poor. The best prognostic indicator has been the child's ability to communicate verbally.

The etiology of the disorder is unclear. Psychodynamic, biochemical, neurological, and behavioral theories have been advanced to account for the development and maintenance of autism. Although some supportive data have begun to appear, no theoretical formulation can presently be considered validated.

Behavioral assessment establishes the diagnosis and identifies targets for intervention. History taking, behavioral observation, and the use of empirically validated diagnostic scales contribute data for the clinician to consider in choosing the appropriate diagnosis.

The child's behavioral repertoire is examined to identify potential targets for treatment. Maladaptive behaviors in need of reduction or elimination may include self-destructive behavior, tantrums, aggressive and disruptive behavior, and stereotyped self-stimulation. Adaptive responses which need to be increased or established may include toilet training, eye contact, imitation skills, verbal behavior and language skills, prosocial behavior, and classroom behavior. In addition, at this point in the assessment, potential primary and conditioned reinforcers are identified for use in the programs to be developed.

Maladaptive behaviors are generally reduced or eliminated through contingent reinforcement withdrawal (e.g., time-out rooms), contingent aversive stimulation, and reinforcement of incompatible behavior. The behavioral repertoire is expanded through the use of contingent reinforcement, shaping, instructions, modeling, guided participation, behavior rehearsal, fading, and negative reinforcement.

A substantial treatment literature has developed, suggesting that behavioral interventions are associated with real therapeutic gain for autistics. Since much of this literature is preexperimental in nature, however, more methodologically rigorous research is required to substantiate this finding. In addition, it should be noted that the repertoire of the treated autistic child only grossly approximates that of the normal child.

Ethical considerations include the use of aversive stimulation (e.g., electric shock) and the seemingly mechanistic nature of behavioral interventions. The National Society for Autistic Children addresses such considerations and endorses behavior modification treatment for autistics.

Recommendations for the future include the development of an operational definition of early infantile autism and further inquiry into the etiology of the disorder. Finally, treatment outcome research must be designed with increased methodological rigor. Firm support for the effectiveness of behavioral procedures with autistics awaits data from experimental and quasi-experimental designs.

REFERENCES

Ando, H. Training autistic children to urinate in the toilet through operant conditioning techniques. *Journal of Autism and Childhood Schizophrenia,* 1977, *7,* 151-163.

Bandura, A. *Principles of Behavior Modification.* New York: Holt, Rinehart & Winston, 1969.

Bonvillian, J. D., & Nelson, K. E. Sign language acquisition in a mute autistic boy. *Journal of Speech and Hearing Disorders,* 1967, *41,* 339-347.

Boullin, D. J., Coleman, M., & O'Brien, R. A. Abnormalities in platelet 5-hydroxytryptamine efflux in patients with infantile autism. *Nature,* 1970, *226,* 371–372.

Brady, D. O., & Smouse, A. D. A simultaneous comparison of three methods for language training with an autistic child. An experimental single case analysis. *Journal of Autism and Childhood Schizophrenia,* 1978, *8,* 271–279.

Breger, L. Comments on "Building social behavior in autistic children by use of electric shock." *Journal of Experimental Research in Personality,* 1965, *1,* 110–113.

Brooks, B. D., Morrow, J. E., & Gray, W. F. Reduction of autistic gaze aversion by reinforcement of visual attention responses. *Journal of Special Education,* 1968, *2,* 307–309.

Brown, R. A., Pace, Z. S., & Becker, W. S. Treatment of extreme negativism and autistic behavior in a six-year-old boy. *Exceptional Children,* 1969, *36,* 115–122.

Campbell, D. T., & Stanley, J. C. *Experimental and quasi-experimental designs for research.* Chicago: Rand McNally, 1963.

Cantwell, D. P., Baker, L., & Rutter, M. Families of autistic and dysphasic children: II. Mothers' speech to the children. *Journal of Autism and Childhood Schizophrenia,* 1977, *7,* 313–327.

Casel, L. O. Development of communicative behavior in autistic children: A parent program using manual signs. *Journal of Autism and Childhood Schizophrenia,* 1978, *8,* 45–59.

Coleman, S. L., & Stedman, J. M. Use of a peer model in language training in an echolalic child. *Journal of Behaviour Therapy and Experimental Psychiatry,* 1974, *5,* 275–279.

Cox, A., Rutter, M., Newman, S., & Bartak, L. A comparative study of infantile autism and specific developmental receptive language disorder: II. Parental characteristics. *British Journal of Psychiatry,* 1975, *126,* 146–159.

Craighead, W. E., O'Leary, K. D., & Allen, J. S. Teaching and generalization of instruction following in an "autistic" child. *Journal of Behavior Therapy and Experimental Psychiatry,* 1973, *4,* 171–176.

Creak, M. Schizophrenic syndrome in childhood: Further progress report of a working party. *Developmental Medicine and Child Neurology,* 1964, *6,* 530–535.

Davison, G. C. An intensive long-term social-learning treatment program with an accurately diagnosed autistic child. *Proceedings of the 73rd Annual Convention of the American Psychological Association,* 1965, 203–204 (summary).

DeMyer, M. K., Barton, S., DeMyer, W. E., Norton, J. A., Allen, J., & Steele, R. Prognosis in autism: A follow-up study. *Journal of Autism and Childhood Schizophrenia,* 1973, *3,* 199–246.

DeMyer, M. K., Churchill, D. W., Pontius, W., & Gilkey, K. M. A comparison of five diagnostic systems for childhood schizophrenia and infantile autism. *Journal of Autism and Childhood Schizophrenia,* 1971, *1,* 175–189.

Eisenberg, L., & Kanner, L. Early infantile autism, 1943–1955. *American Journal of Orthopsychiatry,* 1956, *26,* 556–566.

Ferster, C. B. Positive reinforcement and behavioral deficits of young children. *Child Development,* 1961, *32,* 437–456.

Fineman, K. R. Visual-color reinforcement in establishment of speech by an autistic child. *Perceptual and Motor Skills,* 1968, *26,* 761–762. (a)

Fineman, K. R. Shaping and increasing verbalizations in an autistic child in response to visual-color stimulation. *Perceptual and Motor Skills,* 1968, *27,* 1071–1074. (b)

Folstein, S., & Rutter, M. Infantile autism: A genetic study of 21 twin pairs. *Journal of Child Psychology & Psychiatry & Allied Disciplines,* 1977, *18,* 297–321.

Foxx, R. M., & Azrin, N. H. The elimination of autistic self-stimulatory behavior by overcorrection. *Journal of Applied Behavior Analysis,* 1973, *6,* 1-14.

Fraknoi, J., & Ruttenberg, B. A. Formulation of the dynamic economic factors underlying infantile autism. *Journal of the American Academy of Child Psychiatry,* 1971, *10,* 713-738.

Fulwiler, R. L. & Fouts, R. S. Acquisition of American Sign Language by a noncommunicating autistic child. *Journal of Autism and Childhood Schizophrenia,* 1976, *6,* 43-51.

Gold, M. S., & Gold, J. R. Autism and attention: Theoretical considerations and a pilot study using set reaction time. *Child Psychiatry and Human Development,* 1975, *6,* 68-80.

Halpern, W. I. The schooling of autistic children: Preliminary findings. *American Journal of Orthopsychiatry,* 1970, *40,* 665-671.

Hanson, D. R., & Gottesman, I. I. The genetics, if any, of infantile autism and childhood schizophrenia. *Journal of Autism and Childhood Schizophrenia,* 1976, *6,* 209-234.

Hartung, J. R. A review of procedures to increase verbal imitation skills and functional speech in autistic children. *Journal of Speech and Hearing Disorders,* 1970, *35,* 203-217.

Hermelin, B., & O'Connor, N. *Psychological experiments with autistic children.* Oxford, England: Pergamon Press, 1970.

Hewett, F. M. Teaching speech to autistic children through operant conditioning. *American Journal of Orthopsychiatry,* 1965, *35,* 927-936.

Hingtgen, J. N., Coulter, S. K., & Churchill, D. W. Intensive reinforcement of imitative behavior in mute autistic children. *Archives of General Psychiatry,* 1967, *17,* 36-43.

Husted, J. R., Hall, P., & Agin, B. The effectiveness of time-out in reducing maladaptive behavior of autistic and retarded children. *Journal of Psychology,* 1971, *79,* 189-196.

Jellis, T., & Grainger, R. The back projection of kaleidoscopic patterns as a technique for eliciting verbalizations in an autistic child: A preliminary note. *British Journal of Disorders of Communication,* 1972, *7,* 157-162.

Jensen, G. D., & Womack, M. G. Operant conditioning techniques applied in the treatment of an autistic child. *American Journal of Orthopsychiatry,* 1967, *37,* 30-34.

Kanner, L. Autistic disturbances of affective contact. *Nervous Child,* 1943, *2,* 217-240.

Kanner, L. Problems of nosology and psychodynamics of early infantile autism. *American Journal of Orthopsychiatry,* 1949, *19,* 416-426.

Koegel, R. L., & Covert, A. The relationship of self-stimulation to learning in autistic children. *Journal of Applied Behavior Analysis,* 1972, *5,* 381-387.

Koegel, R. L., Firestone, P. B., Kramme, K., & Dunlap, G. Increasing spontaneous play by suppressing self-stimulation in autistic children. *Journal of Applied Behavior Analysis,* 1974, *7,* 521-528.

Koegel, R. L., & Rincover, A. Treatment of psychotic children in a classroom environment: I. Learning in a large group. *Journal of Applied Behavior Analysis,* 1974, *7,* 45–59.

Koegel, R. L., & Rincover, A. Research on the difference between generalization and maintenance in extra-therapy responding. *Journal of Applied Behavior Analysis,* 1977, *10,* 1–12.

L'Abate, L. Early infantile autism: A reply to Ward. *Psychological Bulletin,* 1972, *77,* 49–51.

Lichstein, K. L., & Schreibman, L. Employing electric shock with autistic children: A review of the side effects. *Journal of Autism and Childhood Schizophrenia,* 1976, *6,* 163–173.

Lotter, V. Epidemiology of autistic conditions in young children: I. Prevalence. *Social Psychiatry,* 1966, *1,* 124–137.

Lotter, V. Factors related to outcome in autistic children. *Journal of Autism and Childhood Schizophrenia,* 1974, *4,* 263–277.

Lovaas, O. I. Strengths and weaknesses of operant conditioning techniques for the treatment of autism. *Proceedings of the Conference and Annual Meeting of the National Society for Autistic Children,* 1970, 30–41.

Lovaas, O. I., Koegel, R., Simmons, J. Q., & Long, J. S. Some generalization and follow-up measures on autistic children in behavior therapy. *Journal of Applied Behavior Analysis,* 1973, *6,* 131–166.

Lovaas, O. I., Schaeffer, B., & Simmons, J. Q. Building social behavior in autistic children by use of electric shock. *Journal of Experimental Research in Personality,* 1965, *1,* 99–109.

Margolies, P. J. Behavioral approaches to the treatment of early infantile autism: A review. *Psychological Bulletin,* 1977, *84,* 249–264.

Marshall, G. R. Toilet training of an autistic eight-year-old through operant conditioning therapy: A case report. *Behaviour Research and Therapy,* 1966, *4,* 242–245.

Marshall, N. R., & Hegrenes, J. R. Programmed communication therapy for autistic mentally retarded children. *Journal of Speech and Hearing Disorders,* 1970, *35,* 70–83.

Martin, G. L., England, G., Kaprowy, E., Kilgour, K., & Pilek, V. Operant conditioning of kindergarten class behavior in autistic children. *Behaviour Research and Therapy,* 1968, *6,* 281–294.

Matson, J. L. Simple correction for treating an autistic boy's encopresis. *Psychological Reports,* 1977, *41,* 802.

McConnell, O. L. Control of eye contact in an autistic child. *Journal of Child Psychology and Psychiatry and Allied Disciplines,* 1967, *8,* 249–255.

Means, J. R., & Merrens, M. R. Interpersonal training for an autistic child. *Perceptual and Motor Skills,* 1969, *28,* 972–974.

Metz, J. R. Conditioning generalized imitation in autistic children. *Journal of Experimental Child Psychology,* 1965, *2,* 389–399.

Miller, N. E. Experimental studies of conflict. In J. McV. Hunt (Ed.), *Personality and the behavior disorders.* New York: Ronald, 1944.

Moore, B. J., & Shiek, D. A. Toward a theory of early infantile autism. *Psychological Review,* 1971, *78,* 451–456.

Murray, M. The treatment of autism: A human protest. *Journal of Humanistic Psychology,* 1974, *14,* 57–59.

National Society for Autistic Children. White paper on behavior modification with autistic children. Mimeo, 1975.

National Society for Autistic Children. Definition of the syndrome of autism. *Journal of Autism and Childhood Schizophrenia,* 1978, *8,* 162–167.

Nordquist, V. M., & Wahler, R. G. Naturalistic treatment of an autistic child. *Journal of Applied Behavior Analysis,* 1973, *6,* 79–87.

Ornitz, E. M. Neurophysiologic studies. In M. Rutter & E. Schopler (Eds.), *Autism: A reappraisal of concepts and treatment.* New York: Plenum Press, 1978.

Ornitz, E. M., & Ritvo, E. R. The syndrome of autism: A critical review. *American Journal of Psychiatry,* 1976, *133,* 609–621.

Phillips, E. L. Contributions to a learning theory account of childhood autism. *Journal of Psychology,* 1957, *43,* 117–124.

Polan, C. C., & Spencer, B. L. Checklist of symptoms of autism in early life. *West Virginia Medical Journal,* 1959, *55,* 198–204.

Rabb, E., & Hewett, F. Developing appropriate classroom behaviors in a severely disturbed group of institutionalized kindergarten-primary children utilizing a behavior modification model. *American Journal of Orthopsychiatry,* 1967, *37,* 313–314.

Rimland, B. *Infantile autism: The syndrome and its implications for a neural theory of behavior.* New York: Appleton-Century-Crofts, 1964.

Rimland, B. Comment on Ward's "Early infantile autism." *Psychological Bulletin,* 1972, *77,* 52–53.

Rimland, B. A risk/benefit perspective on the use of aversives. *Journal of Autism and Childhood Schizophrenia,* 1978, *8,* 100–104.

Rimm, D. C., & Masters, J. C. *Behavior therapy: Techniques and empirical findings.* New York: Academic Press, 1974.

Rincover, A., & Koegel, R. L. Setting generality and stimulus control in autistic children. *Journal of Applied Behavior Analysis,* 1975, *8,* 235–246.

Risley, T. R., & Wolf, M. M. Establishment of functional speech in echolalic children. *Behaviour Research and Therapy,* 1967, *5,* 73–88.

Ritvo, E. R., Rabin, K., Yuwiler, A., Freeman, B. J., & Geller, E. Biochemical and hematologic studies: A critical review. In M. Rutter and E. Schopler (Eds.), *Autism: A reappraisal of concepts and treatment.* New York: Plenum Press, 1978.

Russo, D. C., & Koegel, R. L. A method for integrating an autistic child into a normal public-school classroom. *Journal of Applied Behavior Analysis,* 1977, *10,* 579–590.

Rutter, M. The development of infantile autism. *Psychological Medicine,* 1974, *4,* 147–163.

Rutter, M. Diagnosis and definition of childhood autism. *Journal of Autism and Childhood Schizophrenia,* 1978, *8,* 139–161.

Rutter, M., & Bartak, L. Causes of infantile autism: Some considerations from recent research. *Journal of Autism and Childhood Schizophrenia,* 1971, *1,* 20–32.

Sailor, W., & Taman, T. Stimulus factors in the training of prepositional usage in three autistic children. *Journal of Applied Behavior Analysis,* 1972, *5,* 183–192.

Salvin, A., Routh, D. K., Foster, R. E., & Lovejoy, K. M. Acquisition of Modified American Sign Language by a mute autistic child. *Journal of Autism and Childhood Schizophrenia,* 1977, *7,* 359–371.

Schell, R. E., & Adams, W. P. Training parents of a young child with profound behavior deficits to be teacher-therapists. *Journal of Special Education,* 1968, *2,* 439–454.

Schell, R. E., Stark, J., & Giddan, J. J. Development of language behavior in an autistic child. *Journal of Speech and Hearing Disorders,* 1967, *32,* 51–64.

Schopler, E. On confusion in the diagnosis of autism. *Journal of Autism and Childhood Schizophrenia,* 1978, *8,* 137–138.

Schreibman, L., & Lovaas, O. I. Rejoinder to Murray's article. *Journal of Humanistic Psychology,* 1974, *14,* 61–62.

Stark, J. Language training for the autistic child using operant conditioning procedures. *Journal of Communication Disorders,* 1972, *5,* 183–194.

Stark, J., Giddan, J. J., & Meisel, J. Increasing verbal behavior in an autistic child. *Journal of Speech and Hearing Disorders,* 1968, *33,* 42–48.

Stevens-Long, J., & Rasmussen, M. The acquisition of simple and compound sentence structure in an autistic child. *Journal of Applied Behavior Analysis,* 1974, *7,* 473–479.

Tramontana, J., & Stimbert, V. E. Some techniques of behavior modification with an autistic child. *Psychological Reports,* 1970, *27,* 498.

Ward, A. J. Early infantile autism: Diagnosis, etiology, and treatment. *Psychological Bulletin,* 1970, *73,* 350–362.

Webb, R. A. A comment on D. J. Moore and D. A. Shiek's "Toward a theory of early infantile autism." *Psychological Review,* 1972, *79,* 278–279.

Wells, K. C., Forehand, R., Hickey, K., & Green, K. D. Effects of a procedure derived from the overcorrection principle on manipulated and nonmanipulated behaviors. *Journal of Applied Behavior Analysis,* 1977, *10,* 679–687.

Wetzel, R. J., Baker, J., Roney, M., & Martin, M. Outpatient treatment of autistic behavior. *Behaviour Research and Therapy,* 1966, *4,* 169–177.

Williams, C. D. The elimination of tantrum behavior by extinction procedures. *Journal of Abnormal and Social Psychology,* 1959, *59,* 269.

Wing, L. *Autistic children: A guide for parents.* New York: Bruner-Mazel, 1972.

Wolf, M., Risley, T., Johnston, M., Harris, F., & Allen, E. Application of operant conditioning procedures to the behavior problems of an autistic child: A follow-up and extension. *Behaviour Research and Therapy,* 1967, *5,* 103–112.

Wolf, M. M., Risley, R. R., & Mees, H. Application of operant conditioning procedures to the behavior problems of an autistic child. *Behaviour Research and Therapy,* 1964, *1,* 305–312.

Yeakel, M., Salisbury, L., Greer, S., & Marcus, L. An appliance for auto-induced adverse control of self-injurious behavior. *Journal of Experimental Child Psychology,* 1970, *10,* 159–169.

2
Female
Sexual
Inhibition

R. Taylor Segraves

The etiology and treatment of disturbances of the female sexual response cycle is a confusing area of inquiry, partly because of the imprecise terminology employed by different investigators. Several diagnostic schemes are in current usage, and there is an absence of consensus as to which diagnostic scheme should be employed or, in some cases, as to what specifically denotes a female sexual aberration necessitating treatment.

In the older literature, frigidity was a blanket term employed to designate many female sexual disturbances. This term was too imprecise, since certain clinicians defined frigidity as the absence of a vaginal orgasm as opposed to a clitoral orgasm (Sotile & Kilman, 1977). Although currently there is some disagreement about possible subjective differences between masturbatory and coital orgasms (Fisher, 1973; Shainess, 1975), most investigators have seriously questioned whether a distinction between clitoral and vaginal orgasms is possible since all orgasms appear to be produced at least in part by clitoral stimulation (Kaplan, 1974; Masters & Johnson, 1966).

The diagnostic scheme proposed by Masters and Johnson (1970) primarily differentiates between primary orgasmic dysfunction and situational (secondary) orgasmic dysfunction. Primary orgasmic dysfunction is defined as the total lack of orgasmic attainment by any means during an entire lifetime. A woman is defined as having situational orgasmic dysfunction if she gives a history of having experienced an orgasm at least once by any means. This category is subdivided into three subcategories: masturbatory orgasmic inadequacy, coital orgasmic inadequacy, and random orgasmic inadequacy.

Kaplan (1974) criticizes Masters and Johnson's nosology on the grounds that it does not adequately distinguish between disturbances of sexual excitement and disturbances of orgasm. She maintains on clinical grounds that these are two different syndromes with differing etiologies and treatment considerations. Thus, she proposes that we differentiate between general sexual dysfunction (frigidity) and orgasmic dysfunction. General sexual dysfunction refers to the woman who is essentially devoid of sexual feelings and shows minimal signs of genital vasocongestion (lubrication) in response to genital stimulation.

Orgasmic dysfunction refers to a specific inhibition of the orgasmic component of the sexual response cycle. Similar to Masters and Johnson's diagnostic system, orgasmic disorders can be subdivided into primary or secondary and into absolute or situational.

The American Psychiatric Task Force on Nomenclature and Statistics is currently devising the third edition of the Diagnostic and Statistical Manual (DSM-III) for release in 1978–1979 (Spitzer et al., 1977). The task force subcommittee on Psychosexual Disorders has proposed that a distinction be made between psychosexual disorders with inhibited sexual excitement and those with inhibited female orgasm. Under this scheme, the sexually inhibited female patient may be indexed twice—once as having a psychosexual disorder with inhibited sexual excitement, and again as having a psychosexual disorder with inhibited orgasm.

Although it is currently unclear whether such a distinction is relevant to clinical practice, it appears that future diagnostic schemes will include this distinction. This scheme has the advantage of linking the dysfunction to specific, observable, and potentially measurable aberrations in the human sexual response cycle. Clinically, disorders of sexual excitement frequently coexist with disorders of orgasm (i.e., women who don't become aroused enough to lubricate usually don't reach orgasm either). Most treatment programs do not distinguish between disorders of arousal and disorders of orgasm. Thus, this chapter is devoted to a discussion of the treatment of female disturbances in arousal and orgasm. The diagnostic schemes and definitions are listed in Table 1.

Differing estimates of the prevalence of disturbances in orgasmic capacity have been obtained in different investigations. Part of the difficulty in obtaining reliable estimates of orgasmic capacity is related to the fact that orgasmic capacity appears to vary in relation to marital happiness, length of marriage, and birth later in this century (Morokoff, 1978) as well as to particular aspects of male sexual behavior

Table 1. **Classification schemes for female sexual inhibitions.**

A. Masters and Johnson (1970)
  1. Primary orgasmic dysfunction—lack of orgasmic attainment during an entire lifetime
  2. Situational orgasmic dysfunction—at least one instance of orgasm attainment
     a. masturbatory orgasmic inadequacy—not achieved orgasm by self-stimulation
     b. coital—never achieved orgasm during coitus
     c. random—infrequent orgasm attainment
B. Kaplan (1974)
  1. General sexual dysfunction—no signs of genital vasocongestion and little erotic feeling
  2. Orgastic dysfunction—inhibition of the orgastic component of the sexual response
     a. primary—never experienced an orgasm
     b. secondary—disorder develops subsequent to adequate sexual functioning
     c. absolute—cannot achieve either coital or masturbatory orgasm
     d. situational—reaches orgasm only under certain specific conditions
C. Proposed DSM III Psychosexual Dysfunctions
  1. With inhibited sexual desire—persistent inhibition of desire
  2. With inhibited sexual excitement—failure of the lubrication response of sexual excitement
  3. With inhibited female orgasm—delay or absence of orgasm attainment

(Gebhard, 1978). With these reservations in mind, it is of note that several investigators agree in finding that only 5 to 10 percent of women report never having experienced an orgasm (Chesser, 1956; Fisher, 1973; Frank et al., 1977; Hunt, 1974; Kinsey et al., 1953). Similarly, several surveys agree in finding that 30 to 50 percent of women experience orgasm somewhat infrequently (Dickinson & Beam, 1971; Hamilton, 1929; Terman, 1951). Frank et al. (1977) report that 30 to 50 percent of women also complain of difficulty with the excitement phase of sexual activities.

THEORETICAL ANALYSIS

Nonbehavioral

The primary nonbehavioral treatment for psychogenic sexual inhibition in the female is individual psychotherapy. The most prevalent form of individual psychotherapy has been psychoanalytically oriented psychotherapy. This therapeutic approach hypothesizes that the sexual symptom is the result of a conflict within the individual between a drive toward sexual satisfaction and equally strong repressive forces. These repressive forces probably derive from the patient's childhood experiences, have been extruded from awareness, and thus are inaccessible to modification by rational thought. A key element in this treatment approach is the resolution of transference. Transference in this case refers to the in vivo reenactment with the therapist of the original conflict (Meyer, 1976). Psychoanalytically oriented therapists also tend to stress that sexual symptoms are related to fears of interpersonal intimacy (Crown & Lucas, 1976). The effectiveness of this treatment approach is difficult to assess as the length of treatment typically precludes the use of waiting-list controls or the compilation of large series of patients. Also, the alleviation of the specific sexual symptom is not the primary goal of this treatment orientation. The largest clinical series employing this treatment approach reported a 25 percent cure rate and a 36 percent improvement rate for female disorders (O'Connor & Stern, 1972). Psychoanalytically oriented group therapy (Burbank, 1976) and hypotherapy (Levit, 1971; Richardson, 1963) have also been reported to be useful in the treatment of female sexual inhibitions.

Behavioral

A precise designation of the effective components in the treatment of female sexual inhibitions is difficult to describe; most therapy programs have consisted of a varied mixture of approaches and little work has been devoted to pinpointing the essential components of treatment. Unfortunately, many contemporary clinicians employ multitheoretical treatment approaches (Kaplan, 1975; Schmidt & Lucas, 1976). This confusion of theoretical models is highly unlikely to lead to genuine advances in our knowledge of effective treatment components (Eysenck & Beech, 1971; Segraves, 1976).

Most behaviorally oriented clinicians have conceptualized a lack of female sexual arousal as learned behavior maintained by anxiety and a partner who reinforces the existing behavioral deficit (Lobitz & LoPiccolo, 1972). Wolpe (1958) and Lazarus (1963) were among the first behaviorists to use a respondent-conditioning paradigm as unifying explanation for both the etiology and treatment of sexual dysfunction. According to this model, lack of female sexual arousal is the result of conditioned anxiety to sexual stimuli: thus the therapy consists of some method of deconditioning anxiety. Both systematic desensitization in imagination and in vivo desensitization are logical treatment approaches based on this theoretical model. It is of note that

Masters and Johnson (1970) also emphasize the role of anxiety in human sexual disorders, and the graduated sexual exercises employed in their treatment program appear to be a variant of in vivo desensitization (Franks & Wilson, 1974). Evidence to support the role of anxiety in human sexual disorders is primarily clinical. There is little empirical evidence for this crucial assumption.

Most behavioral treatment approaches supplement anxiety-reduction techniques with other procedures. These procedures include:

1. Imparting sexual information (Lazarus, 1978)
2. Teaching the male partner how to reinforce sexual behavior in his female partner (Lobitz & LoPiccolo, 1972)
3. Attempts at attitude change (Zussman & Zussman, 1976)
4. Teaching both partners to be more aware of their bodily sensations (Tyler, 1975)
5. Attempts to teach communication skills (LoPiccolo, 1978a, 1978b).

Some behavior therapists have basically considered failure to achieve orgasm as a skills deficit, and the treatment approach has accordingly been primarily instructional (Lobitz & LoPiccolo, 1972). The patient is instructed how to achieve orgasm through masturbation, and then steps are taken to transfer the newly acquired skill to coitus (Barbach, 1974). This technique has been employed for women who experience difficulties in initial arousal as well as in orgasm attainment. Most treatment approaches to date have not differentiated between treatment of disturbances in initial arousal and treatment of disturbances in orgasm. Kaplan (1974) distinguishes between treatment approaches to disturbances in arousal and orgasm, but her orientation is predominantly psychoanalytic and poorly investigated.

ASSESSMENT

With the increasing popularity of sex therapy in the media, the clinician encounters many self-referred and self-diagnosed sex therapy patients. Considerable clinical skill and experience are required to judge the appropriateness of this therapy approach for any given individual or couple. Because this treatment approach emphasizes provision of sexual information, anxiety reduction, and skills training in human sexuality, it is most appropriate for individuals and couples whose sexual difficulty appears linked to these etiological factors. Thus, the first task with many self-referred patients is to identify whether other treatment approaches might be more appropriate. Various categories of events mitigate against the effectiveness of behavioral sexual therapy and should be considered in the initial patient evaluation. These factors include faulty self-assessment, hidden agendas, severe marital discord, organic basis to the problem, severe co-existing psychopathology, and poor motivation.

Thorough medical screening of all patients is required to rule out the possibility of an organic basis to the problem. However, on occasion a careful sexual interview can establish a probable psychogenic etiology. For example, most organic lesions interfering with sexual functioning produce a uniform loss of function. Therefore, a situational aspect to the dysfunction is strongly suggestive of a psychogenic etiology (Segraves, 1978). It is difficult to conceive of organic lesions that might interfere with marital sexual responsivity and not also diminish masturbatory or extramarital sexual responsivity. An often overlooked but frequent contributor to disturbances in sexual functioning is pharmacological agents. Although the effects of drugs on female sexual functioning have been investigated minimally to date, there are strong reasons to suspect that drugs with anticholinergic and antiadrenergic side effects may interfere with human female sexual functioning (Segraves, 1977). Thus, many of the commonly prescribed antihypertensive, antidepressant, and antipsychotic drugs may interfere with female responsivity. Unless there is a medical contraindication, these drugs should be discontinued for at least a trial period.

Many patients who request sex therapy may have other hidden agendas or may have arrived at a faulty self-diagnosis (Lobitz & Lobitz, 1978). On occasion, it may require considerable clinical skill to discern the hidden agenda or real problem and to devise a more appropriate treatment intervention. Some individuals use the guise of seeking treatment for a sexual disturbance to engage a depressed mate in psychotherapy or to get the mate to face longstanding marital disagreements. Similarly, many individuals may be aware of longstanding psychological suffering and use their sexual dissatisfactions as a simple explanation for their plight in life, whereas in actual fact their sexual dissatisfactions are the least significant of a long list of interpersonal difficulties.

Numerous clinicians have reported that severe marital discord seriously limits the effectiveness of sex therapy treatment programs, and thus they attempt to limit treatment to couples with less severe marital problems (Brady, 1976; Lobitz & LoPiccolo, 1972). This reasonable approach often can be difficult to implement as most sexual dysfunction is accompanied by a certain degree of marital discord. Other clinicians have suggested that the assessor discriminate between cases of sexual dysfunction which are the result of marital discord and those which have caused the discord (Sager, 1976). Again, this discrimination can be extremely difficult to make. Ultimately, the clinician has to assess to the best of his or her judgment whether the marital discord is so severe that the couple will not comply with the treatment program.

The question of whether certain psychopathologies are contraindications to sex therapy remains unsettled. Several investigations have reported that the presence of severe coexisting psychopathology decreases the liklihood of a successful outcome in sex therapy (Lansky & Davenport, 1975; Meyer, Schmidt, Lucas, & Smith, 1975; Munjack & Kanno, 1977). Other investigators suggest that sex therapy may have a deleterious effect on certain personality types (Wright, Perreault, & Mathieu, 1977), and Kaplan and Kohl (1972) report evidence suggestive of a deleterious effect of sex therapy. In spite of this, many clinicians have successfully treated patients with severe psychopathology (Leiblum & Kopel, 1977; Lobitz & Lobitz, 1978), and the incidence of adverse effects appears to be extremely low (Segraves, 1976). Thus, the presence of coexisting psychopathology is not an absolute contradiction to sex therapy. It does appear, however, to decrease the likelihood of a successful outcome (Wright et al., 1977).

At the point that the assessment excludes the previously mentioned factors as being of major etiological significance and the evidence indicates the problem to be primarily a sexual difficulty of psychogenic etiology, it becomes necessary to detail explicity the exact nature of the difficulty, its onset and course, and the particular circumstances under which the problem occurs. The therapeutic approach may vary, depending on the chronicity and particular situations under which the problem occurs. For example, behavioral treatment of female sexual disturbances have been tested primarily on women with longstanding difficulties in arousal or orgasm attainment. Less work has been reported on the treatment of sexual difficulties of acute onset in women who were previously sexually functional. These women may be inappropriate for traditional therapy since they possess appropriate interpersonal and sexual skills by history, but are not using them at present. In fact, behaviorally oriented sex therapy programs have reported less success in the treatment of such cases (Masters & Johnson, 1970; McGovern, 1978; LoPiccolo & Lobitz, 1973). Similarly, partner-specific difficulties may suggest a different therapeutic approach. Clearly, a woman who is orgasmic and responsive with a lover but not with her spouse merits different treatment goals and methods. Likewise, a woman who has been orgasmic with previous lovers but not with her present one may require modifications of the standard sex-therapy treatment regime.

To date, assessment of pretreatment conditions and treatment effects has been primarily clinical. Such an assessment requires a meticulous detailing of baseline measures such as frequency of intercourse, frequency of lubrication, frequency of orgasm, frequency of sexual initiations, and estimates of subjective satisfaction. Because of variation in the frequency of sexual activities, several authors (Masters & Johnson, 1970; Obler, 1973) have suggested standardization of measures by using percentages or ratios of the proportion of successful experiences to the number of coital occasions. Thus, Masters and Johnson arbitrarily define successful treatment of anorgasmia as occurring when the woman is orgasmic on at least 50 percent of intercourse occasions. The Masters and Johnson definition of treatment success has the advantage of a clearly defined end point, thus allowing comparison between the effectiveness of different treatment approaches. The disadvantage of the Masters and Johnson assessment approach is that evaluation of treatment outcome rests entirely on a single measure. It does not allow for a more precise measure of gradations of change prior to the criterion or for measures of change in sexual attitudes, satisfaction, and comfort.

Various questionnaire measures have been devised to measure sexual behavior in a broader context. Of these measures, the Sexual Interaction Inventory (LoPiccolo & Steger, 1974) has been used most extensively. This instrument consists of a list of 17 heterosexual behaviors. Each spouse is required to answer six questions about each sexual behavior on the list. These responses are then summed across the behaviors and 11 derived scales are obtained. These scales include measures of satisfaction, self-acceptance, pleasure, acceptance of mate, and perceptual accuracy. A recent factor analytic study of this instrument has raised serious questions about its construction (McCoy & D'Agostineo, 1977). The Derogatis Sexual Functioning Inventory (Derogatis, Meyer, & Dupkin, 1976) is a 247-item self-report inventory which is scored on eight primary domains; information, experience, drive, attitudes, symptoms, affects, gender role definition, and fantasy. This relatively new instrument has had minimal clinical testing to date. Preliminary reports of this scale are promising, and it has been shown to differentiate organic from psychogenic impotence. A large number of other instruments are available to assess change in areas related to human sexuality. These include psychoanalytically oriented questionnaires (Blum, 1949), behavioral checklists (Brady & Levitt, 1965), sexual knowledge questionnaires (Miller & Lief, 1976), and modifications of the semantic differential (Marks & Sartorius, 1968). The reader is referred elsewhere for more comprehensive reviews of these instruments (LoPiccolo & Steger, 1974; Schiavi, Derogatis, Kuriansky, et al., 1978).

There have been notable advances in the psychophysiological measurement of human female sexual responsivity (Geer, 1976; Heiman, 1976). Most measures have assessed the degree of genital vasocongestion to sexual stimulation. Both vaginal blood flow as assessed by a photoplethysmograph and labial temperature as measured by a thermistor clip have been employed (Henson & Rubin, 1978). The clinical application of these measures is uncertain at present. In particular, it is unclear to what extent sexual responsiveness under laboratory conditions is predictive of sexual responsivity with partners in natural surroundings.

TREATMENT PROCEDURES

Most of the behavioral approaches to the treatment of female sexual inhibition have consisted of treatment packages. The different treatment packages frequently overlap to varying degrees and little work has been done to isolate their essential components. The main treatment approaches can be separated into three groups: systematic desensitization in imagination studies, conjoint in vivo desensitization, and masturbatory training.

Systematic Desensitization Studies

These studies are summarized in Table 2. Although numerous case reports of the use of systematic desensitization in the treatment of female sexual dysfunction have been reported (Asirdas & Beech, 1975; Fabbri, 1977; Haslam, 1965; Kraft & Al-Issa, 1962; Madsen & Ullman, 1962), only clinical and research reports containing at least five cases are considered in this review.

The first large series of cases was reported by Lazarus (1963) on the treatment of chronic recalcitrant frigidity in 16 women by systematic desensitization in imagination. It appears that all or most of his patients suffered from severe chronic disturbances in sexual arousal and orgasm attainment. His treatment consisted primarily of gradual evocation of imaginary sexual scenes during a state of deep muscular relaxation. Nine of the 16 patients became orgasmic in an average of 28 sessions, and a 15-month follow-up revealed that the changes were sustained. The criteria of a successful outcome included pleasurable anticipation of intercourse, sexual initiation behavior, and almost always reaching an orgasm.

Brady (1966) reported successfully treating four out of five women with chronic disturbances in sexual arousal and orgasmic capacity by systematic desensitization in imagination, using intravenous brevital to pharmacologically induce relaxation. The average number of treatment sessions was 11.5 and a 4½ month follow-up indicated that

Table 2. Systematic desensitization studies.

Investigator	Screening procedure	Number of cases	Other psychotherapy procedures	Average number of sessions	Number of successes[a]	Follow-up	DQR
Lazarus (1963)	Selected cases from private practices	16	Unspecified	28	9 (56%)	15 mo	3
Brady (1966)	unspecified	5	Anamnesic experiences	11.5	4 (80%)	4.5 mo	1
Jones & Park (1972)	Refused patients with marital discord, severe psycho-pathology	55	Abreaction, supportive questioning	14	44 (82%)	None	0
Obler (1973)	Refused patients with other psychological problems; accepted 64 of 235 referrals	13	Assertiveness training	15	11 (85%)	1½ yrs	20
Wincze & Caird (1976)	Accepted only those with essential sexual inhibition	21	None	10	5 (25%)	1–3 mo	30

[a]Success is defined as being orgasmic on 50% of coital opportunities post-treatment.

treatment gains were sustained. Brady indicated that anamnesic experiences occurred during the desensitization process.

The largest clinical series using systematic desensitization was reported by Jones and Park (1972). They reported that 45 out of 55 women previously coitally or totally anorgasmic with their husbands became orgasmic in an average of 14 sessions. The sample apparently included women with disturbances in arousal and orgasm, as the group included five virgin wives. The frequency of orgasm attainment at termination was not reported. Similarly, Jones and Park did not include follow-up data. It is of note that they also reported successfully treating 10 out of 14 wives with late-onset orgasmic dysfunction in a mean of 6 sessions.

The first controlled study of the effectiveness of systematic desensitization in the treatment of sexual dysfunction was reported by Obler (1973). Referred sexual dysfunction patients were allocated into three matched groups: systematic desensitization, psychoanalytically oriented group therapy, and a no-treatment control. The systematic desensitization therapy group was superior to the two other groups on various indices including behavioral, galvanic skin response, and anxiety scales. The systematic desensitization group contained 22 subjects, 13 of whom were female. The significance of this study is difficult to evaluate for the following reasons: (1) the systematic desensitization group also received assertiveness training and confidence training; (2) the exact diagnostic grouping of the female patients was not clearly specified; and (3) the criterion of success on the behavioral outcome measure was not specified.

Wincze and Caird (1976) reported the only controlled study of the effect of systematic desensitization alone on sexual dysfunction in women. Twenty-one women with essential sexual dysfunction were randomly assigned to a videotape systematic desensitization group, a systematic desensitization-in-imagination group, or a no-treatment control group. Treatment effects were evaluated on numerous scales at termination and at 1 to 3-month follow-up. The results indicated that videotape desensitization and, to a lesser degree, imaginary desensitization were effective in reducing heterosexual anxiety but extremely ineffective in treating orgasmic dysfunction. Only about 25 percent of the women who were unable to reach orgasm at the beginning of the study were able to reach orgasm after treatment.

In summary, it appears that systematic desensitization procedures may be effective in reducing sexual anxiety and increasing responsivity during the arousal phase of the sexual response cycle. Evidence to date suggests that systematic desensitization alone is seldom sufficient for the treatment of anorgasmia. It probably contributes to the successful treatment of anorgasmia, but other unknown treatment components also are needed.

Conjoint in Vivo Desensitization

These studies are summarized in Table 3.

The largest clinical series using conjoint in vivo desensitization (directed practice) techniques to treat sexual disorders was reported by Masters and Johnson (1970). Their approach is a highly specific treatment package including a 2-week intensive treatment commitment, a dual-sex co-therapy team, and conjoint treatment sessions. The treatment focuses on sexual education, short-term directive couple therapy, and graduated sexual homework assignments (in vivo desensitization). Using this methodology, they reported treating 193 women with primary anorgasmia and having only 32 failures, an 83.4 percent success rate. A five-year follow-up revealed only 2 cases of symptom recurrence. They also reported treating 149 cases of situational orgasmic dysfunction, with 34 failures or a 77.2 percent success rate. Only 3 cases of symptom recurrence were noted on follow-up. The situational orgasmic dysfunction group contained three subgroups with differing initial success rates. Of 11 women having masturbatory orgasmic dysfunction, there was only one treatment failure. Coital orgasmic dysfunction was diagnosed in 106 women, and only 21 failures were recorded. There were, however, 12 failures in 32 cases of random orgasmic dysfunction, a 37.5 percent failure rate. Because of the absence of a controlled comparison group in their report, it is difficult to ascertain to what extent their high success rate was due to self-selection of patients, or to what extent the outcome was due to specific aspects of the treatment intervention.

Numerous other clinicians have reported clinical studies employing some or all of the Masters and Johnson treatment package. These studies are difficult to evaluate in comparison to Masters and Johnson's work for various reasons. Some clinicians have not reported clear outcome data (Kaplan, 1974; Hartman & Fithian, 1972). Others have not clearly specified the diagnostic grouping treated (Haslam, 1976) or have reported ambiguous outcome data (Brown & Kolaszynska-Carr, 1972; McCarthy, 1973; Meyer et al. 1975). Other clinicians have modified the Masters and Johnson treatment package so that it is unclear as to which components were involved in the treatment given (Blakeney, 1976; Cooper, 1970; Powell, Blakeney, Croft, & Pulliam, 1974; Prochaska and Marzilli, 1973).

Although there have been controlled studies of the Masters and Johnson approach in the treatment of male disorders (Ansari, 1976),

Table 3. Conjoint in vivo desensitization studies.

Investigator	Screening procedure	Number of cases	Other psychotherapy procedures	Average number of sessions	Number of successes[a]	Follow-up	DQR
Masters & Johnson (1970)	High cost, long waiting list, travel to St. Louis	193 primary anorgas-mia	Education; couple therapy	2-wk intensive program	161 (83.4%)	5 yrs	5
Masters & Johnson (1970)	High cost, long waiting list, travel to St. Louis	149 situa-tional anorgas-mia	Education; couple therapy	2-wk intensive program	115 (77.2%)	5 yrs	5
Munjack et al. (1976)	Excluded severe marital discord	22 anorgas-mia women	Assertion training; modeling; education; behavioral rehearsal	20 sessions	33%	9 mo	17
Mathews et al. (1976)	Excluded severe marital discord	36 anorgas-mia women	Factorial design (see text)	10 wks	Only 2 out of 13 women increased on orgasm ratings (see text)	4 mo	21½

[a]Success is defined as being orgasmic on 50% of coital opportunities post-treatment.

there have been only two controlled studies relevant to the directed-practice treatment of anorgasmia. Munjack and his associates (1976) reported treating 22 anorgasmic women in a multiple-technique behavioral therapy including in vivo desensitization. Symptomatic women were assigned randomly either to behavioral treatment or to a waiting-list control group. Assessment of treatment effects included independent assessors and multiple questionnaires. Significant differences were noted between the treatment and no-treatment groups in frequency of orgasm attainment and increase in sexual satisfaction. Approximately one-third of the treated women became orgasmic after treatment and maintained treatment gains at 9-month follow-up. Approximately two-thirds of the treated women reported increased sexual satisfaction after treatment. The waiting-list control group evidenced no change on these dimensions. Follow-up indicated frequent recurrence of symptoms in cases of primary anorgasmia and continued improvement in cases of secondary anorgasmia. This study has produced suggestive evidence that a multiple-technique behavioral therapy including in vivo desensitization is superior to no treatment. As the authors state, the comparison of treatment with no treatment has to be made cautiously, since treatment lasted 20 weeks and the waiting list was for 10 weeks. In view of the usual chronicity of these problems (Kinsey et al., 1953), however, this methodological flaw is probably of minor consequence. The study is difficult to interpret, primarily because treatment was compared with no treatment. This design allows us to conclude that contact with the therapist was better than no contact; it does not allow us to infer that specific treatment interventions were effective. It is difficult to compare this study with the Masters and Johnson study as Munjack et al. made significant modifications in the Masters and Johnson treatment approach. The most serious of these modifications was that not all treatment sessions were conjoint.

Mathews and associates (1976) investigated the relative effectiveness of three treatment approaches: systematic desensitization with counseling, directed practice with counseling, and directive practice with minimal counselor contact. Thirty-six couples with a variety of sexual difficulties were assigned randomly to one of the three treatment procedures and to either one or two therapists within a balanced factorial design. Treatment outcome was assessed by blind evaluations as well as by numerous questionnaires. A 4-month follow-up was included. The sample included 18 female patients. Of these, 17 complained of orgasmic disorders. For the total sample of male and female disorders, few significant differences were found between the treatment approaches. The treatment approach most similar to the Masters and Johnson approach (directed practice with counseling) was approximately twice as effective as desensitization. The lack of significant differences among the approaches was apparently due to wide variations in treatment response. There was also suggestive evidence that the dual-sex co-therapy team approach enhanced the Masters and Johnson type of treatment. Although outcome data was reported primarily for the total sample, female disorders apparently were more resistant to change than male disorders in this study. Only 2 women were rated to have improved orgasm response at follow-up.

In conclusion, it appears that Masters and Johnson's report of high success rates for the treatment of anorgasmia have not been convincingly replicated or refuted. Other investigations have included insufficient numbers of subjects or too many modifications of the treatment approach to be truly comparable with the Masters and Johnson report. Similarly, evidence suggests that the success of this approach is correlated with poorly specified patient variables, such as coexisting psychopathology and interaction difficulties (Segraves, 1978), which precludes comparison across studies in many instances. The only controlled study that attempted to replicate the Masters and Johnson approach was reported by Mathews et al. (1976). This study, however, is not a fair appraisal of their approach to the treatment of anorgasmia for several reasons. They do not report the therapists' ability, training, or experience in their treatment approach. Pretreatment screening of treatment appropriateness appeared to be minimal. Finally, the sample contained 18 couples with females as the symptomatic partner. These 18 females were allocated in a factorial design, meaning that only 3 females were assigned to directed practice plus counseling with a dual-sex co-therapy team. Only 13 of the 18 females had primary orgasmic difficulties. Thus, fewer than 3 females with orgasmic difficulties might have been assigned to the appropriate cell. It is doubtful that this small number of anorgasmic females per cell in a factorial design is a sufficient test of the effectiveness of this approach for anorgasmia.

Masturbatory Training Approaches

The underlying rationale for masturbatory training approaches to the treatment of anorgasmia is the assumption that orgasm attainment is a learnable skill. For several reasons, learning to masturbate to orgasm appears to be a logical first step in the process of learning coital orgasm attainment:

1. Research has indicated that masturbatory orgasms are more in-
    tense than coital orgasms (Masters & Johnson, 1966).
2. Masturbatory orgasms are more easily and reliably produced than
    coital orgasms (LoPiccolo & Lobitz, 1978).
3. Evidence suggests that all orgasms are basically clitoral in origin
    (Sherfey, 1972).

Thus, clinicians have employed a two-step masturbatory training approach to anorgasmia (Caird & Wincze, 1977; Kohlenberg, 1974;
Reisinger, 1974; Zeiss, Rosen, & Zeiss, 1978). The first step is to use
masturbatory training to teach the perceptual motor skills necessary
for orgasm attainment. The second step involves the use of "bridging
maneuvers" to transfer the newly acquired skill to coitus. Evaluation of
outcome for these approaches is confusing unless the investigators
precisely define their criteria of success (Kuriansky, Sharpe, & O'Conner, 1977). For example, any of the following designations of success
could be used: reliably orgasmic with masturbation; reliably orgasmic
through manual manipulation by partner; reliably orgasmic with
manual manipulation accompanying coitus; or reliably orgasmic with
coitus, and without accompanying manual stimulation.

Lobitz and LoPiccolo (1972) have evolved a masturbatory training approach to the treatment of primary anorgasmia. This approach
has four main components. The first component consists of a 9-step
masturbation program proceeding from visual and tactile self-explora-
tion to masturbation and orgasm. The second component consists of
skill training for the mate. The female partner teaches her male com-
panion how to bring her to orgasm first manually and then coitally.
The third component focuses on role playing orgasm attainment to
disinhibit fears of losing control and embarrassment about intense
sexual arousal. The fourth component consists of teaching the woman
certain behaviors such as pelvic thrusting or breath holding which may
help to trigger orgasm. The outcome of this treatment approach is
unclear. Lobitz and LoPiccolo have published at least three separate
reports, each consisting of a different number of cases. It is unclear
whether each report is a separate clinical series. In one report, this
technique was reported to have successfully treated 13 women with
primary anorgasmia (Lobitz & LoPiccolo, 1972). The definition of
success was that the female partner was satisfied in at least 50 percent
of coital interactions. In a separate report (LoPiccolo & Lobitz, 1973),
they stated that all 11 women treated by this approach experienced
orgasm during manipulation by the husband and, of these women, 9
were orgasmic during intercourse. Apparently, some of the 9 coitally
orgasmic women required concurrent manual stimulation. A more

recent clinical study of 8 women was reported by LoPiccolo and Lobitz (1978). Of these women, all were able to learn to masturbate to orgasm. Six were able to experience orgasm during intercourse, 4 of them without concurrent stimulation. From this study it appears that most anorgasmic women can be taught to become orgasmic during masturbation, but only approximately 50 percent are able to transfer this skill to coitus without requiring concurrent stimulation.

Barbach incorporated part of the LoPiccolo and Lobitz procedure into a group therapy format (Barbach, 1974, 1975; Wallace & Barbach, 1974). Primary anorgasmic women were treated in women's conscious-ness-raising groups led by female co-therapists with an emphasis on exploring sexual attitudes and utilizing a graduated approach to sexual stimulation through masturbatory "home play" assignments. Of 83 women treated, 91.6 percent were able to learn to masturbate to orgasm. An 8-month follow-up study was reported for 17 women. Of these, 11 were found to be orgasmic in more than 50 percent of partner-related coital activities. The percentage of women experiencing orgasm during coitus, with or without concurrent stimulation, is unclear.

Several other studies have suggested that many women who be-come orgasmic during masturbation training in group settings have difficulty transferring this skill to coitus. Schneidman and McGuire (1976) reported using the directed-masturbation group therapy method to treat two groups of women, one group of women below 35 years old and one group of women over 35 years old. In the younger group, 70 percent of the women learned to masturbate to orgasm in 10 weeks of treatment, and a 6-month follow-up demonstrated that treatment gains were sustained. In the older group, only 40 percent learned to mastur-bate to orgasm in 10 weeks of therapy. It is of note that only one woman out of the total sample of 20 women learned to transfer this skill to coitus.

Similar findings were reported by Kuriansky and associates (1977). Twenty-five women with anorgasmia were treated in the women's preorgasmic group format, and outcome was assessed by an inde-pendent evaluator. The directed-masturbation group therapy procedure was effective in teaching 93 percent of the women how to masturbate to orgasm. However, only two women subsequently became orgasmic during intercourse. These studies are summarized in Table 4.

In summary, it appears that directed masturbation is an effective way to teach anorgasmic women to become orgasmic during mastur-bation. More investigation is needed to help identify the treatment components necessary to transfer this skill to partner-related activities. On theoretical grounds, it seems that conjoint couple approaches would be more effective in achieving this transfer than same-sex group

Table 4. Directed masturbatory training studies.

Investigator	Screening procedure	Number of cases	Average number of sessions	Number masturbatory orgasms 50% occasions	Number coital orgasms	Follow-up	DQR
LoPiccolo & Lobitz (1978)	Eliminated severe psychopathology	8[a]	15	8 (100%)	4 (50%)	6 mo	2
Barbach (1974)	Unknown	83	10	76 (91.6%)	Unknown	None	1
Wallace & Barbach (1974)	Unknown	17	10	17 (100%)	Unknown	8 mo	4
Schneidman & McGuire (1976)	Excluded singles without partners	20	10	11 (55%)[b]	1 (5%)	6 mo	4
Kuriansky et al. (1971)	Unknown	25	10	23 (93%)	2 (8%)	None	5

[a] See text.
[b] Slightly higher success rates were noted on follow-up.

therapy approaches. More investigation is required to ascertain if conjoint couple therapy is more effective than group therapy for achieving orgasm in heterosexual contexts. In this regard, it is of note that Schneidman and McGuire (1976) reported occasional male resistance to their partner's participation in the female group masturbation program and even a few instances of male erectile dysfunction apparently elicited by the treatment approach for their mates. It is also unclear whether coital orgasm without concurrent manual stimulation should be a treatment goal for all anorgasmic women (Kaplan, 1974).

Other Approaches

A promising alternative approach to the treatment of sexual dysfunction is mixed-disorder couple's group therapy. This technique has the advantage of allowing more efficient usage of professional time, thus lowering treatment costs and potentially extending treatment availability to lower socioeconomic groups. The approach is theoretically sound, since a sizable proportion of behavioral sex therapy consists of instructional material which is uniform across syndromes and across individuals. The couples group approach has the clinical advantage of providing group support and encouragement, a sense of sharing problems, and a unique opportunity to learn intimate details of how other couples have coped with similar difficulties.

Leiblum, Rosen, & Pierce (1976) reported treating six couples in a 10-session group treatment format with a 6-week follow-up. The couples in treatment were heterogenous as to presenting complaint. The treatment format was a modification of the Masters and Johnson approach to a group therapy format. The Sexual Interaction Inventory was administered before and after treatment and indicated significant improvement in five of the six couples. Four of the couples had female members with disorders of sexual arousal and orgasm. Two of these women became orgasmic.

Segraves et al. (1977) attempted to replicate these findings. Four couples with mixed sexual disorders were treated in a similar treatment format. Two of the four couples included female members with sexual inhibitions. One nonorgasmic woman became orgasmic during treatment. Another woman with a complaint of sexual refusal began initiating sexual activities by the end of treatment. She, however, did not become orgasmic.

McGovern, Kirkpatrick, & LoPiccolo (1978) reported similar findings in their group treatment of four couples, each couple consisting of an anorgasmic female and a male with premature ejaculation. Treatment consisted of 15 3-hour weekly sessions. All previously nonorgasmic women were able to learn to masturbate to orgasm, but follow-up data indicated low generalization of this skill to coitus.

Baker and Nagata (1978) reported the largest clinical series utilizing this approach. They have treated 44 couples to date utilizing this approach and have reported promising results. Their report does not specify outcome separately for female orgasmic dysfunction.

In summary, cost-effectiveness considerations make this a very feasible treatment approach; however, minimal investigation with it has been done.

Auxilliary Procedures

Although audiovisual materials have been incorporated into many sex therapy programs, their effectiveness remains to be demonstrated (Bjorksten, 1976). On the rationale that vicarious learning has been demonstrated to be a highly effective means of anxiety reduction, Nemetz and associates (1978) investigated the use of a treatment program in which videotapes of sexual activities played a central role. Women with anorgasmia were allocated to symbolic modeling (videotapes) in groups, symbolic modeling in individual therapy, or to a waiting list. Various questionnaires indicated that the women exposed to the videotapes had significantly less sexual anxiety, initiated intercourse more frequently, and engaged in longer foreplay. The videotapes, however, had minimal impact on orgasm attainment. It is unclear to what extent the films augmented the effectiveness of the standard sex therapy approach, because the women also were instructed to practice the viewed activities at home with their partners. It is hoped that this approach will be investigated further since audiovisual materials have the potential of reducing therapist time and thus patient costs.

Recognizing that pubococcygeal muscle contraction accompanies female coital orgasm and that there is evidence of decreased pubococcygeal muscle tone in anorgasmic women (Kline-Graber & Graber, 1978), many clinicians have hypothesized that strengthening the pubococcygeal muscle through vaginal excercises might facilitate orgasm attainment and have included this procedure into their treatment approach. This procedure has evolved from an incidental finding by Kegel (1952). He advocated pubococcygeal muscle excercises for the treatment of urinary incontinence and reported the incidental finding that some women also experienced enhanced sexual responsivity. There is no empirical evidence to date substantiating Kegel's claim.

Numerous clinicians have observed that some coitally nonorgasmic women are orgasmic during masturbation and their masturbatory fantasies preceding orgasm frequently do not include heterosexual activities with their usual partners (Nims, 1975; Zeiss et al., 1978). Thus, clinicians have experimented with purposely manipulating the masturbatory fantasy. The most common approach is masturbatory conditioning. The client is instructed to masturbate to whatever fantasy she finds sexually arousing, but to switch to an "appropriate" partner-related activity at the point of impending orgasm. After she can do this successfully, she is asked to introduce the switch to the partner-related fantasy slightly earlier in the masturbatory sequence. In this manner, the patient can very gradually progress to the point where she is masturbating solely to the fantasy of a partner-related activity (Segraves, 1977).

Two experimental paradigms can be used as explanatory models for this procedure. According to the classical conditioning model, the goal of treatment is to pair an appropriate partner-related fantasy (i.e., penile thrusting) with the sexual arousal of orgasm (unconditioned response). With enough pairings, the conditioned stimulus (penile thrusting) should elicit orgasm. An alternate explanatory paradigm is that of stimulus control. According to this paradigm, the purpose of treatment is to alter the stimulus that elicits the response. Therefore one would proceed by "fading in" the appropriate stimulus while the response is being emitted. Eventually the new stimulus would predominate in eliciting the response. This approach has been reported to augment the treatment of coital anorgasmia (Zeiss et al., 1978). Lobitz and LoPiccolo (1972) initially employed this procedure in the treatment of secondary anorgasmia. More recently, they have stressed the importance of modifying nonsexual marital problems which contribute to the maintenance of secondary anorgasmia, and thus have shifted their treatment emphasis (McGovern, Stewart, & LoPiccolo, 1975; Snyder, LoPiccolo, & LoPiccolo, 1975). This procedure, although theoretically sound, has not been demonstrated to an essential component in the treatment of anorgasmia.

CLINICAL PRESCRIPTION

Behavioral sex therapy appears to be the treatment of choice for primary disorders of arousal and/or orgasm attainment. This approach is specifically indicated for couples with monosymptomatic complaints of psychogenic sexual dysfunction. It is less appropriate for couples in whom the sexual inhibition coexists with serious interpersonal difficulties in intimacy and attachment. Likewise, the presence of severe marital discord suggests that an alternative treatment approach should be utilized.

In the absence of definitive research on the essential components in the behavioral treatment of anorgasmia, a conservative approach is to combine behavioral approaches from several well investigated treatment packages. The recommended treatment approach should contain the following five components.

A *conjoint treatment technique* involving both partners is recommended. Anecdotal clinical evidence suggests that, in many cases, the husband may be reinforcing sexual unresponsivity in his spouse. There is also evidence that couples' sexual and nonsexual communication and interactional patterns may contribute to anorgasmia in the identified patient. In many cases, the interactional patterns are discernible only by in vivo observation of the couple's behavior in conjoint therapy sessions.

Education about relevant sexual physiology should be included in the treatment approach. Clinical experience indicates that many highly sophisticated and well-educated couples are suprisingly uniformed or misinformed about basic sexual information.

The treatment approach should include *a graduated approach to sexual intimacy* under conditions of minimal or at least tolerable anxiety levels. Available empirical studies do not indicate clearly whether in vivo graduated exercises (the Masters and Johnson conjoint approach) are superior to imaginary or videotape desensitization procedures. The author recommends the conjoint in vivo procedure over standard desensitization procedures for the following reasons. In vivo procedures consistently have been found to be more effective than imaginary procedures in the treatment of nonsexual phobias when analogous approaches are employed (Leitenberg, Agras, Edwards, et al., 1970). A larger number of cases have been treated using the in vivo procedure and thus more information is available about the subtleties of treatment. If successful, the in vivo approach specifically deconditions anxiety about sexual intimacy with the present partner, whereas imaginary deconditioning procedures are frequently less specific. The conjoint in vivo approach enlists both partners in the treatment process and thus is more likely to engender a sense of cooperation between spouses. The conjoint in vivo approach permits easy monitoring of the asymptomatic spouse's reaction to symptom reversal in his mate. If the clinician prefers to use a technique other than in vivo desensitization, evidence suggests that video desensitization is preferable to imaginary desensitization.

In many cases of female sexual inhibition, *conjoint in vivo desensitization (graded practice)* may be sufficient to treat disorders of arousal and orgasm attainment. However, evidence to date suggests that this approach may not be sufficient for all women to attain orgasmic capacity. In cases in which the Masters and Johnson approach is insufficient, specific skill training in orgasm attainment appears indicated. Since numerous investigators have reported difficulties in teaching the transfer of this skill from masturbatory to coital activities, a conjoint rather than woman's group approach is recommended. It also appears that the masturbatory training approach should enlist the partner's participation early in the process so that transfer of this skill to partner-related activities is maximized.

Most of the clinical studies reporting high success rates in the treatment of primary anorgasmia have included some form of *directive couple therapy*. Until adequate empirical investigation establishes whether or not this is an essential component in therapy, clinical anecdotal evidence indicates the wisdom of including such a therapy component. In many cases, nonsexual interactional difficulties create an interpersonal climate less than conducive to sexual intimacy. Although a number of behaviorally oriented couple therapy techniques have been developed in recent years (Azrin, Naster, & Jones, 1973; Jacobson & Martin, 1976; Stuart, 1969), the technique most frequently employed by sex therapists has been a form of communication training (Segraves, 1976). This approach is similar to the therapy approach advocated by Satir (1967) and subsequently elaborated by others (Nunnally, Miller, & Wachman, 1975). The approach primarily focuses on teaching each spouse how to communicate his or her wishes and desires directly and in a manner least likely to arouse antagonism in the partner.

The treatment of choice for secondary anorgasmia is less clear. The author's personal experience and clinical evidence from other investigators (Masters & Johnson, 1970; McGovern, McMullen, & LoPiccolo, 1978) suggest that the treatment of such cases frequently requires a greater emphasis on marital interaction difficulties. On theoretical grounds, one might predict that marital therapy would be preferable to sex therapy as these women by history possess adequate sexual skills but are not employing them at present.

The treatment of women who do not experience orgasm during coitus is a confusing area. Kaplan (1974) suggests that the absence of coital orgasm may be a normal physiological variation without psychiatric significance. She hypothesizes that some psychologically healthy and sexually well-adjusted women simply require more intense stimulation than coitus in order to reach orgasm. Criteria for treatment are ambiguous since some women do achieve coital orgasmic capacity as the result of behavioral sex therapy. The issue of whether the absence of coital orgasm is a condition meriting the professional time of highly trained specialists is unclear.

The treatment of women who can achieve masturbatory orgasm in solitary activities but cannot achieve similar orgasms in partner-related activities is a different issue. These women have been treated successfully by both the conjoint in vivo desensitization procedure and the directed masturbation approach with an emphasis on partner-related sexual activity.

The treatment of women who experience orgasm without manifesting an arousal phase of the human sexual response has been minimally investigated to date. In the absence of research, there are no recommended guidelines to therapy. In the author's limited clinical experience with this syndrome, severe problems in interpersonal intimacy coexisted with the sexual abnormality, and treatment by conventional behavioral sex therapy was unsuccessful.

In recent years, several clinicians (Kaplan, 1974; Levay & Kagle, 1977; Sollod, 1975) have advocated a multimodal therapy combining behaviorally oriented sex therapy with psychoanalytically oriented psychotherapy. There is no empirical evidence to date to support such a combined approach. Unless such evidence is forthcoming, the author specifically advises against such an approach. The combination of techniques and explanatory concepts from different theoretical systems may result in "a gigantic mish-mash of theories, methods, and outcomes that is forever beyond the capacity of scientific research to resolve" (Eysenck & Beech, 1971).

CASE REPORT

This couple was treated by the author in 1977. A graduate student couple, both in their late 20s, was referred by an analytically oriented psychotherapist for behavioral treatment of female anorgasmia. The couple had been in psychoanalytically oriented couple therapy for the preceding year. A gynecological exam excluded an organic etiology to the problem.

Initial assessment of husband and wife revealed no signs of significant psychopathology in either. Likewise, their marital adjustment appeared healthy with the exception of anorgasmia in the wife. The couple had a wide variety of shared activities and demonstrated adequate conflict resolution and decision-making skills. The sexual history revealed that both were sexually inexperienced prior to their marriage. During their four years of marriage, the female partner became sexually aroused but consistently failed to reach orgasm. There was no evidence of erectile or ejaculatory disturbance in her husband. Both came from sexually repressive homes, and the female had never masturbated to orgasm. In summary, the assessment indicated the probable appropriateness of a behavioral sex-therapy approach.

A review of sexual information revealed several pieces of misinformation that apparently contributed to their problem. Both partners felt that normal female orgasms should occur through coitus alone and clitoral stimulation during foreplay might distract from "genuine" sexual arousal. Both partners felt that female lubrication signalled that the woman was ready for penile penetration. The wife somehow felt that her husband should know what aroused her without any verbal instructions on her part. The couple was informed that most women prefer indirect clitoral stimulation during foreplay, lubrication is the first sign of female sexual arousal and does not necessarily indicate readiness for penetration, and adequate sexual interaction might well require the partners to communicate their wishes to one another.

A behavioral analysis of their interaction also revealed several contributory factors. Their pattern of sexual initiations were such as to mitigate against a successful sexual union. Initiation was predominantly by the husband. He frequently made sexual initiations while his wife was watching her favorite television program. Similarly, his voice tone usually conveyed irritation and his expectation of a refusal. She usually declined his initiations indirectly and never informed him of his poor timing from her perspective. It is also of note that sexual initiations usually occurred during periods of minimal physical or emotional intimacy. The contribution to their sexual difficulty of faulty sexual initiations and refusals and their mutual responsibility for this behavior was stressed by the therapist. Steps to alter this behavior were instigated. The therapist stressed that he wished the couple to take turns initiating the sexual activities which were to be prescribed. He then asked each spouse to instruct the mate as to his or her preferred style of initiation and refusal. They were asked to role play these behaviors in the therapist's office.

At this point, the couple appeared ready to begin the directed-practice behavioral sex therapy program. They were instructed not to have intercourse until instructed by the therapist and told that the treatment would take approximately 10 to 15 outpatient visits and one to two hours, three times a week, for behavioral homework assignments. After they expressed their apprehensions about treatment, they were instructed in the first stage of sensate focus. They were instructed to alternate actively caressing and passively receiving tactile pleasure from one another the next week and specifically to avoid sexual areas.

In the session the following week, both were pleased about the exercises and reported no difficulties. They were instructed to proceed to the next assignment, which included sexual areas in their mutual caressing. The program at this stage was delayed for several weeks. First, the therapist discovered that the husband had decided to leave the television on during the exercises. After specifically advising the couple to turn the television off the next week, the therapist found that the couple had become "so aroused that they had to have intercourse" and so violated his instructions. They then became depressed that coitus had not led to orgasm. Their apprehensions about the treatment program were discussed again, and thereafter they cooperated with the therapeutic regime.

The program consisted of a series of graduated exercises involving progressive sexual intimacy and led to the wife becoming increasingly sexually aroused but not orgasmic. At this point, the therapist began prescribing a series of masturbatory exercises to occur concurrently with the directed-practice exercises. Three weeks subsequent to the prescription of masturbatory exercises, the wife reported first masturbatory and then coital orgasms. She expressed fear of her newly discovered sexuality and specifically her fear of becoming promiscuous. Over the next few weeks, she experienced orgasm with greater ease and began initiating sexual activities almost daily. At this point, her husband became increasingly anxious and reported several erectile failures. His wife reported being ashamed of her hypersexuality and had renewed difficulty reaching orgasm. The husband's attitudes about male sexuality were explored. He felt that normal males should be eager for sex at any opportunity. The destructiveness of his attitude was pointed out, and he was asked to role play sexual refusals and to ask his wife if she felt that "he was less of a man" for occasionally not desiring intercourse. Fortunately, she had different stereotypes about male sexuality.

Two more sessions were scheduled to ensure maintenance of the behavioral change and to examine whether the marked change in their sexual interaction had caused serious disequilibrium in their marital-interaction system. After a period of initial readjustment, they stabilized in this new pattern of relating without adverse sequelae. A 1-year follow-up indicated that the changes were permanent and their marital relationship was satisfactory.

The objective of including this case report is to illustrate the five recommended components of therapy in actual clinical use. The role of education and directed couple therapy in the treatment of this case are self-evident. Likewise, the advantages of the conjoint approach are obvious. This case involved the combination of a Masters and Johnson directed-practice approach with masturbatory training. The in vivo desensitization technique appeared to facilitate increased sexual arousal but did not produce orgasm attainment. The inclusion of the masturbatory exercises preceded the development of orgasmic capacity and appeared to be a necessary treatment component.

Therapist Training

It is presently unclear how much or what type of training is necessary to become a competent sex therapist. There is considerable reason to believe that sex therapists need general psychotherapeutic skills as well as specific knowledge in the treatment of sexual dysfunction. Sex clinics are frequently besieged with self-referred patients. The therapist needs to be able to assess the appropriateness of this therapy technique for self-referred patients. Sexual dysfunction frequently coexists with other psychological difficulties. The treatment of such cases requires general clinical competence. Such general clinical training is usually not included in sex therapy training programs. (Kaplan, 1977).

Most experts agree that the training of sex therapists should include a didactic portion and a supervised clinical apprenticeship (LoPiccolo, 1978a; Money & Alexander, 1975; Waggoner, Mudd, & Shearer, 1978).

The didactic portion should probably include basic information about sexual physiology, biological causes of sexual dysfunction, principles of couple therapy, basic principles of behavior therapy, and a review of treatment techniques in sex therapy. This information is relatively easy to teach, although there might be minor disagreements about the required content. The teaching of clinical skills in the area of sex therapy is more problematic. Clearly, the student needs to have his or her clinical activity supervised by a more experienced therapist. The dual-sex team approach to therapy allows a practical means of accomplishing this goal. Each student can be assigned to a more experienced co-therapist during the training period. This procedure allows direct observation of the student's therapy skills and protects the patient from an inexperienced therapist.

This training approach has been adopted by many centers, including a program at the University of Chicago.

ETHICAL AND LEGAL ISSUES

The pivotal point in most discussions of the ethics of sex therapy procedures is whether a given procedure serves the patient's needs or instead appears primarily to benefit the therapist (Redlich, 1977). Most clinicians of varying theoretical persuasions would agree that the therapist should not exploit the patient for his or her own purposes.

This is an excellent abstract principle; however, its application to clinical practices is occasionally ambiguous.

The treatment of sexual dysfunction is unavoidably enmeshed with cultural values and standards concerning human sexuality. These societal values appear to be changing, and there is considerable societal disagreement as to which values are correct and "healthy" versus repressive and crippling. Understandably, the field of human sexuality has attracted individuals with political as well as therapeutic missions. Many of these individuals feel a strong moral obligation to free patients from the crippling effects of cultural prohibitions and thus attempt to convert the patient to their own value system. Most clinicians would agree that the psychotherapeutic setting should not be used as a political arena. The issue is ambiguous, however, in that most psychotherapeutic activity either implicitly or explictly requires attitude change. The issue then is how much attitude change is necessary to help the given patient. In a recent publication, Marmor attempted to delineate the criteria for appropriate attitude change.

> We could say, then, that patients' values require modification only to the degree (and no more) that will enable them to overcome the sexual dysfunction for which they have sought help. For a sex therapist to attempt more—for example, to proselytise for group sex, indiscriminate sex, bisexual behavior, or even heterosexual behavior, if that is not what the patient has come for—would certainly constitute the kind of missionary zeal that Dr. Redlich is decrying and would stretch the limits of ethical propriety to a questionable degree." (Marmor, 1977, pp. 157-158)

To guard against less obvious proselytizing, I suggest that each therapist attempt to become aware of his or her own value system, and the value changes in patients necessary for successful therapy to occur. Prospective patients should be informed of the value system necessarily underlying the treatment modality. Masters and Johnson (1977) suggest that the dual-sex team may protect the patient from undesirable indoctrination as it is unlikely that the values of two therapists will be identical.

Sexual activity between therapists and patients appears to be a more frequent occurrence than previously thought (Kardener, Fuller, & Mensh, 1973). In most cases, this activity appears to serve the therapist's needs and constitutes exploitation of the patient. The available evidence suggests that the typical case involves a male therapist with a younger, attractive female patient. It is of note that sex between therapists and old, ugly, and crippled patients appears to be a somewhat uncommon event (Lowry & Lowry, 1975). The available evidence suggests that such activity is seldom helpful to the patient and occasionally has disasterous effects (Stone, 1976; Taylor and Wagner, 1976; Witkin, 1977). The code of ethics of the American Association of Sex Education, Counselors and Therapists (Witkins, 1977) and the Hippocratic oath specifically prohibit such activity. Hare-Mustin (1974) has suggested that the ethical standards of psychologists indirectly condemn such activity. These standards require the psychologist to offer treatment only within the boundaries of his competence, and there is no evidence to suggest that training in psychology improves sexual technique. Some professional liability insurance policies specifically exclude coverage of legal action resulting from sexual acts between therapist and patient. Such activity can result in large legal awards to the patient if legal action is pursued (Schultz, 1975).

Ethical questions regarding the use of sexual surrogates have mainly concerned the use of female surrogates for dysfunctional males without partners, although some sexual dysfunction clinics also provide male surrogates for female patients without partners (Apfelbaum, 1978; Wolfe, 1978). The ethical questions concerning this practice can be temporarily shelved, as there is minimal evidence documenting the long-term effectiveness of this prodecure or the extent to which behavior change with the surrogate transfers to natural partners in the environment. Many sexually dysfunctional patients without partners have severe coexisting difficulties with interpersonal relations. One could argue that these interpersonal difficulties create greater impairment in living than sexual symptoms and merit treatment priority. It is questionable whether surrogate therapy adequately addresses these problems. The use of sexual surrogates may render the therapist subject to legal action as well (Masters, 1977). If the surrogate is married, the spouse may charge alienation of affection. The applicability of prostitution laws to the use of surrogates is also unclear.

Another ethical concern of some complexity and requiring considerable clinical skill to evaluate is the question of the impact of symptom remission on the patient's subsequent life. Most patients present the therapist with interactional patterns that they have evolved after a lifetime of trial-and-error learning. These seemingly maladaptive interactional patterns may be quite functional in the patient's present relationship. One should appreciate this and anticipate that symptom remission and other changes in interpersonal behavior will be in the patient's best overall interest.

A variety of seldomly enforced laws may unwittingly be violated by sexual therapists. Most states have a bewildering array of laws concerning approved sexual behavior. For example, cunnilingus is illegal in Tennessee, and female masturbation therapy may be illegal in Arkansas and Nevada (Barnette, 1973).

SUGGESTIONS FOR FUTURE RESEARCH

Human sexuality remains an almost virgin research territory. In view of the massive investment of interest and activity in this field since the publication of *Human Sexual Inadequacy* in 1970, it is remarkable that we do not have definitive answers as to the essential therapeutic components for the treatment of sexual dysfunction, the population for whom these treatment approaches are appropriate, or conclusive information about the differential effectiveness of alternative treatment approaches. The impact of Masters and Johnson's work appears to have been twofold. It has opened a new field of inquiry by challenging many widely held assumptions. In another way, the publication of complete treatment packages for a wide variety of disorders has probably inhibited basic clinical research. For a period of time, it almost appeared as if Masters and Johnson had answered all of the important questions in this area. Subsequent failures to replicate their work in certain instances has reminded the scientific community of how little we really know in this important area.

I will briefly outline what I consider to be clinical research priorities concerning the treatment of anorgasmia. First, there is little information concerning the population for whom behavioral sex therapy is appropriate. Clinical anecdotal evidence suggests that vaguely defined difficulties in intimacy and vaguely defined maladaptive marital interaction difficulties decrease the probability of a successful therapeutic outcome in the treatment of anorgasmia. There has been little if any controlled research on these prognostic factors. Likewise, there has been little effort to quantify these dimensions objectively. This information is of particular importance because the typical clinician encounters many self-referred and self-diagnosed patients who request specific treatment approaches.

Research on the natural history of untreated disorders is necessary for the clinician to know when treatment intervention is mandated. The earlier survey data by Kinsey on the relationship of the experience of orgasm to the number of years of marriage suggested that natural exposure to sexual activity in marriage increased the probability of orgasm attainment for some women with primary anorgasmia. This data may not be relevant to current clinical populations since there has been considerable change in societal values concerning female sexuality in the last decade. Many contemporary young married women with anorgasmia may enter marriage with histories of fairly extensive sexual activity and thus be quite different from the women included in the Kinsey surveys. To the author's knowledge, there is no information available on the natural history of secondary anorgasmia. Presumably a large number of these cases spontaneously remit without treatment. Inclusion of such cases in a treatment evaluation study would produce spuriously high success rates.

There is a pressing need for research designed to isolate the essential components of therapy for the treatment of anorgasmia. Numerous clinics and clinicians have evolved complete treatment packages for anorgasmia. These programs frequently emphasize different clinical procedures and theoretical orientations, although they also have many components in common. This unfortunate situation makes it virtually impossible to decide which treatment components are essential to successful therapy. A preferable course would be to identify the necessary and sufficient conditions for the treatment of anorgasmia and then to improve and refine the identified effective components by careful clinical research. The studies by Wincze and Caird (1976) represent beginning efforts in this direction.

Other research needs to address questions of differential effectiveness of certain procedures for given subpopulations. Comparisons of directed masturbation approaches with the conjoint in vivo desensitization approach for the treatment of primary anorgasmia are needed. Similarily, treatment procedures for secondary anorgasmia have been investigated minimally.

In conclusion, the behavioral treatment of anorgasmia appears to be a promising clinical approach. The available evidence suggests that this approach is more effective than traditional psychotherapeutic techniques. There has, however, been a paucity of well-designed research in this area.

SUMMARY

Disorders of sexual arousal and orgasm attainment appear to exist in approximately 30 to 50 percent of the married female population. Both behavioral and psychoanalytically oriented treatment approaches exist for these disorders. Psychoanalytically oriented approaches stress both the importance of unconscious past origins for these disorders and the use of insight as a curative mechanism. The effectiveness of these approaches is unclear. Behaviorally oriented treatments for anorgasmia are based on the hypothesis that sexual dysfunction is learned behavior maintained by sexual anxiety and a nonreinforcing sexual partner. Behavioral treatment packages for anorgasmia usually include sexual education, directive couple counseling, attitude change, a graduated reexposure to sexual stimuli, and masturbatory skill training.

Assessment of the appropriateness of a given patient for behavioral treatment of anorgasmia requires considerable clinical skill.

Such an assessment should examine the presence of hidden agendas, poor motivation, marital discord, organic factors, and severe coexisting psychopathology. Assessment of treatment outcome should specify the exact conditions under which orgasm occurs.

There are three main behavioral treatment techniques for anorgasmia. Systematic desensitization approaches appear to be effective in reducing sexual anxiety. Video desensitization appears to be more successful than imaginary desensitization. Neither approach appears to be particularly effective in increasing orgasmic capacity. Directive practice approaches (in vivo desensitization) have been utilized with larger clinical populations. Controlled-outcome studies with this approach have yielded conflicting results. It appears to decrease sexual anxiety and possibly to increase orgasmic capacity. Directed masturbation approaches appear to be successful in teaching most women how to masturbate. Studies of the extent to which this skill transfers to partner-related activities have yielded ambiguous results.

The recommended treatment approach for primary anorgasmia includes sexual education, directive couple therapy, conjoint in vivo graduated-exposure exercises, and masturbatory training. The treatment of choice for secondary anorgasmia is unclear.

Ethical considerations in the treatment of anorgasmia include assuring that the therapist does not exploit the patient for the therapist's own benefit. Attempted conversion of the patient to the therapist's sexual value system is a form of political persuasion and not a legitimate therapeutic activity. However, the boundary between necessary attitude change for therapy and political activity is ambiguous.

Training for sex therapy should include didactic teaching in sexual physiology, behavioral procedures, and marital counseling skills as well as supervised clinical activity. Sex therapists need general therapy skills as well as specialized sexual counseling skills.

REFERENCES

Ansari, J. M. A. Impotence: Prognosis (a controlled study). *British Journal of Psychiatry,* 1976, *128,* 194–198.

Apfelbaum, B. *The question of surrogates.* Paper presented at the Eastern Association for Sex Therapy, New York, March 1978.

Asirdas, S., & Beech, H. R. The behavioral treatment of sexual inadequacy. *Journal of Psychosomatic Research,* 1975, *19,* 345–353.

Azrin, N. H., Naster, B. J., & Jones, R. Reciprocity counseling: A rapid learning-based procedure for marital counseling. *Behaviour Research and Therapy,* 1973, *11,* 365–382.

Baker, L. D., & Nagata, F. S. A group approach to the treatment of heterosexual couples with sexual dissatisfactions. *Journal of Sex Education Therapy,* 1978, *4,* 15–18.

Barbach, L. G. Group treatment of preorgasmic women. *Journal of Sex and Marital Therapy,* 1974, *1,* 139–145.

Barbach, L. G. *For yourself: The fulfillment of female sexuality.* Garden City, N.Y.: Doubleday, 1975.

Barnette, W. *Sexual freedom and the Constitution.* Albuquerque: University of New Mexico Press, 1973.

Bjorksten, O. J. Sexually graphic material in the treatment of sexual disorders. In J. K. Meyer (Ed.), *Clinical management of sexual disorders.* Baltimore, Williams and Wilkins, 1976.

Blakeney, P., Kinder, B. N., Creson, D., Powell, L. C., & Sutton, C. A short-term intensive workshop approach for the treatment of human sexual inadequacy. *Journal of Sex and Marital Therapy,* 1976, *2,* 124–129.

Blum, G. S. A study of the psychoanalytic theory of psychosexual development. *Genetic Psychology Monographs,* 1949, *39,* 3–99.

Brady, J. P. Brevital-relaxation treatment of frigidity. *Behaviour Research and Therapy,* 1966, *4,* 71–77.

Brady, J. P. Behavior therapy of sexual disorders. In B. J. Sadock, H. I. Kaplan, & A. M. Freedman (Eds.), *The sexual experience.* Baltimore: Williams and Wilkins, 1976.

Brady, J. P., & Levitt, E. E. The relationship of sexual preferences to sexual experience. *Psychological Record,* 1965, *15,* 377–384.

Brown, P. T., & Kolaszynska-Carr, A. *The relevance of Master and Johnson's methodology to the treatment of sexual disorders in an outpatient clinic.* Paper presented at the Second European Conference on Behavior Modification, Wexford, Ireland, March 1972.

Burbank, F. The treatment of sexual problems by group therapy. In S. Crown (Ed.), *Psychosexual problems.* New York: Academic Press, 1976.

Caird, W., & Wincze, J. P. *Sex therapy: A behavioral approach.* New York: Harper and Row, 1977.

Chesser, E. *The sexual marital and family relationship of the English woman.* London: Hutchinson's Medical Publications, 1956.

Cooper, A. J. Frigidity: Treatment and short-term prognosis. *Journal of Psychosomatic Research,* 1970, *14,* 133–147.

Crown, S., & Lucas, C. J. Individual psychotherapy. In S. Crown (Ed.), *Psychosexual problems.* New York: Academic Press, 1976.

Derogatis, L. R., Meyer, J. K., & Dupkin, C. N. Discrimination of organic versus psychogenic impotence with the DSFI. *Journal of Sex and Marital Therapy,* 1976, *2,* 229–240.

Dickinson, R. K., & Beam, L. *A thousand marriages. A medical study of sex adjustment.* Baltimore: Williams and Wilkins, 1971.

Eysenck, H. J., & Beech, R. Counter-conditioning and related methods. In A. E. Bergin & S. L. Garfield (Eds.), *Handbook of psychotherapy and behavioral change.* New York, Wiley, 1971.

Fabbri, R. Jr. *Guided fantasy in sexual therapy.* New Haven, Conn.: Behavioral and Educational Consulting Corporation, 1977.

Fisher, S. *The female orgasm.* New York: Basic Books, 1973.

Frank, E., Anderson, C., & Curtis, E. *The incidence of sexual difficulties in normal couples.* Paper presented at Eastern Association for Sex Therapy, New York, March 1977.

Franks, C. M., & Wilson, G. T. Behavior therapy and sexual disorders: Commentary. In C. M. Franks & G. T. Wilson (Eds.), *Annual review of behavior therapy.* New York: Brunner/Mazel, 1974.

Gebhard, P. H. Factors in marital orgasm. In J. LoPiccolo & L. LoPiccolo (Eds.), *Handbook of sex therapy.* New York: Plenum, 1978.

Geer, J. Genital measures: Comments on their role in understanding human sexuality. *Journal of Sex and Marital Therapy,* 1976, *3,* 165–172.

Hamilton, G. V. *A research in marriage.* New York: Albert and Charles Boni, 1929.

Hare-Mustin, R. T. Ethical considerations in the use of sexual contact in psychotherapy. *Psychotherapy,* 1974, *11,* 308–310.

Hartman, W. E., & Fithian, M. A. *Treatment of sexual dysfunction.* Long Beach, Cal.: Center for Marital and Sexual Studies, 1972.

Haslam, M. T. The treatment of psychogenic dysparenia by reciprocal inhibition. *British Journal of Psychiatry,* 1965, *3,* 280–282.

Haslam, M. T. The psychosexual clinic. *Practitioner,* 1976, *217,* 958–962.

Heiman, J. R. Issues in the use of psychophysiology to assess female sexual dysfunction. *Journal of Sex and Marital Therapy,* 1976, *3,* 197–204.

Henson, D. E., & Rubin, H. B. A comparison of two objective measures of sexual arousal of women. *Behaviour Research and Therapy,* 1978, *16,* 143–152.

Hunt, M. *Sexual behavior in the 70s.* Chicago: Playboy Press, 1974.

Jacobson, N. S., & Martin, B. Behavioral marriage therapy, current status. *Psychological Bulletin,* 1976, *83,* 540–556.

Jones, W. J., & Park, P. M. Treatment of single-partner sexual dysfunction by systematic desensitization. *Obstetrics and Gynecology,* 1972, *39,* 411–417.

Kaplan, H. S. *The new sex therapy.* New York: Brunner/Mazel, 1974.

Kaplan, H. S. Sex therapy: An overview. In E. T. Adelson (Ed.), *Sexuality and psychoanalysis.* New York: Brunner/Mazel, 1975.

Kaplan, H. S. Training of sex therapists. In W. H. Masters, V. E. Johnson, & R. C. Kolodny (Eds.), *Ethical issues in sex therapy and research.* Boston: Little, Brown, 1977.

Kaplan, H. S., & Kohl, R. N. Adverse reactions to the rapid treatment of sexual problems. *Psychosomatics,* 1972, *13,* 185–190.

Kardener, S. H., Fuller, M., & Mensh, I. N. A survey of physicians' attitudes and practices regarding erotic and monoerotic contact with patients. *American Journal of Psychiatry,* 1973, *130,* 1077–1081.

Kegel, A. Sexual functions of the pubococcygeus muscle. *Western Journal of Surgery, Obstetrics and Gynecology,* 1952, *60,* 521–524.

Kinsey, A. C., Pomeroy, W., Martin, C., & Gebhard, P. *Sexual behavior in the human female.* Philadelphia: Saunders, 1953.

Kline-Graber, G., & Graber, B. Diagnosis and treatment procedures of pubococcygeal deficiencies in women. In J. LoPiccolo & L. LoPiccolo (Eds.), *Handbook of sex therapy.* New York, Plenum, 1978.

Kohlenberg, R. Directed masturbation and the treatment of primary orgasmic dysfunction. *Archives of Sexual Behavior,* 1974, *3,* 349–356.

Kraft, T., & Al-Issa, I. A. Behavior therapy and the treatment of frigidity. *American Journal of Psychotherapy,* 1962, *21,* 116–120.

Kuriansky, J., Sharpe, L., & O'Connor, D. *Tell me doctor, am I cured?* Paper presented at the Eastern Association for Sex Therapy, New York, March 1977.

Lansky, M. R., & Davenport, A. E. Difficulties in brief conjoint treatment of sexual dysfunction. *American Journal of Psychiatry,* 1975, *132,* 177–179.

Lazarus, A. A. The treatment of chronic frigidity by systematic desensitization. *Journal of Nervous and Mental Diseases,* 1963, *136,* 272–278.

Lazarus, A. A. Overcoming sexual inadequacy. In J. LoPiccolo & L. LoPiccolo (Eds.), *Handbook of sex therapy.* New York: Plenum, 1978.

Leiblum, S. R., & Kopel, S. A. Screening and prognosis in sex therapy: To treat or not to treat. *Behavior Therapy,* 1977, *8,* 480–486.

Leiblum, S. R., Rosen, R. C., & Pierce, D. Group treatment format: Mixed sexual dysfunctions. *Archives of Sexual Behavior,* 1976, *5,* 313–321.

Leitenberg, H., Agras, W. S., Edwards, J., Thomson, L. E., & Wincze, J. P. Practice as a psychotherapeutic variable: An experimental analysis within single cases. *Journal of Psychiatric Research,* 1970, *7,* 215–225.

Levay, A. N., & Kagle, A. Ego deficiencies in the areas of pleasure, intimacy, and cooperation: Guidelines in the diagnosis and treatment of sexual dysfunctions. *Journal of Sex Marital Therapy,* 1977, *3,* 10–18.

Levit, H. L. Marital crisis intervention: Hypnosis in impotence/frigidity cases. *American Journal of Clinical Hypnosis,* 1971, *14,* 56–60.

Lobitz, W. C., & Lobitz, G. K. Clinical assessment in the treatment of sexual dysfunctions. In J. LoPiccolo & L. LoPiccolo (Eds.), *Handbook of sex therapy.* New York: Plenum, 1978.

Lobitz, W. C., & LoPiccolo, J. New methods in the behavioral treatment of sexual dysfunction. *Journal of Behavior Therapy and Experimental Psychiatry,* 1972, *3,* 265–271.

LoPiccolo, J. The professionalization of sex therapy. In J. LoPiccolo & L. LoPiccolo (Eds.), *Handbook of sex therapy.* New York: Plenum, 1978.(a)

LoPiccolo, J. Direct treatment of sexual dysfunction. In J. LoPiccolo & L. LoPiccolo (Eds.), *Handbook of sex therapy.* New York: Plenum, 1978.(b)

LoPiccolo, J., & Lobitz, W. C. Behavior therapy of sexual dysfunction. In L. S. Hamerlynck, L. C. Hardy, & E. J. Mash (Eds.), *Behavior change: Methodology, concepts and practice.* Champaign, Ill.: Research press, 1973.

LoPiccolo, J., & Lobitz, W. C. The role of masturbation in the treatment of orgasmic dysfunction. In J. LoPiccolo & L. LoPiccolo (Eds.), *Handbook of sex therapy.* New York: Plenum, 1978.

LoPiccolo, J., & Steger, J. C. The sexual interaction inventory: A new instrument for assessment of sexual dysfunction. *Archives of Sexual Behavior,* 1974, *3,* 585–595.

Lowry, T. S., & Lowry, T. P. Ethical considerations in sex therapy. *Journal of Marriage and Family Counseling,* 1975, *1,* 229–236.

Madsen, L., & Ullman, L. Innovations in the desensitization of frigidity. *Behaviour Research and Therapy,* 1962, *5,* 67–68.

Marks, I. M., & Sartorius, N. H. A contribution to the measurement of sexual attitude. *Journal of Nervous and Mental Diseases,* 1968, *145,* 441–451.

Marmor, J. Designated discussion. In W. H. Masters, V. E. Johnson, & R. C. Kolodny (Eds.), *Ethical issues in sex therapy and research.* Boston: Little, Brown, 1977.

Masters, W. H. General discussion. In W. H. Masters, V. E. Johnson, & R. C. Kolodny (Eds.), *Ethical issues in sex therapy and research.* Boston: Little, Brown, 1977.

Masters, W. H., & Johnson, V. E. *Human sexual response.* Boston: Little, Brown, 1966.

Masters, W. H., & Johnson, V. E. *Human sexual inadequacy.* Boston: Little, Brown, 1970.

Mathews, A., Bancroft, J. Whitehead, A., Hackmann, A., Julier, D., Brancroft, J., Gath, D., & Shaw, P. The behavioral treatment of sexual inadequacy: A comparative study. *Behaviour Research and Therapy,* 1976, *14,* 427–436.

McCarthy, B. W. A modification of Masters and Johnson's sex therapy model in a clinical setting. *Psychotherapy,* 1973, *10,* 290–293.

McCoy, N. N., & D'Agostino, P. A. Factor analysis of the sexual interaction inventory. *Archives of Sexual Behavior,* 1977, *6,* 25–35.

McGovern, K. B., Kirkpatrick, C. C., & LoPiccolo, J. A behavioral group treatment program for sexually dysfunctional couples. In J. LoPiccolo & L. LoPiccolo (Eds.), *Handbook of sex therapy.* New York: Plenum, 1978.

McGovern, K. B., McMullen, R. S., & LoPiccolo, J. Secondary orgasmic dysfunction: Analysis and strategies for treatment. In J. LoPiccolo & L. L. LoPiccolo (Eds.), *Handbook of sex therapy.* New York: Plenum, 1978.

McGovern, K. B., Stewart, R., & LoPiccolo, J. Secondary orgasmic dysfunction: Analysis and strategies for treatment. *Archives of Sexual Behavior,* 1975, *4,* 265–275.

Meyer, J. K. Psychodynamic treatment of the individual with a sexual disorder. In J. K. Meyer (Ed.), *Clinical management of sexual disorders.* Baltimore: Williams and Wilkins, 1976.

Meyer, J. K., Schmidt, C. W., Lucas, M. J., & Smith, E. Short-term treatment of sexual problems: Interim report. *American Journal of Psychiatry,* 1975, *132,* 172–176.

Miller, W. R., & Lief, H. I. Masturbatory attitudes, knowledge and experience: Data from the Sex Knowledge and Attitude Test. *Archives of Sexual Behavior,* 1976, *5,* 447–468.

Money, J., & Alexander, H. Sex therapist certification program. *Journal of Sex Education and Therapy,* 1975, *1,* 44–47.

Morokoff, P. Determinants of female orgasm. In J. LoPiccolo & L. LoPiccolo (Eds.), *Handbook of sex therapy.* New York: Plenum, 1978.

Munjack, D., Cristol, A., Goldstein, A., Phillips, D. Goldberg, A., Whipple, K., Staples, F., & Kanno, P. Behavioral treatment of orgasmic dysfunction: A controlled study. *British Journal of Psychiatry,* 1976, *129,* 497–502.

Munjack, D., & Kanno, P. H. Prognosis in the treatment of female sexual inhibition. *Comprehensive Psychiatry,* 1977, *18,* 481–488.

Nemetz, G. H., Craig, K. D., & Reith, G. Treatment of female sexual dysfunction through symbolic modeling. *Journal of Consulting and Clinical Psychology,* 1978, *46,* 62–73.

Nims, J. P. Imagery, shaping and orgasm. *Journal of Sex and Marital Therapy,* 1975, *3,* 198–203.

Nunnally, E. W., Miller, S., & Wachman, D. B. The Minnesota couples communication program. *Small Group Behavior,* 1975, *6,* 57–71.

Obler, M. Systematic desensitization in sexual disorders. *Journal of Behavior Therapy and Experimental Psychiatry,* 1973, *4,* 93–101.

O'Connor, J. F., & Stern, L. O. Results of treatment in functional sexual disorders. *New York State Journal of Medicine,* 1972, *12,* 1927–1934.

Powell, L. C., Blakeney, P., Croft, H., & Pulliam, G. Rapid treatment approach to human sexual inadequacy. *American Journal of Obstetrics and Gynecology,* 1974, *119,* 89–97.

Prochaska, J. O., & Marzilli, R. Modifications of the Masters and Johnson approach to sexual problems. *Psychotherapy,* 1973, *10,* 294–296.

Redlick, F. The ethics of sex therapy. In W. H. Masters, V. E. Johnson, & R. C. Kolodny (Eds.), *Ethical issues in sex therapy and research.* Boston: Little, Brown, 1977.

Reisenger, J. J. Masturbatory training in the treatment of primary orgasmic dysfunction. *Journal of Behavior Therapy and Experimental Psychiatry,* 1974, *5,* 179–183.

Richardson, T. A. Hypnotherapy in frigidity. *American Journal of Clinical Hypnosis,* 1963, *5,* 194–199.

Sager, C. J. The role of sex therapy in marital therapy. *American Journal of Psychiatry,* 1976, *133,* 555–559.

Satir, V. *Conjoint family therapy.* Palo Alto, Cal.: Science and Behavior Books, 1967.

Schiavi, R. C., Derogatis, L., Kuriansky, J. B., O'Conner, D. G., & Sharpe, L. *Assessment of sexual and marital functioning: A preliminary test of instruments and their relevant characteristics.* Report from the Research Committee of the Eastern Association for Sex Therapy, 1978 (available from R. Schiavi, Mount Sinai School of Medicine, Fifth Ave. & 100th St., New York, N.Y. 10029).

Schmidt, C. W., & Lucas, N. J. The short-term, intermittent, conjoint treatment of sexual disorders. In J. K. Meyer (Ed.), *Clinical management of sexual disorders.* Baltimore: Williams and Wilkins, 1976.

Schneidman, B., & McGuire, L. Group therapy for nonorgasmic women. *Archives of Sexual Behavior,* 1976, *5,* 239–247.

Schultz, L. G. *Avoiding legal problems in sex therapy.* Paper presented at the Second Annual Conference of Sex Therapists and Counselors, Galveston, March 1975.

Segraves, R. T. Conditioning of masturbatory fantasies in sex therapy. *Journal of Sex Education Therapy,* 1976, *1,* 53–54. (a)

Segraves, R. T. Primary orgasmic dysfunction: Essential treatment components. *Journal of Sex and Marital Therapy,* 1976, *2,* 115–123. (b)

Segraves, R. T. Pharmacological agents causing sexual dysfunction. *Journal of Sex and Marital Therapy,* 1977, *3,* 157–176.

Segraves, R. T. Treatment of sexual dysfunction. *Comprehensive Therapy,* 1978, *4,* 38–43.

Segraves, R. T., Horton, K., & Lipgar, R. *Group treatment of mixed sexual dysfunction.* Unpublished manuscript, 1977.

Shainess, N. Authentic feminine orgastic response. In E. T. Adelson (Ed.), *Sexuality and psychoanalysis.* New York: Brunner/Mazel, 1975.

Sherfey, N. J. *The nature and evolution of female sexuality.* New York: Random House, 1972.

Snyder, A., LoPiccolo, L., & LoPiccolo, J. Secondary orgasmic dysfunction: Case study. *Archives of Sexual Behavior,* 1975, *4,* 227–283.

Sollod, R. N. Behavioral and psychodynamic dimensions of the new sex therapy. *Journal of Sex Marital Therapy,* 1975, *1,* 335–340.

Sotile, W. M., & Kilman, P. R. Treatments of psychogenic female sexual dysfunctions. *Psychological Bulletin,* 1977, *84,* 619–633.

Spitzer, R. Sex in DSM-III. Panel discussion at the Eastern Association for Sex Therapy, New York, March 1977.

Stone, M. H. Boundary violations between therapists and patients. *Psychiatric Annals,* 1976, *6,* 670–677.

Stuart, R. B. Operant-interpersonal treatment for marital discord. *Journal of Consulting and Clinical Psychology,* 1969, *33,* 675–682.

Taylor, B. J., & Wagner, N. N. Sex between therapists and clients: A review and analysis. *Professional Psychologist,* November 1976, pp. 593–601.

Terman, L. M. Correlates of orgasm adequacy in a group of 556 wives. *Journal of Psychology,* 1951, *32,* 115–172.

Tyler, E. A. Sexual incapacity therapy. In D. X. Freedman & J. E. Dyrud (Eds.), *American handbook of psychiatry: Treatment* (Vol. 5). New York: Basic Books, 1975.

Waggoner, R. W., Mudd, E. H., & Shearer, M. L. Training dual sex teams for rapid treatment of sexual dysfunction: A pilot program. In J. LoPiccolo & L. LoPiccolo (Eds.), *Handbook of sex therapy.* New York: Plenum, 1978.

Wallace, D. H., & Barbach, L. G. Preorgasmic group treatment. *Journal of Sex and Marital Therapy,* 1974, *1,* 146–154.

Wincze, J. P., & Caird, W. K. The effects of systematic desensitization and video desensitization in the treatment of essential sexual dysfunction in women. *Behavior Therapy,* 1976, *7,* 335–342.

Witkin, N. H. Ethical issues and sex therapy. *Journal of Sex Education Therapy,* 1977, *2,* 8–12.

Wolfe, L. The question of surrogates in sex therapy. In J. LoPiccolo & L. LoPiccolo (Eds.), *Handbook of sex therapy.* New York, Plenum, 1978.

Wolpe, J. *Psychotherapy by reciprocal inhibition.* Stanford: Stanford University Press, 1958.

Wright, J., Perreault, R., & Mathieu, M. The treatment of sexual dysfunction. *Archives of General Psychiatry,* 1977, *34,* 881–890.
Zeiss, A. M., Rosen, G. M., & Zeiss, R. A. Orgasm during intercourse: A treatment strategy for women. In J. LoPiccolo & L. LoPiccolo (Eds.), *Handbook of sex therapy.* New York, Plenum, 1978.
Zussman, L., & Zussman, S. Continuous time-limited treatment of standard sexual disorders. In J. K. Meyer (Ed.), *Clinical management of sexual disorders.* Baltimore: Williams and Wilkins, 1976.

SUGGESTED READINGS

Barbach, L. G. *For yourself: The fulfillment of female sexuality.* Garden City, N.Y.: Doubleday, 1975.
Belliveau, F., & Richter, L. *Understanding human sexual inadequacy.* Boston: Bantam Books, 1970.
Frank, E., Anderson, C., & Rubinstein, D. Frequency of sexual dysfunction in normal couples. *New England Journal of Medicine,* 1978, *299,* 111–115.
Group for the Advancement of Psychiatry. *Assessment of sexual function.* New York: Jason Aronson, 1974.
Kaplan, H. S. *The illustrated manual of sex therapy.* New York: Quadrangle, 1975.
LoPiccolo, J., & LoPiccolo, L. *Handbook of sex therapy.* New York: Plenum, 1978.
Sotile, W. M., & Kilman, P. R. Treatments of psychogenic female sexual dysfunctions. *Psychological Bulletin,* 1977, *84,* 619–633.
Tyler, E. A. Sexual incapacity therapy. In D. X. Freedman & J. E. Dyrud (Eds.), *American handbook of psychiatry: Treatment* (Vol. 5). New York: Basic Books, 1975.

3
Smoking

Harry A. Lando

The health implications of cigarette smoking are staggering. It is perhaps the leading preventable cause of death in the United States. Each year approximately 80,000 deaths from lung cancer, 22,000 from other cancers, 19,000 from chronic pulmonary disease, and perhaps as many as 225,000 from cardiovascular disease are directly attributable to smoking (USPHS, 1979). These figures translate into a reduction in life expectancy of between 8 and 9 years in the 30 to 35-year-old, two-pack-a-day smoker. Health costs related to smoking are now estimated to run between $5 and $8 billion annually. When lost productivity, wages, and increased absenteeism caused by smoking-related illnesses also are considered, the annual cost is increased by an additional $12 to $18 billion.

Almost from the time of its introduction into Europe in 1558, the *Nicotiana tabacum* aroused concern over potentially deleterious effects on health. Within a period of less than 60 years, tobacco became a major crop in Virginia and was, in fact, the principle currency. Although the primary use of tobacco in the United States prior to World War I was for chewing, by the 1920s cigarette consumption had increased dramatically. This trend was accelerated by the availability of prefabricated cigarettes. At the same time, health concerns also began to increase. As early as 1900, statisticians noted an increase in the incidence of lung cancer. In 1928 Lombard and Doering reported

Preparation of this chapter was facilitated by Grant 1 R01 CA22102-01, awarded by the National Cancer Institute, Department of Health, Education, and Welfare.

Table 1. Summary of reports of behavioral treatments.

Authors	Number of Subjects	Age of Subject	Type of Report	Treatments	Follow-up	Design Quality Rating
Berecz (1976)	10	—	Experimental	Electric shock	6 mo, 2 yr	Very good (26)
Best et al. (1978)	60	36	Experimental	Satiation, rapid smoking, self-management	3 mo, 6 mo	Very good (27.5)
Blittner et al. (1978)	54	38	Experimental	Cognitive expectancy, stimulus control	6 mo, 14 mo	Very good (28)
Brockway et al. (1977)	27	18–50	Experimental	Self-control, stimulus control	6 mo, 12 mo	Very good (27.5)
Conway (1977)	108	21	Experimental	Aversion, self-management	8 wk, 20 wk	Very good (26.5)
Danaher (1977)	50	33	Experimental	Self-management, rapid smoking	13 wk	Very good (27.5)
Dubren (1977)	61	—	Experimental	Telephone support	1 mo	Very good (24)
Elliot & Denney (1978)	63	29	Experimental	Multicomponent booster, rapid smoking	3 mo, 6 mo	Very good (28.5)
Elliot & Tighe (1968)	25	—	Multiple case study	Contingency management	3 mo, 15–17 mo	—
Flaxman (1978)	64	—	Experimental	Rapid smoking target date	1 mo, 2 mo, 6 mo	Very good (26)
Glasgow (1978)	52	33	Experimental	Self-help manual, rapid smoking	3 mo, 6 mo	Very good (23.5)

Frederiksen et al. (1976)	16	23	Experimental	Contingency contracting, controlled smoking	3 mo, 6 mo	Very good (26.5)
Lando (1977)	34	31	Experimental	Self-management, satiation	4 mo, 6 mo	—
Levinson et al. (1971)	52	—	Experimental	Gradual reduction	12 wk, 3 mo	Very good (24)
Lichtenstein et al. (1973)	40	29	Experimental	Rapid smoking	6 mo	Very good (26)
Norton & Barske (1977)	62	—	Experimental	Rapid smoking	3 mo, 6 mo	Very good (21.5)
Pomerleau et al. (1978)	100	38	Experimental	Multicomponent, self-help manual	1 yr, 2 yr	Very good (23.5)
Resnick (1968)	60	19	Experimental	Satiation	2 wks, 4 mo	Very good (25.5)
Russell et al. (1976)	70	39	Experimental	Electric shock	2 wks	Very good (24)
Wagner & Bragg (1970)	54	40	Experimental	Covert sensitization, systematic desensitization, relaxation	30 days, 90 days	Very good (25.5)
Winett (1973)	45	37	Experimental	Contingency management	3 mo, 6 mo	Very good (25)

It should be noted that in some cases the Design Quality Ratings provide a misleading estimate of the methodological adequacy of the studies cited. A study might, for example, meet a number of major design criteria (i.e., random assignment of subjects to conditions, absence of experimenter bias, appropriate statistical analyses, etc.), yet still suffer important deficiencies. Common shortcomings included the lack of a plausible control condition, failure to confirm adherence to treatment procedures, and the absence of validity checks upon self-reported abstinence. The study reported by Resnick (1968), for example, contains all of these shortcomings but meets a sufficient number of other DQR criteria to receive a high rating.

that cancer patients were more likely than nonsmoking controls to be distinguished by heavy smoking. Trends in diseases such as lung cancer became more evident in the 1930s, and by the 1950s the data implicating cigarettes as a major health hazard began to be overwhelming (USPHS, 1979).

In 1978 estimated cigarette consumption was 615 billion cigarettes for 54 million adult smokers. Despite continuing publicity concerning the health hazards of smoking, consumption among teenage boys has remained virtually constant, and among teenage girls it has shown a sharp increase. On the other hand, there have been a number of encouraging trends. More than 30 million Americans are now ex-smokers. Per capita consumption of cigarettes dropped from 4,345 in 1963 to 3,965 in 1978, the lowest level in 20 years. The prevalence of regular cigarette smoking in the adult population is approximately 33 percent, down from 42 percent in 1964 (USPHS, 1979). These trends are especially heartening in light of recent health findings that clearly indicate declining overall mortality ratios among former smokers as the years of abstinence increase.

The cigarette product has itself changed dramatically. Consumption of filter cigarettes has increased manyfold since 1954 when less than 1 percent of cigarettes were filter-tipped. At the same time, the average tar content has declined from approximately 36 mg to 17 mg, and the average nicotine delivery from over 2 mg to 1.1 mg. Development of low tar and nicotine cigarettes has accelerated in the past five years, and in 1977 almost one-half of the industry's advertising budget was devoted to the promotion of these cigarettes.

Most smokers clearly recognize the risks involved in smoking (Gallup, 1974). Recent surveys reveal that over 60 percent of adult smokers have made at least one serious attempt to break the habit. An additional 30 percent indicate that they would try to do so provided that an easy and effective method were made available (National Clearinghouse For Smoking and Health, 1976). Thus the problem is not one of a lack of awareness among smokers, but rather that a substantial majority of those desiring to quit have been unsuccessful (Guilford, 1966). If these smokers could stop, there might be substantial fringe benefits in the form of reduced smoking among children. Smoking is far less common among children in households where neither parent smokes than in households where both parents smoke. Although the focus of this chapter is upon treatment rather than prevention, anything that can be done to minimize the likelihood of new smokers taking up the habit has obvious advantages. Programs emphasizing prevention have been developed only comparatively recently, although some favorable preliminary data are beginning to be reported (cf. Evans, 1979).

THEORETICAL ANALYSIS

Smoking has been found to be a surprisingly complex behavior, the determining factors of which are not fully understood. A variety of theories and explanations for the persistence of the smoking habit have been developed (Bernstein, 1969; Borgatta & Evans, 1968). Emphasis has been placed upon both pharmacological and psychological factors, as well as upon various combinations of these influences.

Pharmacological Determinants

Many investigators have focused upon the role of nicotine in maintaining dependence upon tobacco. Some investigators prefer the term "dependence" (Russell, 1971), whereas others have used the term "addiction" (Brecher, 1972). Whichever term is chosen, there is convincing evidence for the role of nicotine in cigarette consumption. The work of Schachter and his associates in particular has supported the importance of nicotine as a reinforcer (Schachter, 1978). These workers have construed smoking as an escape-avoidance response stemming from the aversive effects of periodic nicotine withdrawal in the heavy smoker (Pomerleau, 1979). They suggest the existence of an internal regulatory mechanism that operates like a thermostat in maintaining the level of nicotine within set upper and lower limits by regulating cigarette consumption.

In an innovative series of experiments, Schachter and his colleagues have concluded that long-term heavy smokers are clearly sensitive to the nicotine content of cigarettes. Subjects given high and low nicotine cigarettes on alternate weeks adjusted their smoking to maintain nicotine intake at fairly constant levels (Schachter, 1977). Biochemical studies indicated that although some nicotine is detoxified in the liver, a proportion escapes this process and is eliminated directly in the urine (Pomerleau, 1979). The rate of urinary excretion is affected by the pH of the urine, increasing as the urine becomes more acid. Schachter, Kozlowski, and Silverstein (1977) demonstrated that when urinary pH was manipulated by the administration of acidifying (e.g., ascorbic acid) or alkalizing (e.g., sodium bicarbonate) agents, the rate of smoking changed accordingly. Consumption increased when urine was acidified relative to when it was either uncontrolled or made more basic.

Additional studies assessed the possibility that some of the determinants of smoking rate previously ascribed to psychological causes might actually be a function of the urinary pH excretion mechanism. It has been commonly observed, for example, that smoking increases at parties. Silverstein, Kozlowski, and Schachter (1977) reported that party-going reliably leads to acidification of the urine. Acidification of the urine also was found to be produced by stress induced in a variety of settings (Schachter, Silverstein, Kozlowski, Herman, & Liebling, 1977). In each case, increased smoking was also observed. More convincing evidence was obtained in a study by Schachter, Silverstein, and Perlick (1977) which partialed out the effects of stress and urinary pH. It was found that smoking responded to urinary pH and not to stress. Schachter and his colleagues therefore interpreted this series of experiments as demonstrating both that heavy smokers smoke for nicotine and that the crucial mediator of the stress–smoking relationship is the urinary pH mechanism.

Other investigators have reported the effects of nicotine on smoking. Several investigators have obtained reductions in smoking when subjects were given oral or intravenous doses of nicotine (Jarvik, Glick, & Nakamura, 1970; Lucchesi, Schuster, & Emley, 1967). Finnegan, Larson, and Haag (1945) noted that even when smokers were given low nicotine cigarettes, many indicated symptoms essentially the same as those encountered by individuals who quit altogether. Administration of the drug mecamylamine, which functions as a nicotine "antagonist," also has been observed to lead to increased rates of smoking (Stolerman, Goldfarb, Fink, & Jarvik, 1973).

Not all the evidence has supported the nicotine-dependence hypothesis, however. Kumar, Cooke, Lader, and Russell (1977) failed to produce changes in smoking rate when they administered nicotine to subjects intravenously. Jarvik (1977) noted that lettuce cigarettes reinforced with nicotine were no more acceptable to smokers than nonnicotine cigarettes. Schachter, Silverstein, and Perlick (1977) have suggested that some smokers may be addicted to nicotine, whereas others may not. They propose that the study of withdrawal symptoms may hold the key to understanding why this is so.

Heavy smokers have been observed to suffer nicotine withdrawal reactions, including lowered diastolic blood pressure and cardiac slowing, during an experimentally imposed three-day abstinence period (Knapp, Bliss, & Wells, 1963). These investigators concluded that heavy smokers are "true addicts." Jarvik (1977) has suggested, however, that most of the evidence pointing to nicotine as the primary reinforcer in smoking is circumstantial. Although smokers prefer cigarettes with nicotine, they will smoke non-nicotine cigarettes at least temporarily if no others are available. The fact that supplementing lettuce cigarettes with nicotine did not improve their acceptability to smokers indicates that nicotine alone does not provide a sufficient explanation for smoking. Jarvik has suggested that nicotine may be necessary but not sufficient to sustain cigarette consumption.

Pomerleau (1979) argues that the nicotine addiction model is plausible, but it requires further testing. He mentions the need for direct measurements of changes in nicotine titer during withdrawal. He also indicates that the model must deal with such other questions as individual differences in smoking behavior and relapse mechanisms leading to resumption of the habit. The role of environmental stimuli in influencing smoking must also be considered. Despite certain ambiguities in the research evidence, Russell strongly supports the importance of nicotine as a reinforcer and comments that "there is little doubt that if it were not for the nicotine in tobacco smoke, people would be little more inclined to smoke than they are to blow bubbles or light sparklers" (Russell, 1974, p. 793).

Several researchers have attempted to incorporate both pharmacological and psychological factors in developing more comprehensive models of smoking behavior (Dunn, 1973; Eysenck, 1973; Russell, 1974). A particularly interesting approach is taken by Solomon (Solomon, 1977; Solomon & Corbit, 1973, 1974) in his recent opponent process theory. Although his model is not specific to smoking, it is clearly applicable to this behavior. The model includes several major assumptions. Smoking entails a biphasic reaction in which a brief pleasurable response is followed by a more prolonged dysphoric response. These two opposing processes—the pleasurable A state and the dysphoric B state—sum algebraically to produce a discriminable "hedonic tone." The A state is more prominent in the initial stages of the habit. Although there may also be some unpleasant effects the first few times cigarettes are smoked, the reinforcing properties of nicotine are quite strong. With continued use, however, the opponent process begins increasingly to assert itself. The pleasurable A state lessens in intensity, whereas the withdrawal B state becomes more prominent.

In order to terminate the aversive B state quickly, additional smoking is necessary. Smoking is then both positively reinforced by a pleasurable response and negatively reinforced by the termination of withdrawal. An addictive cycle can become established (cf. Pomerleau, 1979). Tolerance is also evidenced as the B state continues to intensify and the pleasurable A state weakens, thus requiring the consumption of greater amounts of tobacco to produce the equivalent pleasurable response.

Psychological factors are also incorporated into the opponent process concept through a conditioning mechanism. Stimuli associated with either the A or B state can eventually elicit the appropriate state as a conditioned response. Stimuli associated with smoking (e.g., a pack of cigarettes, the sight of matches) should elicit a brief conditioned pleasurable A state, whereas the reverse should be true for stimuli associated with withdrawal (e.g., an empty cigarette pack, "no smoking" signs). A chronic smoker may begin to experience anticipatory withdrawal when encountering the latter conditioned stimuli. This can result in reduced intervals between cigarettes, at least until an asymptote is reached. The opponent process model has clear implications in addressing the pervasive phenomenon of relapse. Although the withdrawal B state does eventually diminish, the opponent A state intensifies. If a cigarette is subsequently smoked, the pleasurable A state is again at full strength and the smoker can quickly become locked into an addictive pattern.

Psychological Determinants

Nonbehavioral. Several theoretical models have been developed which attempt to classify smokers by the types of needs provided for by their cigarettes. One of the best known of these models is a formulation by Tomkins (1966, 1968) in which he relates smoking to "affect" management. He argued that for smoking to become habitual, it must consistently be associated with either the enhancement of positive affect or the reduction of negative affect (cf. Lichtenstein & Danaher, 1976). Although he believed that different types of smokers would require different cessation techniques, he failed to provide experimental evidence in support of this position. Ikard, Green, and Horn (1969) subsequently developed a questionnaire that attempted to classify smokers into types according to their reasons for smoking. These reasons included the following six factors when factor analyzed: habitual, addictive, reduction of negative affect, pleasurable relaxation, stimulation, and sensorimotor manipulation. At this point, however, it appears that smoking typologies, at least based upon self-reported reasons for smoking, are only of limited value. A study by Flaxman (1979) examined the types of techniques selected by smokers in a cessation program. Although the study was not conclusive, it failed to support Tomkin's affect management model. Furthermore, Adesso and Glad (1978) reported that the Ikard et al. (1969) factors did not predict smoking behavior patterns observed in the laboratory.

A great deal of work has been done to attempt to correlate personality measures with smoking habits. In general, the results have been quite negative, even with the most reliable personality indicators (i.e., extraversion) explaining perhaps 3 to 5 percent of the variance in smoking patterns (Kozlowski, 1979). A more promising approach appears to be along the lines of the recent study by Best and Hakstian (1978) in which they attempted an analysis of the situations in which subjects smoked.

Behavioral. Several behavioral models of smoking have been proposed, including those of Ferraro (1973), Logan (1970, 1973), and Premack (1970). Hunt and Matarazzo (1970) have proposed an influential formulation that emphasizes the habitual, overlearned aspects of the smoking habit. The sheer repetitiveness of the behavior is staggering: at 10 puffs per cigarette, a pack-a-day smoker takes 70,000 puffs per year, a frequency unmatched by any other form of drug taking (Pomerleau, 1979; Russell, 1977). Furthermore, each of these puffs is capable of delivering a reinforcing "jolt" of nicotine to the brain in only 7 seconds (twice as fast as would be possible from an injection into the arm).

The immediate consequences of smoking are extremely salient, whereas the ultimate aversive consequences are considerably removed. This can lead to continuation of the behavior despite the intellectual realization of the extreme seriousness of the potential outcome. Although this situation is analogous to a number of self-management problems (Pomerleau, Bass, & Crown, 1975), the problem is more difficult because the immediately visible, negative consequences of smoking are far more subtle than those resulting from the abuse of alcohol or most other drugs.

Behavioral researchers typically have assumed a relationship between environmental events and smoking. However, cigarette consumption can take place under so many conditions and in association with so many secondary reinforcers that it becomes an almost impossible task to determine the precise antecedents of each smoking episode. The habit is seen as being acquired initially under conditions of social reinforcement which are sufficiently powerful to counteract the aversive aspects of smoke inhalation. Eventually the behavior becomes reinforcing in its own right. Smoking gradually generalizes to other situations, and at the same time discriminations begin to be made between circumstances in which smoking is permissible and those in which it is not (Pomerleau, 1979). The emphasis from the very beginning has been upon smoking as a learned behavior.

In a fashion analogous to Solomon's opponent process model, situations associated with smoking can elicit conditioned cravings. Stimuli preparatory to the response of smoking, such as opening a cigarette pack, begin to serve as secondary reinforcers. Pomerleau

(1978) has argued that if smoking is to be eliminated, treatment must focus not just upon the overt act of smoking, but also upon these conditioned stimuli and secondary reinforcers. The reinforcing properties of smoking are enhanced by its positive association with an incredible array of environmental circumstances. Some smokers, for example, use cigarettes as escape or avoidance from a number of negative emotional states. Pomerleau (1979) has suggested that the act of smoking can generalize from a direct response to physiological withdrawal to a more diffuse response to a variety of dysphoric emotional states such as fear, anger, or boredom. It should be noted that behavioral analyses of smoking essentially have been derived from general theoretical principles and not from functional analyses of smoking per se. Such functional analyses could contribute substantially to our understanding of smoking behavior.

Distinctions must be made between the acquisition and the maintenance of smoking. A number of social factors may contribute to the initiation of smoking, such as peer pressure, parents who smoke, and imitation of adult behavior. Once the habit is acquired, however, addictive as well as psychological variables can become important in maintenance. Smoking patterns stabilize as the behavior increasingly comes under the control of both environmental and physiological determinants. As noted previously, physiological factors may have considerable responsibility in keeping consumption within certain limits.

Thus, the smoker who contemplates breaking the habit is likely to be confronted with an extremely difficult situation. Not only is smoking a powerful acquired reinforcer, the physiological consequences of quitting may also be severe. Pomerleau (1979) provides a concise summary of some of the psychological and physiological symptoms often resulting from abstinence. Unpleasant side effects include reported inability to concentrate, intense cravings for tobacco, insomnia, irritability, restlessness, impairment of psychomotor performance, and gastrointestinal upsets. Additional symptoms are disturbances in EEG rhythms, decreases in heart rate and blood pressure, alterations in REM sleep, and, in some cases, increases in spontaneous jaw clenching. Although these reactions typically persist from several days to perhaps a few months, some former smokers report intense cravings years after having given up cigarettes. Even after overt withdrawal symptoms have been overcome, conditioned reinforcers may continue to elicit strong desires for tobacco. Particularly problematic are tempting situations that occur only infrequently or traumatic events that may be totally unanticipated.

ASSESSMENT

At first glance, the assessment of smoking behavior appears to be a very simple matter. Smoking is readily observable and occurs in discrete units. But what is the best unit of measurement? Tallies can be kept of cigarettes, of actual puffs, or of amount of tar and nicotine ingested (McFall, 1978). Furthermore, these records can be made on an hourly basis, a daily basis, or even a monthly basis. Most investigators have emphasized number of cigarettes smoked per day. As McFall points out, there is nothing magical about this particular measure. Certainly it overlooks a great deal of important information. However, it does have the advantage of providing a common standard of comparison.

Discussion of assessment issues in smoking have focused primarily on determining the outcome of structured interventions. Two fundamental indices have been used: *rate,* using days as the unit of time and typically expressed in percentage of baseline smoking; and *abstinence,* the number or percentage of subjects abstaining altogether (Lichtenstein & Danaher, 1976). Despite the fact that abstinence is a nominal scale datum which necessitates less powerful, nonparametric statistical procedures, it does have several important advantages. It is less susceptible to reactivity effects of self-monitoring, less likely to require transformations in the data due to a marked skewness in the distribution of outcome, and a better indicator of clinically significant, as opposed to statistically significant, treatment effects. Percentage of baseline data can then provide a valuable additional measure for evaluating finer theoretical issues with parametric statistical analyses (Pechacek, 1979).

Reactivity is likely when subjects in treatment self-monitor their smoking rates because of the implicit assumption that these rates will decrease (Kazdin, 1974). McFall (1970) and others have reported that self-monitored smoking rates tend to be lower than subjects' prior estimates of their smoking behavior. Smoking rates are also likely to be susceptible to changes in self-monitoring procedures. Frederiksen, Epstein, and Kosevsky (1975), for example, found continuous reporting to be significantly more reliable than weekly or daily recording. It is obviously desirable that data collection procedures remain constant. Otherwise, changes in rate may be partly a reflection of changes in measurement (Pechacek, 1979). On the other hand, the major concern with abstinence data is not how the self-report data are obtained, but the possibility that subjects might not be telling the truth.

A crucial issue relates to the selection of a method or methods of assessment. This issue is addressed by McFall (1978) in a comprehensive and useful discussion. Possible measures include self-reports, controlled laboratory observations, unobtrusive naturalistic measurements, collaborator reports, and correlates of smoking behavior. Each of these methods has potential advantages and disadvantages.

The most commonly used measure has been self-report. The obvious advantage is that the subject is in a better position than anyone else to observe his or her own smoking behavior continually. Unfortunately, there is no assurance that the subject will be accurate or even honest. False reporting has been documented in a number of studies (Brockway, 1978; Delarue, 1973; Ohlin, Lundh, & Westling, 1976). Self-reports can also be reactive, as noted previously. The fact that many studies have relied solely upon unverified self-reports as a measure of outcome is therefore a cause for concern.

Observing smoking under controlled laboratory conditions is a more precise method, but it also presents significant problems. Smoking behavior observed in the laboratory may be quite different from smoking that occurs under more natural conditions. Unobtrusive naturalistic measurement presents another possibility. McFall (1978) suggests the monitoring of samples of cigarette butts as one example. The butts could be collected in several locations and would provide both an indirect check upon self-reported smoking and some indication of within-subject changes in smoking over time. One of the few studies to use cigarette butts as a measurement of smoking was that of Auger, Wright, and Simpson (1972). Unobtrusive measurement procedures suffer from several shortcomings, including difficulty, expense, impracticality in many situations, and potential invasion of privacy.

Collaborator reports have been used increasingly in recent years. Investigators sometimes ask subjects to provide the names of close friends or relatives who are in a position to observe their smoking and can be contacted periodically for reports. Again, however, the use of collaborators is no guarantee of accuracy. Lichtenstein and Danaher (1976) have observed that the recruitment of friends as observers can lead to increased reactivity. Cooperation may be very difficult to obtain (Ober, 1968), performance may be sloppy (Conway, 1977), and there may be obvious bias (Marrone, Merksamer, & Salzberg, 1970). Because the collaborators are often close friends of the subjects, their reports may be no more objective than those of the subjects themselves. McFall (1978) suggests that the extremely high correlations often obtained between subjects and collaborators may be a reflection of collusion more than of accuracy. Because there is no simple means of ascertaining the validity of collaborator reports, additional checks upon the accuracy of subjects' self-reports are necessary.

Correlates of smoking behavior are a promising possibility. Investigators have attempted to establish reliable indirect measures of smoking for a number of years. They have considered such measures as sputum samples, blood assays, and nicotinic acid stains on the fingers, but with only limited success (McFall, 1978). More promising physiological correlates of smoking recently have been described. Most notable among these physiological indicators are carbon monoxide and thiocyanates. Carbon monoxide levels can be determined from either blood samples (e.g., Cohen, Perkins, Ury, & Goldsmith, 1971; Ringold, Goldsmith, Helwig, Finn, & Schuette, 1962) or samples of alveolar air (Cohen et al., 1971; Stewart, 1975). Carbon monoxide has been used successfully in validation (Danaher, Lichtenstein, & Sullivan, 1976; Lando, 1975a), but has the drawback of possessing a very short half-life (Ringold et al., 1962; Stewart, 1975), since it is subject to a number of other environmental exposures (Stewart, 1975) and shows high diurnal variability (Cohen et al., 1971; Meyer & Henderson, 1974). Thiocyanates have a longer half-life (approximately 14 days; Pettigrew & Fell, 1973) and therefore may be more useful in validating self-reports (Brockway, 1978; Vogt, 1977). Thiocyanate levels can be assessed through blood samples as well as through tests of urine or saliva. Unfortunately, thiocyanates can also be affected by other environmental sources such as diet (Brockway, 1978). Even so, both carbon monoxide and thiocyanate provide a useful check. Together, these two measures could represent a very powerful test of self-reported abstinence (Vogt, 1977).

As will be discussed later, abstinence cannot be the only goal of all treatment programs. Some smokers are either unable or unwilling to quit altogether. For these smokers, measurements of substance and topography should be included in addition to tabulating the rate of smoking (Frederiksen, Martin, & Webster, 1979). Health risks attributable to smoking are related to the dose of harmful elements contained in cigarette smoke, including tar, nicotine, and carbon monoxide. Dosage typically has been assessed by merely calculating the rate of cigarette consumption. However, an analysis limited to rate alone is incomplete. Smoking a cigarette that is low in tar, nicotine, and carbon monoxide is not the same as smoking a cigarette that is high in these elements. Furthermore, individual differences in smoking topography or the way in which people smoke can also have important implications. Two smokers could consume the same brand at the same rate and not derive the same dose of harmful substances. One smoker might take twice as many puffs, each of which is twice as long and is inhaled twice as deeply.

Frederiksen et al., (1979) strongly maintain that three factors—substance, rate, and topography—interact to produce risk. All three factors must be considered in an adequate assessment of smoking episodes. Substance (the brand of cigarette that is smoked) is easily determined. Topography is more complex and involves such variables as interval between puffs, puff frequency, puff duration, puff volume, puff intensity, cigarette duration, amount of tobacco used, and puff distribution (the point on the cigarette from which each puff is taken, e.g., the proximal or distal end). Direct observation of smoking topography primarily has been restricted to laboratory settings, although observations also have been conducted in the smoker's natural environment. To date, measurement of multiple risk areas has been relatively infrequent.

TREATMENT

As increasing evidence has been reported concerning the health hazards of cigarette smoking, research efforts to help the chronic smoker break the tobacco habit have intensified. A seemingly limitless variety of techniques have been employed. These techniques have ranged from "remote control" tactics such as advertising and antismoking legislation to more personalized interventions including nicotinominetic drugs, hypnosis, psychotherapy, group clinics, role playing, systematic desensitization, aversion, contractual management, and so forth (cf. Bernstein & Glasgow, 1979).

Nonbehavioral

Bans on television advertising do not appear to have had a definitive effect upon smoking (Kozlowski, 1979). Foote (1977) has suggested, however, that a decline in per capita cigarette consumption for the years 1967 through 1970 was the result of antismoking advertisements on television. After the ban on cigarette advertising, these antismoking messages became far less frequent and per capita consumption again began to increase. Bernstein (1969) concluded that public health campaigns against smoking had been ineffective. Yet these campaigns clearly have produced notable changes in public awareness of potential health hazards (Hynd, Stratton, & Severson, 1978; National Cancer Institute, 1977). Warner (1977) argues that according to projected figures per capita, consumption in 1975 would have been 20 to 30 percent higher if it had not been for the sustained antismoking activities, including televised messages, that have been conducted since 1964.

Clinics. Public service and proprietary programs have expanded greatly since 1964. Most of these programs have not been subjected to controlled evaluation (Schwartz & Rider, 1977). The most common public service clinics have been offered by the American Cancer Society (ACS, 1976; Hildebrand, 1977) and the Seventh Day Adventists (McFarland, 1977). The 5-day plans of the Seventh Day Adventists offer a standarized program consisting of 1½ to 2-hour sessions which emphasize a lecture format. The focus is on immediate cessation of smoking and discussion is devoted to dietary and physical changes to minimize withdrawal. Initial abstinence rates generally appear to be fairly high (perhaps 60 to 80 percent). Unfortunately, however, the little controlled data that are available suggest pervasive relapse in the first year following the target date for abstinence (Lawton, 1967; Schlegel & Kunetsky, 1977). Guilford (1972) reported abstinence rates of only 16 to 20 percent at 1-year follow-up, rates no higher than might have been achieved through unaided attempts (Thompson & Wilson, 1966). It should also be noted that in all cases the results were based solely on unverified self-reports, and often only on subjects who completed the entire treatment program (Schwartz & Rider, 1977).

Controlled outcome data on the American Cancer Society programs are again quite limited. The data that are available also tend to be disappointing. An evaluation was conducted on 29 clinics held in Los Angeles from 1970 to 1973 (Pyszka, Ruggles, & Janowicz, 1973). Abstinence rates on a randomly selected sample of 354 subjects contacted through telephone inquiries were 41.7 percent at post-treatment and only 22 percent at 1-year follow-up. These programs focused upon group support, the development of insight, and self-selection of specific cessation techniques.

In light of these findings, the more impressive claims of a number of proprietary programs must be viewed with some skepticism. For obvious reasons, these programs are seldom submitted to controlled evaluation. One published evaluation of the SmokEnders program indicated fairly limited success at long-term (3½ to 4-year) follow-up (Kanzler, Jaffe, & Zeidenberg, 1976). Only a subsample of subjects were contacted and even if the smoking rates of that subsample were representative, the actual success rates based on all treatment participants (including dropouts) was approximately 27 percent (Schwartz & Rider, 1977). The impact of most clinical programs thus appears to be rather minimal. At this point, the use of nonvalidated techniques in clinical settings seems to be of little public benefit (Bernstein, 1969).

Individual and Medical Counseling. Professionals in private practice have often engaged in smoking cessation counseling. The potential impact of the physician in encouraging patients to quit smoking could be major. Yet only 25 percent of smokers contacted in a national telephone survey indicated having been advised by their physicians to quit (NCSH, 1976). Physicians appear reluctant to give antismoking advice unless serious symptoms are evident. When physicians do give specific advice relating to smoking cessation, the results are often encouraging. Richmond (1977) reported that 22 percent of a sample of over 500 patients given such advice during annual physicals succeeded in remaining abstinent for at least one year. Peabody (1972) has suggested that well-developed programs incorporating physicians' advice could readily lead to abstinence in 25 percent of smokers seen in counseling and perhaps eventually as many as 70 percent of them would quit. Certainly patients hospitalized with smoking-related problems such as myocardial infarctions appear particularly responsive to such advice. Rose (1977) has warned, however, against unrealistic expectations on the part of the private practitioner. Guidelines are being developed to assist physicians in reaching the smoker (Horn, 1968; Pomerleau, 1976), and a national program is now being initiated to provide physicians with materials that they can display in their waiting rooms (Ellis, 1979).

Large-scale Coronary Prevention Trials. Several major programs have attempted to reduce risk factors leading to coronary heart disease including cigarette smoking. Major programs have included the Multiple Risk Factor Intervention Trial (MRFIT) in this country and the North Karelia Project in Finland. The MRFIT program is directed at middle-aged men and attempts to reduce serum cholesterol and blood pressure levels as well as to encourage smoking cessation (MRFIT, 1976). Over 60,000 men between the ages of 35 to 57 at elevated risk for coronary disease have been seen in the program (Syme & Jacobs, 1977). Intervention related to smoking includes both group and individual treatment sessions and has led to an abstinence rate of approximately 43 percent among smokers at 1-year follow-up. Self-reported abstinence has been validated by means of biochemical assays. Continued intervention and maintenance contacts are built into the program.

The North Karelia Project (Koskela, Puska, & Tuomilehto, 1976) is a community-wide intervention program that has attempted to reduce the very high incidence of cardiovascular disease in that area. A decline was observed in the number of male smokers (from 54 percent to 43 percent), but the number of female smokers remained constant (11 to 13 percent). The Stanford Heart Disease Prevention Program operated on a somewhat more modest scale, but also produced encouraging results. Two California communities were exposed to an intensive 2-year mass-media campaign, and a third community served as a control (Farquhar, Maccoby, Wood, Alexander, Breitrose, Brown, Haskell, McAlister, Meyer, Nash, & Stern, 1977; Maccoby, Farquhar, Wood, & Alexander, 1977). In one of the two media-exposed communities, face-to-face behavioral counseling also was offered to two-thirds of the high-risk subjects. Results indicated that three years after the initiation of the program, the proportion of smokers in the media-plus-counseling community had dropped by 24 percent, as compared to 8 percent in the media-only and 3 percent in the control community. Self-report data were validated by thiocyanate samples.

Antismoking Drugs. In general the use of drugs in aiding the cessation process has proven to be of only limited value. Early work with lobeline sulphate as a substitute for nicotine was not encouraging (Davison & Rosen, 1972). Somewhat better results have been obtained in more recent studies with nicotine chewing gum. Puska, Björkqvist, and Koskela (1979) found an initial effect for nicotine over placebo gum in a double-blind trial, but this effect was no longer significant at 6-month follow-up. Although nicotine gum can provide a dosage comparable to that derived from smoking, it apparently cannot duplicate the "nicotine jolt" that is received by the brain within a matter of seconds after the smoker takes a puff on a cigarette. Work is now underway to develop nicotine mists or sprays that might approximate this effect more closely.

Combinations of drugs to counteract withdrawal symptoms have been ineffective in preventing relapse. Other substances have been used, such as an antismoking chewing gum that presumably causes an unpleasant taste when taken in conjunction with tobacco (Rosenberg, 1977). It appears that pharmacological substances, notably nicotine gum, can have some value when combined in a more comprehensive cessation program, but they are unlikely to be effective in producing long-term abstinence by themselves.

Hypnosis. Individual practitioners have often claimed dramatic success in inducing cessation through hypnosis. Controlled experimental evaluations have tended not to substantiate these claims, however (Johnston & Donoghue, 1971). Much of the research conducted in this area has been very poor from a methodological standpoint. Orne (1977) has suggested that the effects of hypnosis stem primarily from a placebo response. Pederson, Scrimgeour, and Lefcoe (1975) only obtained an 8 percent abstinence rate at follow-up in a group treated with hypnosis alone, although hypnosis did appear somewhat effective when combined with group counseling. The overall success rate produced by hypnosis might be 15 to 20 percent. One unfortunate aspect of this procedure is that it is often viewed by subjects as a magic cure which can erase all desire for cigarettes with the total absence of effort or commitment on their part.

Fear Appeals. A number of attempts have been made to induce smokers to give up cigarettes by means of persuasive communications that typically emphasize the dangers associated with continued smoking. Janis and Mann (1965) reported significant effects for dramatic role-playing in which subjects who were not motivated to reduce smoking assumed the role of a patient who had just been informed that she had lung cancer. Leventhal (1970), in his thoughtful chapter on the effects of fear communications, has pointed to the need to include specific instructions on how to cope with the fear-arousing situation. Rogers and his colleagues (Rogers, Deckner, & Mewborn, 1978) found that both instructions and reassurance as to the efficacy of stopping were important in motivating smokers to reduce their consumption.

The overall evidence concerning the impact of fear appeals on actual smoking behavior has been negative, however (Bernstein & McAlister, 1976). In part this may be due to the fact that most smokers exposed to fear appeals in these studies were not seeking treatment. Lichtenstein, Keutzer, and Himes (1969) also have observed that current smokers may be better "immunized" or defended against fear-arousing material in view of the fact that they continue to smoke in the face of both mounting evidence pointing to the hazards of cigarette smoking and intensive media campaigns designed to persuade them to stop.

Suedfeld and his colleagues (Suedfeld & Ikard, 1974) obtained somewhat more promising results by means of a procedure in which antismoking and pro-nonsmoking messages were combined with sensory deprivation. The efficacy of the messages themselves is brought into question, however, by the fact that sensory deprivation alone produced essentially the same results as sensory deprivation plus messages. Suedfeld and Best (1977) recently reported on an exploratory program that combined sensory deprivation with a number of behavioral techniques including aversion. Four of five subjects were abstinent at 8-month follow-up. It is possible that fear appeals or other attitude change procedures can be beneficial within more comprehensive smoking cessation programs.

Behavioral

Behavioral approaches to smoking cessation have become more so-phisticated in recent years. At one time reliance was placed exclusively upon limited short-term approaches designed to produce initial ab-stinence but which totally ignored the problem of maintenance. Much of the early work was derived from an armchair analysis of smoking behavior and led to the application of principles of theoretical interest with little long-term success. Most outcome studies in the area of smoking have been frankly discouraging. More recently, multicom-ponent programs have been developed which attempt to address the problems of both initial abstinence and long-term maintenance. These efforts have focused upon reducing the likelihood of smoking episodes and increasing the likelihood of alternative nonsmoking responses (Bernstein & Glasgow, 1979).

Stimulus Control. Stimulus control procedures are intended to facili-tate breaking the smoking habit either by divorcing smoking from its usual pleasurable associations (e.g., social occasions, relaxation, after meals, or at parties) or by bringing it under the control of an external cue. Adherents of stimulus control procedures maintain that cigarettes have become linked to a variety of environmental and internal events which serve as discriminative stimuli for the smoking response. Pre-sumably any program that can weaken the link between such stimuli and smoking will increase the likelihood that smokers can remain abstinent.

Several investigators have attempted to regulate smoking by providing subjects with timers and allowing them cigarettes only at set intervals (Levinson, Shapiro, Schwartz, & Tursky, 1971). Despite re-ports of success with individual cases, however, there is little evidence at present to favor stimulus control over other active or even placebo treatments. Although stimulus control theoretically should make ces-sation easier, most subjects report considerable difficulty in reducing their consumption below a "stuck" point of approximately 10 to 12 cigarettes per day. It is possible that when subjects reach this level, each cigarette becomes more reinforcing and therefore more difficult to give up. Stimulus control procedures have been of limited value even within the context of more complex, multicomponent programs (Flaxman, 1978). There have been a few encouraging applications in programs that include a wide variety of behavioral training skills, or cognitive manipulations designed to convince subjects that they have an especially high probability of succeeding (Blittner, Goldberg, & Merbaum, 1978).

Contingency Contracting. An alternative strategy which has been employed by a number of investigators involves directly reinforcing abstinence from cigarettes. Although early results with this procedure were equivocal, several more recent studies have achieved encouraging outcomes. Elliott and Tighe (1968) reported 84 percent initial abstinence and 36 percent long-term abstinence (15 to 17 months) in undergraduates who put up $50 to $65 deposits as a guarantee of abstinence for a 16-week period. Treatment also involved other techniques including group support, stimulus control, and public pledges. The significance of the results is clouded by the fact that no control groups were included and no attempt was made to assess the accuracy of subjects' self-reports despite their direct financial interest in claiming abstinence. Winett (1973) achieved more modest but still encouraging results (50 percent abstinence at 6-month follow-up) in a more carefully controlled assessment that included validation of self-reports by informants.

Miscellaneous. Several investigators have applied systematic desensitization in an effort to help smokers cope with stress-related cravings. Although this technique has proven effective with other problems and is theoretically promising, outcome data have been almost uniformly disappointing. Homme (1965) focused on the use of covert operants (e.g., smoking causes cancer) which were intended to be incompatible with the act of smoking. As in the case of stimulus control, despite individual successes, controlled outcome trials have been negative (Lawson & May, 1970).

Aversion. The most commonly used techniques designed to reduce the probability of smoking have relied upon aversive stimuli. The theoretical bases of many of the individual applications of these procedures are unclear and, perhaps as a result, early outcomes tend to be mixed (Grimaldi & Lichtenstein, 1969). Aversive procedures usually consist of electric shock, covert sensitization, or cigarette smoke.

Most treatments relying upon electric shock have proven ineffective. There appear to be pitfalls in attempting to extrapolate too closely from laboratory work with animals. Human subjects are all too capable of making the distinction between punished laboratory trials and natural ("safe") outside trials. Wilson and Davison (1969) maintained that for aversion to be effective, the selected technique should have some intrinsic relationship to the target behavior. Russell, Armstrong, and Patel (1976), for example, in a very comprehensive study failed to demonstrate the superiority of contingent shock over several noncontingent shock conditions. They concluded that traditional conditioning processes were not clinically significant in the case of cigarette smoking. A few positive results have been achieved, however (Dericco, Brigham, & Garlington, 1977). Berecz (1976) has suggested that shocking imaginal urges rather than actual smoking may improve outcomes.

Covert sensitization, in which the subject vividly imagines unpleasant sensations contingent upon smoking, such as extreme nausea, has proven relatively ineffective in controlled studies (Wagner & Bragg, 1970). This procedure may have value as part of a maintenance program in which subjects attempt to rehearse unpleasant images associated with smoking. Aversion intrinsically related to the actual smoking response (e.g., rapid smoking or satiation) has, on the other hand, sometimes been effective virtually by itself.

Some of the most successful results for aversion (and indeed some of the most successful results in the entire literature) have been reported by Lichtenstein and his colleagues through the use of a rapid-smoking procedure. Subjects are required to puff on a lighted cigarette once every six seconds until they feel that they are unable to continue. These investigators have consistently reported 6-month abstinence rates of 60 percent (Lichtenstein, Harris, Birchler, Wahl, & Schmahl, 1973; Schmahl, Lichtenstein, & Harris, 1972). Unfortunately, studies conducted in other laboratories have been less successful (Lando, 1975b, 1976a, 1976b; Levenberg & Wagner, 1976). Lichtenstein himself has concluded that a warm and personal client–therapist relationship is an essential component of treatment (Harris & Lichtenstein, 1971), and the magnitude of the rapid-smoking effect itself is not large. An extremely aversive procedure described by Norton and Barske (1977), in which subjects were required to continue rapid smoking beyond tolerance to the point of actual vomiting or other visible signs of illness, was found to be no more effective than the standard rapid-smoking technique. Danaher (1977a), in reviewing a number of rapid-smoking studies, has suggested that their generally less favorable outcomes may be explained at least partly by their failure to tailor the procedure to the individual subject and to insure close client–therapist interaction.

In an unusual long-term follow-up (two to six years) of many of the subjects seen in the original rapid-smoking studies, Lichtenstein and Rodrigues (1977) found a continued abstinence rate of 34 percent in the subjects who could still be located. Although this finding is somewhat encouraging, it is qualified by the additional finding that of 33 subjects currently reporting abstinence, 20 stated that they had gone back to smoking at some time since the treatment. The role of the original treatment in producing long-term abstinence is therefore unclear.

A satiation method was reported by Resnick (1968). In this simple
and ingenious procedure, subjects were instructed to increase greatly
their normal smoking consumption for a period of one week. Presumably, as subjects forced themselves to continue smoking to the
point of aversion, the rewarding properties of cigarette smoking would
gradually be eliminated. Resnick reported abstinence rates of 60 percent at 4-month follow-up. Unfortunately, his procedures are subject
to criticism on a number of methodological grounds. Laboratory
contact was minimal, no independent attempt was made to insure that
subjects were in fact smoking to the point of satiation, and no plausible
control condition was included. More recent studies almost uniformly
have failed to replicate Resnick's findings. There is evidence to suggest,
however, that when satiation is included as part of a multicomponent
treatment package, impressive results can be obtained (Best, Owen, &
Trentadue, 1978; Lando, 1977).

Medical Risks of Oversmoking.   One potentially serious drawback to
both rapid smoking and satiation is that these procedures may involve
some degree of medical risk. The extent of this risk is unclear and has
been the topic of considerable debate. Concern has been expressed
particularly over stressful effects upon the cardiovascular system resulting from increased intake of nicotine and carbon monoxide. The
effects of rapid smoking have been studied extensively, and much of
this work is summarized by Lichtenstein and Glasgow (1977); but the
effects of satiation remain virtually unexplored. Horan and his colleagues found significant EKG abnormalities in young, apparently
healthy subjects exposed to rapid smoking and argued on a theoretical
basis that the procedure could result in serious and perhaps fatal
nicotine poisoning (Horan, Linberg, & Hackett, 1977). Russell, Raw,
Taylor, Feyerabend, and Saloojee (1978) conclude that it is very difficult to determine the precise degree of risk resulting from rapid
smoking. They argue, however, that Horan et al. were in error in
warning of potential nicotine poisoning. They maintain that most of
Horan et al.'s information came from an outdated text, and even the
most dedicated smoker would be very unlikely to abstract more than
approximately three times the standard yield of nicotine from a
cigarette.

   The need for adequate medical screening of potential treatment
participants is now generally accepted. Some investigators have concluded that even this safeguard is insufficient and the rapid-smoking
procedure should be abandoned altogether. Weighing against these
concerns is the fact that rapid smoking has been applied to many
thousands of subjects with few serious side effects and no reported

mortality (Lichtenstein & Glasgow, 1977). The search for effective and nonstressful alternative procedures is now underway (Danaher, 1977b; Hackett & Horan, 1978). Tori (1978) reports good results with a safer taste-aversion technique in which subjects were simply required to retain cigarette smoke in their mouths. This study suffers from a number of methodological weaknesses, including nonrandom assignment to conditions and failure to corroborate self-reported abstinence. Although nonaversive alternatives appear promising, it would be unfortunate simply to abandon rapid smoking before the efficacy of these techniques have been demonstrated. A cost-benefit analysis may be appropriate, in which potential risks of the rapid-smoking procedure are weighed against possible increments in the likelihood of successful outcome. Sometimes overlooked is the substantial risk produced by continued smoking in itself.

Multicomponent Interventions. More comprehensive treatment programs incorporating specific behavioral procedures are beginning to be reported. Results are mixed, but the trend in reported outcomes is clearly encouraging. Many of these programs initially employ aversion as part of a treatment designed to suppress smoking urges and later utilize self-control techniques as a means of assisting participants to overcome subsequent cravings successfully.

Conway (1977) found that the addition of self-management techniques to an aversive conditioning program had a specific incremental effect upon successful outcome. Lando (1976a) reported an initial effect for a contractual management procedure as a supplement to aversion, but this effect was no longer evident at 6-month follow-up. Flaxman (1978) achieved a 50 percent abstinence rate at six months with a procedure that included both a self-management program and a specific target date for quitting. In a carefully evaluated clinical demonstration, Pomerleau, Adkins, and Pertschuk (1978) reported success in 61 of their first 100 participants. Thirty-two of these participants remained abstinent at 1-year follow-up, as verified by urinary nicotine assays.

Best and his colleagues have developed a very promising multifaceted program that includes a heavy emphasis upon training subjects in alternatives to smoking (Best, Owen, & Trentadue, 1978). An especially attractive feature of the program is that these alternatives can be flexible according to individual needs and situations. One person might learn deep relaxation as an alternative means of combating tension; another might substitute a few quick exercises as a form of stimulation (Best, 1977). Admittedly, these alternatives are not direct substitutes for smoking. However, they are intended to meet the same needs. Best stresses the point that an urge to smoke should be an automatic cue for subjects to engage in problem solving designed to overcome the urge without resorting to tobacco.

Brengelmann developed a self-control program consisting of up to 37 procedures (e.g., changing brands daily, limiting smoking to certain times and places, postponing lighting after urges). He later found an additional effect with the inclusion of contingency contracting (58 percent of his subjects were abstinent at 2-month follow-up). More recently he has refined his treatment to the point at which results from treatment-by-mail also have been positive (Brengelmann & Sedlmayr, 1977). As many as two-thirds of the subjects who completed treatment have reported initial abstinence (the completion rate was 86 percent). At follow-up, 57 percent of the respondents claimed continued abstinence, although there was no verification of these self-reports. Even though Pechacek (1979) notes that the success rate would be only 33 percent if it were assumed that the nonresponders were smoking, the approach still appears encouraging. Other positive results also have been reported for multicomponent interventions. Elliott and Denney (1978), for example, found that a package including rapid smoking, self-control strategies, covert sensitization, and systematic desensitization was significantly superior at 6-month follow-up to treatment limited to rapid smoking.

Lando (1977) obtained a 76 percent 6-month abstinence rate with a program consisting of aversive conditioning (excessive smoking) and a self-management procedure including contractual management, structured group support, and renewed aversion (rapid smoking) in the event of relapse. A control group limited to aversive conditioning achieved a 6-month abstinence rate of 35 percent. The nature of the design (simultaneously manipulating several independent variables) precluded the isolation of individual treatment components. A subsequent, more complex study that also incorporated fear appeals and stimulus control (Lando, 1978) was not as successful. A high attrition rate resulted, and the overall 6-month abstinence rate was only 28 percent.

In evaluating these more recent findings, it appears likely that subjects were given an overly elaborate program. Evidence has been reported in the literature which suggests that too many specific treatment elements can actually work against effective outcome (Lichtenstein & Danaher, 1976). Not just in smoking (Danaher, 1977b), but also in dealing with fear of public speaking (Meichenbaum, Gilmore, & Fedoravicius, 1971), investigators have found that at least under some circumstances complex treatments are less effective than comparison conditions which eliminate one or more elements. This possibility has received further support from subsequent work by Lando and his colleagues. Lando, Shirley, Gregory, and McCullough (1979) found a trend favoring a 2-stage program of aversion and maintenance over a more elaborate 3-stage program incorporating preparation as well. In both that study and in a clinical demonstration project by Lando and McCullough (1978), the aversion and self-management procedure originally described by Lando (1977) was replicated successfully. Preliminary data have also been collected which indicate that this multifaceted program is more effective than treatment limited to any of the individual components.

Attempts simply to graft on additional contact or booster sessions following the termination of regular treatment have generally been unsuccessful. Apparently it is necessary that subjects view these or other maintenance procedures as an integral part of a continuing treatment program. Most participants fail to make use of booster sessions or telephone support (Best, 1975). Paradoxically, several studies have shown that supportive phone calls during or after treatment can actually lead to less successful long-term outcome (Best, Bass, & Owen, 1977). Best and Bloch (1979) argue that care must be taken in incorporating maintenance programming to ensure continued internal attributions for success.

Admittedly, not all multifaceted programs have produced impressive long-term abstinence (Brockway, Kleinmann, Edleson, & Gruenewald, 1977). Some of the most successful treatments have come about only after painstaking developmental research (Brengelmann & Sedlmayr, 1977; Pomerleau, Adkins, & Pertschuk, 1978). Pechacek (1979) suggests that the most recent successful findings have been the result of an in-depth clinical knowledge of the problem which can guide the application of diverse techniques in treatment.

Treatment Innovations. Several investigators have sought to apply behavioral principles to larger numbers of smokers through use of the media. McAlister (1975) achieved good preliminary results with televising a behavioral counseling program. Dubren (1977a) obtained a small but clinically meaningful effect (9 to 10 percent abstinence) in smokers exposed to a brief televised intervention. He also demonstrated an effect for taped supportive telephone messages in promoting abstinence at a 1-month follow-up (Dubren, 1977b). In a somewhat different innovation, Rosen and Lichtenstein (1977) assessed a contractual management procedure independently developed by an employer. Preliminary results were at least moderately encouraging. Other researchers have begun to distill the basic elements of successful clinical programs into self-help books and manuals, although with mixed success (Best, Bass, & Owen, 1977; Danaher & Lichtenstein, 1978; Glasgow, 1978).

A major treatment innovation is the recent development of controlled smoking procedures (Frederiksen, Miller, & Peterson, 1977; Frederiksen, Peterson, & Murphy, 1976; Russell, 1974). Frederiksen and his associates have successfully taught subjects to alter their smoking topography by reducing smoke inhalation, taking fewer and more shallow puffs, and extinguishing the cigarette more quickly. Frederiksen and Martin (1979) have demonstrated that subjects can be taught to reduce their uptake of carbon monoxide from smoking, and these effects generalize beyond the laboratory training situation and persist over time. Obviously many smokers want to reduce their risks; this desire is largely responsible for the dramatic changes in the cigarette product described at the beginning of the chapter. Frederiksen and Martin suggest that, given the primary role of carbon monoxide and tar (but not nicotine) in chronic heart disease and cancer risk, and given the likelihood that smokers regulate their consumption to maintain nicotine intake, the safer cigarette should be high in nicotine and low in both carbon monoxide and tar delivery. Although controlled smoking technology is virtually in its infancy, it appears to have great potential in reaching large numbers of smokers who remain unaffected by programs that focus solely upon abstinence. Certainly the goal of reduced risk is well worth pursuing.

An additional procedure that can allow for either abstinence or controlled smoking involves the use of "nicotine fading." This is a convenient nonaversive technique in which the smoker progressively switches to designated lower tar and nicotine brands. Typically the smoker proceeds to a new brand each week until he or she finishes with a brand containing only 0.1 mg of nicotine (Foxx & Brown, 1979; Lichtenstein, 1978). The smoker is then encouraged to quit altogether. Initial results have been extremely favorable. Not only has there been a high rate of abstinence (40 percent at 18 months in the Foxx & Brown study), but smokers who have not quit have tended overwhelmingly to resume smoking lower tar and nicotine cigarettes than their baseline brands. Lichtenstein (1978) comments that one attractive feature of the nicotine fading program is that initial success—reduced tar and nicotine consumption—is virtually assured, thus increasing the subject's confidence in the program. One limitation, however, is the fact that the procedure is not applicable to persons who are already smoking low tar and nicotine cigarettes. Another concern is that subjects may be altering their topography of smoking to compensate for reduced nicotine levels and in the process be experiencing significantly higher doses of carbon monoxide. A very promising alternative might be to combine elements of controlled smoking, as described by Frederiksen and others, and nicotine fading. This procedure could be applicable to all smokers regardless of initial brand preference. The goal would be to bring all of these smokers to the same end point—minimal intake of tar and carbon monoxide. (As argued by Frederiksen and Martin, the focus might not be upon the reduction of nicotine content.) From this point, subjects could either abstain altogether or continue smoking at minimum risk.

Comments. Despite recent encouraging findings, a number of treatments continue to be offered without adequate validation or evaluation. Overlooked by many investigators is the possible role of individual differences and particularly situational factors in mediating outcomes, although most research that has attempted to consider individual differences in treatment designs has been either unsuccessful or generated inconclusive findings (cf. Pechacek, 1979). More significant is the fact that little is known about the literally millions of smokers who have quit on their own. These issues are considered further in the section dealing with suggestions for future research.

At this point, controlled research has not produced a definitive treatment that is clearly superior. However, it appears evident that multicomponent programs emphasizing maintenance are superior to short-term treatments which place their sole emphasis upon the attainment of initial abstinence. These interventions are most likely to be effective when they are applied by researchers who are clinically knowledgeable in the area of smoking. The programming of skills designed to assist subjects in developing new nonsmoking life-styles seems to be of particular value. Pechacek (1979) also suggests that the improved results in recent studies may at least in part be a reflection of the increasingly negative social climate with regard to smoking.

A brief evaluative summary of some of the major behavioral studies is presented in Table 1.

CLINICAL PRESCRIPTION

A crucial step in the clinical process is to assist the smoker in reaching a firm decision that he or she will quit and then to specify a target date for doing so. Many smokers never reach this decision. Instead, they continue to avoid personalizing the dangers involved in their smoking habit. Burton (1978) has emphasized the importance of reasons for quitting which are salient to the individual smoker. These reasons need to be sufficiently powerful to sustain the abstinence effort. Emphasis should not be placed solely upon potential life-threatening diseases;

discussion should also focus upon the quality of life. Smokers suffer from a variety of symptoms, including a significant reduction in resistance to illness, bronchitis, chronic smoker's cough, and a vastly reduced wind capacity that can seriously interfere with many otherwise enjoyable activities. The establishment of salient reasons for quitting can lead to the next step: rehearsing the fringe benefits of abstinence. By quitting, the smoker gains more than he or she is losing. Examples of gains include saving money, smelling better, not offending other people, and feeling proud of being successful. The smoker can be encouraged to begin to develop a new and more rewarding healthy lifestyle.

It is also extremely important that the smoker take personal responsibility for quitting. Too many smokers, especially in structured treatment programs, place full responsibility for their success in the hands of the therapist. Attention should be devoted to an analysis of the needs that cigarettes serve in different situations. Alternative behaviors can then be developed which will help the smoker to confront urges for a cigarette. These alternatives should first be tested and promising strategies rehearsed until they become virtually automatic. Smokers should be led to the realization that the difficulty lies more in maintenance than in initial abstinence. They should learn to anticipate potential problems and be firmly aware that a cigarette is not the answer even in a crisis. If they do succumb to temptation, they must not use this as a rationalization for giving up the entire abstinence effort.

A flexible approach is useful in working with individual smokers. Some smokers require much more intensive and structured interventions than others. A range of alternative treatments should be available, from simple advice and self-help materials to extensive individualized or group support systems that incorporate prolonged maintenance contacts. Smokers who fail to respond to a lower level of treatment might then be rerouted through a more intensive program (Lichtenstein, 1978; Shewchuk, 1976). Special concerns should also be dealt with, perhaps most notably the problem of weight gain. Factual information is useful in allaying some of these concerns. In considering weight gain, for example, it can be pointed out that most ex-smokers experience only relatively minimal weight gain and this effect is usually temporary. Suggestions might be presented for self-monitoring of food consumption and moderate exercise (provided there are no medical contraindications). It might also be noted that, from a health perspective, continued smoking is far more dangerous than a few pounds of extra weight. (This should not be interpreted as a justification for unrestrained binges, however!)

Within a given level of intervention, specific techniques will probably not be identical for all smokers. One example is the use of aversive procedures. Cost-benefit analyses may reveal that aversion is indeed indicated for many smokers. Other smokers will not be able to undergo aversion due to medical restrictions. The point is that aversive procedures should not be arbitrarily rejected for all smokers until equally effective nonaversive alternatives have been demonstrated. At the same time, of course, nonaversive techniques should continue to be refined and the best available procedures offered to smokers who are unwilling or unable to follow an aversive conditioning regimen. This issue was considered previously in the section dealing with treatment, but is important enough to be mentioned again in the present context. In addition to the selection of aversive techniques, it is likely that smokers in a multifaceted program will find some components more valuable than others. They should be encouraged to try the various procedures and then to emphasize those that they find most useful.

Thus far, the discussion has been devoted essentially to programs that have total abstinence as their primary treatment goal. As noted previously, however, flexibility is also important in the choice of desired outcome. Smoking does not have to be treated as an all-or-none problem, and to do so is a serious disservice to many smokers. Furthermore, an all-or-none approach carries the risk of providing a convenient rationalization to smokers who decide simply to resume their former habit in the face of difficulties in maintaining complete abstinence.

Some of the same principles can be used in the pursuit of a controlled smoking goal. Smokers might be informed of the different procedures and possible outcomes with the best possible estimates of relative risks. They can then make an intelligent decision that is appropriate to their particular needs. If nicotine fading and/or altered smoking topography is selected, extensive feedback should be provided so that smokers can clearly see their progress. In addition, if treatment is designed to lead to a safer smoking topography, checks should ideally be provided to ensure the generalization of any changes to the natural environment. Furthermore, periodic reevaluations can be made to mimimize the likelihood that smokers will eventually lapse into their accustomed inhalation patterns.

CASE REPORT

A case study by Frederiksen and Simon (1978) was selected because it illustrates several important points. The study focused upon the modification of smoking topography rather than upon abstinence, and it incorporated a controlled multiple-baseline design. The use of single-subject experimental methodologies has been relatively neglected in this area, which is unfortunate because such procedures allow a more flexible format and permit the isolation of potentially important factors that might otherwise be obscured in the typical group design.

The subject was a 24-year-old male who had a 7-year smoking history and averaged approximately one pack of cigarettes per day. His accustomed brand was Marlboro, which contains 17 mg of tar and 1.1 mg of nicotine. Initial carbon monoxide readings were determined both before and after smoking. Sessions took place in a studio that was comfortably furnished with a couch and reading material. Observations of the subject's smoking were recorded by means of a videotape camera.

The subject was first instructed to smoke a cigarette in his usual manner in order to permit the taking of baseline measures. He was then told to restrict himself to six or fewer puffs on each cigarette and subsequently to shorten his puffs. In addition to puff frequency and puff duration, dependent measures included the percentage of tobacco burned, the uptake in carbon monoxide resulting from smoking a cigarette, the actual length of time the cigarette was lit, and the subject's enjoyment ratings of each smoking episode. The generalization of treatment effects was tested by surreptitiously observing the subject's smoking outside of the laboratory. Checks were made on the reliability of laboratory observations by having a second trained rater independently score a random sample of videotapes. Reliability figures were quite high for all dependent measures.

Results indicated a strong treatment effect both within and outside the laboratory. Puff frequency was reduced from 9.0 during laboratory sessions and 8.1 during surreptitious observations to the target level of six puffs or less. Puff duration was reduced from initial averages of 1.5 and 1.4 seconds to post-treatment levels of .78 and .87 seconds. Furthermore, the mean percentage of tobacco burned was reduced from over 60 percent for both types of observations to 50 percent or less. Carbon monoxide levels and carbon monoxide uptake also were substantially reduced. Mean carbon monoxide levels declined from a pretreatment level of 28.7 parts per million (ppm) to a post-treatment level of only 14.4 ppm. Similarly, the average carbon monoxide boost from smoking fell from 4.2 ppm to less than 1 ppm. Perhaps surprisingly, the subject's average number of cigarettes per day also was reduced from 26.2 to 18.6, even though this had not been specifically programmed into treatment. His rated enjoyment of smoking was actually higher following treatment than it had been at baseline.

Surreptitious observations made one week after treatment confirmed the persistence of changes in smoking topography. Approximately four weeks after treatment, however, the subject spontaneously began to abstain and reported continued abstinence at 1-year follow-up. This report was confirmed by informant reports and periodic checks of carbon monoxide levels. The possibility that other subjects who undergo training designed to modify their smoking topography might also subsequently abstain, either spontaneously or as a planned part of treatment, is intriguing and deserves further investigation.

ETHICAL AND LEGAL ISSUES

Two major ethical issues are the deliberate assignment of smokers who are seeking help to theoretically inactive treatments for purposes of experimental design, and the use of aversion without careful screening and safeguards. In the latter case, the therapist could be legally as well as ethically responsible for any complications that developed.

This discussion is not intended to imply that attention-placebo controls should not be used. However, it is the ethical responsibility of the investigator to be very judicious in the application of such procedures. Admittedly, plausible attention-placebo conditions often produce outcomes equal to the experimental treatments under study. Before designing such a control, the experimenter should be sure that it provides a reasonable baseline for assessing treatment effects and that similar controls have not been totally ineffective in other studies, since it has been repeatedly demonstrated that virtually any credible placebo condition is capable of producing highly significant temporary effects. The experimenter should also seriously consider whether the study is truly likely to be worthwhile or potentially to add to available knowledge. Frivolous manipulations should not be performed. Investigators cannot afford to assume that unsuccessful subjects simply have remained unaffected by treatment. Unfortunately, some subjects are likely to consider themselves to be hopeless failures, especially after having participated in what they view as a professional treatment program. This attitude can then be used as an excuse to abandon further efforts at modifying their smoking behavior. The investigator is ethically bound to take every possible step to prevent this from happening. Subjects should be reminded that many people fail at a particular time in a particular program, only to succeed in a subsequent attempt.

One alternative to attention-placebo controls is the use of active comparison conditions. These conditions could provide an especially stringent standard against which to evaluate newer untested programs. An example might be the use of a combined rapid-smoking and contractual management program as a point of comparison for a more elaborate multifaceted intervention. It is helpful to remember that volunteer smokers are not usually in experimental treatments primarily because they desire to participate in a research project. This point is sometimes easy to overlook in research programs conducted in academic settings.

If aversive procedures, most notably rapid smoking, are to be used, minimum safeguards should include physician consent and the taking of a health history. In addition, informed consent of the subject is also necessary. Potential risks and unpleasant side effects should be outlined clearly and alternative procedures made available if the subject so desires. If the procedure is implemented, total exposure should be limited and the subject's reactions should be closely monitored. He or she should be instructed to discontinue the procedure immediately in the event of either dizziness or nausea.

SUGGESTIONS FOR CLINICAL AND EXPERIMENTAL RESEARCH

Many suggestions for future research are implicit in the preceding discussion. At this point, it is useful to highlight some of the most important issues briefly. Major concerns relate to problems of experimental design, incorporation of adequate multicomponent treatment procedures, and appropriate clinical application in a diversity of settings.

The methodological sophistication of smoking-cessation research has clearly improved in the 10 years since Bernstein's (1969) influential and highly critical review of the literature. Yet this fact is hardly justification for complacency. McFall complains in his 1978 article that investigators have sometimes continued to overlook fundamental methodological recommendations made by Bernstein and others. He strongly urges the detailed reporting of subject characteristics and recruitment procedures. A minimum description should include smoking history and demographic factors, i.e., number of subjects, duration and nature of the tobacco habit, previous attempts to quit, age, sex, occupational and educational status, and where recruited from (e.g., university population, community, hospital).

The problem of subject mortality must also be carefully considered. This has been a serious problem in previous research. Every reasonable effort should be made to minimize attrition. Names and addresses of persons who are well acquainted with the subjects should be solicited at the outset of treatment to facilitate follow-up contacts. Follow-up data should ideally be based upon all subjects who entered treatment and not merely on those who completed the program and happened to respond to initial inquiries: these subjects are, of course, much more likely to be successes. Follow-up measures should also be as rigorous as those employed in the early phases of the study. Unconfirmed self-reported smoking levels obtained through postcards or telephone conversations are inadequate (McFall, 1978).

Reporting of results should also become more standardized. Minimum requirements include a detailed record of percentage reduction data at all post-treatment intervals and the percentage of subjects achieving abstinence. These data should be provided for all treatment conditions and should include all subjects. In addition, reliance should be placed on appropriate physiological measures to validate self-reports. The use of such measures in the past has not uncommonly revealed inaccuracies. Judicious application of physiological assessments (perhaps combined with other indicators described previously) can provide potential convergent validation of abstinence data and, to a lesser extent, of percentage reductions.

It is essential that future experimental designs advance beyond what McFall has referred to as "horse races," in which several promising treatments are lined up with no a priori rationale and given a "run for the money." Effective treatment programs are being established and can provide the basis for more advanced constructive and dismantling procedures. Thus a successful intervention can serve as a starting point for the systematic addition of further treatment elements or be broken down into its components to determine how each of them contributed to the total treatment effect. It may be naive, however, in light of the complex and refractory nature of smoking, to expect the isolation of extremely precise or specific treatment elements. A somewhat more global level of analysis may be necessary in which it is determined, for example, that a comprehensive program of self-management is superior to a maintenance intervention limited to contingency contracting. The most advanced strategy would be to proceed directly from a theory of smoking behavior to testing specific hypothesis. Unfortunately, as noted by McFall (1978), at present there are few promising theoretical leads to pursue.

Future research must obviously emphasize the maintenance as well as the initiation of change (Best & Bloch, 1979). Best and Bloch argue that the two processes may be relatively separate. Somewhat independent methodologies may be needed at each point. Efforts should be made to assess the specific effects of both initiation and maintenance components. Future work should also be attentive to both relapse processes and issues of compliance with treatment instructions. Almost nothing is known currently about the relapse process, despite its fundamental importance, although promising beginnings have been made (Lichtenstein, Antonuccio, & Rainwater, 1977). Compliance typically has been assumed rather than measured. Careful study should be undertaken of the extent of compliance as a function of treatment condition and the relationship between compliance and outcome.

Tailoring treatment to the needs of the individual or to particular subject characteristics has been relatively uncommon. Results of efforts that have been made to match treatments to clients have been inconsistent. It seems ironic in view of an increasingly sophisticated assessment methodology that, for the most part, there is virtually no relationship between initial assessment of smoking history or other individual difference variables and prescription of treatment. It would be logical to provide different treatments for individuals who differ along relevant dimensions (Pechacek, 1979). Unfortunately, the isolation of such relevant dimensions has proven extremely difficult. Much of the work has focused upon personality variables such as locus of control (Best, 1975), but a more promising direction may involve examination of situational factors and their potential relationship to relapse episodes in individual smokers.

Also overlooked has been the very important question of methods used by smokers who have been successful in modifying their smoking behavior on their own. The great majority of ex-smokers have quit in the absence of formal treatment programs. It is possible that knowledge of the techniques they used could provide valuable insights in the design of improved self-help and clinical procedures. A preliminary survey of a limited sample of both successful and unsuccessful subjects was reported by Perri, Richards, and Schultheis (1977).

Issues of application are obviously crucial. Existing community programs have generally remained relatively unaffected by empirical findings. Public service and proprietary treatments have an obligation to engage in systematic evaluations. These evaluations and a greater awareness of the research literature should lead to improved treatment methods. Involvement of the consumer in the development of a range of credible and attractive procedures is also extremely important (Pechacek, 1979). Physicians and other health professionals can play a major role in maximizing public awareness of these programs.

Ideally, as noted previously, several levels of intervention should be available including minimal-contact or self-help programs, formal group treatments, and intensive, more individualized interventions for smokers in need of special treatment (Lichtenstein, 1978). Again, each of these programs should be carefully evaluated, and the relationship between basic research and clinical application maximized. Results of public service programs could provide useful insights in the design of additional controlled studies.

Ideally, a productive interplay would be established between laboratory and clinic. Results from a number of behavioral programs appear to have definite promise for clinical application. Prior to such application, however, these programs should be replicated in different treatment settings by different investigators to insure the generalizability of the treatment effect. On the other hand, it would be both unrealistic and shortsighted to wait for the development of "perfect" treatment techniques before offering the best available methods to the millions of smokers who seem genuinely motivated to break the smoking habit, but who have been unable to do so thus far. Cost effectiveness can be maximized by using paraprofessional volunteers who are perhaps themselves ex-smokers and donated facilities such as churches or schools. Preliminary evidence indicates that paraprofessionals can be just as effective as trained clinicians in treating smokers after relatively brief programs of instruction (Best, 1977; Best, Owen, & Trentadue, 1978).

SUMMARY

There is overwhelming evidence as to the serious health consequences of cigarette smoking. In 1979 it was estimated that more than 300,000 excess deaths each year in the United States alone were directly attributable to cigarette smoking. Per capita consumption of cigarettes has declined, and more than 30 million Americans are now ex-smokers. The cigarette product itself has been reduced substantially in average tar and nicotine delivery.

Smoking has been discovered to be a surprisingly complex behavior, the determining factors of which are not fully understood. Both pharmacological and psychological determinants have been investigated. There is some evidence that smokers regulate their consumption to maintain a relatively constant nicotine intake, but there are contradictory findings as well. Solomon has attempted to incorporate both pharmacological and psychological factors in his opponent-process theory. Tomkins has related smoking to affect management. Hunt and Matarazzo in a specifically behavioral formulation, have emphasized the sheer repetitiveness of the habit. In evaluating the theoretical determinants of smoking, a distinction must be made between acquisition and maintenance.

A number of assessment issues have been considered. Treatment outcomes can be evaluated by either rate or abstinence data, although abstinence data are more likely to be reliable and clinically significant. Assessment should not be limited simply to number of smoking episodes, but should also include the substance consumed and the topography of the smoking behavior. Unvalidated self-reports should not be accepted as the sole indicator of treatment effectiveness. Additional measures which can be used include observation under controlled laboratory conditions, unobtrusive observations in the natural environment, collaborator reports, and especially physiological correlates of smoking.

A variety of both behavioral and nonbehavioral treatment procedures have been employed. "Remote control" tactics such as advertising and antismoking legislation have been used, although evidence of their effectiveness is equivocal. A large number of nonvalidated clinical procedures have been applied on both a public service and proprietary basis, generally with fairly minimal impact. Use of hypnosis and fear appeals also are common, but these procedures usually are ineffective. More promising results have been obtained with recent large-scale coronary prevention trials. Also effective in many cases is simple cessation advice from physicians. Unfortunately, however, physicians often appear reluctant to give such advice. Antismoking drugs have been of little value in aiding the cessation process, although nicotine chewing gum may be helpful to some individuals.

Behavioral interventions have included stimulus control procedures, contingency contracting, systematic desensitization, aversion, and a number of miscellaneous techniques and multicomponent interventions. Most techniques are ineffective in isolation, although favorable long-term results sometimes have been achieved with aversion, particularly when the procedure is intrinsically related to the natural smoking response. Application of aversion is limited by the fact that it can present certain medical risks, and careful screening of participants is necessary. Although not always successful, the most promising results have been obtained by more comprehensive multifaceted interventions which have emphasized maintenance as well as initial abstinence. Recent innovations include the use of the mass media, taped telephone-support messages, interventions in the work place, and controlled smoking.

A clinical prescription for helping smokers to achieve abstinence includes assisting them in reaching a firm decision to quit and then setting a specific target date for doing so. Smokers must take personal responsibility for their behavior. Their reasons for quitting should be sufficiently powerful and personally salient to sustain the abstinence effort. They should also be fully aware of the fringe benefits of nonsmoking. Satisfying alternatives to smoking should be rehearsed for different situations. Flexibility should be maintained in selecting the level of intervention and the treatment components to be included. The choice of treatment goal also must be flexible; subjects who are unable or unwilling to abstain altogether should be trained to reduce their level of risk.

A case study has been presented that illustrates the use of a single-subject experimental design in attempting to modify an individual's smoking topography. Two major ethical issues are considered. The first involves the deliberate assignment of smokers who are seeking help to theoretically inactive attention-placebo control conditions. Care must be taken to ensure that unsuccessful subjects in such conditions do not subsequently abandon further efforts at modifying their smoking behavior. The second issue involves the use of aversion. Aversive procedures require the implementation of appropriate safeguards, including medical authorization, the taking of a health history, informed consent of the subject, and carefully monitored exposure.

Suggestions for future research focus upon issues of methodology and application. Methodological recommendations include the need for carefully describing subject characteristics, guarding against subject mortality, and reporting results in a standardized fashion. Use of more sophisticated experimental designs (constructive strategies, dismantling strategies, theoretical research) is advocated as an alternative to what has been described by McFall as unsystematic "horse races."

Future research must emphasize maintenance as well as the initiation of change. Individual differences should be given a greater influence in the assignment of treatment procedures. Investigators may also profit from a close study of the techniques used by the substantial majority of smokers who have quit entirely on their own.

Public service programs should incorporate relevant empirical findings. Several levels of intervention should be available to the smoker, ranging from minimal contact or self-help programs to highly structured individualized interventions. The need for effective self-help programs is particularly evident in light of survey data which have shown that fewer than one-third of smokers who are motivated to quit express an interest in attending formal treatment programs (Gallup, 1974). A productive interchange between laboratory and clinical treatments can lead to the betterment of both. Cost effectiveness can be maximized by offering validated techniques administered by trained paraprofessionals in donated facilities such as churches or schools.

ACKNOWLEDGMENT

The author is grateful to Lois I. Hamilton for her assistance in reviewing and helping to prepare the final draft of the manuscript.

REFERENCES

Adesso, V. J., & Glad, W. R. A behavioral test of a smoking typology. *Addictive Behaviors*, 1978, *3*, 35–38.

American Cancer Society. *Task force on tobacco and cancer. Report to the board of directors.* New York: American Cancer Society, 1976.

Auger, T. J., Wright, E., & Simpson, R. H. Posters as smoking deterrents. *Journal of Applied Psychology,* 1972, *56,* 169–171.

Berecz, J. Treatment of smoking with cognitive conditioning therapy: A self-administered aversion technique. *Behavior Therapy,* 1976, *7,* 641–648.

Bernstein, D. A. Modification of smoking behavior: An evaluative review. *Psychological Bulletin,* 1969, *71,* 418–440.

Bernstein, D. A., & Glasgow, R. E. The modification of smoking behavior. In O. F. Pomerleau and J. P. Brady (Eds.), *Behavioral medicine: Theory and practice.* Baltimore: Williams & Wilkins, 1979.

Bernstein, D. A., & McAlister, A. The modification of smoking behavior: Progress and problems. *Addictive Behaviors,* 1976, *1,* 89–102.

Best, J. A. Tailoring smoking withdrawal procedures to personality and motivational differences. *Journal of Consulting and Clinical Psychology,* 1975, *43,* 1–8.

Best, J. A. *Clinical guidelines for smoking modification.* Paper presented at the 13th Annual Meeting of the Society of Prospective Medicine, San Diego, October 1977.

Best, J. A., Bass, F., & Owen, L. E. Mode of service delivery in a smoking cessation programme for public health. *Canadian Journal of Public Health,* 1977, *68,* 469–473.

Best, J. A., & Bloch, M. On improving compliance: Cigarette smoking. In R. B. Haynes and D. L. Sackett (Eds.), *Compliance and Public Health.* Baltimore: Johns Hopkins University Press, 1979.

Best, J. A., & Hakstian, A. R. A situation-specific model for smoking behavior. *Addictive Behaviors,* 1978, *3,* 79–92.

Best, J. A., Owen, L. E., & Trentadue, L. Comparison of satiation and rapid smoking in self-managed smoking cessation. *Addictive Behaviors,* 1978, *3,* 71–78.

Blittner, M., Goldberg, J., & Merbaum, M. Cognitive self-control factors in the reduction of smoking behavior. *Behavior Therapy,* 1978, *9,* 553–561.

Borgatta, E. F., & Evans, R. R. (Ed.), *Smoking, health, and behavior.* Chicago: Aldine, 1968.

Brecher, E. M. *Licit and illicit drugs.* Boston: Little, Brown, 1972.

Brengelmann, J. C., & Sedlmayr, E. Experiments in the reduction of smoking behavior. In J. Steinfeld et al., (Eds.), *Health consequences, education, cessation activities, and governmental action.* Washington, D.C.: U.S. Department of Health, Education, and Welfare, 1977.

Brockway, B. S. Chemical validation of self-reported smoking rates. *Behavior Therapy,* 1978, *9,* 685–686.

Brockway, B. S., Kleinmann, G., Edleson, J., & Greunewald, K. Non-aversive procedures and their effect on cigarette smoking. *Addictive Behaviors,* 1977, *2,* 121–128.

Burton, D. Motivating smokers to assume personal responsibility for quitting. In J. L. Schwartz (Ed.), *Progress in Smoking Cessation.* New York: American Cancer Society, 1978.

Cohen, S. I., Perkins, N. M., Ury, H. K., & Goldsmith, J. R. Carbon monoxide uptake in cigarette smoking. *Archives of Environmental Health,* 1971, *22,* 55–60.

Conway, J. B. Behavioral self-control of smoking through aversive conditioning and self-management. *Journal of Consulting and Clinical Psychology,* 1977, *45,* 348-357.

Danaher, B. G. Research on rapid smoking: Interim summary and recommendations. *Addictive Behaviors,* 1977, *2,* 151-166. (a)

Danaher, B. G. Rapid smoking and self-control in the modification of smoking behavior. *Journal of Consulting and Clinical Psychology,* 1977, *45,* 1068-1075. (b)

Danaher, B. G., & Lichtenstein, E. *Become an ex-smoker.* Englewood Cliffs, N.J.: Prentice Hall, 1978.

Danaher, B. G., Lichtenstein, E. & Sullivan, J. M. Comparative effects of rapid and normal smoking on heart rate and carboxyhemoglobin. *Journal of Consulting and Clinical Psychology,* 1976, *44,* 556-563.

Davison, G. C., & Rosen, R. C. Lobeline and reduction of cigarette smoking. *Psychological Reports,* 1972, *31,* 443-456.

Delarue, N. C. The anti-smoking clinic: Is it a potential community service? *Canadian Medical Association Journal,* 1973, *108,* 1164-1192.

Dericco, D. A., Brigham, T. A., & Garlington, W. K. Development and evaluation of treatment paradigms for the suppression of smoking behavior. *Journal of Applied Behavior Analysis,* 1977, *10,* 173-181.

Dubren, R. Evaluation of a televised stop-smoking clinic. *Public Health Reports,* 1977, *92,* 81-84. (a)

Dubren, R. Self-reinforcement by recorded telephone messages to maintain nonsmoking behavior. *Journal of Consulting and Clinical Psychology,* 1977, *45,* 358-360. (b)

Dunn, W. L. Experimental methods and conceptual models as applied to the study of motivation in cigarette smoking. In W. L. Dunn (Ed.), *Smoking behavior: Motives and incentives.* Washington, D.C.: Winston and Sons, 1973.

Elliott, C. H., & Denney, D. R. A multiple-component treatment approach to smoking reduction. *Journal of Consulting and Clinical Psychology,* 1978, *46,* 1330-1339.

Elliott, R., & Tighe, T. Breaking the cigarette habit: Effects of a technique involving threatened loss of money. *Psychological Record,* 1968, *18,* 503-513.

Ellis, B. *The role of the private practitioner in promoting abstinence.* Paper presented at the Fourth World Conference of Smoking and Health, Stockholm, June 1979.

Evans, R. I. Smoking in children and adolescents: Psychosocial determinants and prevention strategies. In *Smoking and health: A report of the Surgeon General.* Washington, D.C.: United States Public Health Service, 1979.

Eysenck, H. J. Personality and the maintenance of the smoking habit. In W. L. Dunn (Ed.), *Smoking behavior: Motives and incentives.* Washington, D.C.: Winston and Sons, 1973.

Farquhar, J. W., Maccoby, N., Wood, P. D., Alexander, J. K., Breitrose, H., Brown, B. W., Jr., Haskell, W. L., McAlister, A. L., Meyer, A. J., Nash,

J. D., & Stern, M. P. Community education for cardiovascular health. *Lancet,* 1977, *1*(8023), 1192–1195.

Ferraro, D. P. Self-control of smoking: The amotivational syndrome. *Journal of Abnormal Psychology,* 1973, *81,* 152–157.

Finnegan, J. K., Larson, P. S., & Haag, H. B. The role of nicotine in the cigarette habit. *Science,* 1945, *102,* 94–96.

Flaxman, J. Quitting smoking now or later: Gradual, abrupt, immediate, and delayed quitting. *Behavior Therapy,* 1978, *4,* 260–270.

Flaxman, J. Affect-management and habit mechanisms in the modification of smoking behavior. *Addictive Behaviors,* 1979, *4,* 39–46.

Foote, E. The time has come: Cigarette advertising must be banned. In M. E. Jarvik et al., (Eds.), *Research on smoking behavior.* Washington, D.C.: National Institute on Drug Abuse, 1977.

Foxx, R. M., & Brown, R. A. A nicotine fading and self-monitoring program to produce cigarette abstinence or controlled smoking. *Journal of Applied Behavior Analysis,* 1979, *12,* 111–125.

Frederiksen, L. W., Epstein, L. H., & Kosevsky, B. P. Reliability and controlling effects of three procedures for self-monitoring smoking. *The Psychological Record,* 1975, *25,* 255–264.

Frederiksen, L. W., & Martin, J. E. Carbon monoxide and smoking behavior. *Addictive Behaviors,* 1979, *4,* 21–30.

Frederiksen, L. W., Martin, J. E., & Webster, J. S. Assessment of smoking behavior. *Journal of Applied Behavior Analysis,* 1979, *12,* 653–664.

Frederiksen, L. W., Miller, P. M., & Peterson, G. L. Topographical components of smoking behavior. *Addictive Behaviors,* 1977, *2,* 55–61.

Frederiksen, L. W., Peterson, G. L., & Murphy, W. D. Controlled smoking: Development and maintenance. *Addictive Behaviors,* 1976, *1,* 193–196.

Frederiksen, L. W. & Simon, S. J. Modification of smoking topography: A preliminary analysis. *Behavior Therapy,* 1978, *9,* 946–949.

Gallup Opinion Index. Public puffs on after ten years of warnings. *Gallup Opinion Index,* 1974, *108,* 20–21.

Glasgow, R. E. Effects of a self-control manual, rapid smoking, and amount of therapist contact on smoking reduction. *Journal of Consulting and Clinical Psychology,* 1978, *46,* 1439–1447.

Grimaldi, K. E., & Lichtenstein, E. Hot, smoky air as an aversive stimulus in the treatment of smoking. *Behavior Research and Therapy,* 1969, *7,* 275–282.

Guilford, J. S. *Factors related to successful abstinence from smoking.* Pittsburgh: American Institutes for Research, 1966.

Guilford, J. S. Group treatment versus individual initiative in the cessation of smoking. *Journal of Applied Psychology,* 1972, *56,* 162–167.

Hackett, G., & Horan, J. J. Focused smoking: An unequivocably safe alternative to rapid smoking. *Journal of Drug Education,* 1978, *8,* 262–265.

Harris, D. E., & Lichtenstein, E. *Contribution of nonspecific social variables to a successful, behavioral treatment of smoking.* Paper presented at the meeting of the Western Psychological Association, San Francisco, April 1971.

Hildebrand, G. I. Improving the adult community through hospital-based smoking education and cessation programs. In J. Steinfeld et al., (Eds.), *Health consequences, education, cessation activities, and governmental action.* Washington, D.C.: U.S. Department of Health, Education, and Welfare, 1977.

Homme, L. E. Perspectives in psychology: XXIV. Control of coverants, the operants of the mind. *Psychological Record,* 1965, *15,* 501–511.

Horan, J. J., Linberg, S. E., & Hackett, G. Nicotine poisoning and rapid smoking. *Journal of Consulting and Clinical Psychology,* 1977, *45,* 344–347.

Horn, D. An approach to office management of the cigarette smoker. *Diseases of the Chest,* 1968, *54,* 203–209.

Hunt, W. A., & Matarazzo, J. D. Habit mechanisms in smoking. In W. A. Hunt, (Ed.), *Learning mechanisms in smoking.* Chicago: Aldine, 1970.

Hynd, G. W., Stratton, T. T., & Severson, H. H. Smoking treatment strategies, expectancy outcomes, and credibility in attention-placebo control conditions. *Journal of Clinical Psychology,* 1978, *34,* 182–186.

Ikard, F. F., Green, D. E., & Horn, D. A scale to differentiate between types of smoking as related to the management of affect. *International Journal of the Addictions,* 1969, *4,* 649–659.

Janis, I. L., & Mann, L. Effectiveness of emotional role-playing in modifying smoking habits and attitudes. *Journal of Experimental Research in Personality,* 1965, *1,* 84–90.

Jarvik, M. E. Biological factors underlying the smoking habit. In M. E. Jarvik et al., (Eds.), *Research on smoking behavior.* Washington, D.C.: National Institute on Drug Abuse, 1977.

Jarvik, M. E., Glick, S. D., & Nakamura, R. K. Inhibition of cigarette smoking by orally administered nicotine. *Clinical Pharmacology and Therapeutics,* 1970, *11,* 574–576.

Johnston, E., & Donoghue, J. R. Hypnosis and smoking: A review of the literature. *American Journal of Clinical Hypnosis,* 1971, *13,* 265–272.

Kanzler, M., Jaffe, J. H., & Zeidenberg, P. Long- and short-term effectiveness of a large-scale proprietary smoking cessation program—a four-year follow-up of Smokenders participants. *Journal of Clinical Psychology,* 1976, *32,* 661–669.

Kazdin, A. E. Self-monitoring and behavior change. In M. J. Mahoney & C. E. Thoresen (Eds.), *Self-control: Power to the person.* Monterey, Ca.: Brooks/Cole, 1974.

Knapp, P. H., Bliss, C. M., & Wells, H. Addictive aspects in heavy cigarette smoking. *American Journal of Psychiatry,* 1963, *119,* 966–972.

Koskela, K., Puska, P., & Tuomilehto, J. The North Karelia project: A first evaluation. *International Journal of Health Education,* 1976, *19,* 59–66.

Kozlowski, L. T. Psychosocial influences on cigarette smoking. In *Smoking and health: A report of the Surgeon General.* Washington, D.C.: United States Public Health Service, 1979.

Kumar, R., Cooke, E. C., Lader, M. H., & Russell, M. A. H. Is nicotine important in tobacco smoking? *Clinical Pharmacology and Therapeutics,* 1977, *21,* 520–529.

Lando, H. A. Measurement and technique innovations. An objective check upon self-reported smoking levels: A preliminary report. *Behavior Therapy,* 1975, *6,* 547–549. (a)

Lando, H. A. A comparison of excessive and rapid smoking in the modification of chronic smoking behavior. *Journal of Consulting and Clinical Psychology,* 1975, *43,* 350–355. (b)

Lando, H. A. Aversive conditioning and contingency management in the treatment of smoking. *Journal of Consulting and Clinical Psychology,* 1976, *44,* 312. (a)

Lando, H. A. Self-pacing in eliminating chronic smoking: Serendipity revisited. *Behavior Therapy,* 1976, *7,* 634–640. (b)

Lando, H. A. Successful treatment of smokers with a broad-spectrum behavioral approach. *Journal of Consulting and Clinical Psychology,* 1977, *45,* 361–366.

Lando, H. A. Issues and new directions in multifaceted behavioral smoking intervention programs. In J. L. Schwartz (Ed.), *Progress in Smoking Cessation.* New York: American Cancer Society, 1978.

Lando, H. A., & McCullough, J. A. Clinical application of a broad-spectrum behavioral approach to chronic smokers. *Journal of Consulting and Clinical Psychology,* 1978, *46,* 1583–1585.

Lando, H. A., Shirley, R. J., Gregory, V. R., & McCullough, J. C. *Broad-spectrum treatment in eliminating smoking: Preparation, aversion, and maintenance.* Paper presented at the meeting of the American Psychological Association, New York, September 1979.

Lawson, D. M., & May, R. M. Three procedures for the extinction of smoking behavior. *Psychological Record,* 1970, *20,* 151–157.

Lawton, M. P. Group methods in smoking withdrawal. *Archives of Environmental Health,* 1967, *14,* 258–265.

Levenberg, S. B., & Wagner, M. K. Smoking cessation: Long-term irrelevance of mode of treatment. *Journal of Behavior Therapy and Experimental Psychiatry,* 1976, *7,* 93–95.

Leventhal, H. Findings and theory in the study of fear communications. In L. Berkowitz (Ed.), *Advances in experimental social psychology* (Vol. 5). New York: Academic Press, 1970.

Levinson, B. L., Shapiro, D., Schwartz, G. E., & Tursky, B. Smoking elimination by gradual reduction. *Behavior Therapy,* 1971, *2,* 477–487.

Lichtenstein, E. Future needs and directions in smoking cessation. In J. L. Schwartz (Ed.), *Progress in smoking cessation.* New York: American Cancer Society, 1978.

Lichtenstein, E., Antonuccio, D. O., and Rainwater, G. *Unkicking the habit: The resumption of cigarette smoking.* Paper presented at the annual meeting of the Western Psychological Association, Seattle, Wash., 1977.

Lichtenstein, E., & Danaher, B. G. Modification of smoking behavior: A critical analysis of theory, research, and practice. In M. Hersen et al., (Eds.), *Progress in behavior modification* (Vol. 3). New York: Academic Press, 1976.

Lichtenstein, E., & Glasgow, R. E. Rapid smoking: Side effects and safeguards. *Journal of Consulting and Clinical Psychology,* 1977, *45,* 815–821.

Lichtenstein, E., Harris, D. E., Birchler, G. R., Wahl, J. M. & Schmahl, D. P. Comparison of rapid smoking, warm, smoky air, and attention placebo in the modification of smoking behavior. *Journal of Consulting and Clinical Psychology,* 1973, *40,* 92–98.

Lichtenstein, E., Keutzer, C. S., & Himes, K. H. Emotional role-playing and changes in smoking attitudes and behavior. *Psychological Reports,* 1969, *25,* 379–387.

Lichtenstein, E., & Rodrigues, M. P. Long-term effects of rapid smoking treatment for dependent cigarette smokers. *Addictive Behaviors,* 1977, *2,* 109–112.

Logan, F. A. The smoking habit. In W. A. Hunt (Ed.), *Learning mechanisms in smoking.* Chicago: Aldine, 1970.

Logan, F. A. Self-control as habit, drive, and incentive. *Journal of Abnormal Psychology,* 1973, *81,* 127–136.

Lombard, H. L., & Doering, C. R. Cancer studies in Massachusetts: Habits, characteristics, and environment of individuals with and without cancer. *New England Journal of Medicine,* 1928, *198,* 481–487.

Lucchesi, B. R., Schuster, C. R., & Emley, G. S. The role of nicotine as a determinant of cigarette smoking frequency in man with observations of certain cadiovascular effects associated with the tobacco alkaloid. *Clinical Pharmacology and Therapeutics,* 1967, *8,* 789–796.

Maccoby, N., Farquhar, J. W., Wood, P. D., & Alexander, J. Reducing the risk of cardiovascular disease: Effects of a community-based campaign on knowledge and behavior. *Journal of Community Health,* 1977, *3,* 100–114.

Marrone, R. L., Merksamer, M. A., & Salzberg, P. M. A short duration group treatment of smoking behavior by stimulus saturation. *Behaviour Research and Therapy,* 1970, *8,* 347–352.

McAlister, A. L. Toward the mass communication of behavioral counseling: A preliminary experimental study of a televised program to assist in smoking cessation. (Doctoral dissertation, Stanford University, 1976). Ann Arbor, Mich.: *University Microfilms,* 1975. (University Microfilms No. 77-7128)

McFall, R. M. Effects of self-monitoring on normal smoking behavior. *Journal of Consulting and Clinical Psychology,* 1970, *35,* 135–142.

McFall, R. M. Smoking-cessation research. *Journal of Consulting and Clinical Psychology,* 1978, *46,* 703–712.

McFarland, J. W. The role of church groups in smoking and health. In J. Steinfeld et al., (Eds.), *Health consequences, education, cessation activities, and governmental action.* Washington, D.C.: U.S. Department of Health, Education, and Welfare, 1977.

Meichenbaum, D. H., Gilmore, J., & Fedoravicius, A. Group insight vs. group desensitization in treating speech anxiety. *Journal of Consulting and Clinical Psychology,* 1971, *36,* 410–421.

Meyer, A. J., & Henderson, J. B. Multiple risk factor reduction in the prevention of cardiovascular disease. *Preventive Medicine,* 1974, *3,* 225–236.

Multiple Risk Factor Intervention Trial (MRFIT). A national study of primary prevention of coronary heart disease. *Journal of the American Medical Association,* 1976, *235,* 825–827.

National Cancer Institute. *Progress report on a nation kicking the habit.* Washington, D.C.: NCI, 1977.

National Clearinghouse for Smoking and Health. *Adult use of tobacco, 1975.* Washington, D.C.: NCSH, 1976.

Norton, G. R., & Barske, B. The role of aversion in the rapid-smoking treatment procedure. *Addictive Behaviors,* 1977, *2,* 21–25.

Ober, D. C. Modification of smoking behavior. *Journal of Consulting and Clinical Psychology,* 1968, *32,* 543–549.

Ohlin, P., Lundh, B., & Westling, H. Carbon monoxide blood levels and reported cessation of smoking. *Psychopharmacology,* 1976, *49,* 263–265.

Orne, M. T. Hypnosis in the treatment of smoking. In J. Steinfeld et al., (Eds.), *Health consequences, education, cessation activities, and governmental action.* Washington, D.C.: U.S. Department of Health, Education, and Welfare, 1977.

Peabody, H. D., Jr. A practical approach to the office management of cessation of cigarette smoking. In R. G. Richardson (Ed.), *Proceedings of the Second World Conference on Smoking and Health.* London: Health Education Council, 1972.

Pechacek, T. F. Modification of smoking behavior. In *Smoking and health: A report of the Surgeon General.* Washington, D.C.: United States Public Health Service, 1979.

Pederson, L. L., Scrimgeour, W. G., & Lefcoe, N. M. Comparison of hypnosis plus counseling, counseling alone, and hypnosis alone in a community service smoking withdrawal program. *Journal of Consulting and Clinical Psychology,* 1975, *43,* 920.

Perri, M. G., Richards, C. S., & Schultheis, K. R. Behavioral self-control and smoking reduction: A study of self-initiated attempts to reduce smoking. *Behavior Therapy,* 1977, *8,* 360–365.

Pettigrew, A. R., & Fell, G. S. Microdiffusion method for estimation of cyanide in whole blood and its application to the study of conversion of cyanide to thiocyanate. *Clinical Chemistry,* 1973, *19,* 466–471.

Pomerleau, O. F. You can get patients to change their habits. *Medical Times,* 1976, *104,* 149–158.

Pomerleau, O. F. Strategies for maintenance: The problem of sustaining abstinence from cigarettes. In J. L. Schwartz (Ed.), *Progress in smoking cessation.* New York: American Cancer Society, 1978.

Pomerleau, O. F. Behavioral factors in the establishment, maintenance, and cessation of smoking. In *Smoking and health: A report of the Surgeon General.* Washington, D.C.: United States Public Health Service, 1979.

Pomerleau, O., Adkins, D., & Pertschuk, M. Predictors of outcome and recidivism in smoking cessation treatment. *Addictive Behaviors,* 1978, *3,* 65–70.

Pomerleau, O., Bass, F., & Crown, V. Role of behavior modification in preventive medicine. *New England Journal of Medicine,* 1975, *292,* 1277–1282.

Premack, D. Mechanisms of self-control. In W. A. Hunt (Ed.), *Learning mechanisms in smoking.* Chicago: Aldine, 1970.

Puska, P., Björkqvist, S., & Koskela, K. Nicotine-containing chewing gum in smoking cessation: A double blind trial with half year follow-up. *Addictive Behaviors,* 1979, *4,* 141–146.

Pyszka, R. H., Ruggels, W. L., & Janowicz, L. M. *Health behavior change: Smoking cessation.* Menlo Park, Calif.: Stanford Research Institute, 1973.

Resnick, J. H. Effects of stimulus satiation on the overlearned maladaptive response of cigarette smoking. *Journal of Consulting and Clinical Psychology,* 1968, *32,* 501–505.

Richmond, H. W. A fifteen-year prospective study of the incidence of coronary heart disease related to cigarette smoking habits in Cummins Engine Company management personnel with results of a vigorous antismoking education campaign. In J. Steinfeld et al., (Eds.), *Health consequences, education, cessation activities, and governmental action.* Washington, D.C.: U.S. Department of Health, Education, and Welfare, 1977.

Ringold, A., Goldsmith, J. R., Helwig, H. L., Finn, R., & Schuette, F. Estimating recent carbon monoxide exposures: A rapid method. *Archives of Environmental Health,* 1962, *5,* 308–318.

Rogers, R. W., Deckner, C. W., & Mewborn, C. R. An expectancy-value theory approach to the long-term modification of smoking behavior. *Journal of Clinical Psychology,* 1978, *34,* 562–566.

Rose, G. Physician counseling and personal intervention. In J. Steinfeld et al., (Eds.), *Health consequences, education, cessation activities, and governmental action.* Washington, D.C.: U.S. Department of Health, Education, and Welfare, 1977.

Rosen, G. M., & Lichtenstein, E. An employee incentive program to reduce cigarette smoking. *Journal of Consulting and Clinical Psychology,* 1977, *45,* 957.

Rosenberg, A. An investigation into the effect on cigarette smoking of a new anti-smoking chewing gum. *Journal of International Medical Research,* 1977, *5,* 68–70.

Russell, M. A. H. Cigarette smoking: Natural history of a dependence disorder. *British Journal of Medical Psychology,* 1971, *44,* 1–16.

Russell, M. A. H. Realistic goals for smoking and health: A case for safer smoking. *Lancet,* 1974, *1*(7851), 254–258.

Russell, M. A. H. Smoking problems: An overview. In M. E. Jarvik et al., (Eds.), *Research on smoking behavior.* Washington, D.C.: National Institute on Drug Abuse, 1977.

Russell, M. A. H. Smoking problems: An overview. In M. E. Jarvik et al., electric aversion therapy for cigarette smoking. *Behaviour Research and Therapy,* 1976, *14,* 103–123.

Russell, M. A. H., Raw, M., Taylor, C., Feyerabend, C., & Saloojee, Y. Blood nicotine and carboxyhemoglobin levels after rapid-smoking aversion therapy. *Journal of Consulting and Clinical Psychology*, 1978, *46*, 1423–1431.

Schachter, S. Nicotine regulation in heavy and light smokers. *Journal of Experimental Psychology: General*, 1977, *106*, 5–12.

Schachter, S. Pharmacological and psychological determinants of smoking. *Annals of Internal Medicine*, 1978, *88*, 104–114.

Schachter, S., Kozlowski, L. T., & Silverstein, B. Effects of urinary pH on cigarette smoking. *Journal of Experimental Psychology: General*, 1977, *106*, 13–19.

Schachter, S., Silverstein, B., Kozlowski, L. T., Herman, C. P., & Liebling, B. Effects of stress on cigarette smoking and urinary pH. *Journal of Experimental Psychology: General*, 1977, *106*, 24–30.

Schachter, S., Silverstein, B., & Perlick, D. Psychological and pharmacological explanations of smoking under stress. *Journal of Experimental Psychology: General*, 1977, *106*, 31–40.

Schlegel, R. P., & Kunetsky, M. Immediate and delayed effects of the "five-day plan to stop smoking" including factors affecting recidivism. *Preventive Medicine*, 1977, *6*, 454–461.

Schmahl, D. P., Lichtenstein, E., & Harris, D. E. Successful treatment of habitual smokers with warm, smoky air and rapid smoking. *Journal of Consulting and Clinical Psychology*, 1972, *38*, 105–111.

Schwartz, J. L., & Rider, G. Smoking cessation methods in the United States and Canada: 1969–1974. In J. Steinfeld et al., (Eds.), *Health consequences, education, cessation activities, and governmental action*. Washington, D.C.: U.S. Department of Health, Education, and Welfare, 1977.

Shewchuk, L. A. Special report. Smoking cessation programs of the American Health Foundation. *Preventive Medicine*, 1976, *5*, 454–474.

Silverstein, B., Kozlowski, L. T., & Schachter, S. Social life, cigarette smoking and urinary pH. *Journal of Experimental Psychology: General*, 1977, *106*, 20–23.

Solomon, R. L. An opponent-process theory of acquired motivation: IV. The affective dynamics of addiction. In J. D. Maser & M. E. P. Seligman (Eds.), *Psychopathology: Experimental models*. San Francisco: W. H. Freeman, 1977.

Solomon, R. L., & Corbit, J. D. An opponent-process theory of motivation: II. Cigarette addiction. *Journal of Abnormal Psychology*, 1973, *81*, 158–171.

Solomon, R. L., & Corbit, J. D. An opponent-process theory of motivation: I. Temporal dynamics of affect. *Psychological Review*, 1974, *81*, 119–145.

Stewart, R. D. The effect of carbon monoxide on humans. *Annual Review of Pharmacology*, 1975, *15*, 409–423.

Stolerman, I. P., Goldfarb, T., Fink, R., & Jarvik, M. E. Influencing cigarette smoking with nicotine antagonists. *Psychopharmacologia*, 1973, *28*, 247–259.

Suedfeld, P., & Best, J. A. Satiation and sensory deprivation combined in smoking therapy: Some case studies and unexpected side-effects. *International Journal of the Addictions*, 1977, *12*, 337–359.

Suedfeld, P., & Ikard, F. F. Use of sensory deprivation in facilitating the reduction of cigarette smoking. *Journal of Consulting and Clinical Psychology,* 1974, *42,* 888–895.

Syme, S. L., & Jacobs, M. J. Smoking cessation activities in the Multiple Risk Factor Intervention Trial: A preliminary report. In J. Steinfeld et al., (Eds.), *Health consequences, education, cessation activities, and governmental action.* Washington, D.C.: U.S. Department of Health, Education, and Welfare, 1977.

Thompson, D. S., & Wilson, T. R. Discontinuance of cigarette smoking: "Natural" and with "therapy." A ten-week and ten-month follow-up study of adult participants in a five-day plan to stop smoking. *Journal of the American Medical Association,* 1966, *196,* 1048–1052.

Tomkins, S. S. Psychological model for smoking behavior. *American Journal of Public Health,* 1966, *12,* 17–20.

Tomkins, S. S. Psychological model for smoking behavior. In E. Borgatta & R. Evans (Eds.), *Smoking, health and behavior.* Chicago: Aldine, 1968.

Tori, C. D. A smoking satiation procedure with reduced medical risk. *Journal of Clinical Psychology,* 1978, *34,* 574–577.

United States Public Health Service. *Smoking and health: A report of the Surgeon General.* Washington, D.C.: USPHS, 1979.

Vogt, T. M. Smoking behavioral factors as predictors of risks. In M. E. Jarvik et al., (Eds.), *Research on smoking behavior.* Washington, D.C.: National Institute on Drug Abuse, 1977.

Wagner, M. K., & Bragg, R. A. Comparing behavior modification approaches to habit decrement-smoking. *Journal of Consulting and Clinical Psychology,* 1970, *34,* 258–263.

Warner, K. E. The effects of the anti-smoking campaign on cigarette consumption. *American Journal of Public Health,* 1977, *67,* 645–650.

Wilson, G. T., & Davison, G. C. Aversion techniques in behavior therapy: Some theoretical and metatheoretical considerations. *Journal of Consulting and Clinical Psychology,* 1969, *33,* 327–329.

Winett, R. A. Parameters of deposit contracts in the modification of smoking. *Psychological Record,* 1973, *23,* 49–60.

4
Erectile Dysfunction: A Review of Behavioral Treatment Approaches

Barry S. Reynolds

Erectile dysfunction may be defined as the persistent inability to obtain or maintain a penile erection that is sufficient to allow intromission, pelvic thrusting, and, in the absence of ejaculatory difficulties, ejaculation during sexual intercourse (Reynolds, 1977). The client may complain of an inability to attain an erection, or he may gain an erection and then lose it during extended foreplay, during the process of intromission, or after several pelvic thrusts. He may ejaculate without an erection or with a partial erection. Chronic erectile difficulties may cause the man to experience exacerbated feelings of personal and sexual inadequacy, concerns about "manliness," and anxiety about his ability to satisfy his sexual partner (Heinrich, 1979). Men with a steady relationship with a partner may report a marked reduction of sexual activity as a means of avoiding failure experiences, and men without a steady partner may report either a cessation of dating activity or a greatly increased frequency of sexual encounters with different partners, usually motivated by a recurrent and anxious desire to test erectile responsiveness.

Masters and Johnson (1970) reported that erectile dysfunction was the presenting complaint for 245 of the 790 couples (31 percent) treated during the initial 11 years of their pioneering treatment program. The percentage of male patients who sought treatment for erection difficulties was slightly greater than the percentage who sought treatment for premature ejaculation. In a recent study of married couples who were not seeking help for marital or sexual problems (Frank, Anderson, & Rubinstein, 1978), 7 percent of the men reported difficulties in getting an erection, and another 9 percent reported difficulty in maintaining erection. However, a much greater percentage of nonpatient men (36 percent) reported difficulties with rapid ejaculation. A comparison of the results of these two studies suggests that men may be more likely to seek therapy for erectile dysfunction than for other male sexual dysfunctions.

Erectile dysfunction may result from a wide variety of physiological conditions, including numerous systemic diseases, endocrine disorders, genital diseases, surgical conditions, neurological disorders, and vascular diseases (Kaplan, 1974). Erectile dysfunction may also result from the acute or chronic use of a variety of drugs and medications, including alcohol, barbiturates, narcotics, anticholinergic drugs used in the treatment of gastrointestinal disturbances, and antiadrenergic medications used in the treatment of hypertension and other vascular disorders (Kaplan, 1974). Extensive reviews of the organic causes of erectile dysfunction can be found in Kaplan (1974), Weiss (1972), and Julty (1975), and Segraves (1978) has written an excellent review of pharmacological agents affecting sexual response. The focus of this chapter is psychogenic erectile dysfunction, which refers to a recurrent disturbance of the erectile response for which no known organic cause can be found and for which the current psychological functioning of the individual or couple is viewed as the primary cause. It has been estimated that from 80 to 97 percent of the cases of erectile dysfunction have a psychological etiology (Kaplan, 1974). Furthermore, many men with organic conditions that are known to disrupt erection may benefit from the application of the psychological treatment approaches reviewed in this chapter.

THEORETICAL ANALYSIS

Nonbehavioral

The major nonbehavioral psychological treatment approaches to erectile dysfunction are derived from classical psychoanalytic theory and from other psychodynamic formulations concerning the development of erectile disorders. The psychoanalytic and psychodynamic formulations begin with the premise that the erectile disorder is symptomatic of underlying unconscious conflicts (Cooper, 1971; Kaplan, 1974).

Classical psychoanalytic theory holds that erectile dysfunction is a result of sexual fear and guilt that can be traced to unresolved oedipal conflict (Freud, 1910/1953; Layman, 1972; Stekel, 1927). Sexual excitement and behavior are believed to re-evoke both unconscious, unresolved incestuous wishes and the castration anxiety and guilt feelings engendered by these wishes. Erectile dysfunction develops as a defense against the emergence of these conflicting effects (Kaplan, 1974). Bieber (1974) also argues that parental reaction to the oedipal phase is one important interpersonal dynamic associated with later erection difficulties. He states that parents who fear the child's sexual responses to them, who are sexually competitive with the same-sex child, or who view the child as a spouse substitute provide a model of rejection, domination, or exploitation. The child's own subsequent sexual relationships are perceived as threatening, and erectile dysfunction becomes a means of resisting the threatening relationship. Because of the defensive nature of the erectile disorder, classical psychoanalytic theory maintains that the oedipal conflict must be brought into consciousness and resolved before any lasting improvement in the erectile symptom can occur.

Although classical psychoanalytic theorists focus almost exclusively on oedipal conflict as a causal factor in erectile dysfunction, other psychodynamic writers have focused on additional intra- and interpersonal factors. Salzman (1972), Friedman (1973), and Kaplan (1974) suggest that the sexual symptom may serve a significant function in the individual's present interpersonal dynamics. For example, Salzman (1972), Kaplan (1974), and Gill and Temperly (1974) state that erectile dysfunction may serve as a means of expressing anger toward the female partner. Goldberg (1973) and Proctor (1973) mention depression as an underlying cause for erection difficulties. These authors discuss cases in which the erectile dysfunction appeared to be associated with the individual's generalized feelings of incompetence and lack of power. They state that both the erection difficulties and the depression disappeared when the man explored the historical roots of his feelings of incompetence and was aided in taking a more active role in all aspects of his life.

Reviews by Cooper (1971), Reynolds (1977), and Kilmann and Auerbach (1979) found that the evidence regarding the effectiveness of various forms of psychoanalysis and depth psychotherapy generally is limited to single-case studies or relatively uncontrolled clinical observations. O'Connor and Stern's (1972) retrospective analysis of outcome results obtained at the Columbia Psychoanalytic Clinic is the only study that reports on more than just a few clients. O'Connor and Stern (1972) report that 11 of 15 men (73 percent) who received either psychoanalysis (4 sessions weekly for a minimum of 2 years) or psychoanalytically oriented therapy (semiweekly sessions for a maximum of 2 years) were judged to have improved on the basis of therapist's report. Although these results are encouraging, the study suffers from some serious methodological problems. No specific definition of improvement is provided, but the authors suggest that improvement "could be a change in attitude, but not in performance" (p. 1928). Furthermore, in the absence of some form of no-treatment control group, the possibility remains that the observed improvement may have been attributable to nonspecific therapeutic experiences occurring outside the treatment situation, particularly since the average client received over two years of therapy.

In summary, there are no well-controlled investigations that support the efficacy of psychoanalysis and other depth therapies for the treatment of erectile dysfunction (Cooper, 1971; Kilmann & Auerbach, 1979; Reynolds, 1977). Furthermore, Kilmann and Auerbach (1979) cite several studies reporting successful treatment of large numbers of men and using procedures that did not involve any attempt at extensive personality reorganization or unconscious conflict resolution (Friedman & Lipsedge, 1971; Masters & Johnson, 1970; Obler, 1973). The results of these studies challenge the assumption that amelioration of erectile dysfunction requires extensive underlying personality change. Finally, Kilmann and Auerbach (1979) also reviewed two studies (Lazarus, 1961; Obler, 1973) that found symptom-focused behavioral techniques to be superior to depth psychotherapy for several male and female sexual dysfunctions.

Behavioral

Professionals from a wide variety of disciplines and orientations have provided valuable contributions concerning the etiology and brief treatment of erectile dysfunction. Hogan (1978) stated that no single theory, including social learning theory, is sufficient to explain all of the phenomena involved in sexual dysfunctions and sex therapy. The theoretical formulations presented here, however, may be considered behavioral for several rather broad reasons:

1. The erectile difficulties are viewed as resulting at least as much from *current* response deficits and environmental consequences as from historical factors.
2. The focus of treatment is on the alteration of the erectile response or other cognitions, affects, and behaviors that directly or indirectly are associated with erectile response or with sexual satisfaction.

The goal of treatment is not extensive personality change or unconscious conflict resolution.

3. The therapy format frequently includes formalized attempts to have clients learn and practice these new behaviors as part of the treatment experience.

Hogan (1978) has presented an interactional systems approach to understanding the causes of sexual dysfunction. In the interactional systems model, events are seen as elements of systems. The different elements affect each other and are affected in turn via positive or negative feedback loops. The system operates in a cyclical fashion; a change in an element that serves as a cause at one moment may become an effect at the next, and vice versa. The interactional model is particularly applicable to understanding the actions of the diverse factors that have been found to be associated with the development and maintenance of erectile dysfunction. These factors follow.

Anxiety. A number of clinical studies have found anxiety to be an important etiological factor for erectile dysfunction (Annon, 1974; Cooper, 1969; Friedman, 1968). Several writers have conceptualized penile erection as a parasympathetic response that is inhibited by the sympathetic components of anxiety (Kaplan, 1974; Wolpe, 1973). Kaplan (1974) views erectile dysfunction as a psychophysiological reaction to anxiety occurring in men who suffer from an excessive vulnerability to stress. Kaplan states that the precipitating stress can bring about the disruption of the erectile response. In contrast to psychoanalytic theory, Kaplan contends that the erectile difficulty need not be symbolically related to conflicts concerning sexuality. Instead, Kaplan uses an "individual response specificity" (p. 264) hypothesis to account for the selection of the specific erectile symptom. According to this notion, psychosomatic disorders of a particular organ system are believed to develop as a result of a chronic tendency to overreact to stress with a somatic symptom (e.g., peptic over-reactivity, hypertension, or genital vasocongestive disruption) that is specific and consistent for a given individual.

Performance concerns. Masters and Johnson (1970) and Kaplan (1974) state that concern about sexual performance is the most important immediate cause of erectile dysfunction. Performance concerns are believed to transform a single episode of erectile difficulties into a chronic sexual dysfunction. Hogan (1978) states that performance concerns have two components: (1) an affective component, termed "performance anxiety," and (2) a cognitive component, termed "spectatoring" (Masters & Johnson, 1970). Masters and Johnson contend that the erectile dysfunction usually is maintained by the man's preoccupation with actively achieving or willing an erection. The preoccupation itself results from a fear of continued erectile difficulty. The preoccupation makes the man a spectator to his own sensual experience rather than a participant, thereby blocking his access to the physical and psychological stimulation which would normally elicit erection. Geer and Fuhr (1976) have demonstrated experimentally that cognitive distraction from the reception of erotic input results in reduced erectile responsiveness. The performance anxiety and concerns may occur at progressively earlier points in a sexual encounter or relationship, so that the fear of failure may eventually result in an avoidance of dating or other activities that include even the possibility of a sexual encounter.

Misinformation and lack of knowledge about sex. A number of clinicians have noted that misinformation and lack of knowledge contribute to erectile difficulties (Kaplan, 1974; LoPiccolo & Lobitz, 1973; Zilbergeld, 1978). For example, many men are not aware of the normal changes in male sexuality that are associated with age; in particular, they are unaware that as men get older they normally require an increasing amount of direct tactile stimulation of the genitals in order to elicit erection (Masters & Johnson, 1966). Other men may be unaware of the importance of clitoral stimulation for female arousal and may believe that the woman's satisfaction is associated with penis size, the "hardness" of the erection, or the depth and number of pelvic thrusts.

Lack of effective communication. Lack of communication between sexual partners has been viewed as a contributing factor for male sexual dysfunctions (Kaplan, 1974; Masters & Johnson, 1970; Zilbergeld, 1978). In the case of erectile dysfunction, the man may be particularly reluctant or unable to communicate verbally or nonverbally about the form and amount of stimulation he requires. He may also feel reluctant to inform his partner on the occasions when he really doesn't wish to have intercourse. In the absence of communication to the contrary, the man's partner may interpret occasional episodes of erectile failure as an indication that he doesn't maintain affection and desire for her or that she is not sexually attractive; these interpretations only serve to increase tension during subsequent sexual encounters.

Reactions by the sexual partner. Masters and Johnson (1970) and Kaplan (1974) have stated that the interference of the man's reception of sensual input frequently is exacerbated by performance demands or negative reactions from his sexual partner. Some women may respond to the explicit and subtle messages in our society which suggest that women should be passive during sexual activities and it is the man who should be responsible for providing her with sexual fulfillment. Due to her own ignorance, antagonism, or discomfort with sexual expression, a partner may fail to provide adequate stimulation for male arousal, either by not providing overt physical stimulation or by being nonexpressive in her reactions to his stimulation.

Historical factors. Masters and Johnson (1970) isolated several psychological factors that they regard as having less immediate but original causal significance for erectile dysfunction. These factors include religious orthodoxy regarding sexual expression, a homosexual orientation based on early meaningful homosexual experience, trauma associated with an initial coital attempt with a prostitute, incestuous encounters, paternal or maternal dominance, iatrogenic influence, and the experience of another sexual dysfunction (primarily premature ejaculation). Reynolds (1977) and Hogan (1978) question the validity of these alleged etiological factors because a significant percentage of men have experienced these conditions without developing sexual dysfunction.

The interactional systems model would predict that the causal factors just outlined would affect each other in a cyclical manner. For example, the man with an excessive erectile vulnerability might react to mild stress with a single episode of erectile difficulties. During subsequent sexual encounters, he might experience mild performance anxiety and spectatoring that he is unable to counteract because he fails to ask for and doesn't receive more direct physical stimulation, or because he and his partner anxiously believe that a firm erection is vital to their sexual satisfaction. Again, the physiological result is reduced erectile responsivity, which serves to elicit even greater performance concerns during later sexual episodes. The combination of inhibitory influences of both partners produces a vicious cycle of distress and flaccidity.

ASSESSMENT

Sexual dysfunctions frequently are presented by clients in nonspecific terms, such as "I'm not performing at all," or "sex isn't what it used to be." The clinician's task is to determine whether the client is indeed experiencing erectile dysfunction; to ascertain whether there is sufficient information to rule out organic causes; and to develop an understanding of the emotional, cognitive, and social factors that are contributing to the client's difficulties. Data pertaining to these general questions can be used to develop a treatment plan.

The differential diagnosis of organic and psychogenic erectile dysfunction is generally made on the basis of a physical examination and a diagnostic interview. Although psychological factors are believed to have primary etiological significance for the great majority of cases of erectile dysfunction, organic causes are implicated more often in cases of erectile dysfunction than in other common sexual dysfunctions (Kaplan, 1974; Masters & Johnson, 1970); therefore, a urological and general physical examination is recommended as an initial diagnostic approach.

The diagnostic interview can aid in the differentiation of organic and psychogenic erectile dysfunction. In particular, it is helpful to determine whether the client reports erection during some sexual encounters with a partner, during solitary self-stimulation, or during nonsexual circumstances such as waking with an erection in the middle of the night or in the morning. Generally speaking, the presence of morning or masturbatory erections indicates that the physical capacity for erectile response is intact and the disorder is more likely caused by psychological factors. The likelihood of a psychological etiology is increased further when the dysfunction occurs under fairly specific circumstances, e.g., with one partner but not another, or only during initial encounters with a new partner.

The differential diagnosis of biogenic and psychogenic erectile dysfunction may require nocturnal tumescence monitoring, particularly in cases where the client does not report morning or masturbatory erections. Nocturnal tumescence-monitoring procedures are based on the finding that physiologically healthy males regularly experience erection during Rapid Eye Movement (REM) portions of the sleep cycle (Karacan, 1966). Nocturnal erection can be measured with a mercury strain gauge (Bancroft, Jones, & Pullan, 1966). This device consists of an elastic rubber tube that is filled with mercury and sealed at both ends with platinum electrodes. The tube is fitted around the penis, and changes in erection produce small changes in electrical resistance of the mercury. The resistance changes are amplified and displayed on a polygraph. Karacan's group has established norms for nocturnal erections for healthy males in various age groups (Karacan, Williams, Thornby, & Salis, 1975) and has begun to establish norms for the differentiation of psychogenic and organic erectile dysfunction in men with physical disorders that may or may not disrupt erection, such as diabetes (Karacan, Salis, Ware, Dervent, Williams, Scott, Attia, & Beutler, 1978). This procedure shows promise as an objective means of differentiating organic from psychogenic erectile dysfunction. However, nocturnal tumescence evaluation is an expensive and time-consuming procedure. An unequivocal evaluation (requiring habituation and verification of REM sleep) may require the client to be monitored in a sleep laboratory for up to three consecutive nights.

Beutler, Karacan, Anch, Salis, Scott, and Williams (1975) evaluated the predictive validity of the Minnesota Multiphasic Personality Inventory (MMPI) (Hathaway & McKinley, 1943) to discriminate between organic and psychogenic erectile dysfunction. Using nocturnal tumescence results as a criterion measure, the combination of the following two rules from the MMPI was found to identify 8 of 9 psychogenic cases and 12 of 13 biogenic cases correctly:

1. *MF* scale *T* score above 60 (call psychogenic).
2. One or more scales above a *T* score of 70 (call psychogenic).

Rule 1, by itself, identified 7 of 9 psychogenic cases but only 3 of 13 biogenic cases. Rule 2, by itself, identified 8 of 9 psychogenic cases and 8 of 13 biogenic cases. The subjects with biogenic and psychogenic etiologies did not differ with respect to absolute elevation of any of the scales, and there was no indication of a clear personality type associated with either psychogenic or biogenic erectile dysfunction.

Assuming that the results of the physical examination, initial interview, psychological tests, or nocturnal tumescence evaluation have established the unlikelihood of an organic cause of the client's erectile difficulties, additional evaluation interviews can focus on the identification of the psychological factors inhibiting the erectile response. The goal of the interview is to obtain a detailed behavioral description of the sexual interactions in which the dysfunction is occurring as well as the behavioral, cognitive, and affective antecedents and consequences of the erectile disorder. Heinrich (1979) suggests the following questions as a guide for the diagnostic interview:

> Do you have problems attaining the erection, sustaining erection, or both?
>
> How long have you been having this problem? Have you had similar problems in the past? What do you think caused the problem previously?
>
> Does the problem occur in specific situations, at certain times, or only with certain partners? Are there times when you do not have the problem? If so, what is different about these situations?
>
> How would you describe your current sexual relationship? How much time do you and your partner spend in foreplay? Is this enough time for you to feel sufficiently aroused? Do you or does your partner expect you to be ready for sex very quickly? How did you and your partner respond when you began having erectile problems?

Heinrich (1979) offers several additional questions that are designed to explore interpersonal, work, and health factors which might be contributing to the dysfunction:

> How is your overall relationship with your partner? Have any changes occurred such as fights, talks about separating, pregnancy, job or role changes, etc.?
>
> How is the sexual relationship with your partner? Does she seem aroused? Does she reach orgasm? Is she satisfied with the sexual relationship? Are you?
>
> Have changes occurred in your work situation such as increased demands, longer hours, threatened layoffs, etc.?
>
> Have there been any recent changes in your health?
>
> Are you using any medications, drugs, or alcohol?

The responses to these and other questions can help to establish whether brief sex therapy is appropriate for the client or whether a referral for alternative treatment is advisable (e.g., marital therapy, or treatment for depression or alcoholism). If sex therapy is appropriate, the responses to these questions will suggest factors that can be the focus of the sex therapy interventions.

A number of questionnaires that are useful for treatment planning and outcome evaluation have been developed. The Sexual Interaction Inventory (LoPiccolo & Stegar, 1974) can provide quantitative information about a variety of sexual interaction factors, including frequency, pleasure, self-acceptance, partner acceptance, and perceptual accuracy. LoPiccolo and Stegar found that all 11 scales of the inventory possess significant test-retest reliability and are sensitive to treatment. Nine of the scales were found to discriminate between sexually adjusted and clinic-referred couples. McCoy and D'Agostino (1977), however, present data that challenge the factoral purity of the psychosexual scales of this measure.

Lobitz and Baker (1979) have applied the Goals for Sex Therapy scaling procedures (Price & Heinrich, 1975; Heinrich & Price, 1975) to the study of erectile dysfunction. Lobitz and Baker designed a 14-item rating scale to assess change in the client's satisfaction with his erectile response and other sexual goals related to erectile responsiveness. The scale is applicable for men with or without partners. Lobitz and Baker (1979) found this measure to be sensitive to group treatment for men without partners who were experiencing erection difficulties. Some convergent validity was demonstrated since the group members also reported significant decreases in the frequency of erection difficulties.

Data on reliability or discriminate validity were not presented. Price, Reynolds, Cohen, Anderson, and Schochet (1980) found that Lobitz and Baker's Goals for Sex Therapy scale discriminated between men who received group treatment and men who were placed on a waiting list.

Reynolds (1978) has developed a 24-item Erection Difficulty Questionnaire (EDQ). This measure includes items that directly reflect the occurrence of erection difficulties (e.g., "my penis remains hard enough for me to stay inside my partner until I ejaculate [reach orgasm]") and items that reflect attitudinal and behavioral reactions to the disorder (e.g., "my erection problem makes me feel like less of a man," or "because of my erection problem I avoid having sex with the same person more than once"). The EDQ has been found to be sensitive to men's group treatment (Price et al., 1980) and biofeedback training (Reynolds, 1980). Reynolds found significant correlations between pre–post change scores on the EDQ and client reports of both global improvement in erectile functioning and frequency of erection difficulties before and during intercourse.

Auerbach and Kilmann (1977) and Reynolds (1980) asked men to keep records of the number of coital attempts during which they attained and maintained a satisfactory erection until orgasm, as well as the total number of coital attempts. A success : experience ratio (Obler, 1973) was computed by dividing the number of successful coital attempts by the total number of attempts for each subject. Auerbach and Kilmann found that the reliability of this ratio was verified by independent records provided by the sexual partner. The success : experience ratio has been shown to be sensitive to treatment when it is computed at both pretreatment and post-treatment periods (Auerbach & Kilmann, 1977).

Projective techniques have not been used widely for treatment planning or outcome evaluation by sex therapists. Lobitz and Baker (1979) assessed changes in fantasy productions to 10 cards of the Thematic Apperception Test (TAT) following men's group treatment for erectile dysfunction. Advanced graduate students rated pre- and post-treatment fantasy productions on seven fantasy dimensions pertaining to sexuality, concept of self, view of females, and so on. The interrater reliability coefficient was .86. Lobitz and Baker found that their group members evidenced more positive and unconflicted attitudes in their fantasy productions following treatment. This study demonstrates the usefulness of projective techniques in assessing general changes in psychological functioning following sex therapy. However, the utility of projective tests for treatment planning has not been demonstrated.

BEHAVIORAL TREATMENT PROCEDURES

An important implication of the interactional systems approach to erectile dysfunction is that the system, including the erectile response and all of the behaviors, cognitions, and affects that enhance or inhibit arousal, can be altered by intervention at a number of different points (Hogan, 1978). It is not surprising, therefore, that the behavioral procedures that are utilized in the treatment of erectile dysfunction have focused on a wide variety of immediate treatment goals, such as the reduction of anxiety, the alleviation of performance concerns, the promotion of sexual assertiveness and effective communication, the reduction of sexual ignorance, the alteration of stereotyped beliefs and myths about male and female sexuality, the redirection of attention toward erotic stimuli, the refinement of sexual stimulation skills, and the direct elicitation and conditioning of erectile arousal. A summary of the reports of behavioral treatments for erectile dysfunction is provided in Table 1.

Systematic Desensitization

Wolpe (1958) advocates the use of systematic desensitization as a means of reducing anxiety in cases of erectile dysfunction. In classical systematic desensitization, the client initially learns to attain a state of deep muscular relaxation. Wolpe (1958) uses Jacobson's relaxation exercises (Jacobson, 1938), although a number of more easily learned relaxation procedures are currently available (Bernstein & Borkovec, 1973; Wolpe & Lazarus, 1966). Following relaxation training, the client is instructed to imagine a series of sexually relevant scenes while attempting to remain in the relaxed state. The scenes are preselected by the client and therapist as being relevant to fears the client is experiencing in sexual situations. Frequently, the content of the scenes refers to specific sexual behaviors (e.g., kissing while clothed, undressing, genital caressing, intercourse) or other aspects of the sexual encounter that elicit anxiety (e.g., fear of injury, disgust or fear of genitals). Scenes may also be developed from fears associated with nonsexual aspects of relationships that contribute indirectly to the erectile disorder (e.g., fear of rejection, fear of assertiveness with women, fear of meeting and communicating with potential partners). The scenes are hierarchically ranked and presented in order of increasing ability to arouse anxiety. No scene is presented until the client has imagined the previous scenes without reporting anxiety. When the client experiences anxiety, he nonverbally signals the therapist, who instructs the client to relax before returning to a scene that is lower on the anxiety hierarchy.

Table 1. *Summary of reports of behavioral treatments for erectile dysfunction.*

Author(s)	Date	Type of Report	No. Ss	Treatment(s)	Outcome	Follow-up	Comments	DQR
Wolpe	1958	Case series	1	System desensitization	Apparently cured	+ for 2 cases at 6–8 mos	Follow-up on others not reported	7
			7	In vivo desensitization	4 apparently cured 3 much improved			
Lazarus	1965	Case report	1	System desensitization	+	+ Unspecified	Masturbation encouraged	1½
Glick	1975	Case report	1	System desensitization	+	None		1½
Kockott et al.	1975	Control group	8	System desensitization	SD produced less subjective anxiety, but groups did not differ on improvement ratings	None	Unimproved Ss did better with modified Masters & Johnson technique	22½
			8	Routine advice & medication				
			8	Waiting list control				
Friedman	1968	Case series	10	System desensitization with methohexitone sodium	8 cured, 1 much improved, 1 slightly improved	+ 12 mo		1½
Friedman & Lipsedge	1971	Case series	19	System desensitization with methohexitone sodium	14 (74%) symptom-free or much improved	+ mean 19.4 mo	Results were at follow-up	6½
Bass	1974	Case report	1	System desensitization with fantasy as anxiety inhibitor	+	+ 6 mo		2
Lazarus	1961	Control group	2	Group system desensitization	Both Ss improved	Unspecified		17½
			3	Interpretive group therapy	None improved			
Auerbach & Kilmann	1977	Control group	8	Group system desensitization	SD group better on several measures	Maintained	Home relaxation encouraged	25½
			8	Group relaxation		3 mo		
Dengrove	1971	Case series	3	In vivo desensitization with medications	+ (3 of 3)	None		½

Study	Year	Design	N	Treatment	Outcome	Follow-up	Comments	Rating
Garfield et al.	1969	Case report	1	System desensitization In vivo desensitization Thought substitution	+	+ Unspecified		2
Jones & Park	1972	Case series	7	System desensitization In vivo desensitization	+ (6 of 7)	None		1½
Salzman	1969	Case report	1	System desensitization In vivo desensitization	+	+ 12 mo	Hypnosis for relaxation	2½
Masters & Johnson	1970	Case series	245	Masters & Johnson (in vivo sensate focus, communication training, & sex education)	59.4% of primary & 73.8% of secondary cases improved	+ (7 of 7) primary & 89% secondary 5 years		6½
			28	Masters & Johnson with surrogate partner	63.1% of primary & 77.8% of secondary cases improved	Not reported		1½
Lobitz et al.	1976	Case report	1	Masters & Johnson	+	+ 10 mo		9½
Lobitz & LoPiccolo	1972	Case series	6	Masters & Johnson weekly sessions	+ (4 of 6)	Unspecified 6 mo		9
Prochaska & Marzilli	1973	Case series	5	Masters & Johnson with single therapist	+ (4 of 5)	None		1½
Lansky & Davenport	1975	Case series	3	Masters & Johnson weekly sessions	− (1 case improved)	None	Two couples didn't complete exercises	½
Ansari	1976	Control group	16 21 18	Chemotherapy Modified Masters & Johnson Nonspecific therapy	No group differences	8 mo	Nonrandom assignment of Ss	8½
Sue	1978	Case report	1	In vivo desensitization	+	+		2

				(couple) Directed masturbation		6 mo		
LoPiccolo et al.	1972	Case report	1	In vivo desensitization (couple)	+	+		10
Wish	1975	Case series	2	Arousal reconditioning Thought stopping Thought substitution	+ (2 of 2)	6 mo None		½
Herman & Prewett	1974	Case report with reversal	1	Continuous erectile biofeedback	+	− 7 mo	Poor social skills	8
Csillag	1976	Comparison group	6 patients 6 volunteers	Erectile biofeedback	Patient group showed progressive improvement in lab; 5 of 6 showed clinical improvement	None		9
Reynolds	1980	Control group	10 10 10	Continuous plus film feedback Film feedback alone Noncontingent film	Film biofeedback enhanced erection in lab, but groups didn't differ in clinical outcome	+ (64%) 1 mo	Therapeutic value remains undemonstrated	24½
Zilbergeld	1975	Single group	6–7	Structured men's group	67% achieved goals; all benefited	+ 4 mo	No statistical verification	1½
Lobitz & Baker	1979	Single group	9	Structured men's group	Pre–post improvement in erectile functioning and attitudes	+ 4–9 mo		15
Price et al.	1980	Control group	7 7 7	Structured men's group Structured men's group (different therapists) Waiting-list control	Men's group Ss showed greater improvement on measures of satisfaction with erectile response and sexual behavior, but not in immediate changes in the frequency of erection difficulties	Same results at 6 weeks; at 6 months, 10 of 14 Ss in men's group reported improved erectile functioning		24

This summary includes only reports that provided separate outcome results for erectile dysfunction.

Wolpe (1958) contends that, as a result of the desensitization process, the client is conditioned to respond with relaxation to stimuli that previously elicited erection-inhibiting anxiety. The ultimate expectation is that the changes which occur in imagination will generalize to the client's actual sexual encounters.

Successful case studies in which individual clients were treated by classical systematic desensitization alone have been reported by Lazarus (1965), Wolpe (1958), Glick (1975). In a control-group evaluation, Kockott, Dittmar, and Nusselt (1975) found that subjects who received systematic desensitization rated themselves as experiencing less subjective anxiety in sexual situations than did subjects who received routine medication and advice or were placed on a waiting list. Statistical analysis of changes in erectile behavior was not conducted, but descriptive statistics indicated that erection behavior increased for both the desensitization therapy and medication-advice therapy groups and decreased for the waiting-list group. However, clinical outcome ratings for the three groups did not differ significantly. The authors concluded that systematic desensitization shows limited therapeutic effect when used alone. Although this study was reasonably well controlled, it is the only negative-outcome report in the literature; the small sample size (N = 8 per group) may have resulted in reduced power to detect real differences, at least between the desensitization and waiting-list groups.

The classical systematic desensitization paradigm has been modified successfully in a number of clinical studies. Friedman (1968) attempted to maximize muscular relaxation by intravenously administering methohexital sodium during scene presentation in desensitization. Friedman also used a standard scene hierarchy for all clients. The hierarchy items ranged from hand-holding to extended intercourse. His criterion for cure was the "ability to have sexual intercourse which was satisfying to both partners without erective or ejaculatory problems" (Friedman, 1968, p. 258). Friedman reported that 8 of 10 treated clients had maintained a cure at a 12-month follow-up. Friedman and Lipsedge (1971) reported that 14 of 19 (74 percent) additional clients were symptom-free or much improved following methohexitone-assisted desensitization.

Systematic desensitization also has been applied in a group therapy format (Auerbach & Kilmann, 1977; Lazarus, 1961). In both of these studies, standardized hierarchies concerning anxiety-arousing aspects of sexual encounters were delivered to several clients at the same time. The pace of the desensitization procedure was determined by the "slower" subject; the therapist withdrew a hierarchy item whenever any subject reported anxiety. Lazarus (1961) compared group desensitization with interpretive group therapy for a variety of phobic disorders;

only five subjects were actually treated for erectile problems. The interpretive group therapy was designed to encourage the personal exploration of emotions, interpersonal relationships, and group dynamics, and the relationship between these factors and the erectile difficulties. Lazarus found that the two men who received group desensitization but none of the three men who received interpretive group therapy were rated as recovered. A recovery referred only to complete absence of the erectile disturbance and not to slight or moderate symptomatic improvement or personality change in the absence of erectile improvement. In one of the better controlled-outcome studies in the sex therapy literature, Auerbach and Kilmann (1977) compared group systematic desensitization with an attention-placebo control condition. The systematic desensitization group received 15 45-minute sessions of relaxation plus exposure to a composite group hierarchy of sexual scenes. The control group received 15 sessions of relaxation alone. Both groups were instructed to practice daily relaxation at home. The desensitization subjects reported an improvement of over 40 percent on the success-experience ratio (Obler, 1973), and the control subjects reported a 3 percent improvement. The desensitization subjects also reported significantly greater satisfaction with nonsexual aspects of their relationship with the most frequent partner. These differences were maintained over a 3-month follow-up period. Auerbach and Kilmann concluded that the hierarchy component of desensitization was the critical variable that produced the differential outcome for the two conditions, and the effectiveness of desensitization was not a function of placebo factors.

Bass (1974) has reported on the use of fantasy-elicited sexual arousal as an alternative anxiety inhibitor in systematic desensitization. His client was a 24-year-old single college student who experienced erectile dysfunction during initial encounters with each new sexual partner. Bass created a hierarchy of items that depicted the client with a number of different women in anxiety-arousing situations. The major dimensions of the hierarchy concerned the perceived sexual experience of the woman and the number of previous unsuccessful attempts the client had experienced with her. Actual incidents from the client's life were built into the hierarchy. Traditional systematic desensitization could not be completed because the client was unable to maintain sufficient relaxation. Bass, therefore, encouraged the client to recall sexual fantasies that he previously had experienced during masturbation or intercourse. For each fantasy, the client suggested a basic theme that was then elaborated by the therapist during treatment. Thus, sexually arousing scenes rather than relaxation were interposed between the anxiety hierarchy items. The client progressed through the 20-item hierarchy in five sessions. A 6-month follow-up revealed that he had maintained erection throughout intercourse during the initial encounter with two new partners and had not experienced further episodes of erectile dysfunction.

Physical stimulation, rather than fantasy, can be used to elicit sexual arousal as an anxiety inhibitor in desensitization. Although he does not describe his procedures in desensitization terms, Zilbergeld (1978) suggests a series of individual exercises in which the client is instructed to masturbate while attending solely to penile sensations or while fantasizing a number of sexual experiences that commonly elicit anxiety.

1. *Losing and regaining erection.*
The client is instructed to masturbate while focusing on penile sensations. After the client attains an erection, he is instructed to stop stimulation and to think about something that is nonsexual. He is instructed to resume masturbation only after the penis becomes completely flaccid. When the erection returns, he is again asked to stop stimulation. If the erection does not return after the resumption of stimulation, the client is asked to get into a more relaxed and sexier frame of mind (e.g., by recalling a good sexual experience, looking at erotic pictures or literature, etc.). The exercise is repeated until the client is confident that an erection can often be regained by the proper atmosphere and stimulation.

2. *Masturbation with Fantasy of Sex with a Partner.*
The client is instructed to masturbate while fantasizing a sexual experience with a partner. The fantasy starts with the first touch or kiss and slowly progresses through all of the activities that might occur in the encounter. If the client experiences anxiety, he is asked to become more relaxed and to imagine himself becoming more relaxed in the fantasized encounter. Masturbation is resumed when the anxiety subsides. This exercise is repeated until the client can fantasize all of the possible activities of a sexual experience.

3. Masturbating with fantasy of losing and regaining erection.
The client is instructed to masturbate while fantasizing that he loses his erection at the point where erection loss has occurred in the past. He is asked to imagine vividly what he and his partner are doing at this point. He is instructed to stop masturbating and to imagine himself doing something to get more comfortable, e.g., asking for a massage, holding his partner, talking, etc. He then resumes masturbation while imagining himself asking for a certain kind of stimulation that he needs or telling his partner what he is feeling. He finally pictures himself getting what he needs to become more aroused and visualizes himself regaining erection and having a good time.

4. *Masturbation with fantasy of no erection.*
The client is instructed to masturbate while fantasizing that he does not get an erection or loses the erection. He is then asked to stop masturbating

and to imagine that he gets all of the conditions and types of stimulation that he prefers but still does not experience erection. He then imagines that he is accepting the fact that he is not going to have an erection. He imagines himself telling his partner this and then imagines himself doing whatever would make the experience an enjoyable one for himself and his partner. At that point he should resume masturbation.

Zilbergeld's exercises reflect a coping model of desensitization, in which the client imagines himself experiencing the difficulties and negative emotions associated with the erectile disorder and then imagines himself coping effectively with the anxiety-arousing situation.

In Vivo Desensitization

There have been several reports of the use of in vivo desensitization in the individual treatment of erectile dysfunction (Dengrove, 1971; Wolpe, 1958; Wolpe & Lazarus, 1966). In vivo desensitization differs from systematic desensitization in that the progressive presentation of situations that have previously aroused fear are behaviorally experienced in the client's natural environment rather than in imagination. Sexual arousal responses that are elicited by self-stimulation and/or stimulation provided by a partner are used to inhibit anxiety in in vivo desensitization. Systematic exposure to the anxiety hierarchy occurs through the assignment of a series of sexual activities that begin with behaviors far removed from intercourse and gradually progress toward coitus. Wolpe (1958) provided the following instructions for the use of sexual responses in the in vivo treatment of erectile problems:

> The patient is told to inform his sexual partner (quoting the therapist if necessary) that his sexual difficulties are due to absurd but automatic fears in the sexual situation, and that he will overcome them if she will help him, i.e., if she will participate on a few occasions in situations of great sexual closeness without expecting intercourse or exerting pressure toward it. He is to ask her to be patient and affectionate and not to criticize. Assured of her cooperation, he is to lie in bed with her in the nude in a perfectly easy, relaxed way, and thereafter to do just what he feels like doing *and no more.* He has no duty at any stage to reach any criterion of performance. It is found that from one love session to the next there is a decrease in anxiety and an increase in sexual excitation and therefore in the extent of the caresses to which the patient feels impelled. He has increasingly strong erections and usually after a few sessions coitus is accomplished and then gradually improves (p. 131)

Wolpe (1958) reported outcome results for seven men treated with in vivo desensitization utilizing sexual responses as anxiety inhibitors. Six men were rated as "apparently cured" and one man was rated as "much improved." Dengrove (1971) briefly described 3 successful cases in which in vivo desensitization was combined with chemotherapy designed to enhance relaxation. Wolpe and Lazarus (1966) reported on a series of 31 cases of male sexual inadequacy. Twenty-one cases (68 percent) were judged to have "achieved entirely satisfactory sexual performance" (p. 112), and another 6 cases (19 percent) were rated as able "to function at a level sufficiently improved to be acceptable to their sexual partners" (p. 112). However, Wolpe and Lazarus (1966) did not report separate results for erectile dysfunction.

In vivo desensitization has been combined with imaginal desensitization in several studies (Garfield, McBrearty, & Dichter, 1969; Jones & Park, 1972; Obler, 1973; Salzman, 1969). The clients in these studies were specifically instructed to practice with their partners only the items (i.e., sexual behaviors) that successfully had been imagined without anxiety during the systematic desensitization sessions. The sexual situations that were encountered during in vivo exercises were slightly lower on the anxiety hierarchy than those encountered during imaginal desensitization. Garfield et al. (1969) and Salzman (1969) reported successful single-case studies using this treatment combination. Jones and Park (1972) reported that six of seven men were "restored to coital competence" (p. 472) in a mean of seven sessions in which systematic desensitization utilizing methohexital sodium-induced relaxation was combined with home practice of desensitized sexual interactions. Obler (1973) additionally utilized graphic aids (films and slides of sexual encounters) that portrayed the subject's sexual dysfunction during the imaginal desensitization sessions. The aids were introduced at a point in the hierarchy when the subject had difficulty imagining a particular item (e.g., imagining himself being unable to maintain an erection during intercourse). The aids portrayed difficulties consistent with the subject's actually experienced anxieties during a given week (e.g., inability to achieve vaginal penetration). Obler (1973) found that this combination of systematic desensitization and *in vivo* instructions was significantly more successful in eliminating a variety of male and female sexual dysfunctions and reducing associated anxieties than psychoanalytically oriented group treatment or an untreated control condition. Unfortunately, Obler (1973) pooled the data and separate results for erectile dysfunction were not reported.

Couple Sex Therapy

The *in vivo* practice of graduated sexual activities is also one major component of the brief couple therapy approaches to erectile dysfunction that have been modeled after the pioneering treatment research of

Masters and Johnson (1970). Couples who participate in the Masters and Johnson program attend daily sessions over a 2-week treatment period. The couple is seen by a therapy team that includes both a male and female therapist. The treatment format consists of educational presentations, discussions, and couple exercises that are designed to alleviate sexual performance concerns, dispel sexual misconceptions, and promote new forms of verbal and nonverbal communication.

The specific couple exercises in the Masters and Johnson approach are designed to allow the couple "to think and feel sexually without orientation to performance" (Masters & Johnson, 1970, p. 202). The couple is directed to avoid attempts at coitus during the initial days of treatment. Instead, the couple is instructed to engage in a series of "sensate focus" activities (p. 201) that are assigned in a sequence involving gradual increase in sexual intimacy. Initially, the partners are instructed to take turns caressing areas of the body other than the genitals or breasts. Masters and Johnson report that many men experience erections during these nondemand exercises. However, such an occurrence is important only in illustrating to the couple that erection cannot and need not be achieved by conscious effort, and the couple is instructed to resist any pressure to proceed to intercourse. The couple is subsequently instructed to include mutual manual stimulation of the genitals as part of the sensate focus activity. The receiver provides verbal and nonverbal feedback to the giver concerning preferences in the positioning, pressure, direction, and rapidity of the genital caresses. This exercise is designed to increase effective stimulation and to insure that the male attends to the giving and receiving of erotic input rather than to erectile performance. However, once the couple has experienced the maintenance of full erection during the early sensate activities, they are instructed to engage in "teasing technique" exercises (p. 206) in which periods of intense genital stimulation are alternated with periods during which penile stimulation is not provided. This exercise is designed to demonstrate to the couple that there is no impairment in the erectile response to effective stimulation and to alleviate the common fear that a loss of erection will not be followed by its return. Coital activities are usually added to the sensate focus exercises in the second week of treatment. Initially the couple is instructed to maintain vaginal containment after intromission without additional stimulation or pelvic thrusting. Vaginal containment begins in the female superior position, and the female partner controls penile insertion. The responsibility for intromission is removed from the male in order to reduce possible sources of performance distraction. After several intromissions have enhanced erectile security, the female is instructed to engage in slow pelvic movements while the male remains motionless. When the male is subsequently directed to begin his own pelvic movements, he is reminded to attend to the giving and receiving of sensate pleasure. Masters and Johnson never formally instruct a couple to resume intercourse as a final exercise. Instead, the couple is encouraged to approach more spontaneous sexual activity with a continued emphasis on mutual intimacy, communication, and pleasuring rather than on erection or orgasm.

Masters and Johnson (1970) reported an initial success rate of 59.4 percent for 32 men who had never completed intercourse because of erectile dysfunction (primary erectile dysfunction) and 73.8 percent for men who had a previous history of successful sexual functioning prior to the development of the erectile disorder (secondary erectile dysfunction). Five-year follow-up evaluations on some of the couples revealed that none of seven couples who were successfully treated for primary erectile dysfunction experienced a return of erectile dysfunction, and 11 percent of the 90 couples with secondary erectile dysfunction experienced a return of the disorder.

Masters and Johnson (1970) utilized surrogate partners in the treatment of 28 men with erectile dysfunction who were unmarried and did not have partners who were willing to participate in therapy. The surrogate partners were volunteers who were carefully screened and trained by Masters and Johnson's staff. The surrogate partners did not attend the daily therapy sessions, but they participated with the client in the full range of between-session sensual activities, including sexual intercourse in many cases. The outcome results for men treated with the aid of a surrogate partner equalled those achieved by cooperative wives and husbands in marital-unit referrals. Masters and Johnson have subsequently discontinued the use of surrogates, partly because of the hazy legal status of this approach. (See the section on ethical and legal issues.)

The Masters and Johnson treatment format was used in a successful case study by Lobitz, LoPiccolo, Lobitz, and Brockway (1976) and is reviewed in detail later in this chapter. Lobitz and LoPiccolo (1972) also successfully treated four of six cases of erectile dysfunction in a modified Masters and Johnson program in which the couples were seen once a week for 15 weeks. Prochaska and Marzilli (1973) reported that four of five men with secondary erectile dysfunction responded favorably when treated by a single male therapist using the weekly-session format. Positive results with the weekly-session variation for a variety of sexual dysfunctions also have been reported by Kaplan (1974), McCarthy (1973), and Meyer, Schmidt, Lucas, and Smith (1975), but these authors did not provide separate statistical results for erectile dysfunction. Negative results were reported by Lansky and Davenport (1975) and Ansari (1976). Lansky and Davenport (1975) reported that only one of three couples improved, but they also reported that the two couples who didn't improve also never attempted the *in vivo* sexual exercises. Ansari (1976) reported on a series of 55 men who received either a modified Masters and Johnson program (biweekly sessions with a single therapist), chemotherapy directed at anxiety reduction, or nonspecific therapy. The three treatment groups did not differ at post-treatment or at an 8-month follow-up. However, Ansari also reported that the assignment of subjects to groups was not random and men without partners who were willing to participate in therapy could not be assigned to the Masters and Johnson condition. Inspection of Ansari's data suggests that the percentage of subjects with acute-onset erectile dysfunction, which was found to be a significant indicator of successful outcome, was disproportionately low in the Masters and Johnson group in comparison with the other groups. These methodological weaknesses prohibit the unequivocable interpretation of Ansari's (1976) results.

Sue (1978) has recently reported a successful case study in which directed masturbation was systematically employed in the hierarchy of *in vivo* desensitization exercises carried out in couple therapy. A 24-year-old male who had never completed intercourse because of erection difficulties was instructed to think about his most erotic fantasies during masturbation in the presence of his partner. The desensitization hierarchy included the following behavioral steps:

1. Male and female lying in bed. Male masturbates to orgasm on his side, facing away from the female.
2. Male masturbates in side position. When near orgasm, he signals his partner (touching her) who caresses him from behind. Orgasm occurs.
3. Male masturbates in side position and signals his partner to caress him earlier in the orgasmic sequence.
4. Male masturbates to orgasm with his partner kissing him and caressing him from the beginning.
5. Male masturbates in side position. When near orgasm he signals his partner who masturbates him to orgasm.
6. Female partner masturbates male to orgasm earlier in the sequence.
7. Female masturbates male to orgasm without any assistance.
8. Female masturbating male who is on his back. When near orgasm, she adopts the female superior position and places his penis in her vagina.
9. Female masturbates male and places his penis in her vagina earlier in the sequence and moves until orgasm occurs.

10. After arousal, male initiates sexual intercourse, moving until orgasm.
11. Male initiates sexual intercourse, moving until orgasm.

The couple practiced these exercises five days a week. The client also was instructed not to masturbate outside of these practice sessions and to continue to provide oral and manual stimulation for his partner's orgasmic release. The couple reported their first instance of successful sexual intercourse after three weeks of the exercises, and the client reported no further erectile difficulties by the end of a 6-month follow-up.

Given that men with partners can be treated with either some form of imaginal desensitization or a variant of the *in vivo* couple exercises (e.g., Masters & Johnson, 1970; Sue, 1978), the question arises as to which is the treatment of choice. The available evidence is not conclusive but does suggest that the directed practice of *in vivo* exercises may hold greater promise of treatment success than imaginal procedures (Kockott et al., 1975; Mathews, Bancroft, Whitehead, Hackmann, Julier, Bancroft, Gath, & Shaw, 1976). In the Kockott et al. (1975) study discussed earlier, 8 of 12 patients who had shown no improvement following imaginal desensitization, medication-advice, or a waiting-list condition were cured or improved when subsequently treated with a modification of the Masters and Johnson procedures. More convincing evidence comes from the study by Mathews et al. (1976) in which couples with a variety of sexual dysfunctions were treated with systematic desensitization plus counseling, directed practice plus counseling, or directed practice with minimal therapist contact. The group differences were not highly significant, but trends in the outcome results consistently suggested that the combination of directed practice and counseling produced the most clinical improvement, particularly when a dual-sex therapy team was used instead of a single therapist. Separate results for erectile dysfunction were not reported, but the authors stated that the type of dysfunction treated was not associated with outcome.

Although available evidence suggests that *in vivo* exercises should be used when possible, Wish (1975) has pointed out that there are situations in which it is impossible or inadvisable to rely on the *in vivo* approach. For example, the fear of failure or rejection may be so intense that the individual is unable to take even the initial steps in the *in vivo* exercises. The imaginal procedures can then be used to prepare the client for in vivo exercises by having him overcome anxieties through the progressive presentation of imagined stimuli apart from the natural sexual setting. Imaginal procedures also become a main therapeutic tool for clients who do not have a steady relationship with a sexual partner who is willing to participate in the *in vivo* exercises.

Arousal Reconditioning

Arousal reconditioning procedures may be helpful in cases of erectile dysfunction in which the client reports deficits in sexual arousal in specific situations or with particular partners or types of partners. McGuire, Carlisle, and Young (1965) have suggested that orgasm during masturbation is the reinforcer that conditions sexual arousal to the fantasy content or other stimuli during masturbation. LoPiccolo, Stewart, and Watkins (1972) made use of this principle in their treatment of a couple whose presenting problems were the male's lack of sexual arousal to his mate, in addition to erectile dysfunction and delayed ejaculation. The male had been an overt homosexual since early adolescence. The couple did not want to eliminate his homosexuality, but they did want to enhance his heterosexual arousal. The arousal reconditioning procedure began with directed masturbation, during which the male was instructed to use his usual homosexual fantasies to attain erection and approach orgasm. At the instant of orgasm, however, he was instructed to switch to fantasies of sexual relations with his mate. Pictures of his partner were initially used to facilitate his visualization of heterosexual stimuli during masturbation. The timing of the switch from homosexual to heterosexual fantasy was gradually moved back from the point of orgasm, and the client was eventually able to use exclusively heterosexual fantasy, without the aid of the pictures, during the entire masturbatory sequence. The fantasy-switching procedure was then incorporated into the couple's *in vivo* desensitization exercises. The male was again instructed to use homosexual fantasies to facilitate arousal, but to return his focus frequently to what he and his partner were actually doing during the encounter and always to switch his focus to the heterosexual reality just prior to orgasm. He eventually came to be highly aroused while focusing exclusively on the heterosexual reality. At termination, the male was able to maintain erection and to ejaculate intravaginally on virtually every occasion solely through the use of heterosexual fantasies and activities. The treatment gains were maintained at 6-month follow-up.

Thought Stopping

Thought stopping and thought substitution procedures (Wolpe, 1958) have been used to inhibit recurrent negative and distracting thoughts experienced by men with erectile dysfunction (Garfield et al., 1969;

Wish, 1975). The negative thoughts not only elicit anxiety but distract the client from the full reception of erotic input. The client who is trained in thought stopping is instructed to imagine an anxiety-arousing thought. When he nonverbally indicates that he has clearly imagined the thought, the therapist shouts "STOP." This procedure is repeated for several trials, and the client is subsequently instructed to block the thoughts by subvocally yelling "stop" whenever he begins to experience the negative cognitions. Wish (1975) reported a case study in which a man with erectile difficulties practiced thought stopping whenever he began to think negatively about his ability to obtain an erection. Wish (1975) reported another case in which thought stopping for concerns about sexual adequacy and penis size was interspersed with the active substitution of more positive thoughts (e.g., "I'm as good at sex as the next guy"). The client treated with desensitization by Garfield et al. (1969) was also trained to use thought stopping and substitution whenever he became preoccupied with his partner's orgasm (e.g., "no, I will not think of that; I will think of enjoying myself"). Wish (1975) also suggested that thought stopping may be helpful in cases in which the client is distracted by extraneous thoughts during sex, such as by concerns about work.

Biofeedback Training

Biofeedback training may be used as an alternative means of teaching clients to attend to the thoughts or feelings that facilitate erection. The measurement of penile erection for biofeedback training can be accomplished by using a mercury strain gauge, described earlier in the discussion of nocturnal tumescence monitoring. The small voltage changes that occur as the gauge is stretched can activate visual or auditory biofeedback devices (e.g., meters, lights, clicks, tones, projectors) which provide the client with immediate feedback concerning small changes in penile diameter. The client might receive continuous or analogue feedback, in which minute increases or decreases in penile tumescence produce analogous changes in the intensity of feedback such as lights or frequency of auditory clicks. Alternatively, or additionally, the client can receive discrete feedback (e.g., tone on versus tone off) that indicates the occurrence of less frequent and relatively large changes in his erectile response. The use of discrete feedback for erectile responses of predetermined magnitude permits the reinforcement and shaping of penile tumescence changes.

Herman and Prewett (1974) conducted a single-subject evaluation of biofeedback training with a 51-year-old male who had never achieved or maintained an erection for more than a few minutes during heterosexual and homosexual encounters. The authors found that the client's erection response to both female and male slides significantly increased during 16 sessions that included contingent analogue feedback, decreased when the feedback was administered noncontingently, and increased again when contingent feedback was reinstated. The changes in penile response during the different portions of the experiment were paralleled by changes in the client's ability to masturbate to orgasm, changes in masturbatory fantasy, and reported changes in homosexual and heterosexual arousal outside of the laboratory. The subject reported two successful sexual encounters near the end of the study. However, when the client was readmitted to the hospital seven months later for medical complications connected with excessive drinking, it was discovered that his erectile response had returned to baseline levels. The client reported that the drinking and a cessation of fantasy and overt sexual behavior began after he was jilted in a homosexual affair. Herman and Prewett cautioned that treatments designed to increase physiological arousal must be combined with efforts to insure that the client has sufficient social skills to implement the arousal.

Csillag (1976) conducted the first comparison group evaluation of biofeedback training for erectile dysfunction. Six men with erectile dysfunction and six volunteers without erection difficulties received 16 sessions of erectile feedback training over an 8-day period. Csillag (1976) found that the increase in erectile response was much greater for the nonpatient subjects than for the patient subjects during the initial treatment sessions. The amount of daily erectile increase for the nonpatients dropped progressively as treatment continued, however, while the patient group demonstrated steadily increasing erectile changes. The clinical evaluation revealed that five of the six patient subjects reported improvement in erectile functioning outside of the laboratory.

Reynolds (1980) conducted a laboratory and clinical evaluation of biofeedback training that included procedures designed to control for such nonspecific treatment factors as repeated exposure to external erotic stimuli (e.g., films, slides) and desensitization to the laboratory task. Thirty men with psychogenic erectile dysfunction were instructed to "concentrate on the thoughts, feelings, or fantasies that allow erection to occur" during one baseline session and four training sessions. The subjects were randomly assigned to three treatment groups that differed in the type of erectile feedback provided during training. One group received continuous visual and auditory feedback of erectile changes in addition to 90-sec segments of erotic films that were delivered contingent upon progressive increases in erectile response. A second group received the contingent erotic film segments but did not receive continuous feedback. The third group received the same number of erotic film segments, but the film segments were delivered on a noncontingent basis. The training trials of each session were followed by an evaluation period, during which the subjects again were instructed to facilitate erection but were not exposed to feedback or film segments. Reynolds found that the subjects who received the film segments on a noncontingent basis showed greater erectile increases than subjects in the contingent feedback groups during early trials of the initial training sessions, perhaps because of a less implicit demand for erectile performance. However, subjects who had received contingent film alone showed greater erectile increases during the evaluation periods than subjects who had received contingent film plus continuous feedback or noncontingent film. These findings raise some doubt about the value of continuous erectile feedback, but the results indicate that contingent, erotic film feedback may enhance the voluntary facilitation of erection in men with erectile dysfunction. However, Reynolds also found that although there was significant improvement from the pretraining to a 6-week clinical follow-up evaluation on a number of self-report measures concerning erectile functioning outside of the laboratory, the three treatment groups did not differ on the outcome measures. The amount of clinical improvement reported by the combined groups of subjects appeared to justify further evaluation of erection facilitation-training procedures. Reynolds suggests that future treatment formats might include modifications designed to reduce possible sources of performance anxiety in the laboratory. For example, clients might initially receive noncontingent erotic stimuli and then be introduced to the contingent stimulus conditions. Alternatively, clients could receive erotic stimulation that would be contingent upon changes in the erectile response without receiving explicit instructions concerning the contingency involved. Finally, Reynolds suggests that further applications of biofeedback treatment for erectile dysfunction should be combined with other sex therapy procedures designed to promote changes in sexual knowledge, beliefs, and attitudes.

Attitude Restructuring

There has been increasing recognition that common erroneous beliefs about male and female sexuality contribute to erectile dysfunction by increasing the client's anxiety and/or despair that he is not living up to a presumed standard of male adequacy. The client's performance anxiety may be increased during sexual encounters if he maintains an underlying belief that neither he nor his partner can have a satisfying sexual relationship because he doesn't live up to such a standard and his relationships are therefore doomed to fail unless he can come to function like the stereotyped models of male adequacy portrayed in both pornographic and nonpornographic media. Masters and Johnson (1970) state that one of their major treatment goals is to dispel sexual misconceptions, and they discuss their educational approaches to misconceptions concerning penis size, the role of clitoral versus vaginal stimulation for female satisfaction, and the effect of attempting to will an erection. Zilbergeld (1978) has written a self-help guide that includes several chapters concerning the fantasy model of male adequacy. His book includes a detailed presentation and exploration of 10 common myths about male adequacy:

1. Men should not have, or at least not express, certain feelings.
2. In sex, as elsewhere, it's performance that counts.
3. The man must take charge of and orchestrate sex.
4. A man always wants and is always ready to have sex.
5. All physical contact must lead to sex.
6. Sex equals intercourse.
7. Sex requires an erection.
8. Good sex is a linear progression of increasing excitement terminated only by orgasm (the myth of the hard-driving fuck).
9. Sex should be natural and spontaneous.
10. In this enlightened age, the preceding myths no longer have any influence on us.

I was unable to find any research reports in which the presentation and exploration of beliefs about male and female sexuality was the only intervention in the treatment of erection difficulties. However, in my own clinical experience, the exploration and restructuring of attitudes concerning male and female adequacy is an important treatment component.

Structured Group Treatment for Men without Partners

There have been three reports concerning the use of structured men's group therapy for men with erectile dysfunction who do not have steady relationships with a sexual partner (Lobitz & Baker, 1979; Price et al., 1980; Zilbergeld, 1975). The group format was similar in these three studies. A group of seven to eight men met with two therapists for 8 to 12 sessions. Zilbergeld and Price et al. included a female cotherapist at all treatment sessions, and Lobitz and Baker had three female therapists attend a single session. The group treatment formats included didactic presentations, group discussions, and homework exercises. The didactic presentations and discussions concerned male and female sexual response, myths and realities of male and female sexuality, sexual assertion (e.g., saying "no" to a sexual request, asking for needed stimulation), effective sexual communication, and suggested exercises and activities to be used when the man became involved in a relationship. Zilbergeld and Lobitz and Baker also utilized role playing among the members or between the members and the female therapist concerning self-disclosure and sexual assertion. For example, Zilbergeld had members divide into pairs to practice reacting to 15 to 20 situations that men often have trouble with, such as "being asked to make love by a date who you like but who you don't feel ready to have sex with," "being stimulated in a way that is uncomfortable or displeasing," and "asking to stop in the middle of love play or intercourse." The homework exercises in the three studies included individually administered sensate focus experiences, a sequence of directed masturbation experiences (e.g., "tease technique," masturbation with fantasy, and masturbation while imagining progressive sexual activities), and role plays to be practiced alone or with another person. The initial portion of each session was used to assess each member's experience with the previous homework assignment, and a new assignment was provided at the end of each session.

The results of these three studies suggest that the structured men's group procedures show considerable promise as a multifaceted treatment approach for men without partners. Zilbergeld (1975) reported that two-thirds of his clients felt that they had completely achieved their goals by the end of therapy. Zilbergeld did not provide more precise data concerning outcome, and his subjects included men who were experiencing erectile dysfunction and/or premature ejaculation. Lobitz and Baker (1979) reported that both the frequency of erectile difficulties and the scores on the Goals for Sex Therapy questionnaire were significantly improved following group treatment. The incidence of erection difficulties was further reduced at the 4- to 9-month follow-up. The three men who did not report a change in erectile functioning also did not once attempt intercourse during the post-treatment or follow-up periods. Price et al. (1980) compared two men's groups with different dual-sex therapy teams against a waiting-list control group. Subjects in the men's groups reported greater improvement than the control subjects on the Goals for Sex Therapy questionnaire, on the Erection Difficulty Questionnaire, and on a variety of other self-report attitudinal measures at both post-treatment and 6-week follow-up periods. The men's group subjects also reported greater satisfaction than control subjects with changes in their erectile functioning, changes in sexual self-esteem, and changes in general self-esteem. The reported change in the actual frequency of erection difficulties did not differ between the group treatment and waiting-list groups at the post-treatment or 6-week follow-up evaluations. Price et al. noted that the great majority of their treated clients did not find a sexual partner during the brief follow-up period, thereby reducing the possibility for treatment effectiveness to be demonstrated. However, Price et al. conducted a second follow-up evaluation at six months post-treatment for the 14 subjects who were in the men's groups. (Control subjects were already in treatment at this period.) Eleven of these 14 subjects (79 percent) had maintained sufficient erection to complete inter-course on at least one occasion during the 6-month follow-up, and 10 subjects (71 percent) reported improvement in their level of satis-faction with the changes in erectile functioning. The authors currently are conducting additional studies using group treatment formats that include greater emphasis on social skills training in order to enable clients to feel more secure about getting involved in heterosexual relationships following treatment.

CLINICAL PRESCRIPTION

The clinician's initial task in working with a client who experiences erectile difficulties is to obtain sufficient medical information about the client to rule out the possibility that the erectile disorder is associated with physical illness, injuries, or prescribed or nonprescribed drug use. Erectile dysfunction can be the initial symptom of previously undiag-nosed conditions (e.g., diabetes mellitus, multiple sclerosis) that re-quire immediate medical treatment. If the client is experiencing other psychiatric conditions that frequently are associated with erection difficulties (e.g., depression, marital discord, alcoholism, psychosis, severely deficient social skills), the clinician will need to determine whether these conditions are severe enough to interfere with the client's full participation in sex therapy and whether treatment of these con-ditions should be initiated prior to sex therapy.

In order to develop a treatment plan, the clinician will need to identify the psychological factors that are inhibiting the erectile re-sponse. It is useful to obtain a detailed behavioral description of the sexual interactions in which the dysfunction occurs; the conditions under which sex is attempted; and the behavioral, cognitive, and affective antecedents and consequences of the occurrence of erectile failure. The clinician should routinely assess the client's level of per-formance anxiety, misconceptions about male or female sexuality, adequacy of physical and psychological stimulation, and ability and willingness to communicate social and sexual needs to a partner. If the client has a current partner, the clinician will need to assess the partner's level of sexual satisfaction in the relationship as well as her usual reaction to the erectile difficulties. Particular attention should be paid to previously attempted treatments and to any conditions that appear to improve or disrupt the client's erectile functioning.

Not all clients will require a formal course of sex therapy. The erectile functioning of some men will improve if they are merely given permission (e.g., to engage or not engage in particular sexual activities), limited information (e.g., about penis size, erectile changes associated with age), and specific suggestions (e.g., only have sex when you are rested and relaxed, have your partner or yourself provide more direct stimulation of the penis) (Annon, 1974).

Some form of graduated *in vivo desensitization* exercises are recommended for clients who have partners and who require more intensive sex therapy. The couple's exercises may include sensate focus activities or a progressive series of directed masturbation activities.

Imaginal desensitization experiences may be helpful for men who do not have partners willing to participate in therapy and for men whose anxiety is so intense as to prevent success in even the initial steps in the *in vivo* approach. Traditional relaxation exercises may be used in desensitization; however, directed masturbation or directed sexual fantasy may be preferable anxiety inhibitors.

Arousal reconditioning procedures can be combined with *in vivo* and/or imaginal desensitization for clients who experience deficits in sexual arousal in specific situations or with particular partners or types of partners. Biofeedback training may help the client attend more fully to what is already arousing to him.

Thought stopping and thought substitution can be used to inhibit recurrent negative thoughts that occur prior to or during the sexual encounter and distract the client from the reception of erotic input. The disruptive power of such negative thoughts can be further reduced, however, via educational and attitude restructuring efforts designed to dispel stereotyped beliefs about male sexual adequacy. Basic education concerning male and female sexual response also promotes the reduction of performance anxiety.

Men with and without partners can benefit from sexual assertiveness and communication training. These procedures are particularly helpful for men who are unable to refuse an unwanted sexual request or who have difficulty with communicating their sexual needs and preferences to a partner. Role play procedures may be useful here.

The interaction of a number of behavioral, cognitive, and affective factors that influence erectile functioning has been stressed throughout this chapter. It usually is appropriate to develop a broad-spectrum treatment plan that includes several of the interventions that have been described.

CASE REPORT

A case originally reported by Lobitz et al. (1976) illustrates the fact that behavioral treatment procedures cannot be administered in a cookbook fashion but must be modified in accordance with the particular client's sexual and nonsexual interactions and forms of resistance to treatment.

Case History

Mr. and Mrs. T were a married couple in their late 50s. Mr. T reported that he was sexually aroused by and attracted to his wife but invariably had been unable to achieve or maintain an erection during their 2-year marriage. Mr. T experienced no erectile difficulties during masturbation; however, Mrs. T was quite unwilling to manipulate Mr. T's genitals manually or orally because she found these activities mildly repugnant. Mrs. T was orgasmic in response to oral or manual stimulation but not during coitus. She had previously been married to a man who usually had an erection *before* beginning any overt sexual activities and never allowed Mrs. T to touch or manipulate his penis. At the time the couple entered treatment, Mrs. T was also clinically depressed, partly in response to her husband's erection difficulties but more centrally in response to Mr. T's impending unemployment due to a reorganization of his company.

Treatment

Mr. and Mrs. T were treated with a modified *in vivo* sex therapy program modeled after Masters and Johnson (1970). They were seen daily by a male–female co-therapy team. The first two sessions were devoted to intake and individual sexual-history taking. Treatment interventions began with the third session.

Session 3. The therapists explained the general dynamics of erectile dysfunction and pointed out that Mr. and Mrs. T both had unrealistic expectations regarding sexual functioning. Mr. T expected to perform as he had in the distant past, and Mrs. T expected her husband to have erections before beginnning sex and in the absence of direct penile stimulation. The male co-therapist revealed that he did not have erections before beginning sexual activity, and the female therapist emphasized the pleasure she obtained from caressing her husband's genitals. Mrs. T was negativistic during this discussion, and she became upset and started to cry when Mr. T was asked to repeat what he reported in the sexual history concerning his wife's hostile remarks about his sexual functioning and her demands for sexual performance. Mr. T made several conciliatory statements. Thus Mrs. T refused to accept her role in Mr. T's problem, and Mr. T refused to confront her. Mrs. T was eventually able to accept some responsibility when the therapists supported her by agreeing that her statements had never meant to be derogatory to Mr. T while insisting that whatever her intentions, the actual statements were quite harmful.

When the treatment strategy was outlined, Mrs. T expressed reservations about beginning because of her depression and busy social schedule. The male therapist simply agreed with Mrs. T, stating that the demands of treatment were probably beyond her present capabilities. Mrs. T then insisted that she could carry out treatment, the female therapist agreed, and the male therapist "reluctantly" allowed himself to be argued into beginning treatment. *Assignment:* full body massage excluding the genitals. All other sexual activity was forbidden, except masturbation if desired.

Session 4. The clients reported pleasure but little arousal during the assignment. *Assignment:* visual examination of the partner's body while massaging it (again excluding genitals) and talking continually about what they saw and felt about the various parts.

Session 5. To their great surprise, Mr. T experienced a partial erection. The therapists repeated that erection would occur naturally when Mr. T was not pressured to perform. *Assignment:* genital caressing was added to the previous assignment. Mr. T was instructed to avoid trying to have an erection or watching for one. He was simply to enjoy his wife's caressing of his flaccid penis.

Session 6. Mr. T was elated over having two brief erections, but Mrs. T reported feeling resentful since he was having erections now that intercourse was forbidden. Eventually, however, she verbalized pleasure that progress was being made. *Assignment:* teasing technique (described in review of Masters and Johnson, 1970).

Session 7. Mr. T experienced repeated erections during the teasing session. Mrs. T reported feeling no arousal, but also no repugnance, while touching Mr. T's penis. *Assignment:* Mrs. T should teach Mr. T how to manipulate her genitals as she did during masturbation. Mr. T was to have Mrs. T caress his genitals and to "try to maintain an erection for 5 to 10 minutes."

Session 8. The therapists regarded the second part of the previous assignment as a tactical blunder since they had placed specific performance demands on Mr. T. In fact, he experienced only three brief, partial erections during this assignment, and he reported feeling anxious and conscious of having to live up to the time expectation. The therapists reassured Mr. T by taking all the blame for his difficulties. However, Mr. T now clearly accepted the formulation concerning the role of performance demands in erectile dysfunction. *Assignment:* mutual caressing of genitals while assuming the body positions recommended by Masters and Johnson (1970). In one position the male sits behind the female and reaches around her to manipulate her genitals. In the other position, the male lies on his back while the female sits between his legs and caresses his genitals.

Session 9. Mr. T continued to experience difficulty in relaxing and focusing on sensation while receiving genital stimulation. However, he experienced full erection during the entire time he caressed Mrs. T's genitals while sitting behind her. They then resumed manual stimulation of his genitals, and he maintained full erection until ejaculation. *Assignment:* the couple was instructed to assume the female superior sitting position, and Mr. T was to place his penis at the entrance to her vagina, but not to insert it. The therapist stressed the fact that this assignment could be accomplished with a flaccid penis.

Session 10. Mr. T reported a strong erection when he caressed Mrs. T's genitals with his penis. The couple was unable to restrain themselves from inserting his penis and engaging in vigorous intercourse. However, they stopped before either of them climaxed. The therapists emphasized both the negative and positive features in this violation of the ban on intercourse. *Assignment:* vaginal containment. Mrs. T was instructed to "stuff" Mr. T's flaccid penis into her vagina. They were not to engage in pelvic thrusting. Since Mrs. T had not been orgasmic for several sessions, Mr. T was instructed to caress her genitals with the aid of a vibrator.

Session 11. Results continued to be positive for Mr. T. Insertion occurred with an erect penis. Mrs. T was still nonorgasmic during this period. *Assignment:* vaginal containment with slow pelvic thrusting but no ejaculation. Mrs. T was also given individual assignments concerning orgasmic functioning.

Session 12. Results were positive for Mr. T. *Assignment:* the couple was instructed to resume a normal sex life without restrictions. However, the therapists predicted to the couple that Mr. T would experience some erectile difficulty at first but this difficulty would be short-lived. The prediction was used to reduce demands for erectile performance further. If the man experiences erectile difficulty, he will be reassured by the prediction. If erection difficulties are not experienced, the man will be too elated by success to worry about the mistaken prediction.

Session 13. The clients engaged in vigorous intercourse until Mrs. T insisted that they stop (just before Mr. T's ejaculation) because she was "hot and tired." After a brief private consultation, the male therapist stated that he felt she was sabotaging the program and at some level did not want to resume a full sexual life with her husband. The male therapist indicated that he thought her statement about their home's lack of air conditioning was just an excuse, and he offered to prove it to Mrs. T by refunding a portion of their fee so that they could spend a weekend at an air-conditioned motel. The couple accepted this challenge.

Sessions 14 and 15. Mr. and Mrs. T reported successful intercourse on both days at a motel. Mr. T also manipulated Mrs. T to orgasm on several occasions. The final step was the development of a maintenance plan for the couple. The plan included lists of factors that contributed to difficulties, specific ways they had learned to correct the problems, and planned sexual activities for a follow-up period.

A variety of self-report measures at post-treatment and 3-month follow-up revealed that Mr. T had little or no trouble in maintaining erection and their sexual life was extremely gratifying to both partners. A 1-year follow-up revealed that these gains had been maintained until Mrs. T's untimely death from a stroke.

ETHICAL AND LEGAL ISSUES

There are currently no state or federal licensure or certification procedures for the practice of sex therapy. The American Association of Sex Educators, Counselors and Therapists (AASECT) certifies sex therapists on the basis of training, experience, and examination results, but this certification has no real legal status. However, the mental health professional who provides sex therapy services is required to operate in accordance with the guidelines provided within the ethics codes and license certification laws pertaining to his or her primary professional affiliation (e.g., psychology, psychiatry, or social work).

Three specific ethical-legal issues that directly pertain to the practice of sex therapy have recently received considerable attention. The first issue concerns erotic contact between the therapist and client. The ethics codes of both the American Psychological Association (APA) and AASECT explicitly prohibit sexual intercourse between the therapist and client, and there have been several court cases in which a therapist was charged with exploiting a client for purposes of the therapist's sexual gratification. The second issue concerns the use of surrogate partners. Since the surrogate receives a fee for engaging in sensual-sexual activities, the use of a surrogate could potentially involve the therapist, client, and surrogate in prostitution charges in spite of the fact that these activities are prescribed for therapeutic reasons. There have been no test cases in the courts concerning this practice, but the legal status of the surrogate approach remains unclear. Many universities specifically prohibit the use of surrogates in university-affiliated clinics, and the approach is generally limited to private practice settings. The third issue concerns differing value systems of the therapist and client. The ethics codes of the APA and AASECT again caution the therapist to avoid imposing his or her value system upon the client. For example, the sex therapist may work with clients whose ethics, upbringing, and values have led them to avoid particular forms of sexual expression. It is appropriate for the therapist to acknowledge the difference in values and even to make an explicit case on behalf of less inhibited behavior if a change in behavior is likely to lead to a more fulfilling sexual life for the client. However, the therapist is obligated to avoid instilling feelings of guilt or inadequacy on the part of the client concerning behaviors that are truly matters of personal choice.

SUGGESTIONS FOR CLINICAL AND EXPERIMENTAL RESEARCH

Clinical research concerning erectile dysfunction has progressed from unsubstantiated pronouncements to single-case reports, single treatment evaluations and, finally, the beginning of systematic control-group evaluations. Extensive discussion of methodological guidelines for future research can be found in several recent methological reviews

(Kilmann & Auerbach, 1978; Reynolds, 1977; Wright, Perreault, and Mathieu, 1977), and the present section focuses instead on suggestions concerning substantive areas for potential inquiry.

First of all, the treatment procedures subsumed under such rubrics as directive sex therapy, Masters and Johnson treatment, systematic desensitization, or men's group treatment obviously consist of a multitude of separate treatment components. Once a new treatment package has been shown to be effective in comparison with a grossly different alternative treatment or a form of no-treatment control condition, further component analysis research is needed to isolate the effective ingredients of the package. A good example of this type of research is Auerbach and Kilmann's (1977) demonstration that the sexual anxiety hierarchy is a vital ingredient of imaginal desensitization. Additional research is needed to assess the relative contribution of such procedures as directed sexual activity, *in vivo* desensitization, communication training, assertiveness training, sex education, and attitude restructuring in the Masters and Johnson or men's group formats.

Systematic experimentation must be done to determine which interventions are most effective for particular types of erectile disorders in clients with particular intra- and interpersonal characteristics. For example, there is no current empirical data that would help the clinician to decide whether to use imaginal desensitization procedures prior to *in vivo* procedures when treating a client who has a partner. Similarly, additional research is needed to provide a more objective basis for determining when the extent of concurrent psychopathology (e.g., alcoholism, depression, psychosis, marital discord, deficient social skills) is sufficient to prohibit the successful application of a particular form of sex therapy.

Research should also address the issue of the cost effectiveness of alternative treatment procedures. For instance, men's group formats may be as effective if not superior to individually administered treatments for men without partners, but this possibility has not been empirically demonstrated. Similarly, biofeedback training may be a helpful treatment procedure, but is the amount of relative improvement derived from such training sufficient to warrant the expense involved in the use of equipment and laboratory facilities for individual therapy? The answers to such research questions ultimately will allow us to match treatment procedures with clients and to offer cost-efficient treatment to a greatly increased range and number of clients.

In summary, the array of behavioral treatment procedures for erectile dysfunction represents a promising multifaceted treatment approach. The therapeutic effectiveness of many of the procedures has been demonstrated in well-controlled research or through repeated replication of positive findings. Additional research is needed to determine the conditions under which each of the behavioral treatment approaches are best administered.

SUMMARY

Erectile dysfunction may be defined as the persistent inability to obtain or maintain a penile erection that is sufficient to allow intromission, pelvic thrusting, and, in the absence of ejaculatory difficulties, ejaculation during sexual intercourse. The client may complain of an inability to attain an erection, or he may gain erection and then lose it during extended foreplay, during the process of intromission, or after several pelvic thrusts.

Erectile dysfunction may result from a wide variety of physiological conditions and may also result from the acute or chronic use of prescribed or nonprescribed medications. The great majority of cases, however, have a psychological rather than an organic etiology.

Psychoanalytic and psychodynamic formulations of erectile dysfunction begin with the premise that the erectile disorder is symptomatic of underlying unconscious conflicts. Classical psychoanalytic theory holds that the erectile difficulty develops as a means of defending against anxiety and guilt associated with an unresolved oedipal conflict. Other psychodynamic writers have suggested that erectile dysfunction may serve as a means of expressing anger toward the female partner or the dysfunction may be associated with the individual's depression concerning generalized feelings of incompetence and a lack of power. The dynamic theorists frequently maintain that the historical roots of these feelings must be explored and the underlying conflicts resolved before lasting improvement in the erectile symptom can occur.

In contrast, behavioral therapists and other professionals who provide brief, directive treatment for erectile dysfunction focus on the current sexual behaviors, cognitions, and affects that are closely associated with the erectile response. The goal of treatment is not extensive personality change. Erectile dysfunction is seen as a psychophysiological disorder that can be elicited by any continued physical or emotional stress but which is usually maintained by the interaction of several immediate intra- and interpersonal factors including anxiety, preoccupation with erectile performance rather than erotic input, lack of sufficient stimulation, misinformation about male and female sexual response, absent or ineffective communication concerning sexual needs and preferences, and stereotyped beliefs about male sexual adequacy.

Sex-therapy treatment approaches and interventions generally are focused on one or more of these contributing factors.

The clinical assessment of erectile dysfunction is primarily based
on a physical examination and evaluation interviews. Generally speaking, the presence of frequent morning erections, masturbatory erections, or erections during some encounters with a partner indicate that
the physical capacity for erectile response is intact and the disorder is
most likely caused by psychological factors. However, the differential
diagnosis of biogenic and psychogenic erectile dysfunction may require
nocturnal tumescence monitoring in cases in which the client reports
minimal morning or masturbatory erections. In order to develop a
treatment plan, the clinician needs to obtain a detailed behavioral
description of the sexual interactions in which the dysfunction occurs
and the behavioral, cognitive, and affective antecedents and consequences of the occurrence of erectile failure. Several questionnaire
measures are now available for purposes of treatment planning and
outcome evaluation.

In vivo desensitization exercises are generally recommended for
clients who have sexual partners and who experience performance
anxiety during sexual encounters. Sexual arousal responses that are
elicited by self-stimulation and/or stimulation provided by the partner
are used in inhibit anxiety in *in vivo* desensitization. Systematic exposure to an anxiety hierarchy occurs through the assignment of a series
of sexual activities that begin with behaviors far removed from intercourse but which gradually progress toward coitus. The couples exercises might include sensate focus on directed masturbation activities.

Imaginal desensitization procedures may be helpful for men who
do not have partners willing to participate in therapy and for men
whose anxiety is so intense as to prevent success in even the initial steps
in the *in vivo* approach. The content of the desensitization hierarchy
items usually refers to actual sexual behaviors (e.g., kissing while
clothed, undressing, genital caressing, intercourse) or other aspects of
sexual encounter that elicit anxiety (fear of injury, disgust or fear of
genitals, fear of rejection). Traditional relaxation training may be
used in desensitization; however, sexual arousal elicited by directed
masturbation or directed sexual fantasy may be a preferable anxiety
inhibitor.

Arousal reconditioning procedures may be applicable to clients
who experience deficits in sexual arousal in specific situations or with
particular partners or types of partners. During masturbation or activities with the partner; the client is instructed to switch his attention to
the stimuli that previously did not elicit arousal just as he approaches
orgasm. He then learns to make this switch at progressively earlier

points in the sexual encounter. Biofeedback training, in which the client receives immediate feedback concerning small changes in erection, may help the client to attend more fully to what is already arousing to him.

Thought stopping and thought substitution may be used to inhibit recurrent negative thoughts that occur prior to or during the sexual encounter and which elicit anxiety and distract the client from erotic input. The disruptive power of negative self statements can be reduced further via education and attitude restructuring efforts designed to dispel stereotyped beliefs about male sexual adequacy. Sexual assertiveness training and communication training can be particularly helpful for men who are unable to refuse an unwanted sexual request or have difficulty with the verbal or nonverbal communication of their sexual needs, preferences, and limits to a partner.

Because of the interaction of the contributing factors that produce or maintain erectile dysfunction, the behavioral treatment approaches have frequently included multiple components designed to address a variety of treatment focuses. Further research is needed to assess the relative contribution of the different treatment components, to determine which interventions are most effective for particular clients, to determine when sex therapy is contraindicated, and to specify the cost effectiveness of alternative procedures. The array of behavioral treatment procedures, however, currently represents a promising multifaceted treatment approach.

REFERENCES

Annon, J. S. *The behavioral treatment of sexual problems: Brief therapy* (Vol. 1). Honolulu: Inabling Systems, 1974.

Ansari, J. M. A. Impotence: Prognosis (a controlled study). *British Journal of Psychiatry*, 1976, *128*, 194–198.

Auerbach, R., & Kilmann, P. R. The effects of group systematic desensitization on secondary erectile failure. *Behavior Therapy*, 1977, *8*, 330–339.

Bancroft, J. H., Jones, H. G., & Pullan, B. P. A simple transducer for measuring penile erection with comments on its use in treatment of sexual disorders. *Behaviour Research and Therapy*, 1966, *4*, 239–241.

Bass, B. A. Sexual arousal as an anxiety inhibitor. *Journal of Behavior Therapy and Experimental Psychiatry*, 1974, *5*, 151–152.

Bernstein, D. A., & Borkovec, T. D. *Progressive relaxation training.* Champaign, Ill.: Research Press, 1973.

Beutler, L. E., Karacan, I., Anch, A. M., Salis, P. J., Scott, F. B., & Williams, R. L. MMPI and MIT discriminators of biogenic and psychogenic impotence. *Journal of Consulting and Clinical Psychology*, 1975, *43*, 899–903.

Bieber, I. The psychoanalytic treatment of sexual disorders. *Journal of Sex and Marital Therapy,* 1974, *1,* 5–15.

Cooper, A. J. A clinical study of "coital anxiety" in male potency disorders. *Journal of Psychosomatic Research,* 1969, *13,* 143–147.

Cooper, A. J. Treatments of male potency disorders: The present status. *Psychosomatics,* 1971, *12,* 234–244.

Csillag, E. R. Modification of penile erectile response. *Journal of Behavior Therapy and Experimental Psychiatry,* 1976, *7,* 27–29.

Dengrove, E. Therapeutic approaches of impotence in the male.: III. Behavior therapy of impotence. *Journal of Sex Research,* 1971, *7,* 177–183.

Frank, E., Anderson, C., & Rubinstein, D. Frequency of sexual dysfunction in "normal" couples. *New England Journal of Medicine,* 1978, *299,* 111–115.

Freud, S. *Standard edition of the complete psychological works* (Vol. 11, J. Strachey, Ed. and trans.). London: Hogarth Press, 1953. (Originally published, 1910.)

Friedman, D. E. The treatment of impotence by Brietal relaxation therapy. *Behaviour Research and Therapy,* 1968, *6,* 257–261.

Friedman, D. E., & Lipsedge, M. S. Treatment of phobic anxiety and psychogenic impotence by systematic desensitization employing methohexitone-induced relaxation. *British Journal of Psychiatry,* 1971, *118,* 87–90.

Friedman, H. J. An interpersonal aspect of psychogenic impotence. *American Journal of Psychotherapy,* 1973, *27,* 421–429.

Garfield, Z., McBrearty, J., & Dichter, M. A case of impotence successfully treated with desensitization combined with *in vivo* operant training and thought substitution. In R. D. Rubin & C. M. Franks (Eds.), *Advances in behavior therapy.* New York: Academic Press, 1969.

Geer, J. H., & Fuhr, R. Cognitive factors in sexual arousal: The role of distraction. *Journal of Consulting and Clinical Psychology,* 1976, *44,* 238–243.

Gill, H., & Temperly, J. Time-limited marital treatment in a foursome. *British Journal of Medical Psychology,* 1974, *47,* 153–162.

Glick, B. S. Desensitization therapy in impotence and frigidity: Review of the literature and report of a case. *American Journal of Psychiatry,* 1975, *132,* 169–171.

Goldberg, M. Selective impotence. *Medical Aspects of Human Sexuality,* 1973 (Aug.), 13–32

Hathaway, S., & McKinley, J. *The Minnesota multiphasic personality inventory.* New York: Psychological Corporation, 1943.

Heinrich, A. G. Sexual dysfunctions. In A. Robbins & J. Tamkin (Eds.), *Manual of ambulatory medicine.* Philadelphia: W. B. Saunders, 1979.

Heinrich, A. G., & Price, S. *Goals for sex therapy—Female.* Unpublished questionnaire, University of California, Los Angeles, 1975.

Herman, S. H., & Prewett, M. An experimental analysis of feedback to increase sexual arousal in a case of homosexual and heterosexual impotence: A preliminary report. *Journal of Behavior Therapy and Experimental Psychiatry,* 1974, *5,* 271–274.

Hogan, D. R. The effectiveness of sex therapy: A review of the literature. In J. LoPiccolo & L. LoPicclo (Eds.), *Handbook of sex therapy.* New York: Plenum Press, 1978.

Jacobson, E. *Progressive relaxation.* Chicago: University of Chicago Press, 1938.

Jones, W. J., & Park, P. M. Treatment of single-partner sexual dysfunction by systematic desensitization. *Obstetrics and Gynecology,* 1972, *39,* 411–417.

Julty, S. *MSP*: *Male sexual performance.* New York: Dell, 1975.

Kaplan, H. S. *The new sex therapy: Active treatment of sexual dysfunctions.* New York: Quadrangle/The New York Times Book Co., 1974.

Karacan, I. The developmental aspect and the effect of certain clinical conditions upon penile erection during sleep. *Excerpta Medica International Congress Series,* 1966, *150,* 2356–2359.

Karacan, I., Salis, P. J., Ware, J. G., Dervent, B., Williams, R. L., Scott, F. B., Attia, S. L., & Beutler, L. E. Nocturnal penile tumescence and diagnosis in diabetic impotence. *American Journal of Psychiatry,* 1978, *135,* 191–197.

Karacan, I., Williams, R. L., Thornby, J. I., & Salis, P. J. Sleep-related tumescence as a function of age. *American Journal of Psychiatry,* 1975, *132,* 932–937.

Kilmann, P. R., & Auerbach, R. Treatments of premature ejaculation and psychogenic impotence: A critical review of the literature. *Archives of Sexual Behavior,* 1979, *8,* 81–100.

Kockott, G., Dittmar, F., & Nusselt, L. Systematic desensitization of erectile impotence: A controlled study. *Archives of Sexual Behavior,* 1975, *4,* 493–500.

Lansky, M. R., & Davenport, A. E. Difficulties in brief conjoint treatment of sexual dysfunction. *American Journal of Psychiatry,* 1975, *132,* 177–179.

Layman, W. A. Pseudo incest. *Comprehensive Psychiatry,* 1972, *13,* 385–390.

Lazarus, A. A. Group therapy of phobic disorders by systematic desensitization. *Journal of Abnormal and Social Psychology,* 1961, *63,* 504–510.

Lazarus, A. A. The treatment of a sexually inadequate man. In L. P. Ullmann & L. Krasner (Eds.), *Case studies in behavior modification.* New York: Holt, Rinehart & Winston, 1965.

Lobitz, W. C., & Baker, E. L. Group treatment of single males with erectile dysfunction. *Archives of Sexual Behavior,* 1979, *8,* 127–138.

Lobitz, W. C., & LoPiccolo, J. New methods in the behavioral treatment of sexual dysfunction. *Journal of Behavior Therapy and Experimental Psychiatry,* 1972, *3,* 265–271.

Lobitz, W. C., LoPiccolo, J., Lobitz, G., & Brockway, J. A closer look at simplistic behavior therapy for sexual dysfunction: Two case studies. In H. J. Eysenck (Ed.), *Case studies in behavior therapy.* London: Routledge and Kegan Paul, 1976

LoPiccolo, J., & Lobitz, W. C. Behavior therapy of sexual dysfunction. In L. A. Hamerlynck, L. C. Handy, & E. J. Mash (Eds.), *Behavior change: Methodology, concepts, and practice.* Champaign, Ill.: Research Press, 1973.

LoPiccolo, J., & Stegar, J. C. The sexual interaction inventory: A new instrument for assessment of sexual dysfunction. *Archives of Sexual Behavior,* 1974, *3,* 585-595.

LoPiccolo, J., Stewart, R., & Watkins, B. Treatment of erectile failure and ejaculatory incompetence of homosexual etiology. *Journal of Behavior Therapy and Experimental Psychiatry,* 1972, *3,* 233-236.

Masters, W. H., & Johnson, V. E. *Human sexual response,* Boston: Little, Brown, 1966.

Masters, W. H., & Johnson, V. E. *Human sexual inadequacy.* Boston: Little, Brown, 1970.

Mathews, A., Bancroft, J., Whitehead, A., Hackmann, A., Julier, D., Bancroft, J., Gath, D., & Shaw, P. The behavioural treatment of sexual inadequacy: A comparative study. *Behaviour Research and Therapy,* 1976, *14,* 427-436.

McCarthy, B. W. A modification of Masters and Johnson sex therapy model in a clinical setting. *Psychotherapy: Theory, Research and Practice,* 1973, *10,* 290-293.

McCoy, N. N., & D'Agostino, P. A. Factor analysis of the sexual interaction inventory. *Archives of Sexual Behavior,* 1977, *6,* 25-35.

McGuire, R. T., Carlisle, J. M., & Young, B. G. Sexual deviation as conditioned behavior: A hypothesis. *Behaviour Research and Therapy,* 1965, *2,* 185-190.

Meyer, J. K., Schmidt, C. W., Lucas, M. J., & Smith, E. Short-term treatment of sexual problems: Interim report. *American Journal of Psychiatry,* 1975, *132,* 172-176.

Obler, M. Systematic desensitization in sexual disorders. *Journal of Behavior Therapy and Experimental Psychiatry,* 1973, *4,* 93-101.

O'Connor, J. F., & Stern, L. O. Results of treatment in functional sexual disorders. *New York State Journal of Medicine,* 1972, *72,* 1927-1934.

Price, S., & Heinrich, A. G. *Goals for sex therapy—Male.* Unpublished questionnaire, University of California, Los Angeles, 1975.

Price, S. C., Reynolds, B. S., Cohen, B. D., Anderson, A., & Schochet, B. *Group treatment of erectile dysfunction for men without partners: A controlled evaluation. Archives of Sexual Behavior,* 1981, in press.

Prochaska, J. O., & Marzilli, R. Modifications of the Masters and Johnson approach to sexual problems. *Psychotherapy: Theory, Research and Practice,* 1973, *10,* 294-296.

Proctor, R. C. Impotence as a symptom of depression. *North Carolina Medical Journal,* 1973, *34,* 876-878.

Reynolds, B. S. Psychological treatment models and outcome results for erectile dysfunction: A critical review. *Psychological Bulletin,* 1977, *84,* 1218-1238.

Reynolds, B. S. *Erection difficulty questionnaire.* Unpublished questionnaire, University of California, Los Angeles, 1978.

Reynolds, B. S. Biofeedback and facilitation of erection in men with erectile dysfunction. *Archives of Sexual Behavior,* 1980, *9,* 101-113.

Salzman, L. F. Systematic desensitization of a patient with chronic total impotence. In R. D. Rubin & C. M. Franks (Eds.), *Advances in behavior therapy.* New York: Academic Press, 1969.

Salzman, L. F. Psychotherapy with patients with sexual disorders. In M. Hammer (Ed.), *The theory and practice of psychotherapy with specific disorders.* Springfield, Ill.: Charles C Thomas, 1972.

Segraves, R. T. Pharmacological agents causing sexual dysfunction. *Journal of Sex and Marital Therapy,* 1978, *3,* 157–176.

Stekel, W. *Impotence in the male.* New York: Liveright, 1927.

Sue, D. Masturbation in the in vivo treatment of impotence. *Journal of Behavior Therapy and Experimental Psychiatry,* 1978, *9,* 75–76.

Weiss, H. D. The physiology of human penile erection. *Annals of Internal Medicine,* 1972, *76,* 793–799.

Wish, P. A. The use of imagery-based techniques in the treatment of sexual dysfunction. *Counseling Psychologist,* 1975, *5,* 52–55.

Wolpe, J. *Psychotherapy by reciprocal inhibition.* Stanford, Ca.: Stanford University Press, 1958.

Wolpe, J. *The practice of behavior therapy* (2nd ed.). New York: Pergamon Press, 1973.

Wolpe, J. A., & Lazarus, A. A. *Behaviour therapy techniques: A guide to treatment of neurosis.* Oxford: Pergamon Press, 1966.

Wright, J., Perreault, R., & Mathieu, M. The treatment of sexual dysfunction. *Archives of General Psychiatry,* 1977, *34,* 881–890.

Zilbergeld, B. Group treatment of sexual dysfunction in men without partners. *Journal of Sex and Marital Therapy,* 1975, *1,* 204–214.

Zilbergeld, B. *Male sexuality: A guide to sexual fulfillment.* Boston: Little, Brown, 1978.

SUGGESTED READINGS

Treatment Models for Erectile Dysfunction

Kilmann, P. R., & Auerbach, R. Treatments of premature ejaculation and psychogenic impotence: A critical review of the literature. *Archives of Sexual Behavior,* 1979, *8,* 81–100.

Reynolds, B. S. Psychological treatment models and outcome results for erectile dysfunction: A critical review. *Psychological Bulletin,* 1977, *84,* 1218–1238.

Physiology of Erection

Masters, W. W., & Johnson, V. E. *Human sexual response.* Boston: Little, Brown, 1966.

Weiss, H. D. The physiology of human penile erection. *Annals of Internal Medicine,* 1972, *76,* 793–799.

Effects of Illness and Drugs

Kaplan, H. S. *The new sex therapy: Active treatment of sexual dysfunctions.* New York: Quadrangle/The New York Times Book Co., 1974.

Segraves, R. T. Pharmacological agents causing sexual dysfunction. *Journal of Sex and Marital Therapy,* 1977, *3,* 157–176.

Clinical Assessment

Lobitz, W. C., & Lobitz, G. K. Clinical assessment in the treatment of sexual dysfunctions. In J. LoPiccolo & L. LoPiccolo (Eds.), *Handbook of sex therapy*. New York: Plenum Press, 1978.

Sex Therapy Treatment Procedures

Annon, J. S. *The behavioral treatment of sexual problems: Brief therapy* (Vol. I). Honolulu: Enabling Systems, 1974.

Annon, J. S. *The behavioral treatment of sexual problems* (Vol. II). Honolulu: Enabling Systems, 1975.

Kaplan, H. S. *The new sex therapy: Active treatment of sexual dysfunctions.* New York: Quadrangle/The New York Times Book Co., 1974.

Masters, W. H., & Johnson, V. E. *Human sexual inadequacy.* Boston: Little, Brown, 1970.

Books for Clients

Kaplan, H. S. *The illustrated manual of sex therapy.* New York: Quadrangle/ The New York Times Book Co., 1975.

Zilbergeld, B. *Male sexuality: A guide to sexual fulfillment.* Boston: Little, Brown, 1978.

5

The Treatment of Marital Problems

Gayla Margolin
Andrew Christensen

Unlike many of the other mental health problems discussed in this book that are defined by virtue of being statistically infrequent (Shepherd, Oppenheim, & Mitchell, 1971), marital problems are notable for their prevalence. It is estimated that over half of the people seeking psychological or psychiatric services mention their marital situation as their primary complaint (Weiss & Birchler, 1978; "Why marriages turn sour," 1975) and that 20 percent of all married couples experience marital problems (Renne, 1970). There are also several sources of information that indirectly offer revealing data regarding the incidence of marital distress. Divorce statistics, for example, have shown a steady increase over the past 20 years. In 1960 there were 393,000 divorces, in 1978 there were 1.12 million divorces, and the projected figure for 1990 is 1.70 million divorces; these figures translate into 2.6 divorces per 100 marriages in 1960, 50 divorces per 100 marriages in 1978, and 63 divorces per 100 marriages by 1990 ("Family trends," 1975; "More marriages," 1979). Further information on the incidence of extreme marital stress can be found in data on violence between spouses. Based on representative samples, it is estimated that 7 percent of wives and 6 percent of husbands have experienced severe physical abuse (Steinmetz, 1977), and that 12 percent to over 20 percent of all homicides are spouse induced (Steinmetz, 1978; "Family violence," 1978). Recent data concerning the prevalence of sexual problems among a relatively large nonclinic sample provide a further index of marital maladjustment: 40 percent of the men and 63 percent of the women reported specific sexual dysfunctions, and 50 percent of the men and 77 percent of the women reported sexual difficulties such as lack of interest or attraction. The sexual difficulties, particularly for women, as compared to the dysfunctions for either sex, were indicative of interpersonal conflict (Frank, Anderson, & Rubinstein, 1978).

How are marital adjustment and maladjustment defined? There is no formally accepted definition, nor has there been much demand for one. However, for the purpose of understanding the development and amelioration of marital distress, studies have been conducted that examine what accounts for the level of marital satisfaction a couple experiences or that compare distressed and nondistressed couples. To conduct these investigations, a couple's status as distressed or non-distressed is determined on the basis of the couple's self-reported level of marital satisfaction. In one such comparison, Mitchell, Bullard, and Mudd (1962) found high agreement between the two sets of couples in the types of content areas they found troublesome: arguments were highest around finances, personality differences, sex, and household management, and lowest around education and religion. However, there was a consistently higher percentage of distressed, as compared to nondistressed, couples who reported disagreements for each content area.

Most investigators assume that marital adjustment is not determined by agreements alone but is a function of the balance between marital benefits and tensions (Orden & Bradburn, 1968). For example, the simple difference between frequency of sexual intercourse and frequency of arguments is a surprisingly good predictor of marital satisfaction (Edwards & Edwards, 1977; Howard & Dawes, 1976; Thorton, 1977). One study showed the ratio of positive to negative time to be 15.3 to 1 for happy couples, but only 6.3 to 1 for distressed couples (Williams, 1977). Furthermore, studies that have examined marital satisfaction as a function of specific behavior exchanges between partners show that distressed, as compared to nondistressed, couples engage in fewer rewarding exchanges, more punishing exchanges, or both (Birchler, Weiss, & Vincent, 1975; Gottman, Markman, & Notarius, 1977; Margolin, 1979a; Vincent, Weiss, & Birchler, 1975). In this brief overview, it should also be noted that the presence of children appears to have a moderating effect on the quality of overall marital interaction. The most consistent finding in this regard is that marital satisfactions and rewards decline sharply during the child-rearing stages of family life and then recover when children are finally launched from the parents' home (Margolin, 1979a; Rollins & Cannon, 1974; Rollins & Feldman, 1970).

Problems of definition are not limited to the construct of *marital distress;* they also exist for the term *marital therapy,* which actually embodies an unwieldy collection of clinical practices. In a landmark paper on the history of marital therapy, Olson (1970) emphasized that marital therapists are not united by either a common theory or similar procedures; in fact, he suggested that the only point of convergence among marital therapists is the value which they place on the marital relationship per se. In the same paper, Olson reviewed the following diverse formats that characterize marital therapy: (1) individual therapy in which the primary focus is on the marital relationship; (2) collaborative therapy in which the two partners are seen individually by two therapists who consult with one another; (3) concurrent therapy in which the two partners are seen by the same therapist but at different times; and (4) conjoint therapy in which the partners are seen together by one or more therapists. Additional options include a combination of these formats and also conjoint group therapy. A further variant of marital therapy is the recent proliferation of marital enrichment programs which teach couples who already perceive their relationships as good to be even more intimate and responsive to each other's needs (Koch & Koch, 1976). These programs will receive only brief mention in this chapter.

One final definition refers to the term *marriage*. Although we will continue to use this term, we acknowledge it to be unnecessarily restricting. Many aspects of the therapies described here are applicable to any two partners in an intimate relationship, regardless of their sexual orientation (see Hall, 1978) and regardless of whether or not they are legally married.

THEORETICAL ANALYSIS

Nonbehavioral

Clinically oriented theorists have written much on marriage and marital therapy. To summarize available nonbehavioral theories in a few pages requires selectivity in the extreme. Therefore, we have chosen only the theories that are well developed, specifically focus on marital relations, and have great influence on the field.

Psychoanalytic Theory. Psychoanalytic theory has influenced psychological thinking far more than any other theory. It is not surprising, then, that concepts of marriage and marital therapy have been affected by this pervasive influence. Very little theoretical development, however, has focused directly on the marital relationship (Gurman, 1978). In this section, we draw on the object relations approach to marriage presented by Dicks (1963, 1967) and the more recent theoretical work of Meissner (1978).

Psychoanalytic views of marital distress emphasize individual factors in the two spouses. Marital discord typically occurs because partners are psychologically deficient. As Paolino (1978) writes: "An unhappy marriage is often the final common pathway that results from a collection of psychic 'symptoms' belonging to one or both partners"

(p. 93). While some psychoanalytic writers have given considerable attention to the interactional determinants of marital discord (Ables & Brandsma, 1977; Martin, 1976; Sager, 1976), the focus on individual psychopathology remains central to psychoanalytic views of marital dysfunction.

The individual inadequacies that contribute to marital distress are a result of early developmental experiences. The spouses' past relationships with their parents determine in important ways their relationship to each other. "For any given husband and wife, the marital dyadic relationship is so inextricably bound to the parent–child relationship in their families of origin . . . that no comprehensive psychoanalytic discussion of marital interaction can avoid the subject of parent–child relations" (Meissner, 1978, p. 26). A residue from past relationships disturbs the present one.

The child who proceeds through the various developmental stages with appropriate need satisfaction will internalize positive models of relationships. He or she will be able to differentiate from parents and develop an autonomous identity, uncontaminated by emotional frustrations from the past. This individual can select a mate, not on the basis of infantile needs which still clamor for satisfaction, but on the basis of adult needs and reality factors. The relationship with one's mate, based on the earlier model of satisfaction and trust, can evolve as the identities of the partners dictate and without distortions created by primitive fears and anger due to infantile frustrations.

In contrast, the child who proceeds through the developmental stages with continued frustration of infantile needs internalizes both the negative qualities of the parents and negative models of relationships. Because of the hate and anger that such continued frustration arouses, the child may repress or split off from himself or herself these internalized negative qualities and models. But the frustrated needs and the repressed aspects of earlier relationships will determine many of the person's responses in later intimate relationships. Psychoanalytic theory suggests that this person will select a mate based on unconscious desires to fulfill infantile needs and to unite with the repressed aspects of oneself (Dicks, 1963). Psychoanalytic theory further suggests that this person will select a mate with a similar level of emotional disorder but with an opposite pattern of defensive style (Meissner, 1978). Thus the pairing will be based on complementary needs. Common examples of such complementary pairings are dominance–submission, sadism–masochism, superiority–inferiority, adequacy–inadequacy, and aggression–victimization.

Sager (1976) and Martin (1976) have used the concept of "marriage contract" to describe this process of marital pairing. Each partner brings to the marriage a set of conscious and unconscious expectations that are a residue of his or her past. In getting married, the partners make a contract, largely unverbalized, about the satsifactions that each will provide the other. Because the contracts have not been openly clarified and agreed upon and involve unconscious material, there is great potential for incorrect assumptions about what each partner wants and what the other wishes to provide.

A common interaction pattern that develops between partners who have paired on the basis of unconscious, infantile needs has been called "projective identification" (Mannino & Greenspan, 1976) or "projective-introjective interactions" (Meissner, 1978). Each partner projects onto the other some unconscious quality of himself or herself and responds to the other as if he or she embodies that quality. Each partner forces the other into a mold dictated by unconscious needs. Both perceptual distortion of the partner's actual characteristics and coercive efforts to change the partner are necessary to achieve this Procrustean fit between the actuality of the partner and the fantasy maintained by the other. "One or both partners fail to confirm the other's real personality or identity. Instead they require the other to conform to an inner role model and punish them if the expectation is disappointed. Much marital conflict can be shown to stem from striv-ings to coerce or mold the partner by very rigid and stereotyped tactics to these inner models" (Dicks, 1963, p. 127). In Sager's (1976) and Martin's (1976) terms, each partner is forcing compliance with a con-tract which has not been openly agreed upon.

While partners resist these attempts at being molded to the other's needs, at another level both participate in a "collusive process" (Dicks, 1963) to support these mutual projections. Partners both resist and internalize (introject) the projections of the other. "Participants in close relationships are often in collusion with one another to sustain mutual projections, i.e., to support one another's defensive operations and to provide experiences through which the other can participate vicariously" (Zinner & Shapiro, 1972, p. 525).

The classical psychoanalytic position about intervention in these pathological patterns argues for separate psychoanalysis for both indi-viduals in the marriage (Giovacchini, 1965). However, recent psycho-analytically oriented therapists (Ables & Brandsma, 1977; Martin, 1976; Sager, 1976) have utilized conjoint therapy with an emphasis on current interactional patterns to alter distressed marital relationships.

Systems Theory. A second nonbehavioral approach which has in-fluenced thinking about marriage and marital therapy is systems theory. This approach is difficult to characterize because several quite different views of marital functioning have all been called "systems theories." The Structural Family Therapy of Minuchin (1974), the strategic therapy of Haley (1963, 1976), the communications therapy of the Palo Alto Group (Watzlawick, 1976a, 1976b; Watzlawick, Beavin, & Jackson, 1967), and the Family Systems Theory of Bowen (1961, 1966, 1976a, 1976c), not known as Bowen theory (1976b), have all been described as systems theories. Yet, with the possible exception of strategic therapy and communications therapy, these approaches are quite different from one another. Furthermore, none was explicitly derived from General Systems Theory (von Bertalanffy, 1962, 1973), although all share its general framework.

In the short space allotted, we only describe a few important aspects of General Systems Theory and explain how these aspects are manifested in the family systems theories just mentioned. We exclude from this analysis the theoretical approaches that are more eclectic in orientation (e.g., Satir, 1967, 1972) and which focus primarily on family rather than marital interaction (e.g., Lidz, Fleck, & Cornelison, 1965). Though Minuchin's work is not primarily directed at marital interaction, his ideas have been included as one example of how systems theory analyzes the relations between marital and child subsystems.

A fundamental idea of General Systems Theory is contained in the old adage that "the whole is greater than the sum of the parts." Parts act in relation to one another; therefore, the whole is a function of the individual characteristics of the parts plus their relationships to one another. Systems theorists emphasize the relationships between parts more than the individual characteristics of these parts. For example, Lederer and Jackson (1968) write of marriage that "most of the important behavior patterns . . . are products of the relationship and not just manifestations of traits peculiar to one spouse" (p. 236).

If the relationship between elements is the crucial unit of analysis, then the tools of intellectual understanding are not isolation and reduction, but molar examination of the structure and function of these relationships as a whole. Thus a primary emphasis is the organization of the system: analysis of the patterning of relationships in hierarchical and horizontal structures provides information about the behavior of their individual parts. A second emphasis is on the function of behavior for controlling the dynamic balance assumed to exist within the system. Positive and negative feedback, for example, are mechanisms by which the system maintains homeostatic balance. These abstract concepts of organization and control in systems will now be illustrated by an explication of particular family systems approaches.

Bowen's theory (1961, 1966, 1976a, 1976b, 1976c) of family functioning emphasizes the organizational concept of "differentiation of
self." Bowen developed this concept as the psychological analogy of
biological differentiation of cells and tissues during growth and development. The concept of differentiation of self actually labels one
side of a dimension that goes from "fusion" at one end to differentiation at the other. This dimension, which can be applied to individuals
or relationships, describes the extent to which autonomy and independence have been achieved. Individuals who are fused to their families
of origin or to their marital partners have not developed separate
identities and are characterized by excessive emotional behavior. Differentiated individuals have established autonomous identities, however, and can guide their behavior with intellect rather than emotion.

A second structural concept within Bowen's theory is the notion
of "triangle," which usually refers to three-person configurations. Tri-
angles are presumed to be the building blocks of emotional systems.
When two undifferentiated individuals form a relationship, each may
attempt to involve a third as a way of stabilizing their position vis-à-vis
the other. Thus marital partners involve a child, an in-law, or a
therapist in their conflicts with each other. The goal of therapy is to
promote the differentiation of individuals by "de-triangling" their relationships. Individuals must learn to make autonomous stands in their
relationships, rather than constantly using third parties for support.

The strategic therapy of Haley (1963, 1976) and the communication approach of the Palo Alto Group (Sluzki, 1978; Watzlawick,
1976a, 1976b; Watzlawick, Beavin, & Jackson, 1967) are quite similar.
Both put more emphasis on dynamic control factors in family systems
than on the structure of family systems. These theories view almost all
behavior as communication: since one cannot not behave, one must
always communicate. While the most obvious aspect of verbal communication is the information reported, a more subtle and sometimes
more crucial dimension is the command aspect—what the communication says about the relationship between the giver and receiver of the
message. When a family member reports a symptom, as in a complaint
of "I have a headache," the most important part of the message may be
the command aspect which communicates "take care of me," or "I can't
do my work," or "I don't want sex tonight."

According to the strategic-communication theorists, symptoms
develop in family systems because of pathological communication. The
most widely discussed pathology is the double bind, in which two
logically inconsistent messages are given along with a third message
that forbids comment about the inconsistency. Other communication
deficits concern the lack of clarity about the origin, direction, and

content of messages. When family members consistently are unable to tell who wants what from whom, symptoms are liable to develop.

Symptoms are not only caused by faulty communications, but they themselves are faulty communications. Symptoms are not just reactions, but are active attempts to control and define the relationship. Thus symptoms have a functional value for both the individual and the system. The child's psychosomatic complaints may command attention for him or her and unite the parents in a common task of aiding their child. Major goals of therapy in the strategic-communications approach are to reduce the controlling value of symptoms and to promote clear communication.

As the name implies, Minuchin's Structural Family Therapy (1974) emphasizes family organization as a central explanatory concept. Boundaries around individuals and subsystems of individuals determine family organization. These boundaries are rules about who can participate in certain activities. For example, if boundaries around the parental subsystem are not clear, children can become "enmeshed" in the marriage; that is, children can participate inappropriately in marital activities. For example, children may form coalitions with the parents that are more powerful than the marital bond itself. Conversely, if boundaries are too strong, individuals become "disengaged" from one another and do not appropriately participate with each other. Minuchin argues for clear but "permeable" boundaries around individuals in the family and the two important subsystems within the family, the marriage and the children. Symptoms in individual family members are a result of pathological family structures which exist when clear, permeable boundaries are absent. A typical pathological family structure involves a father disengaged from the entire family and a mother enmeshed in the child subsystem. The father has only superficial contact with the family while the mother has intense coalitions with the children, often in opposition to the father. The goal of therapy would be greater contact between the mother and father and a weaker coalition between the mother and children. In Minuchin's terms, this change would be described as a strengthening of the boundaries around the marital and child subsystems.

Behavioral

Behavioral views of marital distress developed out of social learning theory (Bandura, 1969, 1977) and social exchange theory (Thibaut & Kelley, 1959). The operant conditioning paradigm from social learning theory has been the focal point for theorizing, and concepts from social exchange theory have been used largely to supplement and elaborate the operant framework. The classical conditioning and cognitive viewpoints in social learning theory have had less impact on behavioral conceptualizations, although the former has been used in analyses of sexual dysfunction.

The operant conditioning approach provides the analytic paradigm of antecedent–behavior–consequent. Using this paradigm, behavioral theorists have analyzed marital interaction as patterns of mutual discriminative stimuli, conditioned responses, and reciprocal reinforcement and punishment. Each partner's behavior is explained by the cueing and reinforcement provided by the other and by the individual's own reinforcement history. It is assumed that partners enter the relationship because of the benefits obtained in the interaction. Once in the relationship, each partner exerts important controlling influences on the other through the patterns of reinforcement they mutually provide.

Deficits leading to marital distress can occur at each of the three points in the antecedent–behavior–consequent model. First, antecedent problems refer to the lack of appropriate stimulus control of marital behavior. If spouses do not have a clear set of signals to cue each other on their readiness for important marital activities (sex, affection, aloneness, etc.), then misunderstanding and frustration are predictable. On a more global level, explicit and implicit rules are needed to guide interaction. Without the stimulus control provided by rules, behavior in the relationship is unorganized and chaotic (Jacobson & Margolin, 1979; Weiss, 1978).

Second, behavior variables reflect each partner's ability to produce adaptive relationship behavior. If couples do not possess sufficient communication skills to listen and understand one another, sufficient problem-solving skills to negotiate conflictual issues, or sufficient behavior change strategies to alter relationship patterns in constructive ways, then marital distress is predictable.

Finally, consequent variables refer to the reinforcement and punishment which accrue to marital partners during their relationship. Clearly, partners enter the marital relationship for benefits obtained and expected. However, over the course of the relationship, spouses lose their reinforcing power through the satiation effects of repeated exposure. If this "reinforcement erosion" (Jacobson & Margolin, 1979) is interpreted as loss of love and if the spouses cannot expand their repertoire of relationship satisfactions, then distress is a likely result.

The loss of reinforcement in distressed couples is often accompanied by an increase in aversive exchange. Patterson and his colleagues (Patterson & Reid, 1970; Patterson, Weiss, & Hops, 1976) used operant concepts to describe the "coercion process," which refers to the development of these aversive exchanges. When spouses are faced with the common situation of wanting to change each other's behavior, a typical response, especially in distressed couples, is to make the request with an aversive stimulus. Rather than simply asking and negotiating for a change, partners use any of a variety of aversive strategies like demanding the change, threatening negative consequences if the partner refuses to change, or inducing guilt until the partner changes. The coerced spouse often will make the change in order to terminate the aversive request. Thus, one partner is positively reinforced for coercion and the other is negatively reinforced for compliance. This short-term benefit for both partners will maintain their respective behaviors. However, the coerced partner may not spontaneously engage in the new behavior on future occasions and may also use coercion for his or her own purposes. Thus, the negative stimulation may escalate into the destructive patterns characteristic of distressed marriages.

Adherence to a strict operant model limits analysis to the immediate consequences of behavior. By borrowing concepts from social exchange theory, behavioral theorists have added a level of complexity to operant analysis. In the economics of exchange theory, the cost of behavior in terms of psychological effort must be examined, as well as the rewards this behavior brings. In addition, the rewards and costs available from a particular interaction or relationship must be compared with the rewards and costs available from alternative possibilities. Finally, norms regarding the exchange of rewards and costs must be examined in order to understand the participants' reactions to these exchanges. A wife, for example, may accept less than an ideal exchange rate because of sex role norms. It is assumed that the aggregate of rewards, costs, alternatives, and norms determine spouses' overall impressions of the relationship.

A second input from social learning theory, the respondent conditioning model, has been employed primarily to explain sexual dysfunctions in marriage. In his early work, Wolpe (1958) suggested that anxiety conditioned to sexual performance is the primary causal factor in sexual dysfunctions. Some years later, Masters and Johnson (1970) independently arrived at a similar formulation of sexual dysfunction, although they did not formally use the respondent conditioning model as Wolpe had done. They argued that performance anxiety becomes associated with the sexual situation for any of a variety of reasons. This anxiety then prevents normal sexual behavior.

The cognitive emphasis in social learning theory, represented by the cognitive behavior modification movement (Mahoney, 1974; Mahoney & Arnkoff, 1978), has had little formal impact on behavioral marriage therapy. The major point of similarity between cognitive behavior modification and behavioral marriage therapy is the common emphasis on problem-solving skill deficits as an explanation for distressed functioning. This common emphasis developed independently, however, and in general there has been little conceptual commerce between the two approaches.

The cognitive emphasis that does exist in behavioral marriage therapy has come more from social psychology than from cognitive behavior modification. Social exchange theory requires attention to cognitive factors like the cost of behavior and the expectations regarding the exchange of behavior. In addition, some recent behavioral writers have drawn notions from attribution theory (Jones, Kanouse, Kelley, Nisbett, Valins, & Weiner, 1972; Kelley, 1973) to explain patterns of behavior in distressed couples (Jacobson & Margolin, 1979; Margolin, Christensen, & Weiss, 1975; Margolin & Weiss, 1978b). These writers propose that distressed couples overly attribute their suffering to the partner ("it's your fault that I'm unhappy in this relationship") rather than to the relationship ("we are both responsible for these problems").

As we shall describe in detail later, the goal of behavioral intervention in marriage is to shift the couple from coercive to positive strategies of behavior change. It is assumed that all couples are faced with conflict issues. Those couples with adequate relationship skills can resolve their problems to the betterment of their marriage and each other.

Summary

The three theoretical approaches presented in this section represent the major conceptual perspectives on marriage and marital therapy. The psychoanalytic approach has probably had the most conceptual influence, but it has provided little in the way of treatment procedures. Systems theory and behavioral theory have been less influential conceptually, but they have provided the bulk of treatment procedures used specifically for treating relationship difficulties. Another theoretical approach, client-centered or nondirective therapy (Carkhuff, 1969, 1972; Rogers, 1951), has not provided a comprehensive view of marriage and marital therapy and therefore was not discussed. However, as we shall see later in this chapter, the client-centered or nondirective therapy movement has provided some important procedures for treating relationships.

The three theoretical approaches represent separate but overlapping viewpoints on marriage and marital therapy. They differ in their emphasis on the individual, the dyad, and the family system. Psychoanalytic theory traditionally has focused on individual developmental history as the casual explanation for distressed functioning, and behavioral theories have emphasized the current, controlling contingencies present in dyadic interaction. In contrast, systems theories have focused on the entire family unit, viewing individual pathology as a function of system properties.

There are many points of contact among the theories. Relationship rules represent a common emphasis for both systems and behavioral theories (Weiss, 1978). Some systems approaches, like Bowen's theory (Bowen, 1961, 1966, 1976a, 1976b, 1976c), share an emphasis with psychoanalytic approaches on the marital partners' families of origin.

Other similarities and differences among the three major theories of marriage and marital therapy could be identified. However, such similarities and differences have practical implication only to the extent that they imply assessment and treatment procedures. It is to these more practical issues that we now turn.

MARITAL ASSESSMENT

The assessment of marital dysfunction stands out from most other forms of assessment in that there is little if any emphasis on traditional diagnosis. Simply labelling a couple as having marital problems has minimal utility from the standpoint of treatment except to suggest that a relationship focus is in order. Actual decisions about how to conduct therapy depend on a more thorough functional analysis of the situation surrounding the couple's problems. Furthermore, according to the policies of most third-party providers, a DSM label of marital maladjustment does not even provide clients with a diagnosis worthy of reimbursement. Thus, differential diagnosis is rarely conducted with couples for the purposes of correctly identifying the marital problems. If used at all, differential diagnosis is likely to serve the purpose of screening out persons whom the therapist views as inappropriate candidates for marital therapy: some therapists for example, exclude from marital therapy any person with a psychotic disorder or borderline personality.

Since there is minimal need for formal diagnosis, marital assessment can be devoted exclusively to the important functions of providing direction for the therapeutic intervention and evaluating the efficacy of that intervention. As such, marital therapists of varying orientations tend to minimize the distinctions between assessment and treatment, viewing them as intimately intertwined rather than as separate phases in the therapeutic process (Ables & Brandsma, 1977; Minuchin, 1974; Sager, 1976; Weiss & Margolin, 1977). Marital therapists have also been informal and practical in their development of assessment procedures, relying most heavily on interview data which they might supplement with objective scales and behavioral measurements. Generally, there is little enthusiasm for individually oriented projective or objective measures among therapists whose primary consideration is the marital relationship.

The Interview

As an assessment procedure, the interview fulfills two aims: it functions as a fact-finding session and as a sample of the couple's interactional style. Marital therapists tend to emphasize one or the other of these objectives as a reflection of their predilections toward content versus process issues. In addition, therapists' theoretical orientations influence whether or not the interview is conducted conjointly and whether the content is present or past-oriented.

Compared to therapists of other theoretical positions, psychoanalytically oriented marital therapists are more likely to have one or more separate sessions with each partner. The goals of these interviews are to assess the individuals' separate histories, psychic processes, and ego functioning, as well as to establish a relationship and allow for the confiding of "secrets" (Nadelson & Paolino, 1978). Other psychodynamically oriented therapists are also interested in the developmental histories of each partner, particularly in their abilities to resolve early symbiotic ties; but they value conjoint interviews as a vehicle for assessing how the spouses respond to the rules and structure of therapy (Ables & Brandsma, 1977). Data from a psychodynamically oriented interview is sometimes catalogued in terms of marriage contracts; that is, conscious and unconscious, verbalized and unverbalized, expectations and terms of the relationship. An assessment of the conflict in the two partners' individually expressed contracts provides a basis for formulating the therapy plan (Martin, 1976; Sager, 1976).

Therapists with a systems orientation are likely to see the marital partners conjointly or perhaps in the context of the entire nuclear family. Within that model, therapist styles differ considerably in the degree to which the partners direct their comments to the therapist (Bowen, 1976) or interact with one another (Minuchin, 1974). Systems therapists collect their assessment data experientially by actively probing family members to interact differently (Sluzki, 1978), a strategy particularly prone to minimizing the distinction between assessment and therapy. The purpose of these probes may be to define family boundaries and coalitions (Minuchin, 1974); to examine whether the relationship is complementary, symmetrical, or parallel (Lederer & Jackson, 1968; Watzlawick et al., 1967); or to identify closed, open, or random family systems (Kantor & Lehr, 1975). Data from this assessment process may be translated into a visual mapping of family structures, showing the original structures and new ones that develop over the course of additional experimental probes.

Assessment interviews in the behavioral approach are conducted conjointly, span two or more sessions, and serve several distinct purposes. The first purpose is to build positive expectancies and trust, to provide a structure that minimizes nonproductive complaining, and to undermine spouses' notions that unilateral goals will be supported (Jacobson & Margolin, 1979; Weiss & Birchler, 1978). A second purpose is to explore spouses' thoughts, feelings, and behaviors that currently affect their marital satisfaction. The third and perhaps most important purpose of the interview is to observe how the partners interact with one another, how they present themselves to a third party, how they attribute the marital problems, and how they formulate requests of one another (Jacobson & Margolin, 1979). For behavioral marital therapists, the interview typically is used in conjunction with one or more objective inventories and observational measures which are described in the next section.

Objective Measures

Most objective inventories of marital functioning measure either marital satisfaction, marital stability, or spouses' perceptions of their interaction in specific realms of the relationship. Among the assortment of these inventories, there is considerable variability in terms of their specificity; some provide a global index of marital adjustment and others identify specific strengths and weaknesses of the relationship. The most well-known index for a global estimate of marital satisfaction is the Locke-Wallace Marital Adjustment Scale (MAS) (Locke & Wallace, 1959), a 15-item questionnaire with scores ranging from high marital distress (2) to high marital adjustment (161). The MAS is frequently adopted as a quick means of screening marital adjustment versus distress, with a score of 100 being the accepted cut-off point. The Dyadic Adjustment Scale (DAS) by Spanier (1976) is similar in format to the MAS and, in fact, includes many of the same items. However, this more recent index contains a greater number of items, eliminates the sex bias found in MAS scoring, and provides information on four factors—dyadic satisfaction, dyadic cohesion, dyadic consensus, and affectional expression. Global measurements of marital satisfaction also have been assessed in an ongoing basis throughout treatment with spouses providing daily ratings of "current marital happiness" on a 7- or 9-point scale, ranging from "completely unhappy" to "completely happy" (Azrin, Naster & Jones, 1973; Weiss & Margolin, 1977).

Another type of objective measure sacrifices the quantifiable nature of data produced by the DAS and MAS but surpasses those measurements in terms of providing detailed information about the perceived strengths and weaknesses of the relationship. The prototypical example is the Marital Pre-Counseling Inventory (MPI) (Stuart & Stuart, 1972) which assesses nine separate areas: Goals for Behavior Change, Resources for Change, Degree of Marital Understanding, Power Distribution, Congruence of Priorities, Communication Effectiveness, Sexual Satisfaction, Congruence in Child Management, and General Marital Satisfaction. For some of the areas, spouses respond to the same set of questions in terms of themselves and the partner, thereby assessing the congruence between partners' separate views of the relationship. Since there are only sparse validity data for the MPI and only some of the sections are scored, this instrument is limited as an evaluative measure. However, the MPI is highly valuable to the clinician in the beginning stages of therapy: it provides organized, comprehensive data relevant to the formulation of therapy goals and also socializes clients into therapy by directing their observations to positive elements of their own and the spouse's behavior.

The Oregon Marital Studies Center designed the Areas of Change Questionnaire (AC), a measure of relationship satisfaction, and the Marital Status Inventory (MSI), a measure of marital stability. The AC (Weiss & Birchler, 1975) serves the dual functions of providing: (1) quantifiable data that indicate level of marital distress and can be used as outcome measures; and (2) specific content information upon which to plan treatment strategies. This instrument assesses marital satisfaction by asking how much each partner wants the other to change. In completing the two-part questionnaire, each spouse first indicates whether the partner should increase, decrease, or not change each of 34 specific behaviors; the respondent then indicates how she or he imagines the partner will mark the same set of items. Scoring of this questionnaire provides information on total change sought by each partner as well as perceptual accuracy between partners. Norms for the AC come from Birchler and Webb (1977) who report total change scores of 28.0 and 6.9 respectively for distressed and nondistressed couples.

The second instrument from this research group, the Marital Status Inventory (Weiss & Cerreto, 1975), is a Guttman scaling of 14 steps toward divorce. Spouses indicate which steps they have taken toward the dissolution of the relationship. For example: Have they thought about divorce? Have they discussed it? Have they established separate checking accounts? This index provides one of the few measurements of relationship stability.

Behavioral Assessment

Behavioral marital assessment encompasses two primary strategies: spouses' monitoring of day-to-day relationship behaviors; and observation by trained coders of the couple's communication or interaction style. Both of these approaches are concerned with the occurrence or nonoccurrence of specific behaviors, but they differ in terms of specificity and naturalness. The first approach is designed to reconstruct the couple's daily behavioral patterns: spouses recall and record behaviors at relatively frequent intervals (e.g., daily, hourly), but the measurement is still based upon self-report. In contrast, the behavioral observations circumvent problems of delayed recall through the moment-to-moment recording of well defined behavioral categories, but the structure for obtaining these observations may cause them to be obtrusive to the participants.

Spouse-monitoring Procedures. The Oregon group developed a third instrument, the Spouse Observation Checklist (SOC) (Patterson, 1976; Weiss, 1978; Weiss & Margolin, 1977), to examine relationship adjustment in terms of the couple's day-to-day exchange of rewarding and punishing behaviors. This eight-page checklist contains approximately 400 items which have been categorized as pleasing and displeasing relationship events; for example, "spouse greeted me affectionately when I came home" and "spouse said something unkind to me." SOC items also have been classified into the following content areas of marital interaction: Companionship, Affection, Sex, Consideration, Communication Process, Coupling Activities, Child Care, Household Management, Financial Decision Making, Employment, Personal Habits, and Self–Spouse Independence. Spouses collect SOC data throughout the assessment and intervention phases of therapy by going through the entire inventory each evening, preferably before bedtime, and checking which items occurred during the previous 24-hour period, Normative data on the SOC indicate that mean please: displease ratios are approximately 4 : 1 for distressed spouses and 12 : 1 to 30 : 1 for nondistressed spouses (Birchler et al., 1975; Margolin, 1979a).

In addition to providing frequency data on the exchange of specific relationship behaviors, the SOC also answers the question of what behaviors are particularly important to a spouse's perceived satisfaction with the relationship (Christensen & Nies, 1980; Jacobson, Waldron & Moore, in press; Margolin, 1979a; Wills, Weiss, & Patterson, 1974). The final step in filling out the SOC requires spouses to indicate their satisfaction for a given day by marking a 9-point scale that ranges from totally dissatisfied (1) to totally satisfied (9). The association between fluctuations in behavioral frequency data and fluctuations in daily satisfaction offers important information about the types of behaviors that account for the greatest variance in daily satisfaction. Identifying the behaviors that have this sort of impact on satisfaction offers direction for planning the therapeutic intervention.

When a couple describes problems that are relatively restricted in range, nonetheless important to the couple's marital well being, the therapist may choose to forego the extensive nature of SOC data collection and utilize other self- or spouse-monitoring measures. Because these procedures are essentially tailor-made to suit the particular problem area, the therapist must decide how best to observe the target behavior(s): Who will observe what behaviors, during what time period, using what unit of measurement, and with what method for recording observations? The behavioral diary is one commonly used method to obtain information about the environmental variables that control a specific behavior. In keeping such a diary, spouses record each occurrence of a behavior in a narrative fashion, indicating the events that preceded or followed the target behavior. Another approach is to have the spouses simply tally the frequency of specified behaviors. When two or more behaviors are monitored, multiple baseline comparisons are possible (see Hersen & Barlow, 1976). These procedures provide an index of the correspondence between change in a particular behavior and the application of a specific intervention.

Observational Procedures. Observational procedures in marital assessment have ranged from relatively structured problem-solving discussions in the laboratory setting (Carter & Thomas, 1973; Gottman, Notarius, Gonso, & Markman, 1976; Hops, Wills, Patterson, & Weiss, 1972) to more naturalistic observations of typical interactions in the home (Follingstad, Sullivan, Ierace, Ferrara, & Haynes, 1976; Patterson, Weiss, & Hops, 1976; Robinson & Price, 1976). Early laboratory-based marital assessments were designed to evoke spouses' decision-making patterns in resolving tasks with built-in conflicts (Jacobs, 1976; Riskin & Faunce, 1972; Winter & Ferreira, 1969). More recently, laboratory assessment has sought to elicit spouses' characteristic patterns of resolving differences of opinion on real-life relationship problems. The problem-solving discussions that evolve from these procedures are videotaped and then coded by observers trained in highly complex coding systems that examine the ongoing sequential interactional patterns. One such system, the Marital Interaction Coding System (MICS) (Hops et al., 1972), contains 29 categories for recording verbal and nonverbal behaviors (e.g., problem solution, compromise, complaint, laugh, not tracking) in the ongoing sequential pattern in which they occur. In an even more complex system by Gottman and his colleagues (Gottman, Notarius, Gonso, & Markman, 1976), each brief segment of behavior is first coded for content and then coded again by different observers for positive or negative nonverbal cues. Both coding systems have been shown to discriminate distressed and nondistressed couples (Gottman et al., 1977; Vincent et al., 1975). According to the Gottman findings, however, adequate discrimination is demonstrated only when content codes are considered in the context of the simultaneous nonverbal codes.

Behavioral assessment of couple interactions has included having the spouses code problem-solving discussions that were also coded by trained observers. Results from studies utilizing these procedures have shown that the nature of the data influence spouses' abilities to code accurately. Gottman's group (Gottman, Notarius, Markman, Bank, Yoppi, & Rubin, 1976), for example, found no differences between distressed and nondistressed couples in the number of positive messages sent; yet distressed, as compared to nondistressed, spouses underestimated the number of positive statements received from the partner. These findings may hold implications for any participant observation method in which spouses' observations are susceptible to the influence of subjective impressions.

One other option is to conduct marital observations in the home setting. While it seems that home observations would hold greater potential for generalizability, these observations are hampered by the effects of introducing observers into the home; significant interactions between spouses are unlikely to occur in the presence of observers (Peterson, 1977). However, there is hope that some new developments in this area will surmount the reactivity problem. Instead of live observers, tape recorders can be installed that automatically activate at certain decibel levels or timed intervals (Bernal, Gibson, William, & Pesses, 1971; Christensen, 1979). Further experimentation is necessary to evaluate the quality of the data that are available through these procedures.

Assessment for Research versus Clinical Purposes

Marital assessment procedures present a trade-off between measures that are methodologically sound and measures that are efficient to administer. Unfortunately, this trade-off creates a distinction between what the researcher is likely to employ to analyze the efficacy of treatment procedures and what the clinician is likely to administer to gain further understanding of a couple's presenting concerns. Objective assessment procedures and the interview are the mainstay of the assessment armamentarium of the clinician who wants to collect a wealth of information with minimal investment. These measurements provide data that relate directly to the formulation of treatment objectives (e.g., the AC and MPI) and that offer a pretherapy and post-therapy comparison (e.g., the DAS, MAS, and AC). On the negative side, the reliability of these instruments may be compromised by spouses' inabilities to recall and report accurately, and their validity may be affected by social desirability factors (Edmonds, Withers, & Dibatista, 1972; Murstein & Beck, 1972).

The second category of assessment measures, the spouse-monitoring procedures, actually span the behavioral and objective methodologies. These procedures are unique in that they provide efficient, ongoing data collection throughout therapy. Compared to objective measures, they present fewer problems of recall and response bias. On the negative side, recent evidence (Christensen & Nies, 1980) suggests that untrained spouses are not very accurate observers of their interpersonal behavior. Also, it is presumed, although not yet proven, that these monitoring procedures are reactive and actually evoke behavior changes. However, the clinician may view this reactivity as a virtue and not a vice.

The category of behavioral observations conducted by trained observers has been of greatest utility for researchers who want an unbiased and reliable evaluation of treatment effects as well as a detailed profile of spouses' communication styles. These procedures are not highly accessible to the clinician in their current form, but modifications could make them more feasible. Audiotaped samples of a couple's interaction in either the home or therapy setting are available to most clinicians. While not trained in a complex coding system, the therapist can listen to these tapes and derive important formulations about the couple's communication style. The tape-recording may present an intrusive influence for the couple, but these procedures generally prove to be more instructive to both the therapist and couple than asking the couple simply to describe their interactions.

For both the researcher and clinician, an issue to be considered is the convergent and discriminant validity among marital assessment measures. Thus far there have been only a few attempts to measure the relationships among different procedures. Within the objective mode of data collection, both AC scores and the frequency of SOC "pleases" correlate in the predicted directions with MAS scores (Margolin, 1978b; Weiss, Hops, & Patterson, 1973). However, there is still little evidence of convergent validity across assessment methodologies. Significant correlations between outside observers' coding and spouses' own coding of similar behaviors have been found in the home (Robinson & Price, 1976) but not in the laboratory (Margolin, 1978a). Low correlations were found between behaviors coded by an outside observer and spouses' subjective impressions of marital satisfaction (Margolin, 1978b; Robinson & Price, 1976). In general, marital assessment procedures and the relationships among them require substantial empirical investigation.

Summary

The aim of marital assessment is twofold: to formulate intervention goals and to assess the efficacy of the intervention. On the basis of an initial assessment, the therapist should be able to determine whether or not marital therapy is appropriate and to identify problematic content issues as well as nonfunctional interactional processes. Ideally, the therapist does not end assessment at this point, but continues to collect information about the effectiveness of the intervention and the factors contributing to its efficacy.

KNOWN TREATMENT PROCEDURES

In this section we address general treatment issues, specific treatment components, and behavior change procedures. Our discussion is limited to the topics in which empirical research has provided at least some tentative leads. In discussing outcome studies that provide the empirical basis for this section, we use Gurman and Kniskern's (1978) design quality rating system for marital and family studies. This system, which includes the categories poor (P), fair (F), good (G), and very good (VG), is based on 14 dimensions that reflect both design and measurement qualities relevant to marital or family outcome studies.

General Treatment Issues

At the outset of treatment, the marital therapist must face three general treatment issues: Who should be seen in therapy, the husband or the wife or both? Who should see the clients, a single therapist or co-therapist team? How long should one anticipate treatment to last?

As indicated earlier, a variety of formats for treating marital problems have been attempted. Probably most marital complaints, like most other presenting complaints, traditionally have been treated by seeing one individual in therapy. Some striking results emerge, however, when the outcomes of individual therapy for marital problems have been compared with formats involving both partners. In their review of the literature, Gurman and Kniskern (1978) have shown that across a variety of studies, individual therapy produces less improvement (48 percent versus 65 percent) and more deterioration (11.6 percent versus 5.6 percent) than formats involving both partners. Clearly, the evidence argues strongly for seeing both members of the marital dyad. The particular format that showed the most improvement and least deterioration was conjoint therapy, although concurrent therapy was a close second.

A second general treatment question asks, "Who should see the marital pair?" Co-therapy by a male-female team is widely advocated by marital therapists (Gurman & Kniskern, 1978). However, comparisons of gross improvement rates across many studies of marital therapy show no practical difference in outcome between co-therapist and single-therapist marital therapy (Gurman, 1973). Until recently, no direct comparisons of co-therapy versus single-therapist treatment had been conducted (Roman & Meltzer, 1977). However, Birchler (1979) reports preliminary results from a study by Turner which does compare the two formats, and initial results support the superiority of co-therapy.

A final general consideration is the length of treatment. Surprisingly, the available data do not indicate that more treatment is better treatment. Several investigators have found no relationship between treatment length and outcome (Freeman, Leavens, & McCulloch, 1969, P; Wattie, 1973, G; Zeigler, 1973, G). In one study (Reid & Shyne, 1969, G) it was found that time-limited couples therapy produces a better outcome than "continuing service" or open-ended treatment. Most marital therapy is similar to crisis intervention in that it typically lasts only about nine sessions (Gurman & Kniskern, 1978).

It is encouraging that the answers to each of these general treatment questions, with the possible exception of the co-therapy question, suggest that the best treatment is also the most cost-effective treatment. Or stated more conservatively, the cost-effective procedures are as powerful as the more expensive procedures.

Specific Treatment Components

Empirical research examines four specific treatment components: basic communication skills, problem solving, behavioral exchange, and behavioral contracting. While all of these components can be construed as developing new relationship or communication skills (Birchler, 1979), it is not clear whether the skills are actually missing from the behavioral repertoires of distressed couples or whether these couples simply fail to exhibit the necessary behaviors in the presence of their spouse.

Basic Communication Skills. The first treatment component, which we shall call Basic Communication Skills (BCS), grew out of the nondirective therapy movement (Carkhuff, 1969, 1972; Guerney, 1977; Rogers, 1951). Its emphasis is on feeling expression and empathic listening. A variety of programs have been developed to train marital partners in these skills; for example, the Conjugal Relationship Enhancement program (Guerney, 1977; Rappaport, 1976) and, to a lesser extent, the Minnesota Couples Communication Program (Miller, Nunnally, & Wackman, 1976). Several individual investigators have given training in these types of skills but have called their programs by other names, such as interpersonal communication skills training (Pierce, 1973) and human relation skills training (Valle & Marinelli, 1975). Many behavioral marriage therapists also have adopted the training of these communication skills in their therapy programs (Jacobson & Margolin, 1979; Turkewitz, 1977; Weiss, 1978). Though all these training programs treat BCS quite differently, they share certain similarities that allow for their combination for the purposes of this chapter.

Basic Communication Skills training usually focuses on both speaker and listener behaviors. When in the role of speaker, marital partners are trained to be direct, emotionally expressive, and specific. Being direct implies speaking for oneself rather than speaking for others, invoking the support of others, or referencing abstract principles. Marital partners are trained to speak in terms of "I want" and "I feel" rather than in terms of "we should," "other people do," or "married couples ought to." Being emotionally expressive implies describing one's own feelings rather than casting accusations and blame. For example, a spouse may be directed to say "I feel angry" rather than "you SOB, you did it again!" And finally, partners are instructed to be specific, to reference their feelings in particular events. The statement "I feel hurt when you forget my birthday" is preferable to "I feel hurt because you don't care about me" because of the greater specificity of the former statement. Specific statements imply less blame and often suggest possible changes.

In addition to speaker skills, couples are trained in how to listen to one another. The central idea is that the listener must behaviorally demonstrate to the speaker that he or she has heard by repeating, paraphrasing, or summarizing the message. This active response by the listener enables the speaker to clarify or correct any miscommunication. In addition to this direct feedback process, emphasis is also placed on the feelings that underlie the speaker's message. As listeners, marital partners are encouraged to reflect the feeling of the spouse's messages as well as to paraphrase its content. If one partner says "I can't seem to catch up with my work," the other can simply paraphrase the message, for example, "you're behind in your work." However, a more desirable response would capture the feeling behind the message, for example, "you're feeling overwhelmed by all your work."

Different communication programs vary greatly in their specific training procedures and their emphasis on particular skills. However, the skeleton description of BCS just presented represents some of the target behaviors common to most training programs.

Some of the empirical support for training in BCS comes from research with marital enrichment programs in which nondistressed couples are provided with training to improve their relationships. The Conjugal Relationship Enhancement Program (Rappaport, 1976) and, to a lesser extent, the Minnesota Couples Communication Program (Miller et al., 1976) are examples. Since marital enrichment programs are not focused on distressed couples and these programs have been reviewed elsewhere (Birchler, 1979; Gurman & Kniskern, 1977), they will not be described here.

Support for BCS training in a clinical context comes from studies comparing this approach to no-treatment controls and groups receiving other treatments. In a well-designed study, Turkewitz (1977, VG) found BCS training to be superior to a waiting-list control group and a variety of self-report measures, and equivalent to a group that combined BCS training and behavior exchange procedures. Cardillo (1971, VG) found BCS training to be superior to another communication training condition, and Cassidy (1973, VG), Pierce (1973, F) and Valle and Marinelli (1975, F) demonstrated the superiority of BCS training over traditional therapy conditions emphasizing insight and catharsis. Most of these studies were limited by their exclusive reliance on self-report measures and an absence of follow-up assessment. Taken as a whole, however, they do offer some support for BCS training.

Problem Solving. The second treatment component has been called problem solving (Jacobson & Margolin, 1979; Weiss, 1978) or conflict resolution skills (Birchler, 1979). The BCS training discussed previously can lead to understanding of problems, but it does not necessarily lead to their resolution. In many cases BCS may be a necessary but not sufficient condition for the resolution of conflictual issues. Therapists who focus on both components emphasize the importance of making a clear distinction between communication for understanding and communication for resolving problems (Jacobson & Margolin, 1979; Weiss, 1978).

Training in problem solving teaches the couple to define their problems, to generate possible solutions for their difficulties, to evaluate those solutions, and finally to negotiate agreements specifying particular solutions. Attention also is given to certain background variables like the value of a planned agenda, a setting where interruptions are unlikely and a collaborative spirit on the part of both partners. Couples initially are trained to define their problems in specific and descriptive, rather than derogatory, terms. Once a problem definition is agreed upon, couples are encouraged to brainstorm about any changes that might solve the problem. A spouse's proposal that "you could call me when you must work late" is appropriate, but the accusation that "you could stop being so inconsiderate" has no place in brainstorming. When all possible solutions have been generated, the couple evaluates and negotiates their options until they formulate an agreement to implement a particular course of action.

Behavioral Exchange.   Behavioral exchange procedures refer to the explicit trading of behaviors that each spouse desires. Though the term "behavioral exchange" can be used to refer to the negotiation procedures involved in problem solving, our usage focuses only on procedures directed at marital activities that are not highly conflictual but, through their absence, detract from marital satisfaction. Therapists often direct couples to increase the frequency of their companionship activities or to exchange pleasing behaviors. Since distressed couples may not know the activities that please their partners, exercises are necessary to identify each spouse's unique likes and dislikes. The Spouse Observation Checklist developed by Weiss and Patterson (Patterson, 1976; Weiss & Margolin, 1977) can be used for this purpose. Once the couple is knowledgeable of what pleases each other, a variety of strategies, described in detail by Jacobson and Margolin (1979), are possible for increasing the frequency of these events. One common strategy is "love days" (Weiss et al., 1973; Wills et al., 1974) or "caring days" (Stuart, 1976). In these procedures, the couple specifies two days during the week when each partner will, respectively, increase the frequency of behaviors pleasing to the other partner.

Behavioral Contracting.   Behavioral contracting, or contingency contracting, refers to written agreements that specify behaviors for each partner to change and consequences to follow the completion of these behaviors. Usually behavioral contracting has been conducted as a final stage in problem solving, although problem solving can be completed without either a written agreement or specific contingencies for enactment of the agreement. Furthermore, contingency contracting can be used to specify the enactment of nonconflictual behaviors, as in the behavior exchange procedures just discussed (Rappaport & Harrell, 1972).

Two kinds of contingency contracts have been discussed in the literature (Jacobson & Margolin, 1979; Weiss, Birchler, & Vincent, 1974). Quid pro quo contracts specify a direct exchange between partners, in which one partner's behavior is contingent on the other's behavior. For example, Sue agrees to talk with Harry about his day for 20 minutes whenever he comes home from work on time. Parallel or "good faith" contracts specify changes for both partners, but these changes are not contingently related. Instead, additional consequences are made contingent on the specified changes. For example, Harry agrees to come home from work on time and will be rewarded with a record album of his choice when he has completed this goal five consecutive times. Sue agrees to talk with Harry about his day for 20 minutes each night and will be rewarded with a book of her choice when she has completed her goal five consecutive times. Parallel contracts can include rewards from the spouse as well as the external rewards listed above, but these rewards should not include behaviors that are directly related to the couple's problems. In the example given, Harry could agree to provide Sue with a back rub each night that she engaged in her contracted behavior, provided back rubs were not a conflictual issue for the couple.

Weiss et al. (1974) have argued that parallel contracts are superior to quid pro quo contracts, at least for severely distressed couples, because they eliminate the problem of "who goes first" and the failure of one partner to make the specified changes does not logically cause the whole contract to break down. However, Jacobson and Margolin (1979) argue that the quid pro quo contract is simpler; powerful reinforcers, apart from the changes requested of the partner, are difficult to find; and the problems of the quid pro quo contract can be alleviated by the therapist specifying who goes first and establishing contingencies for reinstatement of the contract if it is broken.

Empirical Research. Empirical research usually has not made clear distinctions between problem solving, behavioral exchange, and contingency contracting. We present these distinctions because we believe them to be clinically useful and because a few of the studies, which will be discussed later, do differentiate these components. For the moment we shall consider the research that has been globally identified as behavioral marital therapy and has involved some combination of these three procedures. As in the discussion of research on BCS training, outcome results on nondistressed couples are excluded.

Several studies have demonstrated the superiority of behavioral marriage therapy (BMT) over no-treatment or waiting-list control conditions on self-report measures (Jacobson, 1977, G; Jacobson, 1978b, VG; Tsoi-Hoshmand, 1976, F; Turkewitz, 1977, VG). Furthermore, the two Jacobson studies have demonstrated the superiority of BMT using observational measures of the couples' problem-solving behaviors. These two studies are also notable for their demonstration of long-term maintenance at 1-year and 6-month follow-ups respectively.

When BMT has been compared to attention placebo conditions or nondirective therapy conditions, a similar pattern of positive results emerge. Jacobson (1978, VG) and Margolin and Weiss (1978b, VG) demonstrated the superiority of two types of BMT using both self-report and observational measures. Using only self-report measures, Crowe (1973, 1974, G) also showed the superiority of BMT over a supportive-nondirective group. Only Becking (1973, VG) was not able to find differences between BMT and an attention placebo condition.

When contrasted with other treatment approaches, the results of BMT have been more equivocal. Crowe (1973, 1974, G) showed that BMT is generally superior to an interpretive systems approach, and McLean, Ogston, and Graver (1973, G) showed that BMT was superior to a mixed treatment program for depressed outpatients. Liberman et al. (1976, F) found that BMT was superior to an interaction-insight group on some behavioral measures but not on self-report measures. However, Turkewitz (1977, VG) compared BCS training and BCS training plus BMT and found no differences between the two. In post hoc analyses she did discover an interesting treatment-by-age interaction. Younger couples benefited most from BMT and older couples benefited most from communication training. In reviewing the Turkewitz study, Jacobson (in press) notes that the BMT condition did not include much problem-solving training; had the BMT included a strong problem-solving component, differential effects might have been apparent.

Earlier in this chapter, a distinction was made between problem-solving training, behavioral exchange, and contingency contracting. The work of Jacobson has provided the empirical base for these distinctions. For example, Jacobson (1979, VG) has provided some preliminary evidence for the effectiveness of behavioral exchange alone and for the effectiveness of problem solving without contingency contracting. Jacobson (1978, VG) compared four conditions: quid pro quo contracting, parallel contracting, placebo control, and no-treatment control. While both treatments were superior to control conditions, there were no differences between the two behavioral treatments. The two contracting procedures may produce equivalent results, or they may be a superfluous addition to the problem-solving training that occurred in both treatment conditions.

Behavior Change Procedures

The four treatment components just discussed refer to the targets of marital intervention. Therapists assume that couples who use some combination of BCS, problem solving, behavioral exchange, and behavioral contracting will resolve their difficulties and increase their relationship satisfaction. But how does the marital therapist train spouses in these particular skills or bring about these behavior changes? We now focus on strategic questions about inducing behavior change.

Direct Training Procedures. Perhaps the most direct methods for changing behavior are skill training procedures. These procedures, used in BCS training, problem solving, and, to a lesser extent, behavioral exchange and behavior contracting, can be conceptualized as three processes: instruction, practice, and feedback. First the therapist exposes the couple to information about the skills. This exposure may be through some combination of prepared materials (written descriptions or tape-recorded presentations), verbal instruction, or modeling. With sufficient instruction, the couple can then practice the skills. This practice, often called behavior rehearsal or role playing, occurs in both the therapy session and in the home. The therapist sometimes assists the couple in structuring their home practice sessions to increase the probability that practice will occur without interruption (Jacobson & Margolin, 1979). The final element of skill training is feedback. The therapist must provide corrective feedback to the couple and the couple must provide feedback on the success of their efforts to each other. Most often this feedback consists of simple verbal comments. However, audio-taped and audio-visual recordings often are used as an aid. Recently several innovative mechanical devices have been developed to assist couples in providing each other with direct, immediate feedback. Devices developed by Margolin and Weiss (1978a), Thomas and his associates (Thomas, Carter, & Gambrill, 1971), and Gottman and his associates (Gottman, Notarius, Markman, Bank, Yoppi, & Rubin, 1976) can all be used by couples to generate specific and immediate feedback to each other, either during the communication or subsequent to it by means of taped replays.

There is little good empirical data explicitly testing the value of instruction, practice, and feedback in marital therapy. Since these procedures were often used in the outcome studies on BCS training and BMT, however, they receive indirect empirical support. Furthermore, the research on learning suggests the value of procedures like instruction, practice, and feedback for learning any skill (De Cecco, 1968).

Indirect Behavior Change Strategies. Sometimes direct approaches to altering couple behavior are met with resistance and failure, and the therapist must try alternative strategies. We discuss two indirect strategies for altering couple behavior: reattribution or reframing and paradoxical instructions. These strategies are sometimes used alone or as a method of preparing the couple for one of the treatment components discussed previously.

The first strategy, common to both behavioral and systems approaches, is reframing (Watzlawick, 1976a, 1976b; Watzlawick, Beavin, & Jackson, 1967) or reattribution (Margolin, Christensen, & Weiss, 1975; Margolin & Weiss, 1978). In this approach, the couple is presented with an alternative perspective on their marital problems. For example, behavioral applications are directed at reducing spouses' attribution of their distress to deficiencies in each other. The behavior therapist provides the opposing view that marital problems result from inadequacies in the relationship rather than in the individual. If successful, such interventions enable couples to give up some of their mutual blame and engage in more collaborative efforts to improve their relationship.

In a somewhat different vein, systems applications tend to reinterpret negative behavior as positive behavior. The spouse with a complaining partner might be enjoined to view the complaints as a sign of partner concern and caring rather than unkind annoyances. Thus, systems reformulations resolve problems by changing spouses' perspectives rather than altering specific behaviors. Sometimes, however, these reformulations may produce beneficial paradoxical effects on behavior (see below).

Only one empirical outcome study is relevant to the strategies discussed here. Margolin and Weiss (1978b, VG) demonstrated that BMT with a strong focus on attributing success and failure to mutual rather than individual functioning was superior to BMT alone on self-report and observational measures. However, other results from this study were somewhat equivocal in that there were equivalent reductions in negative relationship behaviors for both groups.

Another indirect approach to changing marital behavior is paradoxical intervention (Haley, 1973, 1976; Frankl, 1975; L'Abate, 1978;

Sluzki, 1978). Though no controlled-outcome research has evaluated the effectiveness of these interventions, their widespread use warrants their inclusion in this chapter. Primarily espoused by systems theorists, paradoxical interventions refer to therapist activities that overtly encourage behavior opposite from what is truly desired. Acting in a paradoxical manner, marital therapists occasionally will prescribe problem behavior, compliment partners on problem behavior, encourage relapses, and express doubts that any positive change will endure. The logic for these interventions derives from the belief that symptomatic behavior is a method of controlling interaction and defining relationships. When paradoxical interventions are used successfully, symptoms can no longer control the responses of others in the same manner and then are expected to decrease in frequency and intensity. As an example, consider the spouse whose constant aches and pains serve to control the partner's behavior. The therapist, taking those physical complaints very seriously, might instruct the spouse to go to bed whenever the pains appear and rest without interruption. In addition, the therapist might put the partner in charge of the "sick" spouse. As long as going to bed did not serve as another mechanism of control, the "sick" spouse would be expected to relinquish his or her aches and pains since they could no longer control the partner. The objective of such a strategy would not be to reduce the overall attention to the partner, but to remove the controlling influence of the symptom.

The use of paradoxical interventions with resistant clients is thought to be especially useful. If the client truly resists the paradoxical instruction, she or he will engage in nonsymptomatic behavior. If the client complies with the instruction, then a step has been taken toward cooperation with the therapist. Either decision by the client represents a step toward improvement.

We urge caution in the use of paradoxical interventions. Though many provocative case examples attest to their power, no hard empirical data support their use. Furthermore, because they are deceptive and encourage problem behavior, paradoxical interventions can have unfortunate effects when used carelessly or by inexperienced therapists.

CLINICAL PRESCRIPTION

The previous section described the major components and strategies of marital therapy; this section offers suggestions on how to present these components to the couple in a well integrated, personalized treatment plan. The underlying premise is that the therapist must provide a context conducive to the couple's reception of therapy components if the components are to be effective (Jacobson & Margolin, 1979). This section considers some of the factors that make for such a context, e.g., an overall structure, the role of the therapist, and the difference between technology and strategy. This section is offered in a speculative vein since these issues have not been the object of empirical investigations.

Marital therapy ideally progresses through several phases: (1) an initial evaluation; (2) an interpretive meeting; (3) the intervention; (4) a post-therapy evaluation, and (5) follow-up therapy sessions and evaluation. The discussion here relates to phases 2 and 3, since the other phases are comprised of procedures previously described in the assessment section. Once the initial assessment is completed, the interpretive meeting provides a brief but critical step for introducing the couple to therapy (see Jacobson & Margolin, 1979). In this session, the therapist presents the couple with a formulation of their relationship based on the assessment data and a treatment plan for helping the couple to improve their relationship. If the therapist and couple come to a mutual decision to engage in the therapeutic endeavor, they should formalize their agreement in a treatment contract, i.e., an understanding of what each person may gain by engaging in such a process. Clients are best able to enter this agreement if they understand the overall goals and also have adequate information about the mechanics of therapy, e.g., how much it will cost, how long it may extend, and how much time per week it takes in addition to the therapy hour.

In planning the intervention, the overriding aim is for the couple to learn long-range strategies to handle their relationship more effectively. Thus, the therapist does not immediately strive to rid the couple of their problems, but focuses instead on teaching them coping strategies. Based on this objective, there is a natural progression to the previously discussed treatment components. Behavior exchange procedures, which are usually the first intervention, offer the couple immediate benefits in nonconflictual areas and help to maneuver them into a position of readiness for more demanding changes. Another reason for beginning with this intervention is that it requires no new skills and is comparatively easy to implement in a short period of time. Basic communication training is often selected as the second intervention because it, too, should precede problem-solving training. Unless spouses can take responsibility for their feelings and demonstrate that they have heard and can understand one another's position, problem solving cannot progress.

In addition to this overall sequence of behavior exchange, basic communication skills, and problem-solving training, a general structure for individual therapy sessions also exists. Therapy is present oriented with most of the session time spent on either what happened during the previous week or what is to occur in the upcoming week. Clients come to know they will receive homework assignments, so that between sessions they can practice what was learned in the previous session. Each new session begins with a review of the previous week, and particular emphasis always is paid to the couple's experience with their homework. The agenda for each session is made explicit to elicit the couple's aid in moving the session along and to make sure that the spouses' own agenda items are included. It must be understood that structure is not used to constrict or rigidify therapy. On the contrary, it serves as a way to insure that something is accomplished in each session that the couple can take home with them and continue to use.

Another important factor in developing a context that is conducive to therapeutic change is the therapist's own behavior. Whether or not it is the therapist's intention, his or her behavior influences each therapy session and serves as an important model for the couple. The necessity for the therapist to be directive is consistent with the emphasis on structure. The therapist cannot simply verbalize the conditions of structure but must, in fact, implement them. To facilitate a constructive working atmosphere, for example, requires that the therapist make active efforts to halt destructive and punitive interactions and to elicit cooperative behaviors. In addition, the therapist must be an effective instructor, laying the groundwork for behavior change while allowing the couple to arrive at answers on their own. Yet the therapist's skills at being directive and instructive are meaningless unless she or he develops a positive relationship with the couple and elicits their trust (Alexander, Barton, Schiavo, & Parsons, 1976; Gurman & Kniskern 1978). Trust is likely to develop if both spouses feel supported by the therapist, and if they find the therapy session to be a relatively safe place where their disappointments and pain are lessened rather than heightened. Finally, for the couple to embrace the therapy program and be willing to try new and risky behaviors, the therapist must communicate enthusiasm and confidence for his or her approach.

The brevity of this chapter forces us to talk as though there were a *therapy program* applicable to all couples; unfortunately this is not the case. By discussing the components and strategy of therapy, there is a strong risk that the therapist will become overly dependent on specific therapy components and pay little regard to the individual needs of each couple. We endorse an approach that starts with simple interventions and turns to complicated interventions only when they are needed. The best way to make decisions regarding the pacing of treatment components is continually to evaluate the couple's progress through the course of therapy. Each weekly success or failure tells the therapist what the next step should be. A couple's difficulty with or refusal to engage in a new behavior signals that the intervention is off course: perhaps there is too much emphasis on an unimportant target; perhaps the intervention is moving too quickly; or perhaps a paradoxical directive is in order to permit the couple to "continue" their problem behaviors.

There is no way within the confines of this chapter to do justice to the array of therapeutic decisions involved in improving a marital system. For the therapist who is more accustomed to individual therapy, just learning to refocus one's attention on the relationship rather than on the individual is a major step. For all marital therapists, it is important to be familiar with and employ specific interventions, while at the same time charting an overall treatment that is creative, flexible, and responsive to new input from the couple.

CASE REPORT

The case study that follows employs a behavioral treatment approach but diverges from the previously described strategy in that it includes the management of anger as a primary treatment focus. Sam and Ella R.,[1] aged 47 and 50 years old respectively, had been married for 5 years at the time they sought therapy. Both spouses had completed high school. Sam worked as a semiskilled laborer and Ella was a secretary. This relationship was a second marriage for each. They had three children from Ella's former marriage, one of whom still lived with Sam and Ella. Unlike many marital cases in which one spouse finally initiates therapy after an accumulation of destructive incidents, this referral had a distinct precipitant: Sam had hit Ella in the midst of an argument and drinking bout, causing three fractures to her jaw. Charges filed against Sam led to a referral for therapy by the district attorney.

A 2-week assessment was conducted with the couple to learn about the quality of their interaction in general and specifically about their problems handling anger. Overall, Ella expressed more relationship dissatisfaction than Sam as reflected in their scores on the DAS and AC (DAS = 74 and AC = 11 for Ella; DAS = 91 and AC = 19 for Sam). Despite their dissatisfaction, data from the MSI suggested that neither partner had seriously considered or actually taken steps toward separation. Baseline data on the SOC revealed low please: displease ratios of 6:1 for Sam and 1:10.6 for Ella. Since Ella's ratio of displeases to pleases was quite atypical, even for distressed spouses, her data probably reflected a cry for help.

The purpose in gathering information about the R.'s patterns of expressing anger was to identify what cues elicited and maintained the partners' angry reactions (Margolin, 1979b). It was evident from SOC data that the R.s bickered several times a day and became embroiled in more serious arguments approximately twice a week. The same set of complaints tended to surface in each of the R.s' arguments, regardless of who began the argument or what the central theme was: Ella wanted Sam to drink less, to reestablish a speaking relationship with one of her daughters, to pay attention to his personal hygiene, and to spend more time with her, particularly around the dinner hour. Sam, in turn, also wanted Ella to stop drinking, to stop lying about what she did drink, to keep the house in better order, and to stop criticizing him.

Information about the process of their arguments was derived from laboratory-based problem-solving sessions and from behavioral diaries in which they kept a record of each angry incident. Spouses' records in the behavioral diary were to include details about the circumstances surrounding each expression of anger, the specific angry behaviors that each partner emitted, and the manner in which the conflict was resolved. Regardless of which partner began a particular argument, it quickly turned into a crossfire of complaints with each partner hearing nothing of what the other had to say. Arguments ended when one partner abruptly walked away or refused to respond, or the couple's attention was diverted by a third party. Both partners contributed, but in different ways, to the highly negative tone of their interactions. Ella tended to dominate discussions, overriding Sam's statements and sidetracking the conversation to unrelated issues. In response, Sam unrelentingly maintained and repeated his original position. Although their arguments fell into familiar and well-rehearsed patterns, Sam and Ella still became visibly aroused with each new round: Ella became loud, flushed, and tearful, and Sam became increasingly white-knuckled and tense.

Treatment with the R.s had the triple focus of having the couple establish limits on their expressions of anger, develop problem-solving skills, and show greater appreciation for one another. The immediate objective was to help them feel that they had control over their anger. Work on this goal began during the first session even though the meeting is usually reserved for assessment. The first step required a ground rule establishing that physical violence was unacceptable. A potent contingency for this ground rule came from Ella, who said that she would leave the relationship if Sam ever hit her again. An intermediary contingency plan also was specified in case either partner felt that the ground rule was in jeopardy. That is, at the first sign that physical harm was imminent, Ella was to leave the house and drive to the home of her married daughter. Since both partners agreed that violence had no place in their relationship, the ground rule and contingencies were accepted with relief.

A second important step toward the goal of helping this couple handle anger differently was a reframing of the abusive incident so that responsibility for this incident as well as for future change did not reside solely with Sam. Although these spouses entered therapy with Sam designated as aggressor and Ella designated as victim, the escalation of anger in this couple could not be viewed as Sam's unilateral problem. In the couple's typical format for arguing, Ella launched highly punishing verbal attacks while Sam exercised restraint by ignoring Ella and saying little in return. Similar to other arguments that the R.s had had, the battle that brought them to the attention of the district attorney contained a long chain of events in which each spouse participated in the escalation of anger and lowered the partner's restraints against emitting aggressive behaviors. This particular argument had originated between Sam and Ella's 17-year-old daughter; but then Ella entered the argument, supporting her daughter and calling Sam profane names. Sam, of course, was responsible for the physical violence that occurred, but Ella's taunting was an important precipitant. The therapists' purpose in reframing the responsibility of this incident was not to relieve either partner of responsibility for what had happened but to elicit cooperation from both of them in seeing that the abusiveness could be stopped (Margolin, 1979b).

Perhaps the most important focus of treatment for the R.s was developing problem-solving skills and thereby discovering that they could actually resolve the sources of discontent that had plagued their relationship for years. The frustration and quick tempers displayed by Sam and Ella were related to their sense of impotence at being able to affect change in the areas they viewed as problematic. Problem solving led to the discovery that they could, in fact, resolve some of the problems that had been sources of conflict since the beginning of their relationship. However, problem solving did not come easily for this couple. In order to overcome their well-rehearsed escalations into a match of accusations, the spouses needed to identify and quickly terminate the behaviors that contributed to this destructive interaction. A concrete method for gaining control over these negative interactions involved the use of cue cards, each of which listed an irritating communication behavior of one partner (e.g., criticism, lecturing, not listening, interrupting). During problem-solving discussions, the spouses flashed the cards when they wanted to give feedback to each other that something was amiss in their interaction. The cards served as a vehicle for the delivery of feedback in a nonpunishing manner, and the situation itself was so unique that it increased their involvement in communication training.

Once the negative interactions subsided, Sam and Ella turned their attention to the process of negotiating and formalizing change agreements through written contracts. The relatively concrete requests specified by Sam and Ella lent themselves to the format of parallel change agreements, one of which appears below:

> I, Ella, agree to make sure that there are no glasses with alcohol around on days when I say that I have had nothing to drink.
>
> Reward: 25 roses
>
> I, Sam, agree to shower and shave before dinner on Saturday and Sunday.
>
> Reward; Ella gives Sam a special "thank you."

An additional focus of treatment was for the R.s to express some apppreciation to one another and to derive more enjoyment from each other's company. Initially this consisted of having them identify and write down one specific behavior each day that the partner had done that was pleasing. Sample appreciation notes exchanged during the first week included "I appreciate your giving me a hug this morning" from Ella and "I appreciate the way you handled the call to the phone company" from Sam. Another component of this goal was the identification of activities that both Sam and Ella found enjoyable. When they entered therapy, the R.s rarely spent time together or even shared meals. Through the course of therapy, they identified and engaged in several activities that both reported as enjoyable, e.g., playing craps, watching the World Series, and going out to dinner.

During the course of therapy it became quite evident that the R.'s problems with alcohol played a central role in their relationship problems. Many of their arguments developed around the topic of drinking or occurred under the influence of alcohol. As an initial step in working with the R.s, the therapists needed to prohibit any drinking before coming to therapy sessions. When learning how to solve problems, the R.s decided to apply these new skills to their mutual complaints about drinking. Specifically, they wrote a contract indicating that both partners were to abstain from liquor for two full days during the upcoming week. The contract was difficult to carry out but was a success, and provided one of the few instances that they spontaneously praised one another. Yet it was evident that this couple's drinking problems required a much more comprehensive treatment program and such a treatment was critical to the maintenance of gains from marital therapy. A final and significant goal for the couple was making the transition from marital therapy to a treatment program for alcoholism.

By the time Sam and Ella terminated therapy, self-report and behavioral data suggested substantial improvement in their marriage. Table 1 contains pretreatment and post-treatment scores on three objective measures. Dramatic increases on the DAS and decreases on the AC indicate changes in the couple's subjective impressions of the relationship and in their level of dissatisfaction over specific issues. SOC pleases and displeases also changed in the predicted directions and at post-treatment appeared comparable to SOC data for non-distressed couples.

Table 2 displays data from pretherapy and post-therapy problem-solving sessions that were audiotaped and then coded for nine separate categories of behavior. The most striking change is the reduction in negative responses, reflecting a decrease in critical and blaming statements. Other improvements in the couple's problem-solving abilities are indicated by increases in the categories of problem solution, approval, and acceptance of responsibility. These data suggest that the R.s were actively implementing their newly learned communication skills at termination. Unfortunately, there are no follow-up data to assess whether treatment gains were maintained.

Because of the brevity of this case presentation, there is not much opportunity to portray adequately the intricacies and false starts in this couple's therapy. Although a great deal of time was spent initially on how they handled anger, their concern for this topic faded as the abusive incident became history. Problem-solving training was introduced as a way to work on the anger through specific content issues. In general, therapy moved more quickly than usual into the problem-solving mode because the R.s could not handle behavioral exchanges adequately without the formal procedures of problem-solving. One feature of this case which is characteristic of other couples as well is that the couple had very little idea of what they wanted out of therapy. Their stated goal was to feel better about the relationship, and they appeared to be content simply to air their complaints. The therapists' challenge was in getting this couple involved in actually taking steps toward remedying their complaints and in enacting positive exchanges.

ETHICAL AND LEGAL ISSUES

Marital therapists face ethical and legal issues common to all psychotherapists but, in addition, they confront issues that are unique to the situation of working with two intimately related partners. The American Psychological Association's Ethical Standards and Standards for Providers of Health Services (APA, 1977a, 1977b) offer guidelines for psychotherapists in general, but further recommendations are needed

Table 1. *Self-report indices of marital adjustment at pretherapy and post-therapy.*

Index	Husband		Wife	
	Pretherapy	Post-therapy	Pretherapy	Post-therapy
Dyadic Adjustment Scale (DAS)	91	113	74	93
Areas of Change Questionnaire (AC)	18	4	11	2
Spouse Observation Checklist (SOC)				
Mean daily pleases	14.0	28.3	2.9	31
Mean daily displeases	2.3	.3	30.7	1.3

Table 2. *Rate per minute of communication behaviors at pretherapy and post-therapy.*

Behavior	Husband		Wife	
	Pretherapy	Post-therapy	Pretherapy	Post-therapy
Approval (AP)	.04	.47	.04	.20
Accept Responsibility (AR)	.00	.13	.12	.67
Communication Talk (CT)	.24	.13	.12	.07
Emotional Clarification (ĖC)	.00	.07	.04	.00
Mindread (MR)	.00	.07	.12	.00
Negative Response (NR)	1.16	.13	3.04	.00
Paraphrase/Reflection (PR)	.08	.00	.00	.00
Problem Solution (PS)	.00	.33	.24	.67
Sidetrack (ST)	.12	.00	.24	.00

that apply more directly to marital and family therapists. Ethical issues that continually require thoughtful consideration by marital therapists are those regarding the therapist as an agent, confidentiality, patient privilege, and the role of therapist values.

Whose agent is the therapist? Is therapy designed to meet the goals of the husband, the wife, or the therapist? What if there is not much overlap between the goals of these separate individuals? Thus far we have suggested that the goal of marital therapy is an "improved relationship," thereby making the therapist the agent of the relationship rather than of one or the other spouse. In such a role, the therapist is supportive of actions that strengthen the relationship and not receptive to individual goals at the expense of the relationship. Individual goals that have no particular effect on the relationship may elicit support but will not be a top priority. Carrying out the role of relationship advocate sets a constructive atmosphere for relationship change, avoids collusion with one partner, and tends to be well received by the spouses as long as it matches with their own objectives.

There are some instances, however, in which the therapist needs to acknowledge that the goal of an improved relationship is undesirable, impractical, or of lesser importance than another goal. Weiss and Birchler (1978) offer some guidelines for determining the appropriateness of marital therapy in their triangular model of marital complaints with mutuality, separateness, and self as the three reference points. Therapeutic expectations such as greater sharing, relationship change, or even an appraisal of whether or not to divorce suggest a mutuality focus. The therapist does not want to enter into a therapeutic alliance for relationship improvement, however, if one spouse illicitly seeks therapy as a way to exit from the relationship, to ease the burden of announcing a decision to divorce, or to force the other partner to make unilateral changes. Finally, when the presenting complaint focuses more on the problems of one partner, such as his or her depression or alcoholism, the therapist needs to evaluate whether the individual's problem is maintained by relationship variables or extra-relationship variables, and then design treatment plans accordingly.

Another type of situation that conflicts with the goal of an improved relationship is physical violence among family members. Upon learning that a couple has problems with physical violence, the therapist should immediately attend to the goal of reducing the danger of physical harm. If a conjoint program of anger management proves to be ineffective or inappropriate, it is the therapist's ethical responsibility to abdicate the role of relationship advocate and help the threatened person find protection (Margolin, 1979b). This situation presents an example of when the therapist may need to make a direct recommendation and actively assist one partner to extricate from the relationship. A similar situation occurs upon learning that a couple is depriving, neglecting, or abusing their child. The therapist who suspects that this is occurring should discuss the situation directly with the couple, unless doing so puts the child in further jeopardy, and, according to the Child Abuse Reporting Law, should inform authorities even at the expense of the parents' confidentiality. The primary goal in this situation is the child's well-being.

Finally, and perhaps already understood, relationship improvement is unfeasible if only one partner chooses to participate in the therapeutic process. There are serious ethical problems if the therapist passively agrees to the individual client's desire for an improved relationship without informing the person that conjoint therapy has a greater likelihood of success than individual therapy. As an alternative, the therapist can approach the reluctant partner, encourage that person to participate at least in the evaluation process, and work to dispel misconceptions that make the person hesitant to enter marital therapy. Invitations to enter therapy and efforts to educate a person about therapy are acceptable, but attempts to cajole or coerce a reluctant spouse into marital therapy pose both ethical and therapeutic problems.

Confidentiality

Relatively little in the practice of psychotherapy commands as much agreement as the tenet that it is the psychotherapist's responsibility to safeguard information obtained in the therapy session. Exceptions to this rule (e.g., the Tarasoff decision) are relatively infrequent. Unfortunately, however, there is no simple translation of standard confidentiality practices from individual sessions to conjoint sessions. Marital therapists tend to hold strong and highly divergent preferences about whether they accept the confidences of one spouse and withhold that information from the other partner. Some therapists who hold individual sessions with each spouse actively encourage the divulging of individual confidences and treat the information as though it were from an individual client. Other therapists explicitly discourage the sharing of any information leading to a two-person alliance that excludes the uninformed partner. Whatever the therapist's preferences, it is important that the therapist inform the clients of how confidential material will be treated so that the clients and therapist are not proceeding under discrepant assumptions.

Confidentiality issues also are related to psychotherapist–patient privilege, i.e., the patient's legal right that information communicated to the psychotherapist will not be disclosed unless the patient waives that privilege. Most but not all states have statutes defining patient privilege in the psychotherapy situation. Several state statutes (e.g., Illinois, Maryland, District of Columbia) even define group and family-therapy members as "joint holders of the privilege" such that if one patient waives privilege, the rights of other patients to claim privilege are not affected. For the most part, however, privilege tends to be ill-defined for the situation in which two or more clients are seen simultaneously in therapy. A New Jersey psychologist (Sugarman, 1974), for example, recently faced a situation in which the husband waived privilege and subpoenaed the psychologist's testimony, but the wife was unwilling to waive her privilege. A decision allowing the psychologist to maintain the wife's privilege came only because the psychologist was covered by laws in that state for marriage counselors; on the basis of psychologist–patient privilege, the wife would not have been protected. In similar cases faced by psychiatrists, courts in New York and Tennessee maintained privilege, but a Virginia court denied the psychiatrist such protection (Herrington, 1979). It is likely that marital therapists will continue to fight this battle in divorce and child custody cases until legislation to cover the situation exists in all states.

Therapist Values

Does the therapist express an opinion about whether the couple should separate or divorce? Few therapists would deny formulating opinions about whether a couple should remain together, but therapists vary greatly in how comfortable they feel in sharing such opinions. A five-way debate on this issue (Yoell, Stewart, Wolpe, Goldstein, & Speirer, 1971) produced two somewhat divergent positions. One is expressed in Wolpe's statement, "if every step that could be taken seems to have been taken and has failed. If the prognosis for the relationship in terms of happiness is close to zero, then I accept the responsibility not only to advise the dissolution of the marriage but to help in every practical way to bring it about" (p. 128). Stewart's response represents another position: "I feel discomfiture about making decisions for a person. The thought constantly pops up—'Is this going to be a meaningful decision for the individual if it is made by somebody else?'" (p. 129). Still other therapists endorse an explicit statement of one's opinion to the clients while claiming that the opinion is a personal one rather than a reflection of professional expertise (Halleck, 1976).

The clearest professional standard on this issue is found in the Professional Code of the American Association for Marriage and Family Therapy, which states, "in all circumstances, the therapist will clearly advise a client that the decision to separate or divorce is the responsibility solely of the client" (AAMFT, 1979). While this stance may be appealing in principle, in practice it is difficult if not impossible for a couple in therapy to reach such a decision independent of the therapist's influence. Most people who seek marital therapy have at some time thought about separation, and a good number view therapy as the way to decide whether or not the relationship should continue (Stuart, 1976; Weiss & Birchler, 1979). When clients enter therapy seeking advice on this issue, they are particularly primed to be influenced by the therapist. In light of the therapist's potential for biasing the couple's decision, we recommend two strategies for a cautious exercise of this influence. A couple can be advised to try marital therapy and temporarily postpone a decision about divorce. Through this process they learn what benefits are to be gained from the relationship and then can make a more informed decision about the future of their relationship. Second, the therapist is responsible for exploring his or her own biases regarding divorce. Therapists who consistently find themselves with a predilection toward either the perpetuation or dissolution of marriages should seek consultation to minimize the effects of this unidimensional attitude on couples.

How does the therapist respond to the knowledge that one partner is currently engaging in an extramarital affair? For some therapists, this knowledge does not particularly alter the treatment: the major focus is still on improving the primary relationship which, if successful, may cause the other relationship to dwindle in importance. Since the disclosure of an affair tends to have an impact upon a relationship that cannot be ignored, this strategy may only work if the noninvolved partner is naive about the affair. Other therapists actively discourage extramarital relationships or even stipulate that the extramarital affair must end before marital therapy can commence (Ables & Brandsma, 1977; Jacobson & Margolin, 1979). This stance is strategic rather than moralistic, based on the assumption that it is difficult for spouses to devote themselves fully to improving the relationship if their attention is split between two relationships. Furthermore, if the spouse without a lover is aware of the partner's other involvement, it may be equally difficult for that spouse to commit himself or herself to improving the relationship. A third stance is based on the belief that the therapist should not interfere with the behavior of one spouse as long as it does not cause the partner unhappiness (e.g., Wolpe's position in Yoell et al., 1977). We recommend that the decision about how to handle extramarital relationships not rest solely with the therapist's preconooptions about this matter, but also take into account the couple's comfort with a nonmonogamous relationship. Exploration is necessary to determine the meaning of the behavior for a given couple, e.g., whether it is threatening the future of the marriage, whether it is a danger sign that the marriage is deteriorating, whether it is tolerated but with reservation, or whether it is acceptable or even desirable for the marital relationship.

SUGGESTIONS FOR CLINICAL AND EMPIRICAL RESEARCH

Although marital therapy has become established as a target for scientific inquiry during the past 10 years, a wide gap between therapeutic practice and empirical findings still exists. Many of the therapeutic procedures that clinicians currently employ lack any sort of empirical support. The only specific components that have been empirically validated are basic communication skills, problem solving, behavior exchange, and contracting, which together represent behavioral marital therapy. In general, data show behavioral marital therapy to be more effective than waiting-list controls and placebo treatments, but the data are equivocal on whether or not behavior therapy is more effective than other theoretical approaches. The first wave of studies by behavior therapists is promising, but further research is needed to understand the antecedents of marital adjustment and maladjustment and the process by which change occurs in marital therapy.

In order to conduct definitive outcome studies on marital therapy, preliminary work is needed to eliminate the inadequacies of our assessment measures. There is only limited information on the psychometric properties (e.g., reliability, validity, norms) of measurements currently in use, particularly spouse-monitoring and behavioral observation procedures. Furthermore, as indicated in the assessment section, only a few studies have explored convergent and discriminant validity among marital assessment measures and these have shown mixed results. Additional data are needed to describe the degree of correspondence among measurements as related to (1) the *source* of the reported data (self-reports versus spouse reports versus observers' reports); and (2) the *nature* of the reported data (verbal versus nonverbal and affect-laden versus neutral) (Jacobs, 1976). To conceptualize these assessment options, Olson (1977) offered a 2 × 2 table that considers subjective and objective impressions by "insiders" and "outsiders" of the marital system. Sampling from all four cells and comparing data across these cells would provide needed information on how to measure interpersonal behavior.

A second recommendation toward long-range planning for better outcome studies is to acquire greater understanding of what differentiates maritally satisfied and dissatisfied couples. Along these lines, Meichenbaum (1979) recently called for a moratorium on outcome research until the excesses and deficits associated with a particular problem are identified. It is relatively well established that distressed, as compared to nondistressed, couples engage in more punishing and fewer rewarding exchanges (e.g., Birchler et al., 1975; Gottman et al., 1976; Gottman et al., 1977; Vincent et al., 1975). In addition, there is preliminary support for the hypothesis that the marital satisfaction of happy couples is primarily a function of the frequency of partner-provided positive interaction, and daily satisfaction in distressed couples is a function of the presence or absence of punishing behaviors (Jacobson et al., 1979; Margolin, 1979a). Other formulated differences between distressed and nondistressed couples that deserve further exploration include the hypotheses that distressed as compared to non-distressed couples (1) are not effective reinforcers; (2) are unusually sensitive to immediate as opposed to long-term contingencies; (3) practice coercive rather than positive control strategies in their attempts to influence one another's behavior; and (4) function under discrepant, unrealistic, or an absence of relationship rules.

In addition to cross-sectional comparisons, another important way to examine these questions is through longitudinal research to examine what behaviors are predictive of marital adjustment or maladjustment. Two noteworthy exceptions to the virtual absence of longitudinal studies in the marital literature are by Markman (1977) and by Vincent, Cook, and Brady (1979). Both of these studies found communication skillfulness to be predictive of subsequent relationship satisfaction. More studies of this sort that follow couples across important transition points and into progressive life stages would allow us to model our treatment procedures after the coping strategies of successful couples.

There are several directions to be explored in terms of future therapy-outcome research. Comparative research is needed to clarify the equivocal findings from earlier studies. Component analyses are needed to examine the relative efficacy of treatment ingredients, both specific treatment procedures and nonspecific treatment factors. Another important aim is the clear demonstration of the maintenance of treatment gains over time. Thus far, therapy maintenance has been measured only at 6-month and 1-year follow-ups and with objective self-report measures as the sole data collection procedure. Although training in behavior exchange and communication skills are considered the most promising treatment procedures, it is unknown whether couples continue to employ these skills after therapy has ended.

Based on the assumption that no one treatment approach is effective with all clients, the long-range aim should be to match therapeutic procedures and clients. Turkewitz (1977) provided one step in this direction with her unexpected finding of an interaction between type of treatment and age of client. Several design modifications are in order, however, for research to provide data toward treatment by client matching. A first step is to study more varied client samples with particular emphasis on including minorities, older couples, and non-college-educated couples. Second, greater attention should be paid to the characteristics of couples who are treatment failures. Third, more careful examination of individual couples through single-subject experimental designs would delineate, in the course of treatment, at what point a specific intervention affects change in a given target behavior. Jacobson (1977), for one, demonstrated how to combine single-subject procedures with group designs.

In summary, marital therapy has gained the enthusiasm and interest of clinicians of all orientations, although behavior therapists have been the most active in rigorously evaluating their procedures. It is time, however, for all approaches including behavior therapy to translate a greater number of their clinical speculations into testable hypotheses and to let research findings guide their rapidly expanding clinical endeavors.

SUMMARY

In light of the growing body of data suggesting that approximately half of the persons seeking psychological services present concerns related to their marital situation, mental health providers of all persuasions need to be able to recognize and either treat or refer these persons. Marital adjustment and maladjustment are conceptualized best as end points on a continuum: a couple's subjective placement on this continuum typically reflects how the spouses experience marital benefits relative to marital tensions. Marital maladjustment includes a diverse constellation of problems, some related to specific content issues and others representative of process deficits.

The major theoretical analyses of marital maladjustment come from the psychoanalytic, systems, and social learning perspectives. The psychoanalytic model examines the marital relationship as a function of the spouses' individual developmental histories and their relationship to their families of origin. Marital problems may occur when mate selection is based on a desire to fulfill frustrated infantile needs and then leads to patterns of mutual misperception and projection. In direct contrast, the systems model pays little attention to the individual partners and focuses instead on the relationship as a whole. Although this model contains several viewpoints, two unifying features are the emphasis on structures in family organization and the importance of behavior in controlling a dynamic balance within the relationship. According to the social learning viewpoint, marital distress may result from the use of negative rather than positive control, specific skills deficits, the erosion of relationship benefits, and faulty relationship expectations and attributions. Of these three perspectives, the social learning model translates most directly into specific assessment and treatment procedures.

Marital assessment is not conducted for traditional diagnostic purposes but rather to provide direction for the intervention and to evaluate the efficacy of the intervention. The interview is the most common method of data collection for all theoretical orientations, but its format varies as to whether or not it is conducted conjointly and whether it is present or past oriented. The assessment interview is conducted for three primary purposes: to collect information about either the individuals or the relationship; to actively probe the marital relationship and observe the couple's response; or to obtain a sample of the couple's interactional style. Objective self-report inventories (e.g., the Marital Adjustment Scale, the Areas of Change Questionnaire, the Marital Pre-Counseling Inventory, and the Marital Status Inventory) provide indices of marital satisfaction and/or stability. Some of these instruments offer inexpensive, easily administered outcome measurements, and others are best used in the formulation of treatment goals. The most unique aspect of marital assessment is the use of spouse-monitoring procedures (e.g., the Spouse Observation Checklist, the behavioral diary) to examine the couple's day-to-day exchanges of rewarding and punishing behaviors. Similar to other participant-observer methods, these procedures yield specific behavioral data in the natural environment but may pose a reactivity problem. The most unbiased and reliable procedures are observations of the couple's interactions in the laboratory or home. The couple engages in a problem-solving discussion that is videotaped and then coded by observers trained in a highly complex coding system (e.g., the Marital Interaction Coding System). Data from such systems provide a profile of spouses' communication skills as well as a detailed analysis of ongoing sequential patterns.

The differences between theoretical orientations become somewhat indistinct when it comes to the actual procedures used in therapy. A survey of clinical procedures reveals only several that have received empirical support. While these procedures are most representative of behavioral and nondirective therapy approaches, other therapists also tend to draw upon them. The most commonly described set of procedures in marital therapy is communication training: this includes the separate and yet highly complementary categories of Basic Communication Skills and problem-solving training. Basic Communication Skills training teaches spouses to be active, accurate listeners and direct, emotionally expressive speakers. Training in problem solving teaches spouses to formulate a mutually acceptable problem definition, to brainstorm solutions, and to negotiate a final agreement which may be formalized in a written contract. Another type of intervention, behavior exchange procedures, helps spouses to make nonconflictual requests of one another and to increase their overall exchange of pleasing relationship events. Increases in companionship activities, love days, and simple exchange contracts are examples of behavior exchange procedures. The most typical sequencing of these three treatment components to give the couple some immediate benefits as well as to prepare them for more demanding changes is behavior exchange procedures followed by Basic Communication Skills followed by problem-solving training.

These therapy components are effective only if the therapist provides a context conducive to the couple's acceptance of the therapeutic intervention. This context is more likely if:

1. The therapist and couple formulate a therapeutic contract.
2. The therapy follows a well paced natural progression.
3. The therapist is directive, present oriented, elicits trust, maintains a relationship focus, and is not overly dependent on technology.

Certain ethical and legal issues that are unique to the situation of simultaneously seeing two intimately related clients arise in marital therapy. Questions to be considered in conjoint therapy include: Whose agent is the therapist? Under what circumstances does the therapist dispense with conjoint therapy? How are confidentiality and patient privilege defined? What is the role of the therapist's values regarding extramarital affairs and divorce?

Since marital therapy has had a relatively brief history, many issues regarding this psychotherapeutic endeavor have not been sufficiently explored through scientific inquiry. Behavioral marital therapy is the only treatment demonstrated to be more effective than placebo and waiting-list controls, but it has not been demonstrated conclusively to be more effective than other approaches. The promising research on behavior marital therapy needs to be replicated with different populations, with more attention to the generalization and maintenance of treatment effects, and with components analyses to determine the active treatment variables. Before definitive outcome studies can be conducted, however, more preliminary work is needed to explore the psychometric properties of marital assessment methods, particularly behavioral procedures, and to understand the antecedents of marital dissatisfaction. That is, what excesses and/or deficits are associated with marital distress? This question calls for both longitudinal research to examine what behaviors are predictive of marital maladjustment and further cross-sectional research to compare maritally distressed and nondistressed couples. In light of the first wave of promising data from behavioral marital researchers, it is now time to retrench and reformulate research questions so that they bridge the gap between empirical findings and actual clinical practices.

NOTE

1. All identifying data have been altered to insure the couple's anonymity. Noel Novison served as co-therapist along with Gayla Margolin on this case.

REFERENCES

Ables, B. S., & Brandsma, J. M. *Therapy for couples.* San Francisco: Josey-Bass, 1977.

Alexander, J., Barton, C., Schiavo, R. S., & Parson, B. V. Systems-behavioral intervention with families of delinquents: Therapist characteristics, family behavior and outcome. *Journal of Consulting and Clinical Psychology,* 1976, *44,* 656–664.

American Association for Marriage and Family Therapy. *Code of professional ethics and standards for public information and advertising.* Upland, Ca.: American Association for Marriage and Family Therapy, 1979.

American Psychological Association. *Ethical standards of psychologists* (Rev. ed.). Washington, D.C.: American Psychological Association, 1977. (a)

American Psychological Association. *Standards for providers of psychological services.* Washington, D.C.: American Psychological Association, 1977. (b)

Azrin, N. H., Naster, B. J., & Jones, R. Reciprocity counseling: A rapid learning-based procedure for marital counseling. *Behavior Research and Therapy,* 1973, *11,* 365–382.

Bandura, A. *Principles of behavior modification.* New York: Holt, Rinehart & Winston, 1969.

Bandura, A. *Social learning theory.* Englewood Cliffs, N.J.: Prentice-Hall, 1977.

Becking, E. P. Pretraining effects on maladaptive marital behavior within a behavior modification approach (Doctoral dissertation, California School of Professional Psychology, 1972). *Dissertation Abstracts International,* 1973, *33,* 5007B.

Bernal, M. E., Gibson, D. M., William, D. E., & Pesses, D. I. A device for recording automatic audio tape recordings. *Journal of Applied Behavior Analysis,* 1971, *4,* 151–156.

Birchler, G. R. Communication skills in married couples. In A. S. Bellack & M. Hersen (Eds.), *Research and practice in social skills training.* New York: Plenum, 1979.

Birchler, G. R., & Webb, L. J. Discriminating interaction in behavior in happy and unhappy marriages. *Journal of Consulting and Clinical Psychology,* 1977, *45,* 494–495.

Birchler, G. R., Weiss, R. L., & Vincent, J. P. Multimethod analysis of social reinforcement exchange between maritally distressed and nondistressed spouse and stranger dyads. *Journal of Personality and Social Psychology,* 1975, *31,* 349–360.

Bowen, M. Family psychotherapy. *American Journal of Orthopsychiatry,* 1961, *30,* 40–60.

Bowen, M. The use of family theory in clinical practice. *Comprehensive Psychiatry,* 1966, *7,* 345–374.

Bowen, M. Family therapy and family group therapy. In D. H. L. Olson (Ed.), *Treating relationships.* Lake Mills, Ia.: Graphic Press, 1976. (a)

Bowen, M. Theory in the practice of psychotherapy. In P. Guerin (Ed.), *Family therapy.* New York: Gardner, 1976. (b)

Bowen, M. Principles and techniques of multiple family therapy. In P. Guerin (Ed.), *Family therapy.* New York: Gardner, 1976. (c)

Cardillo, J. P. Effects of teaching communication roles on interpersonal perception and self-concept in disturbed marriages. *Proceedings of the 79th Annual Convention of the American Psychological Association,* 1971, 441–442.

Carkhuff, R. R. *Helping and human relations* (Vols. I & II). New York: Holt, Rinehart & Winston, 1969.

Carkhuff, R. R. *The art of helping.* Amherst, Ma.: Human Resource Development Press, 1972.

Carter, R. D., & Thomas, E. J. Modification of problematic marital communication using corrective feedback and instruction. *Behavior Therapy,* 1973, *4,* 100–109.

Cassidy, M. J. *Communication training for marital pairs.* Unpublished doctoral dissertation, University of California, Los Angeles, 1973.

Christensen, A. Naturalistic observation of families: A system for random audio recordings in the home. *Behavior Therapy,* 1979, 10, 418–422.

Christensen, A., & Nies, D. C. The Spouse observation checklist: empirical analysis and critique, *American Journal of Family Therapy,* 1979, *8,* 69–79.

Crowe, M. J. Conjoint marital therapy: Advice or interpretation: *Journal of Psychosomatic Research,* 1973, *17,* 309–315.

Crowe, M. J. *Conjoint marital therapy: Advice or interpretation?* Unpublished data, Institute of Psychiatry, University of London, 1974.

DeCecco, J. P. *The psychology of learning and instruction: Educational psychology.* N.J.: Prentice-Hall, 1968.

Dicks, H. V. Object relations theory and marital studies. *British Journal of Medical Psychology,* 1963, *36,* 125–129.

Dicks, H. V. *Marital tensions.* New York: Basic Books, 1967.

Edmonds, V. M., Withers, G., & Dibatista, B. Adjustment, conservatism and marital conventionalization. *Journal of Marriage and the Family,* 1972, *34,* 96–103.

Edwards, D. D., & Edwards, J. S. Marriage: Direct and continuous measurement. *Bulletin of the Psychonomic Society,* 1977, *10* (3), 187–188.

Family trends now taking shape. *U.S. News and World Report,* October 27, 1975, p. 32.

Family violence. *California State Psychologist,* March, 1978, pp. 30; 33.

Follingstad, D. R., Sullivan J., Ierace, C., Ferrara, J., & Haynes, S. N. *Behavioral assessment of marital interaction.* Paper presented at the 10th Annual Convention of the Association for the Advancement of Behavior Therapy, New York, 1976.

Frank, E., Anderson, C., & Rubinstein, D. Frequency of sexual dysfunction in "normal couples." *New England Journal of Medicine,* 1978, *299* (3), 111–115.

Frankl, V. Paradoxical intention and dereflection: Two logo therapeutic techniques. In S. Arieti and G. Chrzanowski (Eds.), *New dimensions in psychiatry: A world view.* New York: Wiley, 1975.

Freeman, S. J. J., Leavens, E. J., & McCulloch, D. J. Factors associated with success or failure in marital counseling. *Family Coordinator,* 1969, *18,* 125–128.

Giovacchini, P. Treatment of marital disharmonies: The classical approach. In B. L. Greene (Ed.), *The psychotherapies of marital disharmony.* New York: The Free Press, 1965.

Gottman, J., Markman, H., & Notarius, C. The topography of marital conflict: A sequential analysis of verbal and nonverbal behavior. *Journal of Marriage and the Family,* 1977, *39,* 461–477.

Gottman, J., Notarius, C., Gonso, J., & Markman, H. *A couple's guide to communication.* Champaign, Il.: Research Press, 1976.

Gottman, J., Notarius, C., Markman, H., Bank, S., Yoppi, B., & Rubin, M. E. Behavior exchange theory and marital decision making. *Journal of Personality and Social Psychology,* 1976, *34,* 14–23.

Guerney, B. *Relationship Enhancement.* San Francisco: Jossey-Bass, 1977.

Gurman, A. S. The effects and effectiveness of marital therapy: A review of outcome research. *Family Process,* 1973, *12,* 145–170.

Gurman, A. S. Contemporary marital therapies: A critique and comparative analysis of psychoanalytic, behavioral, and systems theory approaches. In T. J. Paolino & B. S. McCrady (Eds.), *Marriage and marital therapy: Psychoanalytic, behavioral, and systems theory perspectives.* New York: Brunner/Mazel, 1978.

Gurman, A. S., & Kniskern, D. P. Enriching research on marital enrichment programs. *Journal of Marriage and Family Counseling,* 1977, *3,* 3–11.

Gurman, A. S., & Kniskern, D. P. Research on marital and family therapy: Progress, perspective, and prospect. In S. L. Garfield & A. E. Bergin (Eds.), *Handbook of psychotherapy and behavior change: An empirical analysis* (2nd ed.). New York: Wiley, 1978.

Haley, J. *Strategies of psychotherapy.* New York: Grune & Stratton, 1963.

Haley, J. *Uncommon therapy: The psychiatric techniques of Milton H. Erickson, M. D.* New York: Norton, 1973.

Haley, J. *Problem-solving therapy.* San Francisco: Jossey-Bass, 1976.

Hall, M. Lesbian families: Cultural and clinical issues. *Social Work,* 1978, *23,* 380–385.

Halleck, S. L. *The politics of therapy.* San Francisco: Jossey-Bass, 1976.

Herrington, B. S. Privilege denied in joint therapy. *Psychiatric News,* 1979, *14*(a), pp. 1; 9.

Hersen, M., & Barlow, D. H. *Single case experimental designs.* London: Pergamon, 1976.

Hops, H., Wills, T. A., Patterson, G. R., & Weiss, R. L. *Marital interaction coding system.* Eugene, Ore.: University of Oregon and Oregon Research Institute, 1972.

Howard, J. W., & Dawes, R. M. Linear prediction of marital happiness. *Personality and Social Psychology Bulletin,* 1976, *2,* 478–480.

Jacobs, T. Assessment of marital dysfunction. In M. Hersen & A. S. Bellack (Eds.), *Behavioral assessment: A practical handbook.* New York: Pergamon, 1976.

Jacobson, N. S. Problem-solving and contingency contracting in the treatment of marital discord. *Journal of Consulting and Clinical Psychology,* 1977, *45,* 92–100.

Jacobson, N. S. Specific and nonspecific factors in the effectiveness of a behavioral approach to the treatment of marital discord. *Journal of Consulting and Clinical Psychology,* 1978, *46,* 442–452.

Jacobson, N. S. Behavioral treatments for marital discord: A critical appraisal. In M. Hersen, R. M. Eisler, & P. M. Miller (Eds.), *Progress in behavior modification.* New York: Academic Press, in press.

Jacobson, N. S. Increasing positive behavior in severely distressed marital relationships. *Behavior Therapy,* 1979, *10,* 311–326.

Jacobson, N. S., & Margolin, G. *Marital therapy: Strategies based on social learning and behavior exchange principles.* New York: Brunner/Mazel, 1979.

Jacobson, N. S., Waldron, H., & Moore, D. *Toward a behavioral profile of marital distress. Journal of Consulting and Clinical Psychology,* in press.

Jones, E. E., Kanouse, D. E., Kelley, H. H., Nisbett, R. E., Valins, S., & Weiner, B. *Attribution: Perceiving the causes of behavior.* New York: General Learning Press, 1972.

Kantor, D., & Lehr, W. *Inside the family: Toward a theory of family process.* San Francisco: Jossey-Bass, 1975.

Kelley, H. H. The processes of casual attribution. *American Psychologist,* 1973, *28,* 107–128.

Koch, J., & Koch, L. The urgent drive to make good marriages better. *Psychology Today,* Sept. 1976, pp. 33–35.

L'Abate, L. A bibliography of paradoxical methods in psychotherapy of family systems. *Family Process,* 1978, *17,* 95–98.

Lederer, W. J., & Jackson, D. D. *Mirages of marriage.* New York: Norton, 1968.

Liberman, R. P., Levine, J., Wheeler, E., Sanders, N., & Wallace, C. Experimental evaluation of marital group therapy: Behavioral vs. interaction-insight formats. *Acta Psychiatrica Scandinavica* (Supplement), 1976.

Lidz, T., Fleck, S., & Cornelison, A. *Schizophrenia and the family.* New York: International Universities Press, 1965.

Locke, H. J., & Wallace, K. M. Short-term marital adjustment and prediction tests: Their reliability and validity. *Journal of Marriage and Family Living,* 1959, *21,* 251-255.

Mahoney, M. J. *Cognition and behavior modification.* Cambridge, Ma.: Ballinger, 1974.

Mahoney, M. J., & Arnkoff, D. B. Cognitive and self-control therapies. In S. L. Garfield & A. R. Bergin (Eds.), *Handbook of psychotherapy and behavior change: An empirical analysis* (2nd ed.). New York: Wiley, 1978.

Mannino, F. V., & Greenspan, S. I. Projection and misperception in couples treatment. *Journal of Marriage and Family Counseling,* 1976, *2,* 139-143.

Margolin, G. A multilevel approach to the assessment of communication positiveness. *International Journal of Family Counseling,* 1978, *6* (1), 81-89. (a)

Margolin, G. The relationships among marital assessment procedures: A correlational study. *Journal of Consulting and Clinical Psychology,* 1978, *46,* 1556-1558. (b)

Margolin, G. *Behavior exchange in distressed and nondistressed marriages: A life span perspective.* Unpublished manuscript, University of Southern California, 1979. (a)

Margolin, G. Conjoint marital therapy to enhance anger management and reduce spouse abuse. *American Journal of Family Therapy,* 1979, *7* (2), 13-23. (b)

Margolin, G., Christensen, A., & Weiss, R. L. Contracts, cognition, and change: A behavioral approach to marital therapy. *The Counseling Psychologist,* 1975, *5,* 15-26.

Margolin, G., & Weiss, R. L. Communication training and assessment. A case of behavioral marital enrichment. *Behavior Therapy,* 1978, *9,* 508-520. (a)

Margolin, G., & Weiss, R. L. A comparative evaluation of therapeutic components associated with behavioral marital treatment. *Journal of Consulting and Clinical Psychology,* 1978, *46,* 1476-1486. (b)

Markman, H. *A longitudinal investigation of couples planning to marry.* Paper presented at the Annual Meeting of the Association for the Advancement of Behavior Therapy, Atlanta, 1977.

Martin, P. *A marital therapy manual.* New York: Brunner/Mazel, 1976.

Masters, W. H., & Johnson, V. E. *Human sexual inadequacy.* Boston: Little, Brown, 1970.

McLean, P. D., Ogston, K., & Grauer, L. A behavioral approach to the treatment of depression. *Journal of Behavior Therapy and Experimental Psychiatry,* 1973, *4,* 323-330.

Meichenbaum, D. *Cognitive behavior modification: The critical issues and future directions.* Paper presented at the 10th Annual Southern California Conference on Behavior Modification, Los Angeles, 1979.

Meissner, W. W. The conceptualization of marriage and family dynamics from a psychoanalytic perspective. In T. J. Paolino & B. S. McCrady (Eds.), *Marriage and marital therapy: Psychoanalytic, behavioral, and systems theory perspectives.* New York: Brunner/Mazel, 1978.

Miller, S., Nunnally, E. W., & Wackman, D. Minnesota Couples Communication Program (MCCP): Premarital and marital groups. In D. H. L. Olson (Ed.), *Treating Relationships*. Lake Mills, Ia.: Graphic Publishing, 1976.

Minuchin, S. *Families and family therapy*. Cambridge: Harvard, 1974.

Mitchell, H. E., Bullard, J. W., & Mudd, E. H. Areas of marital conflict in successfully and unsuccessfully functioning families. *Journal of Health and Human Behavior*, 1962, *3*, 88-93.

More marriages—and divorces. *Los Angeles Times*, March 20, 1979, p. 13.

Murstein, B. I., & Beck, G. D. Person perception, marriage adjustment, and social desirability. *Journal of Consulting and Clinical Psychology*, 1972, *39*, 396-403.

Nadelson, C. C., & Paolino, T. J. Marital therapy from a psychoanalytic perspective. In T. J. Paolino & B. S. McCrady (Eds.), *Marriage and marital therapy: Psychoanalytic, behavioral, and systems theory perspectives*. New York: Brunner/Mazel, 1978.

Olson, D. H. Marital and family therapy: Integrative review and critique. *Journal of Marriage and the Family*, 1970, *32*, 501-538.

Olson, D. H. Insiders' and outsiders' views of relationships: Research studies. In G. Levinger & H. L. Raush (Eds.), *Close relationships: Perspectives on the meaning of intimacy*. Amherst, Ma.: University of Massachusetts Press, 1977.

Orden, S. R., & Bradburn, N. A. Dimensions of marriage happiness. *American Journal of Sociology*, 1968, *73*, 715-731.

Paolino, T. J. Introduction: Some basic concepts of psychoanalytic psychotherapy. In T. J. Paolino & B. S. McCrady (Eds.), *Marriage and marital therapy: Psychoanalytic, behavioral, and systems theory perspectives*. New York: Brunner/Mazel, 1978.

Patterson, G. R. Some procedures for assessing changes in marital interaction patterns. *Oregon Research Institute Bulletin*, *16* (7), 1976.

Patterson, G. R., & Reid, J. B. Reciprocity and coercion: Two facets of social systems. In K. Neuringer & J. Michael (Eds.), *Behavior modification in clinical psychology*. New York: Appleton-Century-Crofts, 1970.

Patterson, G. R., Weiss, R. L., & Hops, H. Training of marital skills: Some problems and concepts. In H. Leitenberg (Ed.), *Handbook of behavior modification*. New York: Appleton-Century-Crofts, 1976.

Peterson, D. R. A functional approach to the study of person–person interactions. In D. Magnusson & N. S. Endler (Eds.), *Personality at the crossroads: Current issues in interactional psychology*. Hillsdale, N. J.: Lawrence Erlbaum Associates, 1977.

Pierce, R. M. Training in interpersonal communication skills with the partners of deteriorated marriages. *Family Coordinator*, 1973, *22*, 223-227.

Rappaport, A. F. Conjugal relationship enhancement program. In D. H. L. Olson (Ed.), *Treating relationships*. Lake Mills, Ia.: Graphic Publishing, 1976.

Rappaport, A. F., & Harrell, J. A behavioral exchange model for marital counseling. *The Family Coordinator*, 1972, *22*, 203-212.

Reid, W. J., & Shyne, A. W. *Brief and extended casework*. New York: Columbia University Press, 1969.

Renne, K. S. Correlates of dissatisfaction in marriage. *Journal of Marriage and the Family*, 1970, *32,* 54–67.

Riskin, J. M., & Faunce, E. E. An evaluative review of family interaction research. *Family Process*, 1972, *11,* 365–456.

Robinson, E. A., & Price, M. G. *Behavioral and self-report correlates of marital satisfaction.* Paper presented at the Annual Meeting of the Association for the Advancement of Behavior Therapy, New York, 1976.

Rogers, C. R. *Client-centered therapy.* Boston: Houghton Mifflin, 1951.

Rollins, B. C., & Cannon, K. Marital satisfaction over the family life cycle; A reevaluation. *Journal of Marriage and the Family,* 1974. *30,* 271–282.

Rollins, B. C., & Feldman, H. Marital satisfaction over the family life cycle. *Journal of Marriage and the Family,* 1970, *26,* 20–28.

Roman, M., & Meltzer, B. Co-therapy: A review of current literature (with special reference to therapeutic outcome). *Journal of Sex and Marital Therapy,* 1977, *3,* 63–77.

Sager, C. *Marriage contracts and couple therapy: Hidden forces in intimate relationships.* New York: Brunner/Mazel, 1976.

Satir, V. *Conjoint family therapy.* Palo Alto, Ca.: Science and Behavior Books, 1967.

Satir, V. *Peoplemaking.* Palo Alto, Ca.: Science and Behavior Books, 1972.

Shepherd, M., Oppenheim, B., & Mitchell, S. *Childhood behavior and mental health.* New York: Grune & Stratton, 1971.

Sluzki, C. E. Marital therapy from a systems theory perspective. In T. J. Paolino & B. S. McCrady (Eds.), *Marriage and marital therapy: Psychoanalytic, behavioral, and systems theory perspectives.* New York: Brunner/Mazel, 1978.

Spanier, G. B. Measuring dyadic adjustment: New scales for assessing the quality of marriage and similar dyads. *Journal of Marriage and the Family,* 1976, *38,* 15–28.

Steinmetz, S. K. Wife beating, husband beating: A comparison of the use of physical violence between spouses to resolve marital fights. In M. Roy (Ed.), *Battered women: A psychosociological study of domestic violence.* New York: Van Nostrand Reinhold, 1977.

Steinmetz, S. K. Violence between family members. *Marriage and Family Review,* 1978, *1,* 1; 3–16.

Stuart, R. B. Operant-interpersonal treatment for marital discord. *Journal of Consulting and Clinical Psychology,* 1969, *33,* 675–682.

Stuart, R. B. An operant interpersonal program for couples. In D. H. L. Olson (Ed.), *Treating relationships.* Lake Mills, Ia.: Graphic Publishing, 1976.

Stuart, R. B., & Stuart, F. *Marital Pre-Counseling Inventory.* Champaign, Il.: Research Press, 1972.

Sugarman, D. A. Diary of a subpoenaed psychologist. *New Jersey Psychologist,* 1974, *24,* 2:13–18.

Thibaut, J. W., & Kelley, H. H. *The social psychology of groups.* New York: Wiley, 1959.

Thomas, E. J., Carter, R. D., & Gambrill, E. D. Some possibilities of behavior modification with marital problems using "SAM" (signal system for the assessment and modification of behavior). In R. D. Rubin, H. Fensterheim, A. A. Lazarus, & C. M. Franks (Eds.), *Advances in behavior therapy.* New York: Academic Press, 1971.

Thorton, B. Toward a linear prediction of marital happiness. *Personality and Social Psychology Bulletin,* 1977, *3,* 674–676.

Tsoi-Hosmand, L. Marital therapy: An integrative behavioral-learning model. *Journal of Marriage and Family Counseling,* 1976, *2,* 179–191.

Turkewitz, H. *A comparative study of behavioral marital therapy and communication therapy.* Unpublished doctoral dissertation, SUNY at Stony Brook, 1977.

Valle, S. K. & Marinelli, R. P. Training in human relations skills as a preferred mode of treatment for married couples. *Journal of Marriage and Family Counseling,* 1975, *1,* 359–365.

Vincent, J. P., Cook, N. I., & Brady, C. P. *Accomodation to birth of the first child: Contribution of marital skills, satisfaction and infant temperament.* Paper presented at the Western Psychological Association Convention, San Diego, 1979.

Vincent, J. P., Weiss, R. L., & Birchler, G. R. A behavioral analysis of problem solving in distressed and nondistressed married and stranger dyads. *Behavior Therapy,* 1975, *6,* 475–487.

von Bertalanffy, L. General system theory—a critical review. *General Systems,* 1962, *7,* 1-20.

von Bertalanffy, L. *General systems theory.* New York: Braziller, 1973.

Wattie, B. Evaluating short-term casework in a family agency. *Social Casework,* 1973, *54,* 609–616.

Watzlawick, P. *How real is real? Confusion, disinformation, communication.* New York: Random House, 1976. (a)

Watzlawick, P. The psychotherapeutic technique of "reframing." In J. L. Claghorn (Ed.), *Successful psychotherapy.* New York: Brunner/Mazel, 1976. (b)

Watzlawick, P., Beavin, J. H., & Jackson, D. D. *Pragmatics of human communication.* New York: Norton, 1967.

Weiss, R. L. The conceptualization of marriage from a behavioral perspective. In T. J. Paolino & B. S. McCrady (Eds.). *Marriage and marital therapy: Psychoanalytic, behavioral, and systems theory perspectives.* New York: Brunner/Mazel, 1978.

Weiss, R. L., & Birchler, G. R. *Areas of change.* Unpublished manuscript, University of Oregon, 1975.

Weiss, R. L., & Birchler, G. R. Adults with marital dysfunction. In M. Hersen & A. S. Bellack (Eds.), *Behavior therapy in the psychiatric setting.* Baltimore: Williams & Wilkins, 1978.

Weiss, R. L., Birchler, G. R., & Vincent, J. P. Contractual models for negotiation training in marital dyads. *Journal of Marriage and the Family,* 1974, *36,* 321–330.

Weiss, R. L., & Cerreto, M. *Marital status inventory.* Unpublished manuscript, University of Oregon, 1975.

Weiss, R. L., Hops, H. & Patterson, G. R. A framework for conceptualizing marital conflict, a technology for altering it, some data for evaluating it. In L. A. Hamerlynck, L. C. Handy, & E. J. Mash (Eds.), *Behavior change: Methodology, concepts and practice.* Champaign, Il.: Research Press, 1973.

Weiss, R. L., & Margolin, G. Marital conflict and accord. In A. R. Ciminero, K. S. Calhoun, & H. E. Adams (Eds.), *Handbook for behavioral assessment.* New York: Wiley, 1977.

Why marriages turn sour—and how to get help. *U.S. News and World Report,* October 27, 1975, pp. 44–46.

Williams, A. M. *The quantity and quality of marital interaction related to marital satisfaction: A behavioral analysis.* Unpublished doctoral dissertation, University of Florida, 1977.

Wills, T. A., Weiss, R. L., & Patterson, G. R. A behavioral analysis of the determinants of marital satisfaction. *Journal of Consulting and Clinical Psychology,* 1974, *42,* 802–811.

Winter, W. D., & Ferreira, A. J. (Eds.), *Research in family interaction: Readings and commentary.* Palo Alto, Ca.: Science and Behavior Books, 1969.

Wolpe, J. *Psychotherapy by reciprocal inhibition.* Stanford: Stanford University Press, 1958.

Yoell, W., Stewart, D., Wolpe, J., Goldstein, A., & Speirer, G. Marriage, morals and therapeutic goals: A discussion. *Journal of Behavior Therapy and Experimental Psychiatry,* 1971, *2,* 127–132.

Ziegler, J. S. A comparison of the effect of two forms of group psychotherapy on the treatment of marital discord (Doctoral dissertation, University of Pittsburgh, 1972). *Dissertation Abstracts International,* 1973, *34,* 143–144A.

Zinner, J., & Shapiro, R. Projective identifications as a mode of perception and behavior in families of adolescents. *International Journey of Psychoanalysis,* 1972, *53,* 523–530.

6

Functional Headache: Description, Mechanisms, and Treatment

Douglas W. Thomas
Daniel J. Cox

It was clear even to the ancients that some headaches could be accounted for by physical injury or disease. Although we now know more about the nature of such distress than was known in the past, we are only beginning to understand what causes headache in the absence of physical insult or illness. Functional headaches have been considered the therapeutic responsibility of the medical establishment, but medical investigation into their pathophysiology did not begin until the 1930s. As Bakal (1975) points out, psychological investigators have tended to avoid studying them in the belief that they have physical causation, but the medical view is that stress and psychophysiological, predispositional variables are critically implicated.

Migraine headache was recognized as far back as the time of Hippocrates; Galen called it "hemicrania" (Sargent, Green, & Walters, 1973). Treatment ranged from the strong purgatives prescribed by Galen, bloodletting, trephining, and acupuncture to the pharmacotherapy now generally used in medical practice. Mitchell and Mitchell (1971) hold, however, that "psychological or behavioral events are seen as primary antecedents of migraine episodes and the site of migraine as secondary" (p. 153). Only recently have views of the mechanisms responsible for functional headache, and recommendations for its treatment, begun to be integrated.

In 1962 the Ad Hoc Committee on Classification of Headache, a panel of physicians, delineated 15 categories in an attempt to account for the full range of all cephalic pain. Headaches without an organic base are classified as either vascular headache of the migraine type or muscle-contraction headache; allowance also is made for the appearance within a single individual of both types at different times. These two types account for 90 percent of all the headaches reported. (See Table 1 for a summary of the chief characteristics of each.)

Vascular headaches are described as quite labile in respect to frequency, duration, and intensity, and they are usually unilateral and characterized by a throbbing onset. They customarily produce pain in the temporal or parietal areas and are sometimes accompanied by nausea and vomiting. The principal subdivisions of this type of headache are the classic and common varieties of migraine. Classic migraine is characterized by transient sensory and/or motor prodromal symptoms, but the common type has no prodromal symptoms and is less often unilateral. Pain is accounted for by the distention and dilation of extracranial arteries following intracranial vasoconstriction, without associated pathophysiology. It has been hypothesized that the secretion of neurokinins induces localized edema and pain (Budzynski, 1978). A family history of headaches would be one basis for the differential diagnosis of migraine, ruling out the muscle-contraction variety which is known also as nervous tension or psychogenic headache. The latter type is considered labile although the pain is typically a steady ache with tightness or bandlike pressure, usually in the suboccipital or frontal region. It is said to be associated with the sustained contraction of skeletal muscles in the head, neck, and shoulders of a degree that brings no structural damage.

Not surprisingly, this categorization of headaches permits considerable diagnostic and therapeutic confusion. Philips (1977a, 1978), Bakal (1975), Bakal and Kaganov (1977), and Cohen (1978) challenge

Table 1.   Chief characteristics of vascular and muscle-contraction headaches.

	Vascular	Muscle Contraction
Pain laterality	Unilateral	Bilateral
Pain described	Throbbing	Steady pressure Aching Bandlike sensations
Pain location	Parietal Temporal	Suboccipital Frontal
Mechanism of pain	Intracranial vasoconstriction followed by extracranial vasodilation	Sustained contraction of head, neck, and shoulder muscles
Prodromes	Sensory, motor, speech, and gastrointestinal	None

the classification vigorously. Although empirical studies undoubtedly form the basis for some of the Ad Hoc Committee's guidelines, their publication lacks references and one must assume that they depend substantially on the panelists' clinical experience and thus were focused on reported pain and the complaints of individuals seeking medical attention. It seems worth considering that patients who complain of headache symptoms differ in some significant way from those who may very well have the same physical disturbance without complaining of it. Data on the incidence and characteristics of headache in the general population would be useful in assessing this possibility.

Ogden (1952) conducted a study of 4,634 individuals from the population at large to ascertain the prevalence of headaches. He found that 65 percent reported having headaches, with more than 1 percent having them daily; but only 18 percent had consulted a physician. Twenty-nine percent had a family history of headaches. Headache sufferers tended to be from a higher socioeconomic level and significantly younger than subjects without headaches. Fatigue and eyestrain most usually were cited as causes, and 31 percent of the women who were questioned considered menstruation a factor. Twenty percent of the whole group spoke of having prodromal signs and nausea: of these individuals, 30 percent were troubled by throbbing and 37 percent by painful dull pressure.

In comparing migraine sufferers with patients having tension headaches, all of whom had been referred by neurologists, Bakal and Kaganov (1977) reported that the two groups were identical in their complaints of prodromes and throbbing pain (52 percent and 40 percent respectively); quite similar in having family histories of headaches (44 and 48 percent); and significantly different only in respect to nausea and vomiting, from which 72 percent of the migraine patients but only 36 percent of the others suffered. Moreover, the two groups were not different in the frequency or intensity of their headaches, contrary to what traditional criteria would lead one to expect. Waters and O'Connor (1971) and Philips (1977c) worked with samples of medical patients who had been selected without regard to any reports of headache and found, as did Ogden (1952), that classic migraine was unrelated to either the family history or intelligence, but it seemed evident that headache sufferers of a relatively high social status were readier to consult a physician than those further down the scale. Philips (1977a) and Waters and O'Connor (1971) found that 19 percent of the women they studied had migraine during the year under consideration, but only half of the women Waters and O'Connor studied sought medical attention. The only way in which women differed from men in the sample in respect to their headaches was that the men reported tension headaches significantly more often, and the women reported more migraine. Both studies found the severity of headache to be significantly related to prodromes and gastrointestinal symptoms, although about one-quarter of those with less severe tension headaches reported a single vascular symptom. Philips concluded that there is little evidence of identifiable, discrete diagnostic categories for functional headaches.

Ziegler, Hassanein, and Hassanein (1972) made a factor analysis of symptom–patient variables, and offer seven that are clinically meaningful and account for 47 percent of the total variance. They report that prodromes, unilateral pain, and nausea are traditionally associated with migraine, thus suggesting the possibility of three migraine syndromes. All variables tended to overlap, however, and the other factors failed to correspond to the symptoms usually ascribed to muscle-contraction headache, with the possible exception of "steady pain." They make the convincing hypothesis that the many apparently conflicting physiochemical findings are at odds because of the use of invalid diagnostic criteria.

HEADACHE MECHANISMS

Physiological and chemical studies of functional headache have focused on factors related to migraine more than on those at work in the condition attributed to muscle contraction. Although the literature is inconclusive in each case and the comparative work is sparse, the available research does shed light on the diagnostic issues involved.

Migraine

Wolff (1963) and his colleagues are well known for their pioneering investigation of the pathophysiology of migraine vasculature. It is generally accepted that an initial period of intracranial arterial vasoconstriction, associated with prodromal signs, precedes extracranial arterial vasodilation with its accompanying headache.

O'Brien (1973) reported intracranial vasodilation during the phase of extracranial arterial vasodilation. Graham and Wolff (1938) demonstrated that subjects with migraine reported that pain was reduced when they were given ergotamine tartrate, a vasoconstrictive substance. Bakal (1975), reviewing several biochemical investigations of migraine vasculature, concluded that certain potent vasodilative substances may eventually be implicated in headache onset.

Appenzeller, Davison, and Marshall (1963) found that heating the chests of headache-free migraine subjects failed to elicit reflex vasodilation in the hands, although this effect does take place among people not susceptible to headache. No other differences were found between the two groups studied. Elliott, Frewin, and Downey (1974) also demonstrated that reflex vasodilation was absent in the hands of migraine subjects when their contralateral arm was heated. These findings raise the possibility that migraine is a generalized vasomotor dysfunction.

Morley (1977) criticized the studies of Appenzeller et al., and Elliott et al., concluding that there is no evidence of abnormal vasomotor control by migraine subjects, and raised the question as to whether long-term pharmacotherapeutic treatment of migraine would alter vasomotor responsivity. The single study of the heat-dilation reflex of migraine subjects who had never been given traditional vasoconstrictive pharmaceuticals (Hockaday, MacMillan, & Whitty, 1967) failed to support the hypothesis of vasomotor dysfunction. Diamond and Franklin (1975) found that headache sufferers who had become drug-dependent through pharmacotherapy did relatively poorly at learning a treatment regime of hand warming.

Muscle Contraction

Philips (1978) observes that there is little empirical support for the assumptions made in the literature about treating muscle-contraction, or tension, headache. Tunis and Wolff (1954) compared pulse-wave records from several extracranial arteries and EMG readings from the muscle groups they served in two groups of subjects—those troubled by tension headaches and those free from headaches. Subjects who suffered from tension headaches were tested both during headache-free periods and when headache was felt. The average systolic pulse-wave amplitude of the normal subjects was significantly greater than that of muscle-contraction headache subjects when headache-free, and these headache-free values were significantly greater than when the same subjects were experiencing headache pain. The EMG levels during headaches were reported to be 10 times those of the same subjects when they were headache-free. Tunis and Wolff observed that transient vasoconstriction and muscle contraction often occurred in subjects without causing pain; they postulate a connection between concomitant muscle tension, extracranial vasoconstriction, and the onset of headache. Philips (1977a) and van Boxtel and van der Ven (1978) found that persons diagnosed as having muscle-contraction headaches had significantly elevated frontalis EMG levels as compared with controls. In this study they monitored several muscle groups. Vaughn, Pall, and Haynes (1977) found that persons suffering from frequent attacks of tension headache had frontalis EMGs significantly higher than those less often symptomatic. Van Boxtel and van der Ven (1978) showed that headache victims engaged in performing a task that required mental effort had higher EMG levels than the controls only in the frontalis muscle. Philips (1977a) showed that persons diagnosed as having migraine tended toward higher levels of EMG than those diagnosed as having tension headache. Like van Boxtel and van der Ven, Philips found that only the frontalis EMG differed significantly between stress and nonstress recordings for muscle-contraction headache subjects asked to imagine stressful scenes.

Comparative Data

In support of Philips' findings (1977a), Bakal and Kaganov (1977) found that migraine subjects had the most elevated frontalis muscle activity relative to the muscle-contraction headache and control samples, which were similar; and these effects held, regardless of the presence or absence of headache during the recording. These researchers uncovered no effect for extracranial temporal artery reactivity to orienting auditory stimuli specific to a diagnostic group or headache condition. There was, however, a tendency for both headache groups to exhibit reduced reactivity to the stimuli, as measured by pulse-wave velocity, while controls increased on this measure. Working with a headache patient population and controls, Poźniak-Patewicz (1976) demonstrated that controls had lower levels of EMG activity in neck and temporal muscles than the headache-prone or headache-free subjects. Migraine attacks were, on the other hand, associated with the most intense muscle spasms.

Summary

From a substantial array of physiological data, one is inclined to considerable agreement with Cohen (1978). The similarities of tension and migraine headaches include: (1) elevated EMG activity in the frontalis muscle and possibly in other muscles of the head and neck; (2) extracranial arterial vasoconstriction, which is implicated in at least some phase of headache or prodromal activity; and (3) extracranial vasoconstriction in response to apparently innocuous stimuli of the sort to which normals respond with a dilative orienting reflex. The headache types are, however, clearly differentiated in respect to migraine pain onset. The individual with migraine has strong rebound extracranial vasodilation, but those who suffer tension headaches remain vasoconstricted for reasons as yet unexplained. Also, only those with migraine symptoms tend to experience a reduction of discomfort when given ergotamine tartrate preparations. Evidence of a generalized vasomotor dysfunction in migraine cannot be supported at this time.

ASSESSMENT

The subjective and behavioral aspects of functional headache will be examined against a background of epidemiological and physiological data. Philips (1977a) suggests that physiological, subjective, and behavioral analyses and their concordance or discordance are critically important in conceptualizing functional pain.

Pain Behavior

We must ask whether physiological data such as EMG recordings or the blood levels of potent vasoactive substances relate to such subjective and behavioral factors as (1) the location, quality, intensity, frequency, or duration of head pain; (2) the medication used; (3) relaxation or tension as reported by the subject himself; or (4) some other factors not commonly associated with headache. Much of the writing on these issues is oriented toward treatment and deals with muscle-contraction headaches, but a few studies examine headaches outside the therapeutic context and consider headache patients along with controls. Studies comparing headache types are equally few in number.

Subjective and Behavioral Factors

Examining a group of psychiatric patients considered to be tense and anxious, Sainsbury and Gibson (1954) found seven who complained of headaches of unspecified type. Only frontalis muscle tension differentiated these patients from those without headaches. The investigators took this difference as evidence for the close relationship between the location of elevated EMG and reports of pain from that site. Vaughn, Pall, and Haynes (1977) studied student volunteers with muscle-contraction headaches and divided them into high- and low-frequency groups. The high-frequency headache subjects had significantly greater frontalis EMG activity than the comparison group. Although muscle tension levels were reduced in both groups during the course of treatment, only in the low-frequency group was the perceived relaxation level increased. It could be hypothesized that in the high-frequency group this aspect of pain behavior was no longer under the control of muscle tension, and other factors had become significant.

As noted, Bakal and Kaganov (1977) found no relation between the site of headache pain and its diagnosis. In partial support of this finding, van Boxtel and van der Ven (1978) and Epstein, Abel, Collins, and Parker (1978) found no systematic relationship between patterns of muscular activity and the locale of head pain reported by patients with muscle-contraction headaches. Neither study rules out some correspondence between these factors, but a relationship certainly does not appear in all subjects.

In a study of the treatment of tension headaches in subjects who had been recruited by advertisement, Budzynski, Stoyva, Adler, and Mullaney (1973) found that decreasing headache activity is highly correlated with decreasing frontalis EMG levels ($r = .90$). With similarly recruited subjects, Cox, Freundlich, and Meyer (1975) obtained an r of .42 between the same factors, using only pre- and post-treatment EMG recordings in their analysis. In a patient sample referred for tension headaches, Harper and Steger (1978) found low correlations between pretreatment headache activity and frontalis EMG levels. Treating patients referred for tension, Epstein and Abel (1977) observed that change in frontalis EMG activity failed to correspond to reports of headache activity during treatment. They speculate that headache complaints may be influenced by environmental contingencies or that these individuals may have been deficient in discriminating tension. The findings of Vaughn, Pall, and Haynes (1977) with low- and high-frequency headache subjects may relate to this speculation. Only the low-frequency group felt more relaxed in treatment.

The work of Philips (1977a, 1977b, 1977c) systematically examines several subjective and behavioral factors related to headache pain and diagnostic grouping. She notes in her epidemiological study (1977c) that people with even mild headaches are apt to take pills for them, and resorting to medication does not depend on the severity of the pain. Moreover, few people report being able to ignore even mild headache, although such distress very seldom keeps them away from work. In a treatment study, Philips' (1977c) subjects were patients with tension headaches along with some patients whose headaches had been classified as both tension and migraine. She found that felt tension did not decline significantly during treatment although muscle tension and headache pain did. Recordings were taken from the frontalis or temporalis muscles according to an assessment of which muscle was more tense. Considerable dysynchrony was observed between the reported decrease in headache pain and the level of muscle tension; the former changed over a much longer time than muscle tension did. In another and more complex study, Philips (1977a) investigated a group of tension-headache patients ($n = 11$) and patients with mixed tension-migraine headaches (n = 6). Table 2 summarizes intercorrelations among four headache pain measures taken during a 1-month pretreatment assessment. Overall, only intensity and frequency are significantly correlated. When the tension and mixed cases are carefully examined, the latter group fails to show any significant intercorrelations among the measures, and the patients with a pure type of tension headache exhibit higher intensity and frequency correlations (r = .64 to .85) and stronger correspondence between frequency and muscle tension (r = .66) Philips notes the absence of any systematic relationship between the taking of pills and other components of the headache situation. There were considerable individual differences, with some subjects with relatively high levels of pain abstaining from any medication. Since only eight patients had a "true" (nonplacebo) treatment, Philips was unable to give for the treatment and follow-up phases of this study a similar intercorrelational matrix. Muscle tension during treatment did correspond with headache intensity, which showed a continued decline at follow-up whereas EMG increased slightly. Decline in felt pain was the only other measure to relate significantly to lowered muscle tension. The intensity of headaches and changes in their frequency corresponded only in tension cases, and the use of medication was reduced overall only at follow-up. Cox et al. (1975) found significant reduction in the amount of medications used after treatment and at follow-up, with similar reduction in the levels of frontalis EMG. Among the negative findings reported by Philips was the failure of muscle tension to relate to the frequency of headache or to felt tension, which did not vary with felt pain. Philips concludes that there is considerable dysynchrony among physiological, subjective, and behavioral factors in headache pain.

It is difficult to summarize the foregoing studies, particularly in view of the widely varied patterns of time at which the relevant headache features were sampled. Philips also is alone in attempting the

Table 2. Intercorrelations among four headache pain parameters taken at 1-month pretreatment assessment.

	Headache Intensity	Headaches Per Week	Medications Per Week	Muscle Tension
Headache intensity				
Headaches per week	.64*			
Medications per week	.44	.19		
Muscle tension	.38	−.05	−.20	

Note. Pretreatment n = 17.
*$p < .01$

exhaustive analysis necessary for the elucidation of the subjective and behavioral interrelationships involved. Her data would be more meaningful with larger samples and with an examination of headache characteristics by diagnostic category, since some differences among them are apparent. The specific type of therapeutic intervention used in headache treatment could be expected to affect differentially the rate and progress of the alleviation of pain. The discordances noted between the intensity of headache and its frequency and duration make a combined headache activity index, such as is often seen in the literature, a misleading measure in many instances (Philips, 1978). The assessment of headache pain before it is treated, however, could very well point the way to the appropriate therapeutic strategies. These issues are examined more fully in the following section.

Personality Factors

It is not unusual to find assumptions in the literature that point to typical personality characteristics of persons who have functional headache. Mitchell and Mitchell (1971), in a brief review of populations of migraine patients, stated that "migraine sufferers are usually senstitive, worrisome and perfectionistic individuals, often chronically tense, apprehensive, and preoccupied with achievement and success . . . also characterized by superficial interpersonal relationships, sexual maladjustments, and obsessive preoccupation with moral and ethical issues" (p. 137). Mayo Clinic patients diagnosed as having muscle-contraction headaches were studied by Martin (1966, 1972). They were observed to handle emotional conflict by denial, and their chief problem areas were identified as being related to dependence, sexuality, and the control of anger. Psychoneurotic depression also was common. Like Mitchell and Mitchell's complainers (1971), patients with tension headaches were described as rigid, perfectionistic, and compulsive, with evident psychosexual conflicts. Associated psychophysiological disorders were often apparent, and there was often a goal of secondary gain. Philips (1976) commented that distinctions rarely are made between the personality traits of persons suffering from migraine and those who have muscle-contraction headaches; indeed, the descriptions offered by Mitchell and Mitchell and by Martin hardly differ. Martin (1966) ventures to conclude that clinical interviews and tests provide no basis for the identification of a specific headache-prone personality. As indicated, only half of the people who have headache pain consult a physician about it (Waters & O'Connor, 1971), so that data based on patients are obviously less than comprehensive.

Rhodes (1973), working with volunteers who had headaches, was unable to validate a 28-item headache-proneness scale, although scores on this measure did correlate highly with other scales associated with personal discomfort, distress, anxiety, and general emotional upheaval. In their comunity-sample study of women, Waters and O'Connor (1971) found no differences on a derived psychoneuroticism scale between subjects who had migraine and those who did not. They did not use patients in this study.

As indicated, Harper and Steger (1978) found no significant frontalis EMG and headache pain correlations for within-session or weekly activity averages. There were, however, many significant relationships between the EMG levels of the women patients having tension headaches and their complaints of physical and psychological symptoms, according to the Cornell Medical Index and the SCL-90 R. Moreover, within-session as well as weekly averages of pain measures corresponded significantly with the showing on the hypochondriasis, depression, and hysteria scales of the MMPI and with the subjects' complaints of physical and psychological symptoms.

Thomas (1979) found no differences in SCL-90 symptoms among patients referred because of headache, psychiatric patients, and unclassified medical outpatients. The headache patients did, however, have significantly more social supports and fewer life stresses than the psychiatric sample. Budzynski et al. (1973) demonstrated that MMPI hypochondriasis scores decreased significantly during treatment in a group with declining headache activity. A chi-square test showed this change to be significantly greater than that occurring in a pseudo-treatment or control group.

Studying a random sample of patients in a physician's general practice, Philips (1976) selected subjects irrespective of any complaint of headache. Using the Eysenck Personality Questionnaire (PQ), she found that the headache sufferers differed insignificantly from the control norms for all factors examined, and she was unable to demonstrate systematic discordance on the PQ among groups of persons with migraine, tension, or mixed-type headaches. Only female migraine subjects showed significant Lie-scale elevation in comparison with control norms; and women with severe tension headaches, selected on the basis of their desire for treatment, demonstrated significantly elevated neuroticism scores. Seeking some difference in PQ factors between subjects with tension headaches who took medication often and those who did not, she found none that were significant.

Various researchers have helped to clarify issues of personality involved in functional headache, but it seems evident that psychopathology concomitant with headache is likely to be seen, when it occurs, only among those who seek medical attention irrespective of the diagnosis. Persons who turn to physicians for the relief of headaches are by no means among those who suffer most from headaches. Philips reports that many people who take little or no medication for headache dislike the idea of taking pills at all; and since 90 percent of consultations for headache result in prescriptions (Rachman & Philips, 1975), this may be one reason why many people choose to suffer without medical attention. Among patients who do complain, associated physical and psychological symptoms may be found more often than chance would indicate.

TYPES OF HEADACHE TREATMENT

Numerous therapies have been used to treat functional headache, but it is only within the last decade that medical models, which typically involve pharmacotherapy, have been significantly challenged by alternative treatments. An overview of traditional and evolving models of headache therapy follows.

The Medical Model

Physicians have somewhat neglected the control of muscle-contraction headache, and it has had little empirical study. The assumption of a functional musculo-skeletal etiology places the focus on symptoms. Martin (1966, 1972) proposes psychotherapy, symptomatic drug therapy, and physiotherapy that emphasizes the use of heat and massage. Suggested medications include mild analgesics and sedatives or mild tranquilizers (Martin, 1966, 1972); tranquilizers that affect the central nervous system such as chlorpromazine and meprobamate (Bakal, 1975); an analgesic sedative such as fiorinal; and aspirin (Cohen, 1978), which is said to be the drug most commonly used for muscle-contraction headache. Cohen also notes recent interest in tricyclic antidepressants for the management of chronic headache. Table 3 indicates the more commonly prescribed headache medications. Nelson (1976) reports on three cases in which orgone, or Reichian therapy, was used for tension headaches; this approach combines a version of muscular massage with character-analytic psychotherapy.

Drug therapy for migraine headache is rather well standardized and differentiated between use for an acute attack and for prophylaxis; the rationale is based on symptoms and aimed at the prevention of painful dilation of extracranial arteries. The drug of choice for use

Table 3. *Headache medications.*

Migraine	Muscle Contraction
1. Ergotamine tartrate preparations, such as cafergot, wigraine, and genergen, as vasoconstrictors	1. Aspirin
	2. Mild analgesic sedatives, such as fiorinal and fiorinal with codeine
2. Methysergide maleate preparations, such as sansert, for prophylaxis	3. Mild tranquilizers, such as valium and librium
3. Propranolol, such as indiral, for prophylaxis	4. Tranquilizers with central nervous system action, such as meprobamate and chlorpromazine
4. Demerol for those requiring hospitalization	5. Tricyclic antidepressants, such as elavil and tofranil

immediately at onset of headache is one of the ergotamine tartrate preparations, which are potent vasoconstrictors (Bakal, 1975; Cohen, 1978; Gold, 1974; Sargent, Walters, & Green, 1973). Methysergide maleate can be used as a means of prophylaxis (Bakal, 1975; Cohen, 1978; Gold, 1974; Sargent, Walters, & Green, 1973). Its effect is presumably the potentiation of endogenous vasoconstrictors (Bakal, 1975; Gold, 1974). Propranolol, which prevents vasodilation, has been used recently to ward off migraine attacks (Bakal, 1975; Cohen, 1978). For patients requiring hospitalization, demerol is generally the drug of choice (Budzynski, 1978). Bakal (1975) points out that pharmacotherapy ties the headache victim to a drug-dependent life-style. This is not the only objection to its use; virtually every review of the pharmaceuticals mentioned emphasizes the potentially dangerous side effects that accompany chronic use. Alternatives to their administration would be welcome. Mitchell and Mitchell (1971), in an admittedly poorly controlled comparison study, summarized the outcomes of methysergide trials from 1959 to 1969 and compared them to several behavioral interventions. Of the 2,329 patients receiving drug therapy, 13 percent dropped out; 3 percent became headache-free; 52 percent had fewer headaches by about one-half; and 31 percent were without improvement (less than 20 percent reduction). Of the 27 persons in behavior therapy, none withdrew; 22 percent became headache-free; 70 percent had a 50 percent reduction; and 7 percent were unimproved. Fortunately, it appears that alternatives to medical treatment are effective, and their recent proliferation is dramatic.

Alternative Models—Migraine

Nonpharmacological approaches to headache treatment have tended to focus on symptoms. Thus, migraine therapy has involved:

1. The use of biofeedback in learning to control hand temperature and cephalic artery vasomotor activity
2. The elicitation of relaxation through taped, verbal, autogenic, or Transcendental Meditation training
3. The use of cognitive and self-control procedures
4. Hypnotherapy
5. Adjuncts to the foregoing, such as in vivo practice, instruction in all treatment modalities, breathing exercises, and concurrent psychotherapy.

Rationales have been advanced for each of these approaches and are reviewed here.

The use of hand warming to counter migraine activity was first advanced by Sargent, Green, and Walters (1972). Werbach and Sandweiss (1978) reported that migraine patients have significantly lower temperature of the hands than persons with headaches other than migraine or than persons with other medical complaints. Since the peripheral vasculature receives only sympathetic innervation with decreased activity associated with volitional warming, studies bearing on these phenomena require examination. Working with a nonheadache sample, Christie and Kotses (1973) demonstrated significant bi-directional control of the external carotid vasomotor response. Koppman, McDonald, and Kunzel (1974) showed that individuals who suffer from migraine have significant bi-directional control of the cephalic temporal artery. In consideration of the data on the control of hand warming, the volitional manipulation of vasomotor activity seems established among normal and migraine individuals.

Other researchers examined autonomic implications of hand warming control. Price and Tursky (1976) found that both normal and migraine subjects exhibited increases in extracranial blood volume concomitant with hand warming. Their subjects were exposed to only a single session of warming, however, and it would be misleading to consider their group representative of trained subjects. Sovak, Kunzel, Sternbach et al. (1978) reported that extracranial arterial beds may show blood volume changes either similar to or opposite from digital beds. The "orienting reflex" of Pavlov is characterized by simultaneous peripheral vasoconstriction and extracranial dilation. With stressful or intense stimulation, dual vasoconstriction occurs. Sovak et al., demonstrated extracranial arterial vasoconstriction in their trained subjects during hand warming of both normals and migraine sufferers who had improved after treatment; these variables were unrelated for the migraine subjects who experienced no improvement. It is clear that extracranial and digital vasomotor response can be regulated differentially. Bradycardia, or slowing of heart rate, also occurred during volitional hand warming among Sovak's subjects. The opposite effect of tachycardia was observed during hand warming accomplished with hot air. The investigators concluded that a generalized decrease in sympathetic outflow had been conditioned and hand warming was only one component of the physiological pattern.

The trained control of extracranial artery vasoconstriction has been used to counter intense and painful dilation occurring during migraine (Feuerstein, Adams & Beiman, 1976; Friar & Beatty, 1976). This type of learned response has a physiological effect similar to the vasoconstrictive effects of migraine pharmaceuticals. Hypnotherapy for migraine focuses on hand warmth and forehead coolness, something similar in effect to biofeedback training (Daniels, 1976). The use of relaxation procedures is relevant to the supposedly worrisome and perfectionistic migraine-prone personality, and it aims at teaching some degree of self-control in the face of physiologically reactive stimuli (Benson, Klemchuk, & Graham, 1974; Benson, Kotch, & Crassweller, 1977).

Cognitive methods of migraine treatment emphasize the importance of psychological factors in the etiology of the disorder. Mitchell and Mitchell (1971) used applied relaxation, systematic desensitization, and assertiveness training in the belief that coping and self-change strategies are vital to the alteration of migraine responses. Price (1974) speculated that assertiveness training might be the critical element, permitting migraine sufferers to have emotional outlets with fewer cardiovascular consequences. It is usual to require daily practice of the relevant therapeutic procedures in order to generalize the learning effects. Instruction in the control of breathing also has been given (Werbach & Sandweiss, 1978). Adler and Adler (1976) reported in their long-term follow-up of headache patients treated with biofeedback that most of the patients whose improvement continued after treatment had undergone concurrent psychotherapy.

Alternative Models—Muscle Contraction

Until recently, therapies for tension headache focused on relieving the supposedly sustained contraction of muscles in the head, neck, and shoulders. Although this musculo-skeletal rationale is now less accepted than it was (Philips, 1978), deep-muscle relaxation procedures and/or EMG biofeedback have been employed widely (Bakal & Kaganov, 1977; Budzynski, Stoyva, & Adler, 1970; Wickramasekera, 1973b). Feedback has been used in auditory as well as visual modalities (Bakal & Kaganov, 1977; Epstein, Hersen, & Hemphill, 1974), typically from the frontalis muscle, although other muscles have been used (Philips, 1977b). Home practice of trained behaviors virtually always is required. Stress management, a variant of systematic desensitization, is sometimes used (Holroyd, Andrasik, & Westbrook, 1977; Reeves, 1976), and cue-controlled breathing also is employed (Cox, Freundlich, & Meyer, 1975).

McKenzie, Ehrisman, Montgomery, and Burnes (1974) used EEG alpha feedback training in addition to other relaxation procedures. Cognitive self-control modalities recently have been utilized by Holroyd, Andrasik and Westbrook (1977) and Holroyd and Andrasik (1978). In the latter study, these techniques were applied in a group context with the goal of modifying cognitive responses to situations likely to elicit stress, to which tension-headache sufferers are particularly vulnerable.

Operant Models

It is curious that so little attention has been paid to headache pain behavior within this paradigm. Operant techniques have been advanced by Fowler (1975) and Norton and Nielson (1977) to control complaints about headaches without an organic basis. Such a therapeutic model disregards muscular and vascular considerations as well as experiential components and focuses on pain-motivated behavior. Is headache onset associated with social or other environmental rewards such as attention or the consumption of medication? Are those headache-sufferers who behave well reinforced? Yen and McIntire (1971) report on a case referred for psychological evaluation of continuous headache. Using a response-cost approach, they required progressively more written material from the patient for each complaint of headache pain, and the results were quite impressive.

TREATMENT AND OUTCOME
Muscle Contraction

Tables 4 through 6 summarize important data on treatment and outcome from most published studies on functional headache. The more significant studies are discussed in some detail here, and the others are taken into consideration as supportive or contraindicative of various therapeutic procedures.

In 1970 Budzynski, Stoyva, and Adler reported on a pilot study of frontalis EMG feedback in the treatment of medically diagnosed tension headache. Patients were asked to practice their learned relaxation skills at home daily in order to generalize laboratory successes into everyday life. By the end of treatment, significant decline in EMG levels as well as in headache activity was observed. These researchers introduced a headache index that is readily applicable in quantifying frequency, duration, and intensity of pain (Budzynski et al., 1973). It has been used freely by other experimenters since its introduction.

Wickramasekera (1972, 1973b) performed two studies in which he began pilot investigations that examined the additive effects of verbal instructions for relaxation (1973b). He also looked at the effect of "false" or noncontingent feedback on headache. In the first experiment, a series of verbal relaxation sessions was followed by the addition of frontalis EMG feedback. Declines in headache activity were observed during relaxation training, and these continued with added EMG training; concomitant decreases in EMG values also could be seen. Wickramasekera (1972) followed six sessions of noncontingent feedback with six sessions of true feedback and found that only the latter produced a decline in EMG values and headache activity.

Working with 10 neurology referrals in a group setting, Fichtler and Zimmermann (1973) effected significant declines in the duration and intensity of headaches in just four sessions (a total of 2½ hours). They used taped relaxation instructions and encouraged home practice. Tasto and Hinkle (1973) also were able to reduce the frequency and duration of tension headaches to nearly zero for six college students in four sessions. They used an unspecified relaxation training administered by undergraduate paraprofessionals.

In the first controlled group-outcome study, Budzynski et al. (1973) randomly assigned 18 tension-headache subjects to one of three treatment groups: the first group charted headache activity, the second received noncontingent auditory EMG feedback, and the third received contingent auditory feedback of frontalis EMG activity. Only the last group had any significant decline in headache activity and the use of medication after treatment; at 18-month follow-up, four of the six subjects reported low or reduced headache activity. Members of the other two groups were later offered similar treatment and evidenced equal or better improvement at 3-month follow-up.

Epstein, Hersen, and Hemphill (1974) showed that music feedback of frontalis EMG activity reduced headache reports initially and with-

Table 4. Muscle-contraction treatment studies.

Author(s)	Subject(s) & Treatment(s)	No. of Sessions	Headache Activity Change	Associated Changes	Design Quality Rating
Budzynski, Stoyva, & Adler, 1970	Patients n=5, EMG frontalis feedback with home practice used	8–24	Headache activity significantly decreased	Frontalis EMG significantly decreased	13.5
Wickramasekera, 1972	Neurology referrals n=5, EMG frontalis feedback, "false" condition followed by "true"	6 "false" 6 "true"	Headache frequency and intensity fell only during "true" phase	EMG declines paralleled headache decrease	9
Wickramasekera, 1973b	Neurology referrals n=5, verbal relaxation instructions, followed addition of EMG frontalis feedback Home and clinic practice used	9	Headache index fell during verbal relaxation, and more so during feedback	Average EMG levels fell, as did headache activity	15
Fichtler & Zimmerman, 1973	Neurology referrals n=10, group treated with relaxation tapes Home practice used	4	Headache duration and intensity fell significantly	Interference caused by headache decreased	18
Tasto & Hinkle, 1973	Student health-service referrals n=6, muscle relaxation training using paraprofessionals Home practice used	4	Headache frequency and duration decreased to near zero for all subjects		14.5

Study	n	Method	Results	EMG/Physiological findings	
Budzynski, Stoyva, Adler, & Mullaney, 1973	16	Subjects from ads $n=6$, frontalis feedback $n=6$, feedback-type clicks as diversion $n=6$, headache charting only Home practice used	Feedback group significantly reduced headache activity and medications	Weekly averaged EMG correlates .90 with headache index; feedback group significantly decreased Hypochondriasis scale of MMPI	30
McKenzie, Ehrisman, Montgomery, & Barnes, 1974	10	Neurology referrals $n=7$, progressive relaxation, autogenic training, and EEG alpha feedback $n=7$, relaxation tape and instrumentation exposure	Both groups reduced headaches by at least 75%		10
Epstein, Hersen, & Hemphill, 1974	10	VA Hospital patient $n=1$, music feedback from frontalis while inpatient; same plus home practice while outpatient	Headache activity fell during inpatient training, but much more so during outpatient training	EMG fell during feedback and rose during return to baseline; heart rate increased during feedback	16
Haynes, Griffin, Mooney, & Parise, 1975	6	Ads for students $n=8$, frontalis EMG feedback $n=8$, relaxation tapes $n=5$, told to "relax" and applied practice used	Both $n=8$ groups significantly reduced headache frequency and overall headache activity		24

Table 4. *(Continued)*

Author(s)	Subject(s) & Treatment(s)	No. of Sessions	Headache Activity Change	Associated Changes	Design Quality Rating
Cox, Freundlich, & Meyer, 1975	Newspaper ads $n = 9$, weekly medication placebo $n = 9$, EMG frontalis feedback, applied relaxation, and cue-controlled breathing $n = 9$, verbal relaxation instructions, applied relaxation, and cue-controlled breathing Home practice used	8	EMG feedback and verbal relaxation groups both significantly decreased headache activity	Feedback and relaxation groups significantly decreased; EMG and medications used; locus of control shifted toward internality; and psychosomatic complaints fell	22
Hutchings & Reinking, 1976	Medical referrals $n = 6$, progressive relaxation and taped autogenic training $n = 6$, frontalis EMG feedback $n = 6$, combined above treatments Home practice used	10	Both groups receiving feedback significantly reduced headache index by 66%; progressive relaxation group reduced by 20%	All 3 groups reduced EMG activity to low levels, though feedback groups were faster in acquiring skill	21.5
Epstein & Abel, 1977	Patient referrals $n = 6$, music feedback from frontalis No home practice	16	Headache activity fell only for $n = 3$, with low initial EMG levels	Subjects unable to lower EMG in absence of headache	17.5

Reeves, 1976	Neurology referral $n=1$, headache charting, then cognitive skill training, then EMG feedback with stress management	30	30% decrease in headache activity with cognitive training; 66% decrease with EMG added	Frontalis EMG tension fell 38% only with feedback	11
Holroyd, Andrasik, & Westbrook, 1977	Ad recruitment $n=10$, headache charting only $n=11$, EMG frontalis feedback $n=10$, cognitive intervention with stress management Home practice used	8	Only cognitive-intervention group significantly reduced headache activity	Both treatment groups significantly decreased psychosomatic complaints and medications used; only feedback group significantly reduced EMG levels; both treatments seen as equally credible, and practice similar in both groups	22
Holroyd & Andrasik, 1978	Ad recruitment $n=10$, headache charting only $n=9$, headache discussion group without coping strategies $n=10$, group cognitive self-control training with practice at home $n=10$, group cognitive self-control plus muscle relaxation and practice at home	5	All 3 treatment groups significantly decreased headache activity; no differences between groups	EMG change unrelated to headache activity; treatment credibility ratings unrelated to headache activity changes	22

Table 5 *Migraine treatment studies.*

Author(s)	Subject(s) and Treatment(s)	No. of Sessions	Headache Activity Change	Associated Changes	Design Quality Rating
Mitchell, 1971a	Volunteers $n = 3$, headache charting only $n = 7$, applied relaxation $n = 7$, applied relaxation, systematic desensitization, and assertive training (combined desensitization) with home practice encouraged	15	76% frequency and 50% duration reductions for combined training; no significant change for other groups	Positive change in "minor" type life problems for combined group only	20
Mitchell, 1971b	Students $n = 3$, headache charting only $n = 3$, combined desensitization Home practice encouraged	15	Significant reduction in headache frequency for combined desensitization group (no figures)		18.5
Mitchell & Mitchell, 1971 (Study II)	Volunteers $n = 5$, headache charting only $n = 5$, systematic desensitization $n = 5$, combined desensitization with no previous pharmacology $n = 5$, combined desensi-	15	Both combined desensitization groups showed reduced frequency; significant duration reduction only for combined group with no previous pharmacotherapy; other groups showed no significant change	Both combined desensitization groups were significantly improved in "minor" type life problems	20

	tization, with previous pharmacotherapy failures Home practice encouraged				
Lutker, 1971	Patient $n = 1$, applied relaxation with home practice encouraged	6	"Symptoms gone" (no figures)		1.5
Sargent, Green, & Walters, 1972	Patients $n = 32$, autogenic feedback training—home practice used		Authors agree that an average of 79% were clinically improved	Handwarming learned	14
Sargent, Walters, & Green, 1973	Patients $n = 57$, home practice used		Authors say 81% had slight to very good improvement	Handwarming learned	8.5
Wickramasekera, 1973a	Patients $n = 2$, frontalis EMG feedback, followed by thermal-hand feedback, with home practice encouraged	17 EMG ? thermal	No change during EMG training; headache activity nearly zero with thermal feedback	Both skills learned; acquired temperature elevations followed headache reduction	14.5
Benson, Klemchuk, & Graham, 1974	Recruitment unknown $n = 17$, TM relaxation response, with home practice encouraged		13 of 17 had no significant change in headache		20

Table 5 (Continued)

Author(s)	Subject(s) and Treatment(s)	No. of Sessions	Headache Activity Change	Associated Changes	Design Quality Rating
Johnson & Turin, 1975	Patient n = 1, hand temperature-cooling phase, followed by warming phase; home practice used	12 cooling 12 warming	Headache frequency, duration, and medication increased while cooling; decreased for warming	Both responses learned	10
Graham, 1975	Patients n = 2, under hypnosis, hand-warming suggestions; then autohypnosis used; home practice used	5	1 symptom-free; 1 with markedly reduced symptoms	Prodromes occur, though headaches are aborted	14
Andreychuk & Skriver, 1975	Volunteers from ads n = 11, hypnosis n = 11, autogenic headache training n = 11, alpha wave enhancement Home practice used	10	Headache index significantly decreased equally for all groups	Trend for highly suggestible subjects to have greater reduction of headaches	25.5
Mitch, McGrady, & Iannone, 1976	Patients n = 20, autogenic headache training done at home only	6	Headache intensity reduced 75%, duration 60%, frequency 45%, medications 55%		14
Daniels, 1976	Volunteers n = 3, taped hypnotic induction with hand-warming and forehead cooling suggested	6	Headache intensity, frequency, and duration decreased	Subjects highly satisfied with experiment	14

Study	Method		Results		
Lambley, 1976	Patient $n = 1$, assertive training with psychotherapy	15	Headache intensity and frequency decreased to low levels		9
Turin & Johnson, 1976	Volunteers $n = 4$, feedback for hand-warming only $n = 3$, feedback for cooling, then warming	$\bar{x} = 8.7$	Headache frequency, duration, and medications all significantly decreased	2/3 achieved cooling; all acquired warming	20
Friar & Beatty, 1976	Ad recruits $n = 9$, feedback for arterial constriction of digit-control group $n = 9$, feedback for temporal artery constriction with practice at headache onset	8	Temporal artery group significantly reduced duration and decreased intensity and frequency relative to controls	Temporal artery constriction acquired	25
Mitchell & White, 1976	Recruitment unknown $n = 1$, headache charting with cognitive coping strategies		Headache frequency decreased 72.5%	General coping better	8.5
Stambaugh & House, 1977	Patient $n = 1$, muscle relaxation, autogenic training, hypnosis; 22 "phases" used; home practice used		Headache activity near zero		6

Table 5 (Continued)

Author(s)	Subject(s) and Treatment(s)	No. of Sessions	Headache Activity Change	Associated Changes	Design Quality Rating
Blanchard, Theobald, Williamson, Silver, & Brown, 1978	Recruitment by ads $n = 13$, autogenic feedback training $n = 13$, progressive relaxation $n = 13$, waiting list with headache charting, later receiving autogenic feedback training $n = 13$, similar waiting list, later receiving progressive relaxation Home practice used	12	All groups significantly reduced overall headache activity as well as frequency, intensity, and medication; treatments are equally good	At 3-month follow-up, progressive relaxation was somewhat better than autogenic training in reduction of medication usage	2
Mullinix, Norton, Hack, & Fishman, 1978	Patient referrals $n = 6$, "true" feedback of hand temperature $n = 5$, "false" feedback showing increasing hand temperature Home practice used	9	$\bar{x} = 21\%$ improved headache scores with "true" feedback; $\bar{x} = 39\%$ improved with "false" feedback	"True" feedback group achieved significantly greater hand-temperature increases	20.5

Sovak, Kunzel, Sternbach, & Delassio, 1978	$n = 12$, patients receiving taped autogenic feedback training $n = 5$, "normals" recruitment Home practice used	8	At 3-month follow-up, 8 of 12 had 50% improvement in 2/3 of headache frequency, intensity, or medications	Differential cardiovascular activity between migraineurs and normals, and improved and unimproved migraineurs	14.5
Werbach & Sandweiss, 1978	Patient referrals $n = 37$, progressive relaxation, autogenic feedback training, breathing exercises. Feedback from most activated physiological index (EMG, thermal, skin conductance) Home practice used	10	73% decreased on one or more of headache intensity, frequency, medications, or increased ability to abort headaches	Significant inverse relationship between ability to increase hand temperature during first session and treatment success; $r = .01$ between hand-warming ability and treatment success	15

Table 6 Treatment of migraine and muscle contraction headaches.

Author(s)	Subject(s) & Treatment(s)	No. of Sessions	Headache Activity Change	Associated Changes	Design Quality Rating
Sargent, Green, & Walters, 1973	Patient population n = 20, migraine n = 5, tension Autogenic feedback training with home practice		Unanimous clinical agreement on headache improvement for 12/20 migraine and 2/5 tension		9
Warner & Lance, 1975	Neurology referrals n = 12, migraine n = 17, tension Muscle relaxation and mental imagery; home practice used; groups of 2–6 patients treated	4	At 6 months, 8/12 migraine and 11/17 tension decreased frequency of headaches by 50% at least; somewhat better improvement for tension-headache patients		18
Medina, Diamond, & Franklin, 1976	Patient population n = 13, migraine n = 14, mixed EMG frontalis feedback, plus autogenic feedback from hands each session; home practice with home feedback trainers	8 plus boosters	64% of migraineurs improved; 30% of mixed cases improved	Success with 50% of those previously unresponsive to medication	20

Feuerstein, Adams, & Beiman, 1976	Patient $n = 1$, mixed headaches EMG feedback from frontalis for 6 sessions, followed by CVMR training for 6 sessions Home practice used	12	Decrease in headache activity associated with EMG training	No EMG control achieved; CVMR achieved	17.5
Adler & Adler, 1976	Patient follow-up study $n = 22$, migraine, treated with EMG feedback, then thermal feedback $n = 19$, tension, treated with EMG feedback $n = 12$, mixed, same as migraine treatment 3/4 also received psychotherapy	5–60	75–100% remission in 86% of patients at 3 1/2–5-year follow-up; 81% for migraine, 88% for tension, and 60% for mixed	Most unimproved patients did not receive psychotherapy	n/a
Feuerstein & Adams, 1977	Patients $n = 2$, migraine $n = 2$, tension EMG frontalis feedback then CVMR feedback; counterbalanced for each subject Home practice used	6 EMG plus 6 CVMR	$n = 3$, significant decrease in headache activity $n = 1$, some positive change	Migraine subjects tended to decrease headaches with CVMR; tension subjects did so for EMG feedback; all learned to control the physiological responses	23.5

Table 6. *(Continued)*

Author(s)	Subject(s) & Treatment(s)	No. of Sessions	Headache Activity Change	Associated Changes	Design Quality Rating
Philips, 1977b	Postal survey of a medical practice $n = 8$, biofeedback from most tense resting muscle with $n = 5$, tension and $n = 3$, mixed $n = 7$, pseudo-feedback control; with $n = 4$, tension; and $n = 3$, mixed	12	Headache activity decrements only for feedback group; most change occurred after 6–8 weeks, when follow-up done; mixed cases had little change in headache measures	EMG significantly decreased only for feedback group; muscle tension and felt tension unrelated; EMG decline did not follow headache decrements	22
Bakal & Kaganov, 1977	Neurology referrals $n = 5$, migraine $n = 5$, tension Muscle relaxation followed by EMG frontalis feedback Home practice used	15–105 5-min sessions	Both groups significantly decreased headache index scores; greatest decreases came within 5 sessions	Both groups significantly reduced EMG levels, mostly in initial sessions	20

out the addition of practice. When practice was encouraged after a return to baseline, much greater decline was achieved. Again using music feedback, Epstein and Abel (1977) obtained headache decrements in three of six subjects who did not practice at home and were unable to lower EMG activity in the absence of the feedback signal. It appears that generalization procedures are needed for the best results.

McKenzie et al. (1974) compared two treatment procedures for patients referred for tension headache. One group received an elaborate package of progressive relaxation, autogenic training, and EEG alpha-enhancement feedback. The same number of subjects listened to a relaxation tape and had similar exposure to instrumentation. Both groups reduced headaches on the order of 75 percent. The long-term follow-up of these and several other patients by Montgomery and Ehrisman (1976) spanned from six months to three years post-treatment. When questionnaires were mailed, 59 percent returned them; the training effects of these responders, who perhaps were more likely to have had positive outcomes than nonresponders, held at significant levels.

In another comparative study (Haynes, Griffin, Mooney, & Parise, 1975) college students with tension headaches were assigned randomly to one of three conditions: frontalis EMG feedback, relaxation tapes, and the instruction merely to "relax." Both the feedback and tape groups significantly reduced the frequency and overall activity of their headaches, and these declines persisted for the 75 percent who were contacted six months later.

Cox, Freundlich, and Meyer (1975) used a matching procedure with recruited subjects, placing 18 of them in three different conditions. Subjects were used in the study if they met common diagnostic criteria for tension headache. One group received frontalis EMG feedback, applied relaxation, and instructions for cue-controlled breathing; the second was given verbal relaxation instructions along with the applied relaxation and breathing aids; and the third, a control group, was given a placebo with the expectation that it would prove effective in relieving headache. The third group demonstrated no changes in headache activity, but the other two had a significant decrease not only in headache activity but also in EMG levels, the amount of medications used, and the presence of other psychosomatic complaints.

Hutchings and Reinking (1976) found that progressive relaxation and taped autogenic training added nothing to reductions in headache effected by a frontalis EMG-feedback treatment regime. Subjects were assigned randomly to each of three groups: one using frontalis EMG feedback; one receiving taped autogenic instructions for progressive relaxation; and one using a combination of EMG feedback and relaxation instructions. Both groups receiving feedback significantly reduced headache activity by 66 percent, and the other (relaxation) group declined by only 20 percent. This finding is at variance with that of Haynes et al. (1975) and Cox et al. (1975), since both of these groups of researchers found relaxation training and EMG feedback to be effective in headache reduction. In the Hutchings and Reinking study, all three groups evidenced large and equivalent declines in EMG activity; thus it was not differential EMG activity that was responsible for the discrepant findings, but perhaps some other factor, such as generalizability of the relaxation training. Longer training or follow-up might determine the responsible factor. The Hutchings and Reinking sample was composed of medical referrals, all of whom experienced severe and stable headache activity and presumably had tonic elevated muscle tension. They may have been more effectively managed by EMG training than another group would have been. The samples used by Haynes et al., and Cox et al., were composed of recruits who had tension headaches but were not medical patients.

Cognitive coping strategies were applied in migraine headache therapy as early as 1971 by Mitchell and Mitchell, but not for tension headache until Reeves used them in 1976. He successively applied a variety of interventions to a single subject without any true baseline recording. Training in identifying the negative statements the subject made about himself, connected with stressors and with modifying them, caused a 33 percent reduction in his headache activity. With the addition of frontalis EMG biofeedback, headaches dropped 66 percent from the beginning of treatment and EMG activity fell by 38 percent. A serious criticism of this study is that cognitive training was half as long as feedback training and half as successful. It remains for others to continue this line of research.

Holroyd, Andrasik, and Westbrook (1977) advertised for persons subject to tension headaches and then had them medically screened. Within-sample matching yielded three treatment conditions: headache activity recording only; frontalis EMG feedback; and cognitive, stress-coping training. Although subjects perceived the latter two treatments as equally credible and practiced them with similar frequency at the rate of three sessions a week, cognitive training was the only modality to decrease headache activity significantly after treatment and at 15-week follow-up. EMG activity, however, was lowered significantly only by feedback, and both groups reported significantly reduced use of medication and significantly fewer psychosomatic complaints. This study may have been influenced by the fact that the investigators themselves gave the cognitive training, but laboratory assistants gave the biofeedback training. This circumstance might account for failure of EMG feedback to effect a significant reduction in headache activity such as other research has demonstrated.

Holroyd and Andrasik (1978) expanded an earlier investigation into cognitive self-control treatment modalities for the treatment of tension headache. Using methods similar to those in the research just cited, they assigned subjects to one of four conditions: the recording of headache activity only; a headache discussion group without coping strategies; group training in cognitive self-control; and group training in cognitive self-control with the addition of training in muscle relaxation. They found changes in EMG activity unrelated to headache reports and equally significant headache decrements in all three treatment groups. The positive results were maintained at follow-up. The subjects in the discussion group tended to devise their own coping strategies to deal with headaches and stressors, and this may have accounted for their success.

Clinical Prescription. In summary, it is clear that reductions in tension-headache activity occur either with muscle relaxation training or EMG biofeedback, or with both. Cognitive treatment modalities have received attention only recently, but they show promising results. On the basis of current research, biofeedback and muscle relaxation methods do not demonstrate differential treatment outcomes. Definitive comparison of these therapy modalities with cognitive self-control procedures is yet to be made, although recent work suggests that the latter may be superior. Since cognitive training obviates the need for expensive instrumentation and can be carried on in groups, it would be the treatment of choice over biofeedback if superior outcomes can be demonstrated.

Migraine

Lutker (1971) reported the almost total alleviation of a severe migraine by muscular relaxation training and its application in stressful situations. Although other investigators have used relaxation training as part of a treatment package, it is curious that only Blanchard et al. (1978) and Mitchell (1971a) used it exclusively with certain groups in treatment comparison studies. The Blanchard group indicated that it was equivalent to other methods they had used in respect to its success in modifying headache activity, but the Mitchell study failed to confirm this finding. The small number of subjects and less rigorous methodology of the Mitchell study may, however, diminish the relative importance of its findings. In a related effort, Benson, Klemchuk, and Graham (1974) found that eliciting the relaxation response through

Transcendental Meditation was largely unsuccessful in reducing migraine activity, but their work also suffers from lack of adequate controls.

Mitchell (1971a, 1971b) and his colleagues (Mitchell & Mitchell, 1971; Mitchell & White, 1976) pioneered the use of cognitive self-control procedures in migraine therapy. His 1971a study reported that applied relaxation training failed to reduce headaches significantly, while a combined desensitization package produced significant decrements of 76 percent in migraine frequency and 50 percent in duration relative to controls. The combined package consisted of applied relaxation, systematic desensitization, and assertiveness training. There was no change in one group that simply recorded headache activity. It is interesting that applied relaxation did tend to lessen migraine activity, and the combined package failed to attain statistical superiority over the single-treatment method. Mitchell (1971b) again demonstrated his combined desensitization program to be significantly superior to a control group that simply recorded headache activity. In a controlled case study, Mitchell and White (1976) reduced headache frequency by more than 72 percent with the use of self-control and cognitive and relaxation procedures. Lambley (1976) used assertiveness training and psychodynamic insight in a single case study in which headache frequency and intensity fell to low levels. The patient was free of headache at a 9-month follow-up.

Mitchell and Mitchell (1971) have conducted the sole controlled group-outcome experiment with the use of cognitive methods. The subjects were assigned randomly to one of four conditions: headache recording only; systematic desensitization; a combined desensitization package for those with no history of migraine pharmacotherapy; and a combined desensitization package for previous pharmacotherapy failures. Subjects in the combined-treatment groups reported significantly reduced headache frequency, and those without previous pharmacotherapy reported significantly decreased duration. The systematic desensitization group showed improvement (about 40 percent) in both categories, though nonsignificantly. The investigators argue that single-model therapies fail to match the behavioral complexity of migraine. The monitoring of headache activity, strategies for coping with stress, and reeducative efforts are seen as crucial in altering the pain syndrome. As further evidence of the generalizability of their techniques, Mitchell (1971a) and Mitchell and Mitchell (1971) report that combined desensitization techniques reduce complaints of "minor type" life problems concerning family, academic activities, religion, sex, and so on.

The use of thermal biofeedback of digital hand temperature has received considerable attention in research into the treatment of migraine. Sargent, Green, and Walters (1972) report that volitional increases in hand temperature are associated with spontaneous recovery from migraine headache. Sargent, Walters, and Green (1973) made use of autogenic phrases and imagery in addition to providing thermal feedback. They called this method autogenic feedback training (AFT). Home practice of the technique is held to be essential to its successful mastery and use in aborting vascular headaches. These investigators provide only global clinical judgments of improvement for about 90 patients; 80 percent had slight to very good reduction in headache.

Sovak et al. (1978) gave taped AFT to 12 patients and checked their headache activity at 3-month post-treatment. Two-thirds reported a reduction of at least 50 percent in two of three headache pain parameters—frequency, intensity, or medication usage. Mitch, McGrady, and Iannone (1976) gave similar treatment with the home use of portable temperature trainers. No laboratory training was involved, and the investigators had no control group. Headache intensity fell by 75 percent, duration by 60 percent, and the amount of medications taken by 55 percent.

Wickramasekera (1977) observed that elaborate biofeedback instrumentation and laboratory setting could exert a strong nonspecific (placebo) effect on migraine headache activity. This was especially true if suggestions were given that the therapeutic procedure was known to have positive effects. Working with two subjects who had had migraine attacks over 15 to 20 years and were veterans of various therapies, Wickramasekera (1973a) was unable to effect improvement during a long series of frontalis EMG training. After a return to baseline, he offered his subjects thermal feedback only, while minimizing its potential effectiveness. Both subjects acquired the hand warming skill and experienced concomitant decrements in headaches to a near-zero level.

Johnson and Turin (1975) in a systematic case study and Turin and Johnson (1976) examined the placebo-expectancy issue more closely. In the first study, the investigators gave 12 sessions of finger cooling, followed by a similar series of finger warming sessions. Positive expectations were encouraged for both exercises. Each of these vascular responses was mastered, and all headache activity parameters rose during cooling and fell to low levels during warming. Turin and Johnson taught some volunteer subjects to cool their hands and others to warm them; and after one group learned to lower the temperature of their hands, they were instructed in warming them. Significant decreases in migraine frequency, duration, and medication use were observed in both groups only as they acquired mastery of the warming response.

Mullinix, Norton, Hack, and Fishman (1978) provide the only evidence for placebo effects of thermal biofeedback in migraine therapy They gave six patients thermal feedback contingent upon hand temperature and gave five patients noncontingent feedback that indicated control of hand warming. The group averages of 21 percent and 39 percent for headache improvement were unimpressive in both conditions, with the "false" feedback group showing the more positive change, and in spite of significant temperature elevation in the "true" feedback group. It is interesting that these researchers told their subjects that the treatments were experimental and some of them would receive altered feedback.

Hypnotherapy for migraine has been described in several case reports (Ansel, 1977; Daniels, 1976; Graham, 1975), with positive results reported. The procedure typically involves verbal, taped, or autohypnotic suggestions of hand warmth. Ansel offers a procedure for inducing sensations of hand warmth in subjects with low suggestibility; he has them whirl about, arms extended, to allow centrifugal force to increase the blood volume in the hands.

Since the onset of migraine pain is associated with dilation of extracranial arteries, Friar and Beatty (1976) trained subjects to constrict these vessels through biofeedback of arterial pulse waves. Biofeedback control generalized to no-feedback trials after eight training sessions. A second group of control subjects was trained to constrict digital arteries. Results indicated that the controls retained relatively stable headache activity and the treatment group significantly decreased the duration of major attacks. Headache frequency fell to near-significant lows, although the intensity of pain remained virtually unchanged.

Stambaugh and House (1977) report a case study covering 22 separate interventions with interphase baselines. This neurology referral was given relaxation therapy, hypnotherapy, autogenic training, and autohypnotic treatment instructions. With so complicated a treatment over 264 days, it was inevitable that the variables at issue in the case would be confounded. Although follow-up at eight months showed no headache activity, the cumbersome nature of this treatment package hardly makes it the therapy of choice.

Werbach and Sandweiss (1978) used a limited version of the Stambaugh and House "shotgun" approach, teaching 37 patients progressive relaxation, AFT, and breathing exercises in 10 sessions. Feedback came from the most highly activated physiological system (EMG; thermal or skin conductance). Seventy-three percent of the subjects were able to reduce migraine activity in one or more aspects—intensity, frequency, medication usage, or an increased ability to abort the migraine. The investigators report further the absence of correlation between hand warming ability and treatment success; and, more importantly, they note that the lower the patient's initial hand temperature was, the greater his chance was for success in the treatment.

Andreychuk and Skriver (1975) randomly assigned volunteers to one of three treatment conditions; hypnosis, AFT, and alpha EEG-enhancement feedback. Although all three groups significantly reduced migraine headache activity by equivalent amounts, the AFT group had somewhat better improvement. It seemed evident that subjects with high suggestibility, as measured by the Hypnotic Induction Profile, tended to make more positive responses to therapeutic intervention.

Blanchard et al. (1978) made the most systematic investigation of the relative value of AFT as compared to progressive relaxation training. Random assignment of 52 migraine subjects yielded four groups: one using AFT; one using progressive relaxation; a waiting list with headache charting, later to receive AFT; and a waiting list with headache charting, later to receive progressive relaxation. All experienced significant reduction in overall headache activity after treatment and in individual parameters of frequency, intensity, and medication use as well. A slight trend appeared at 3-month follow-up for relaxation training to be superior to AFT in the reduction of medication intake.

Clinical Prescription. In summary, a reduction in migraine headache activity has been effected successfully by a variety of therapeutic interventions, including volitional hand warming, cognitive procedures, hypnotherapy, progressive relaxation, and biofeedback of extracranial artery activity and EEG alpha activity. All have been shown to be effective in treatment regimes. It appears that only EMG biofeedback is ineffective, although it has actually received scant attention. Comparative work largely has failed to distinguish among the various treatment modalities, and further research is indicated. The choice of therapy for any given patient is determined by the presence or absence of activated physiological parameters and the significance of psychological factors, in addition to considerations as to the availability of instrumentation. Therapies that take into account the many factors potentially implicated in migraine are more likely to generate positive outcomes than single-model therapies aimed at a single symptom.

Migraine and Muscle-Contraction Treatment Comparisons

Suprisingly few studies have applied similar treatments to both migraine and tension-headache groups; but four are known, none of which used control groups. An additional weakness in these studies is that they all used different treatment modalities, which makes generalization hazardous. Sargent, Green, and Walters (1975) reported on the use of AFT with both tension-headache and migraine samples; 12 out of 20 migraine patients and 2 out of 5 tension-headache patients were rated as improved, according to the investigators' judgment of improvement. It is unfortunate that the length of treatment was not indicated; in all likelihood, it was variable among the members of the groups.

Warner and Lance (1975) applied muscle relaxation and mental imagery therapy to patients referred by neurologists, 2 of whom were diagnosed as having purely functional headaches. These investigators treated the subjects in groups of 2 to 6 for four sessions and reported results at 6-month follow-up. Tension headache patients performed somewhat better overall; 8 of 12 migraine subjects and 11 of 17 tension subjects demonstrated a decrease in headache frequency of at least 50 percent, and decreases in medication and elevations in mood were generally reported.

A single-subject multiple baseline design was used by Feuerstein and Adams (1977) with two tension patients and two migraine sufferers. They counterbalanced six sessions of frontalis EMG feedback and six of cephalic vasomotor response feedback (CVMR) across subjects and conditions. Three of the four subjects had significant reduction in headache activity, and the remaining subject tended toward similar reduction. These changes tended to occur during CVMR in the case of migraine and during EMG for the tension patients. The investigators hypothesize that CVMR training helped to increase arterial muscle tone and to decrease lability and the painful dilation of migraine headache. The total training time for each subject was only four hours. A study by Feuerstein, Adams, and Beiman (1976) reports the successful application of EMG and CVMR training to a geriatric patient with mixed headaches.

Bakal and Kaganov (1977) taught muscle relaxation and frontalis EMG reduction to five tension-headache and five migraine patients referred by neurologists, with significant EMG decrements obtained within five 5-minute sessions but with no further improvement beyond 15 sessions; as many as 105 were administered. Reductions in headache activity in both groups occurred at significant levels concomitant with EMG reduction.

Two research studies examined therapy packages for migraine and combined muscle-contraction and migraine headaches. Medina, Diamond, and Franklin (1976) applied frontalis feedback and AFT in each treatment session, and the patients were given portable temperature trainers for use at home. Improvement was noted in 64 percent of the migraine subjects but in only 30 percent of the mixed cases. The treatment was successful, however, for 50 percent of subjects previously unresponsive to pharmacotherapy.

Philips (1977b) gave contingent EMG biofeedback from head or neck muscles recorded at their highest tension with the subject at rest; an equivalent group received pseudo-feedback as a control. Only the contingent group achieved EMG decrements and, of this group, only the patients with tension headache showed reduced headache frequency. There was little change in the mixed cases.

Adler and Adler (1976) conducted the longest post-treatment follow-up of headache patients to date. They made their assessments from three-and-a-half to five years after therapy was completed. The tension-headache patients received frontalis EMG feedback, and the migraine and mixed patients were given EMG followed by thermal feedback. Of all patients, 86 percent showed major improvement in headache symptoms immediately after treatment, as defined by 75 to 100 percent remission, and the results were similar at long-term follow-up: tension, 81 percent; migraine, 81 percent; and mixed, 60 percent. Three-fourths of the patients had concomitant psychotherapy; the investigators consider this to be a critical treatment component, since most of those reporting no improvement had not been given adjunctive therapy.

CLINICAL EXAMPLES

This chapter focuses to a considerable extent on treatment research in which one procedure is compared with another. In clinical practice, however, the treatment package must be specifically designed to fit the patient's personality, physiology, and presenting problems. With the patient who has an obsessional style, for example, the feedback loop is probably more efficacious when the feedback gets louder as the patient becomes more relaxed. This procedure gives him the task of producing rather than turning something off. If a patient experiences tension first in his abdomen and then in his forehead, breathing exercises should probably come before progressive relaxation training. The general superiority of individualized plans is reflected in two recent reports. Medina, Diamond, and Franklin (1976) report a 50 percent success rate with the various headache types when biofeedback was applied mechanically by nurse-technicians. Adler and Adler (1976), on the other hand, report a success rate of 80 to 90 percent at 3 to 5-year follow-up when biofeedback was administered in the context of psychotherapy. The following cases illustrate some of the clinical subtleties involved in actual practice that indicate the need to go beyond electronics and techniques to meet the needs of the individual patient.

Case 1

J. was a 21-year-old woman, a college senior with a 5-year history of tension headaches. Current stressors included the recent divorce of her parents and the uncertainty of her postgraduate career. Her only readily accessible social support was a roommate. She described herself on the SCL-90 as obsessive, acutely sensitive to rejection, and aware of marked depression and anxiety. She was an angry and hostile young woman suffering from onset insomnia and early morning awakening. A neurological work-up proved negative, and a trial of librium was unhelpful.

Initial physiological recordings indicated marked distress, with frontalis EMG of 4.1 uv and peripheral skin temperature of 76° F. Although she exhibited significant physiological relaxation while listening to Budzynski's relaxation tapes, she was unable to maintain this state when listening to auditory biofeedback or resting quietly. It was not until the fourth session, when she found herself laughing at "how absurd it is to control a machine with my forehead" that she demonstrated marked relaxation during feedback conditions. On immediate debriefing, she reported that she had stopped forcing herself to relax and found humor in the situation. She had been told to "let go" instead of trying to force relaxation, but until this incident the instructions had not had any personal meaning for her. Further exploration and experimentation with the feedback equipment revealed that whenever she was truly amused her EMG dropped and her skin temperature climbed. This led to a discussion which revealed that she was a very serious student who seldom had fun and who kept up her guard defensively in expectation of the worst from reality.

She was told to smile often throughout the day, especially when she recognized tension, and to see the humor in daily living. She exhibited rapid improvement during the four biofeedback sessions that followed. When her treatment concluded, her EMG was down to 1.6 uv, her skin temperature was up to 92.4° F, and her headache score had dropped to 3.0 from a baseline of 27.9. Her mental state also underwent a radical change; depression, anxiety, obsessional thoughts, and interpersonal sensitivity were greatly reduced. During post-treatment debriefing, she reported that the most beneficial aspect of her treatment was "learning how to breathe and smile at life." It is important to recognize that although the mechanical application of biofeedback did not directly lead to significant control of physiological or headache activity, it does not seem likely that the very real gains she made would have been achieved without biofeedback.

Case 2

Mrs. M. was a 66-year-old married housewife who was admitted to the hospital for psychiatric care because of depression and her habitual abuse of analgesic headache medication. She had a long history of depressive episodes and chronic headache. Her problems, seen psychodynamically, seemed to arise from early childhood experiences of rejection by her biological parents. As the oldest of six children, she had been the only one "farmed out" to grandparents. She had spent much of her adult life in a futile attempt to gain love and recognition from her father.

She had her first biofeedback session while in the hospital. During the session, she showed psychomotor retardation and wept. She was frightened and had difficulty concentrating, as shown by her inability to complete the standard psychometrics. Her EMG was elevated (3.4 uv) but peripheral skin temperature was within normal limits (95.6). At the conclusion of the first session, her EMG dropped to 1.8 uv and her skin temperature to 92.4°F. She recognized that "the feedback noise went off when I wasn't thinking of anything . . . when I had an empty mind . . . when I was just staring at the blinds." This acknowledgment led to talk about how she could control her body. She said, "my body must feel better when I am not thinking those depressive thoughts." She was an outpatient when she had her final four sessions, and the death of her father occurred between sessions seven and eight. When her treatment terminated, she experienced no headache; her frontalis EMG was 1.5 uv and her skin temperature was 97.3°F. These gains were achieved and maintained in spite of tremendous stress caused by her father's death. She was discharged from biofeedback to the care of a psychiatrist who sees her on an as needed basis.

LEGAL AND ETHICAL ISSUES

Behavioral treatment of headaches represents an interface between medicine and the behavioral sciences and is a prime example of the new field referred to as behavioral medicine. Professionals working in this area need to respect the input of both specialities. Consequently, it is both unethical and representative of legal liability for a behavioral clinician to accept and treat a patient for headache without a thorough medical exam that would rule out any organicity. Diamond (1978) estimates that 1 headache patient in 10 has some positive and significant organic dysfunction that should at least be documented and at best remediated. If this is not done, the obvious possibility exists of implementing innappropriate treatment that prevents appropriate and possibly life-saving treatment.

To what type of physician does one turn for such preliminary medical screening? If the case represents a classic symptom pattern, reliance on any competent general practitioner is appropriate. If the complaint has any atypical patterns, however, referral to a neurologist—the medical headache specialist—is indicated. Failure to secure a medical assessment is not only poor patient care, but amounts to malpractice. As elaborated elsewhere (Cox, 1979), such behavioral-medical contacts have the potential for many positive spin-offs: ruling out any organicity, communicating to the referring physician a responsible approach to patient care, functioning as part of a mutual educational experience, and potentially leading to reciprocal referrals from the physician.

Is it ethical to provide treatment for headaches without available biofeedback equipment? Though there is no data clearly documenting the efficacy of biofeedback over the nonelectronic relaxation techniques, it seems that doing so would be analogous to fitting a person who complains of leg pain with a cast without x-raying to assess the presence of a broken bone. That is, biofeedback equipment, besides being a treatment tool, plays a critical role in the documentation of whether excessive muscle contraction or vasoconstriction exists prior to treatment, and it allows evaluation of treatment effectiveness on the same physical parameters. Providing relaxation training for headaches to someone who has neither elevated tonic EMG nor labile electromyographic activity in response to stress is not only a waste of time and money, but also postpones more accurate diagnosis and treatment.

Specifics about the necessary type of equipment and facilities have been enumerated elsewhere (Cox, 1979). Briefly, however, it is important to have equipment that reliably and validly assesses the physiological parameter intended, is durable and reliable in its performance, and is flexible in its monitoring and generation of feedback.

FUTURE RESEARCH ISSUES

To conduct yet another study that compares any two standard treatment procedures (biofeedback versus muscle-relaxant medication) would be a tremendous waste of resources. Because of the infinite number of comparisons, procedural variations, and patient characteristics, such studies tell the clinician little about optimal treatment procedures for a specific patient. At best, such research suggests the treatment approach with which to start. What clinical research needs to address, as suggested by Bergin (1971) almost 10 years ago, is patient–treatment interaction studies that isolate patient characteristics, successfully predicting the patients who will and will not benefit from a specific program. It makes little difference what the treatment procedure is. If we can identify for whom it works and does not work, then a significant service has been done for the field of behavioral medicine and for patients in general. After identifying the subgroup that will not respond, alternative interventions can be explored for subsequent research.

This point is illustrated by the Cox, Freundlich and Meyer (1975) study that documented progressive relaxation training and EMG frontalis biofeedback to be equivalent in reducing group-mean headache activity. An erroneous conclusion often drawn from such a study is that these two treatment procedures are equally effective for all patients. Such a conclusion, however, is not justified on the basis of the experimental procedure used. The Cox, Freundlich and Meyer (1975) project could have had more clinical and scientific significance if it had documented whether these techniques were equally effective with the same type of patient, or whether one technique worked better with one type of patient and the other worked best with a different patient subtype.

Potentially significant patient variables to consider in future research are initial scalp EMG levels; general body EMG levels (limb EMG); liability of EMG activity; patient characteristics such as obsessive-compulsive, passive-dependent, hypochondriacal, and hysterical; health locus of control; field dependency; and existence of additional psychiatric symptomotology. Additional factors include positive and negative reinforcement, expectancy, motivation to change (including differing methods of free payment), severity of functional pain, and patient–therapist rapport.

We know that various techniques work with various patients. Now we need to know what patient works best with what techniques.

SUMMARY

Functional headache has been described and treated by various procedures for thousands of years. It was long considered the sole province of the medical establishment, yet research into its pathophysiological

266   *Douglas W. Thomas and Daniel J. Cox*

mechanisms began only about four decades ago. As the role of stress
has become more clearly detailed in the onset and maintenance of
headache symptoms, psychologists have become increasingly active in
conceptualizing and treating functional headache. Two main diagnostic categories, migraine and muscle contraction, are described.
Headache studies generally fail to distinguish these headache diagnoses
from one another, and the notion of a headache-prone personality is
not supported. It has been suggested that the best way to view functional headache is in terms of the physiological, behavioral, and subjective interrelationships involved.

Numerous therapeutic strategies have been advanced for the treatment of functional headache, including interventions based on pharmacology, cognitive approaches, biofeedback, general muscle-relaxa-
tion training, and hypnosis, either singly or in combination. These
strategies are examined as to outcome and relative to experimental
rigor employed. Case examples illustrate considerations involved in
clinical procedures. Ethical and future research issues are also examined.

REFERENCES

Ad Hoc Committee on Classification of Headache. Classification of headache.
Journal of the American Medical Association, 1962, *179,* 127–128.
Adler, C. S., & Adler, S. M. Biofeedback-psychotherapy for the treatment of
headache: A 5-year follow-up. *Headache,* 1976, *16,* 189–191.
Andreychuk, T., & Skriver, C. Hypnosis and biofeedback in the treatment of
migraine headache. *International Journal of Clinical and Experimental
Hypnosis,* 1975, *23,* 172–183.
Ansel, E. L. A simple exercise to enhance response to hypnotherapy for
migraine headache. *International Journal of Clinical and Experimental
Hypnosis,* 1977, *25,* 68–71.
Appenzeller, O., Davison, K., & Marshall, J. Reflex vasomotor abnormalities
in the hands of migrainous subjects. *Journal of Neurology, Neurosurgery,
and Psychiatry,* 1963, *26,* 447–450.
Bakal, D. A. Headache: A biopsychological perspective. *Psychological Bulletin,* 1975, *82,* 369–382.
Bakal, D. A., & Kaganov, J. A. *Muscle contraction and migraine headache: A
psychophysiological comparison.* Paper presented at the Annual Meeting
of the American Association for the Study of Headache, June 1977.
Benson, H., Klemchuk, H., & Graham, J. The usefulness of the relaxation
response in the therapy of headache. *Headache,* 1974, *14,* 49–52.
Benson, H., Kotch, J. B., & Crassweller, K. D. The relaxation response: A
bridge between psychiatry and medicine. *Medical Clinics of North
America,* 1977, *61,* 929–938.
Bergin, A. E. The evaluation of therapeutic outcome. In S. L. Garfield & A. E.

Bergin, (Eds.), *Handbook of psychotherapy and behavior change.* New York: Wiley, 1971.

Blanchard, E. G., Theobald, D. E., Williamson, D. A., Silver, B. V., & Brown, D. A. Temperature biofeedback in the treatment of migraine headaches: A controlled evaluation. *Archives of General psychiatry,* 1978, *35,* 581–588.

Budzynski, T. H. Biofeedback strategies in headache treatment. In J. V. Basmajian, (Ed.), *Biofeedback: A handbook for clinicians.* Baltimore: Williams and Wilkins, 1978.

Budzynski, T. H., Stoyva, J., & Adler, C. Feedback-induced muscle relaxation: Application to tension headache. *Journal of Behavior Therapy and Experimental Psychiatry,* 1970, *1,* 205–211.

Budzynski, T. H., Stoyva, J., Adler, C. S., & Mullaney, D. J. EMG biofeedback and tension headache: A controlled outcome study. *Psychosomatic Medicine,* 1973, *35,* 484–496.

Christie, D., & Kotses, H. Bidirectional operant conditioning of the cephalic vasomotor response. *Journal of Psychosomatic Research,* 1973, *17,* 167–170.

Cohen, M. J. Psychophysiological studies of headache: Is there similarity between migraine and muscle contraction headaches? *Headache,* 1978, *18,* 189–196.

Cox, D. J., Freundlich, A., & Meyer, R. G. Differential effectiveness of electromyograph feedback, verbal relaxation instructions, and medication placebo with tension headaches. *Journal of Consulting and Clinical Psychology,* 1975, *43,* 892–898.

Cox, D. J. *Development of behavioral medicine services within a medical setting.* Paper presented at the November, 1978 meeting of the AABT, Chicago.

Cox, D. J. *Development of a biofeedback facility.* Unpublished manuscript, 1979.

Daniels, L. K. The effects of automated hypnosis and hand warming on migraine: A pilot study. *American Journal of Clinical Hypnosis,* 1976, *19,* 91–94.

Diamond, S. *Biofeedback treatment of headaches.* Paper presented at the November, 1978 meeting of the AABT., Chicago.

Diamond, S., & Franklin, M. F. *Intensive biofeedback therapy in the treatment of headache.* Paper presented at the Sixth Annual Meeting of the Biofeedback Research Society, Monterey, February 1975.

Elliott, K., Frewin, D. B., & Downey, J. A. Reflex vasomotor responses in the hands of patients suffering from migraine. *Headache,* 1974, *13,* 188–196.

Epstein, L. H., & Abel, G. G. An analysis of biofeedback training effects for tension headache patients. *Behavior Therapy,* 1977, *8,* 37–47.

Epstein, L. H., Abel, G. G., Collins, F., Parker, L., & Cinciripini, P. M. The relationship between frontalis muscle activity and self-reports and headache pain. *Behavior Research and Therapy,* 1978, *16,* 153–160.

Epstein, L. H., Hersen, M., & Hemphill, D. P. Music feedback in the treatment of tension headache: An experimental case study. *Journal of Behavior Therapy and Experimental Psychiatry,* 1974, *5,* 59–63.

Feuerstein, M., & Adams, H. E. Cephalic vasomotor feedback in the modification of migraine headache. *Biofeedback and Self-Regulation,* 1977, *2,* 214–254.

Feuerstein, M., Adams, H. E., & Beiman, I. Cephalic vasomotor and electromyographic feedback in the treatment of combined muscle contraction and migraine headaches in a geriatric case. *Headache,* 1976, *16,* 232–237.

Fichtler, H., & Zimmermann, R. R. Changes in reported pain from tension headaches. *Perceptual and Motor Skills,* 1973, *36,* 712.

Fowler, R. S. Operant therapy for headaches. *Headache,* 1975, *15,* 63–68.

Friar, L. R., & Beatty, J. Migraine: Management by trained control of vasoconstriction. *Journal of Consulting and Clinical Psychology,* 1976, *44,* 4.

Gold, J. D. *Migraine headache: Its causes and treatments.* Unpublished manuscript, 1974.

Graham, G. W. Hypnotic treatment for migraine headache. *International Journal of Clinical and Experimental Hypnosis,* 1975, *23,* 165–171.

Graham, J. R., & Wolff, H. G. Mechanism of migraine headache and the action of ergotamine tartrate. *Archives of Neurology and Psychiatry,* 1938, *39,* 737–763.

Harper, R. G., & Steger, J. C. Psychological correlates of frontalis EMG and pain in tension headache. *Headache,* 1978, *17,* 215–218.

Haynes, S. N., Griffin, P., Mooney, D., & Parise, M. Electromyographic feedback and relaxation instructions in the treatment of muscle contraction headaches. *Behavior Therapy,* 1975, *6,* 672–678.

Hockaday, J. M., MacMillan, A. L., & Whitty, C. W. M. Vasomotor reflex response in idiopathic and hormone dependent migraine. *Lancet,* 1967, *1,* 1023–1026.

Holroyd, K. A., Andrasik, F. Coping and self-control of chronic tension headache. *Journal of Consulting and Clinical Psychology,* 1978, *46,* 1036–1045.

Holroyd, K. A., Andrasik, F., & Westbrook, T. Cognitive control of tension headache. *Cognitive Therapy and Research,* 1977, *1,* 121–133.

Hutchings, D. F., & Reinking, R. H. Tension headaches: What form of therapy is most effective? *Biofeedback and Self-Regulation,* 1976, *1,* 183–190.

Johnson, W. G., & Turin, A. Biofeedback treatment of migraine headache: A systematic case study. *Behavior Therapy,* 1975, *6,* 394–397.

Koppman, J. W., McDonald, R. O., & Kunzel, M. G. Voluntary regulation of temporal artery diameter by migraine patients. *Headache,* 1974, *14,* 133–138.

Lambley, P. The use of assertive training and psychodynamic insight in the treatment of migraine headache: A case study. *Journal of Nervous and Mental Disease,* 1976, *163,* 61–64.

Lutker, E. R. Treatment of migraine headache by conditional adaptation: A case study. *Behavior Therapy,* 1971, *2,* 592–593.

Martin, M. J. Tension headaches, a psychiatric study. *Headache*, 1966, *6*, 47-54.

Martin, M. J. Muscle-contraction headache. *Psychosomatics*, 1972, *13*, 16-19.

McKenzie, R. E., Ehrisman, W. J., Montgomery, P. S., & Barnes, R. H. The treatment of headache by means of electroencephalographic biofeedback. *Headache*, 1974, *13*, 164-172.

Medina, J. L., Diamond, S., & Franklin, M. A. Biofeedback therapy for migraine. *Headache*, 1976, *16*, 115-118.

Mitch, P. S., McGrady, A., & Iannone, A. Autogenic feedback training in migraine: A treatment report. *Headache*, 1976, *15*, 267-270.

Mitchell, K. R. A psychological approach to the treatment of migraine. *British Journal of Psychiatry*, 1971, *119*, 533-534. (a)

Mitchell, K. R. Note on treatment of migraine using behavior therapy techniques. *Psychological Reports*, 1971, *28*, 171-172. (b)

Mitchell, K. R., & Mitchell, D. M. Migraine: An exploratory treatment application of programmed behavior therapy techniques. *Journal of Psychosomatic Research*, 1971, *15*, 137-157.

Mitchell, K. R., & White, R. G. Control of migraine headache by behavioral self-management: A controlled case study. *Headache*, 1976, *16*, 178-184.

Montgomery, D. S., & Ehrisman, W. J. Biofeedback-alleviated headaches: A follow-up. *Headache*, 1976, *16*, 64-65.

Morley, S. Migraine: A generalized vasomotor dysfunction? A critical review of evidence. *Headache*, 1977, *17*, 71-74.

Mullinix, J. M., Norton, B. J., Hack, S., & Fishman, M. A. Skin temperature biofeedback and migraine. *Headache*, 1978, *17*, 242-244.

Nelson, A. Orgone (Reichian) therapy in tension headache. *American Journal of Psychotherapy*, 1976, *30*, 103-111.

Norton, G. R., & Nielson, W. R. Headaches: The importance of consequent events. *Behavior Therapy*, 1977, *8*, 504-506.

O'Brien, M. The haemodynamics of migraine—a review. *Headache*, 1973, *10*, 160-162.

Ogden, H. D. Headache studies, statistical data. I. Procedure and sample distribution. *Journal of Allergy*, 1952, *23*, 58-75.

Philips, C. Headache and personality. *Journal of Psychosomatic Research*, 1976, *20*, 535-542.

Philips, C. A psychological analysis of tension headache. In S. Rachman (Ed.), *Advances in Medical Psychology*. Oxford, England: Pergamon Press, 1977. (a)

Philips, C. The modification of tension headache pain using EMG biofeedback. *Behavior Research and Therapy*, 1977, *15*, 119-129. (b)

Philips, C. Headache in general practice. *Headache*, 1977, *16*, 322-329. (c)

Philips, C. Tension headache: Theoretical problems. *Behavior Research and Therapy*, 1978, *16*, 249-261.

Poźniak-Patewicz, E. "Cephalgic" spasm of head and neck muscles. *Headache*, 1976, *15*, 261-266.

Price, K. P. The application of behavior therapy to the treatment of psychosomatic disorders: Retrospect and prospect. *Psychotherapy: Theory, research and practice,* 1974, *11,* 138–155.

Price, K. P., & Tursky, B. Vascular reactivity of migraineurs and non-migraineurs: A comparison of responses to self-control procedures. *Headache,* 1976, *16,* 210–217.

Rachman, S., & Philips, C. *Psychology and medicine.* London: Temple-Smith, 1975.

Reeves, J. L. EMG-biofeedback reduction of tension headache: A cognitive skills-training approach. *Biofeedback and Self-Regulation,* 1976, *1,* 217–225.

Rhodes, R. J. Failure to validate an MMPI headache scale. *Journal of Clinical Psychology,* 1973, *29,* 237–238.

Sainsbury, P., & Gibson, J. F. Symptoms of anxiety and tension and accompanying physiological changes in the muscular system. *Journal of Neurology, Neurosurgery and Psychiatry,* 1954, *17,* 216–224.

Sargent, J. D., Green, E. E., & Walters, E. D. The use of autogenic feedback training in a pilot study of migraine and tension headaches. *Headache,* 1972, *12,* 120–124.

Sargent, J. D., Green, E. E., & Walters, E. D. Preliminary report on the use of autogenic feedback techniques in the treatment of migraine and tension headaches. *Psychosomatic Medicine,* 1973, *35,* 129–135.

Sargent, J. D., Walters, E. D., & Green, E. E. Psychosomatic self-regulation of migraine headaches. *Seminars in Psychiatry,* 1973, *5*(4), 415–428.

Sovak, M., Kunzel, M., Sternbach, R. A., & Delassio, D. J. Is volitional manipulation a valid rationale for biofeedback therapy of migraine? *Headache,* 1978, *18,* 197–202.

Stambaugh, E. E., & House, A. E. Multimodality treatment of migraine headache: A case study utilizing biofeedback, relaxation, autogenic and hypnotic treatments. *American Journal of Clinical Hypnosis,* 1977, *19,* 235–240.

Tasto, D. L., & Hinkle, J. E. Muscle relaxation treatment for tension headaches. *Behavior Research and Therapy,* 1973, *11,* 247–349.

Thomas, D. W. Comparison of functional headache referrals to psychiatric outpatients. Paper presented at the meeting of the Virginia Psychological Association, Richmond, April 1979.

Tunis, M. M., & Wolff, H. G. Studies on headache: Cranial artery vasoconstriction and muscle contraction headache. *Archives of Neurological Psychiatry,* 1954, *71,* 425–434.

Turin, A., & Johnson, W. G. Biofeedback therapy for migraine headaches. *Archives of General Psychiatry,* 1976, *33,* 517–519.

van Boxtel, A., & van der Ven, J. Roozeveld. Differential EMG activity in subjects with muscle contraction headaches related to mental effort. *Headache,* 1978, *17,* 233–237.

Vaughn, R., Pall, M. D., & Haynes, S. N. Frontalis EMG response to stress in subjects with frequent muscle-contraction headaches. *Headache,* 1977, *16,* 313–317.

Warner, G., & Lance, J. W. Relaxation therapy in migraine and chronic tension headache. *Medical Journal of Australia,* 1975, *1,* 298–301.

Waters, W. E., & O'Connor, P. J. Epidemiology of headache and migraine in women. *Journal of Neurology, Neurosurgery and Psychiatry,* 1971, *34,* 148–153.

Werbach, M. R., & Sandweiss, J. H. Peripheral temperatures of migraineurs undergoing relaxation training. *Headache,* 1978, *17,* 211–214.

Wickramasekera, I. W. Electromyographic feedback training and tension headache: Preliminary observations. *American Journal of Clinical Hypnosis,* 1972, *15,* 83–85.

Wickramasekera, I. W. Temperature feedback for the control of migraine. *Journal of Behavior Therapy and Experimental Psychiatry,* 1973, *4,* 343–345. (a)

Wickramesekera, I. W. The application of verbal instructions and EMG feedback training to the management of tension headache—preliminary observations. *Headache,* 1973, *13,* 74–76. (b)

Wickramasekera, I. W. The placebo effect and medical instruments in biofeedback. *Journal of Clinical Engineering,* 1977, *2,* 227–230.

Wolff, H. G. *Headache and other head pain,* 2nd ed. New York: Oxford University Press, 1963.

Yen, S., & McIntire, R. W. Operant therapy for constant headache complaints: A simple response-cost approach. *Psychological Reports,* 1971, 267–270.

Ziegler, D. K., Hassanein, R., & Hassanein, K. Headache syndromes suggested by factor analysis of symptom variables in a headache-prone population. *Journal of Chronic Diseases,* 1972, *25,* 353–363.

Author Index

Numbers in *italic* refer to reference lists at the end of chapters.

Subject Index

Abstinence, in smoking, 83, 85, 101
American Association for Marriage and Family Therapy, Professional Code of, 207-208
American Association of Sex Educators, Counselors and Therapists (AASECT), certification of sex therapists by, 156-157
American Cancer Society smoking program, 87
American Psychological Association (APA), ethics code of, 157, 202
Anger
  in erectile dysfunction, 123
  as marital problem, 198-202
Anorgasmia, 44
  components in treatment of, 54-55
  as normal physiological variation, 55
  number of years of marriage and, 62
  pubococcygeal muscle in, 52
  secondary, 55
Anxiety
  in erectile dysfunction, 125
  in female sexual inhibition, 36-37
Approach-avoidance conflict theory, 5
Areas of Change Questionnaire (AC), 181
Arousal and orgasm disturbances in female, 43
Arousal reconditioning, 145
Aspirin, for headaches, 235
Assertiveness training, in migraine headaches, 237
Attention-placebo control

group systematic desensitization versus, 137
  in smoking, 103
Attitude restructuring, in erectile dysfunction, 148-149
Attribution theory, in marital problems, 177
Audiotape, in marital problems, 185
Audiovisual techniques
  in erectile dysfunction, 147-148
  in sex therapy, 52
Autism, 1-26
  age of onset of, 2
  approach-avoidance conflict theory in, 5
  assessment of, 5-7
  aversive stimulation in, 23
  behavior modification in, 23
  "behavioral ego" in, 3
  behavioral repertiore expansion in, 12-19
  behavioral theories of, 5
  behavioral treatment procedures in, 7-20
  biochemical influences on, 4
  case report on, 21-23
  classroom behavior in, 19
  clinical prescription in, 20-21
  cognitive deficit in, 4-5
  contingent reinforcement in, 16
  contingent shock in, 10, 11
  definition of, 1
  diagnosis of, 5
  electric shock in, 23-24
  eliminating maladaptive behavior in, 7-8
  ethical considerations in, 23-24

Marital problems (*cont.*)
  divorce rates as indication of, 167
  future research on, 209–211
  physical abuse, 167
  prevalence of, 167
  psychoanalytic theory of, *see* Psychoanalytic theory of marital problems
  sex role in, 176
  sexual dysfunction as, 176
  systems theory of, *see* Systems theory
  theoretical analysis of, 169–178
  treatment of, 186–195
    assessment versus, 178–179
    behavioral exchange in, 190
    "coercion process" in, 175–176
    conjoint versus individual therapy in, 187
    contingency contracting in, 191
    direct training procedures in, 193–194
    directness of communication in, 188
    emotional expressiveness in, 188
    empirical research on, 191–193
    feedback in, 193
    "good faith" contract in, 190
    indirect behavior change strategy in, 194–195
    individual versus conjoint therapy in, 187
    negative behavior as positive behavior in, 194
    parallel contract in, 191
    problem-solving skills in, 200
    reattribution in, 194
    reframing in, 194, 200
    specificness of communication in, 188
    taped replays in, 193
Marital satisfaction
  children and, 168
  measuring, 168
  objective measures of, 180–182
Marital Status Inventory (MSI), 181
Marital therapy

confidentiality in, 206–207
conjoint versus individual, 187
"continuing service" versus open-ended, 187
cost effectiveness of, 187
co-therapist versus single therapist in, 187
defining, 168–169
diverse formats of, 169
ethical issues in, 202–209
extramarital affairs and, 208–209
goal of, 205
individual versus conjoint, 187
interpretive meeting in, 196
legal issues in, 202–209
length of treatment in, 187
phases of, 196–197
psychoanalytically oriented, 179
psychotherapist-patient privilege in, 206–207
separation or divorce in, 207–208
systems orientation in, 179–180
therapist in
  role of, 205–206
  values of, 207–209
time-limited, 187
Marriage, as term, 169
"Marriage contract," 170–171
Masturbation
  anorgasmia treatment by, 47–53
  components of, 48
  conditioning in, 53
  in erectile dysfunction, 138–139, 145, 147
  fantasies in, 52–53, 138–139, 145
  in female sexual inhibition, 47–53
  in group therapy, 49
  male response to, in female group therapy, 51
  and orgasm transference to coitus, 49
  physical behavior in, 48
  role playing in, 48
  skill training in, 48
  training studies in directed, 50
Masturbatory erections, 128
Mecamylamine, in smoking, 78